Literary and Cultural Theory

Literary and Cultural Theory:

From Basic Principles to Advanced Applications

Donald E. Hall
California State University, Northridge

Houghton Mifflin Company   Boston   New York

Senior Sponsoring Editor: Suzanne Phelps Weir
Editorial Development: Bruce Cantley
Editorial Assistant: Bridgit Brown
Project Editor: Carla Thompson
Editorial Assistant: Magdalena Carpenter
Associate Production/Design Coordinator: Lisa Jelly
Senior Cover Design Coordinator: Deborah Azerrad Savona
Senior Manufacturing Coordinator: Marie Barnes
Senior Marketing Manager: Nancy Lyman
Marketing Assistant: Sandra Krumholz

Cover Design: Len Massiglia/LMA Communications
Cover Image: Diana Ong/SuperStock

Library of Congress Catalog Card Number: 00-133852
ISBN: 0-395-92919-9

89-FFG-09 08 07 06 05

Contents

Preface

This book serves as a succinct and accessible overview of some of the basic concepts underlying contemporary literary and cultural analysis. The impetus behind its writing was my own frustration with the lack of availability of a brief, clear, and practical guide to literary and cultural theory that I could use as a supplemental text for my literature classes.

The study of literature has changed dramatically in the past few years. Today, students are not only expected to read and understand the novels, plays, and poems assigned in class; they are also expected to reflect on how their understanding is shaped by presuppositions and affected by cultural forces. Furthermore, as they conduct research on, analyze, and write about literature, students are urged to use a consistent and appropriate methodology that builds on this self-awareness. Indeed, at all levels, students are increasingly expected to write essays and term papers whose analysis has a clear theoretical base. But given these increasing demands and expectations of sophistication, where can students turn for a source of very basic information about the latest critical methodologies? Most textbooks on and overviews of the subject are lengthy and written explicitly for theory classes, with advanced readers in mind. Collections of primary materials by theorists are even more difficult to comprehend and use efficiently.

Literary and Cultural Theory: From Basic Principles to Advanced Applications is different. It is designed explicitly as a supplemental text for undergraduate students in a wide range of courses, from sophomore-level classes covering the basics of literary analysis through junior- and senior-level literature classes for English majors and nonmajors. Students who are completely unfamiliar with theory will find in it clear explanations and quick tips for immediate use. More advanced students who need a broad refresher or exposure to fields outside their own specializations will find it comprehensive as well as practical and accessible. It can also be used as a text in undergraduate critical theory courses, easily supplemented for that purpose with a standard reader of primary materials. *Literary and Cultural Theory: From Basic Principles to Advanced Applications* fills a current gap in available theory texts, for unlike others, it presents in the most succinct and jargon-free manner possible the "basics" of recent developments in literary and cultural theory. It gives students quick access to the fundamentals of contemporary theory as they begin to work on projects and essays, and it encourages them to move in a self-directed fashion from basic principles to advanced applications in ways reflecting their individual needs and levels of comprehension.

The book can meet such a wide range of needs and foster such self-directed study because of its unique design. The Introduction, which should be read by all students, presents a basic overview of the changing nature of the critical analysis of literature, art, and culture, from Plato to the present. It also includes a list of key principles that are relevant to all forms of written analysis, whatever the methodology chosen. This Introduction provides enough general information that a reader interested primarily in feminist analysis, for example, may go immediately to that chapter of the text without reading intervening sections yet still understand some of the issues facing contemporary critics. Of course, students are encouraged, time permitting, to read all chapters (or all potentially relevant chapters) before choosing a methodology for their own use. Each chapter opens with a brief overview of the methodology under consideration and provides details about controversies and subfields within it. But the most distinctive component of each chapter is its list of key principles and concise explanations of those principles, a careful reading of which will allow students to begin generating their own analysis. It is important to remember that these principles are not formulas, but rather are starting points for interpretation and investigation. While they are necessarily broad in nature, they provide students with enough information to choose a methodological base for their analysis and to begin to shape that analysis to maximize their insights. Following the list of principles is an annotated bibliography, which students are encouraged to consult for more detailed information about the methodology discussed in the chapter. And, finally, each chapter concludes with an essay-length example of applied analysis, written by a specialist in the field under consideration. These scholarly applications are preceded by reading prompts, so students will know what to look for in the application, and are followed by a succinct explanation of how the application exemplifies the methodology and principles delineated in the chapter. These scholarly applications will be of greatest interest to intermediate and advanced readers, but in order to meet the needs of the widest possible audience, all examine well-known literary texts by authors such as William Shakespeare, William Faulkner, Maya Angelou, and Richard Wright. By reading each chapter carefully, delving into appropriate works from the bibliography, and reviewing the example offered, students are able to move, in self-motivated fashion, from basic principles to advanced applications.

Literary and Cultural Theory: From Basic Principles to Advanced Applications is arranged topically, with all the major methodologies of the twentieth century receiving attention, from the New Criticism through the latest developments in the New Historicism and queer theory. Its breadth of coverage and clarity of presentation will save instructors valuable classroom time, for they will no longer be required to lecture on and answer questions concerning the "basics" of contemporary theory or make difficult, time-driven choices about which theories to cover and which to ignore. This book will also save students substantial time in their paper preparation process, for its organization allows for an efficient investigation of potential methodologies and avenues for research. Its careful use will lead to more sophisticated student projects and more rewarding classroom discussions.

Acknowledgments

Many helpful and supportive people at Houghton Mifflin have aided in the creation and production of *Literary and Cultural Theory*. I would like especially to thank Suzanne Phelps Weir, Bruce Cantley, Bridgit Brown, and Carla Thompson for their superb editorial work and production assistance. It has been a great pleasure working with Houghton Mifflin.

Also, the following reviewers offered very helpful readings of and commentary on this text:

Dennis Allen, West Virginia University
Kristin Carter-Sanborn, Williams College (MA)
Laura Fasick, Moorhead State University (MN)
Tom Goldpaugh, Marist College (NY)
Frederick Horn, Westminster College (PA)
Joseph Janangelo, Loyola University Chicago (IL)
James R. Kincaid, University of Southern California
Mary Klages, University of Colorado, Boulder
Charles Lewis, Westminster College (MO)
Ed Madden, University of South Carolina, Columbia
Jean-Michel Rabaté, The University of Pennsylvania
Michael Ragussis, Georgetown University (DC)
Mark Rollins, Ohio University, Athens
Michael Selmon, Alma College (MI)
Cheryl B. Torsney, West Virginia University

I would like to thank the faculty, administration, staff, and students of California State University, Northridge, for their inspiration and assistance.

And, finally, I would like to dedicate this book, with gratitude and love, to William K. Maruyama for his patience and support, and for the many ways he has enriched my life.

Donald E. Hall

From Aesthetics to Cultural Studies: The Many Productive Forms of Critical Analysis

Overview

The history of literary and cultural theory is long, dense, and complex, but recent years have seen developments in theory that share a basic characteristic. The following pages will focus on a general shift from *transhistorical* to *contextual* points of reference in understanding the ways in which texts make meaning and the corresponding multiplication of possible emphases and approaches in the analysis of literary and other cultural texts. Following this overview eight principles are presented that are key to the successful written analysis of texts, whatever the critical approach taken. The chapter concludes with an annotated bibliography that points interested students to longer and more advanced introductions to the history of literary and cultural theory. After reading this Introduction carefully, students will be ready to evaluate the appropriateness of methodologies covered in later chapters for their own use. If time permits, students are urged to read all the chapters of this book before choosing a methodology. For those students already sure of the methodology they want to use, chapters are designed to stand alone as practical guides to the many exciting fields making up literary and cultural studies today.

As this Introduction's title indicates, the millennia-long history of literary and cultural analysis is one of dramatic metamorphosis and expansion, from aesthetics—the study of beauty and the delineation of precise standards for judging art and expression—to an emphasis today on the study of culture and how aesthetic notions are produced in a given time and place. While earlier forms of analysis assumed that critics could discover and articulate fixed standards against which all poetry, drama, and fiction could be judged, most recent studies of literature and culture have given up claims to transhistorical (enduring or timeless) frames of reference, suggesting instead that meanings are made contextually. While aestheticians debated how most accurately to judge a text's degree of perfection or imperfection, cultural criticism has opened up for discussion how both literary texts and critical standards are produced and what social forces they may reflect. In the twentieth century, not just drama, fiction, and poetry, but also the political (sub)texts of literature and other cultural forms, even those of literary history itself, became available for analysis.

    This is not to suggest that the social realm surrounding literature and art had received no attention before the twentieth century. In many ways, aesthetic analysis began as social analysis, with Plato (427–347 B.C.) and Aristotle (384–322 B.C.) working to define the social role of art and what effects drama and poetry should have on their audience (see Chapter 1). Thus at its inception, literary criticism had clear ties to sociopolitical critique, even though such ties were forgotten or even repudiated in later centuries. Aestheticians such as Horace (65–8 B.C.), Sir Philip Sidney (1554–1586), Alexander Pope (1688–1744), Samuel Taylor Coleridge (1772–1834), and Matthew Arnold (1822–1888) focused much more directly on the critic's role in accurately defining, defending, and judging "beauty" in literature and art. Of course, implicit social standards and political judgments are apparent throughout such writings (and even more so in book and theater reviews published during the eighteenth and nineteenth centuries), but their importance was largely denied or downplayed by philosophers and theorists as aesthetic and critical "truth" was sought, with that "truth" often assumed to be a real, fixed, and discoverable entity.

    In many ways, this search culminated in the New Criticism of the early to middle decades of the twentieth century. The New Critics took aesthetic criticism to something of an extreme, attempting to divorce both critical standards and the practice of criticism from social context and historical specificity (see Chapter 1). Yet even though their exclusive focus on literature's formal properties and ways of making meaning may seem extraordinarily narrow to us today, the analysis of form has always played and will continue to play an important role in most fields of critical inquiry. Even for those critics who explicitly reject the apolitical stance of the New Criticism, an exploration of the rules and effects of form, as they were understood and used in a particular time and place, often allows for a richer appreciation of the complexity of a given text.

The significance of form cannot be denied, but political and social interests in critical analysis also reemerged as important considerations for many critics of the twentieth century. As the writings of the nineteenth-century political theorist Karl Marx (1818–1883) circulated widely (see Chapter 3), and as the work of the psychoanalyst Sigmund Freud (1856–1939) shifted attention to how literature might reveal individual personalities and broad psychosocial tensions (see Chapter 4), criticism's possible avenues of inquiry expanded beyond these perspectives. If literary texts were not transcendent entities wholly separate from society, if they were instead products of social forces and belief systems that demanded critique and change, then literary critics were able, and even expected, to probe beyond the formal limits of the text; many redefined themselves as social critics working openly to achieve certain political goals through the study of cultural forms. Accompanying this redefinition has been a much more self-conscious probing of the implicit political agenda of literary criticism itself—both that of the present and that of the past. Thus critics have shifted their focus to examine the complex interplay between text and context, including the context of their own writings. In a nutshell, this is the shift from strictly literary analysis to a more expansive notion of cultural studies.

It is useful to think of this process as an expansion of the questions that the critic might ask. Instead of providing highly directive examples that might predetermine student conclusions, the following chapters will suggest possible questions that each methodology might pose as it investigates a text, while using a few examples to illuminate the topic at hand. Chapter 1 ("The New Criticism and Formalist Analysis") discusses principles and issues derived from a focus on the internal properties of literary and other cultural texts. Chapter 2 ("Reader-Response Analysis") shifts the emphasis to external factors, offering commentary and posing questions about the role of the reader in making textual meaning(s). Chapter 3 ("Marxist and Materialist Analysis") examines the role of texts in exposing belief systems about social class and economic status. Chapter 4 ("Psychoanalytic Analysis") probes theories and asks questions about the psychological functions and origins of literary and other cultural texts. Chapter 5 ("Structuralism and Semiotic Analysis") examines how texts reveal the underlying ways in which cultures make meaning through binary relationships and interrelated references. Chapter 6 ("Deconstruction and Post-Structuralist Analysis") builds on Chapter 5 by considering ways that critics can destabilize binary oppositions and work to alter those structures by which meaning is made. Chapter 7 ("Feminist Analysis") asks questions about the gender belief systems of society and how texts may reflect and/or revise them. Chapter 8 ("Gay/Lesbian/Queer Analysis") probes somewhat similar issues but focuses specifically on the ways texts reflect social views of sexuality—in particular, narrow designations of "normal" sexuality. Chapter 9 ("Race, Ethnicity, and Post-Colonial Analysis") examines how texts may reveal society's beliefs regarding race and nationality, suggesting that critics have an important role to play in changing those beliefs. And, finally, Chapter 10 ("The New Historicism and Pluralistic Cultural Analysis") probes ways of combining methodologies covered in previous chapters and offers insights into recent perspectives on how history is defined and how historical research is conducted.

But as indicated above, not only the methodologies of textual analysis but also the definitions of "text" have proliferated dramatically in recent years. Today, literary and cultural critics examine not only poetry, drama, and fiction but also texts as diverse as film, advertising, political prose, suburban shopping malls, and literary and cultural theory itself. Students should always be guided by their instructors regarding what constitutes an acceptable text for analysis in a given course or project, but certainly the field of literary and cultural studies today is an expansive one. New forms of literary and cultural analysis encourage innovative thinking and dense sociopolitical inquiry, as long as the text itself provides evidence that can be used to support generalizations and defend a well-articulated thesis.

The following principles include and build on such general reminders. These principles underlie all successful literary and cultural analysis, whatever the methodology. Some hark back to the guidelines covered in freshman composition courses; others point more directly to how one can apply literary and cultural theory today. While a few may seem simple and even obvious, these are principles too often forgotten or ignored as students proceed with their exciting and perhaps highly innovative research projects. Following these guidelines is an annotated bibliography of works that provide in-depth investigations of the history of literary and cultural criticism as well as useful collections of primary texts. Students should explore as many of these works as possible as they consider the many methodologies available today.

Key Principles

1 *After carefully considering your options, choose a text, topic, and methodology to which you can devote yourself enthusiastically.*

This may seem like the most obvious principle possible, but it is one that is frequently forgotten. Too many students choose a topic because they think it is easy or will impress the instructor rather than selecting one in which they have a genuine interest. From the freshman and sophomore through the graduate level, the first key to successful literary and cultural analysis is enthusiasm for the project at hand. Excitement and a sense of personal commitment will take you through the hard tasks of research, writing, and revision. One of the most noteworthy aspects of the newest forms of literary and cultural criticism is that such enthusiasm is often generated by a profound sense of political commitment as well as an energizing sense of intellectual commitment. Indeed, there is no one source from which enthusiasm for a topic can or must arise. Ask yourself the following question: Of the texts available for analysis, which one (or several) grabbed and held your attention? Do not worry at first about why it did so; instead focus simply on picking the one that generated, for whatever reason, excitement and a sense of attachment. Only after pinpointing the text(s) that you find most interesting should you ask "why?" Isolating the reasons behind that interest will help you choose a topic and methodology. Is there a connection between the text's plot, theme, setting, or characters and your own life? Does the text explore a personal or social problem or suggest a resolution to such a problem that you feel is particularly intriguing and compelling—or, alternatively, wholly misconceived? Does the text present a worldview or lifestyle that seems so foreign to you that you feel compelled to explore and understand it? These are just a few of the many possible reasons that we may be drawn to a text, but in asking why we are so drawn, it is possible to begin taking a more expansive, critical view of the text and to move toward choosing a methodology for its analysis. Indeed, all the methodologies covered in this book explore the power that texts have over individual audience members and/or society as a whole.

2 *Acquaint yourself thoroughly with your text.*

Choosing a text that excites you will help carry you through the time-consuming task of acquainting yourself thoroughly with it. If you are working with a novel, you will return to its pages time and again, reading and rereading certain passages and chapters. A play, poem, or short story may require rereading in its entirety many times. But do not simply read and reread your text—also interact with it. This brings us to another obvious, but often forgotten, rule of thumb: Read with a highlighter, pencil or pen, and Post-it notes in hand (in fact, the reading prompts preceding the applications in every chapter urge you to locate and flag key passages for later reference and use). While we may admire or even love a particular text, we should never be shy about interacting with it in very basic, physical ways. Indeed, the freedom to approach and grapple with the text as a thoroughly human—rather than intimidating, sacred, or transcendent—creation is one of the most important aspects of recent theoretical trends. Being an interactive reader means energetically marking up the text (assuming that it belongs to you, of course) and flagging places in it to which you want to return and probe more deeply. Look for and mark passages of tension, confusion, contradiction, symbolic resonance, character revelation, and so forth. Take extended notes as you read and as project ideas occur to you. While you may feel that such digressions from the act of reading compromise your enjoyment of the text, you are actually engaging in a tradeoff, for simple acts such as note-taking and passage-marking make the process of developing and completing a project much more enjoyable. The more work you do as you read, the less tedious time you will have to spend later reconstructing half-forgotten ideas. And the more thoroughly you acquaint yourself with your text, the more likely it is that you will be able to anticipate possible objections to your thesis and deal with these effectively in the body of your essay. If you know which passages may complicate or contradict your own generalizations, and address these effectively and carefully, then a hostile or skeptical reader will have little basis on which to mount a forceful objection to your argument. The satisfaction of constructing a compelling and enjoyable work of analysis will more than offset the momentary distraction of making a note or marking a passage.

3 *Reflect on several methodological possibilities and choose a methodology appropriate for the text under consideration.*

This is another seemingly obvious principle, but one that too often fails to guide analysis. While you may be quite innovative in your approach to and analysis of a text, it is clear that some methodologies will carry you far in analyzing a given text and others will be difficult to apply. If you know why a text intrigues you, then you will probably be able to isolate a methodology that allows you to explore that textual power, whether it is psychological, gender-related, formal, or historical. But too often students are drawn to a particular text because they find it exciting or complex in some vague way, and then choose a methodology that they also find exciting or complex, only to discover much later that the two do not match up well. After acquainting yourself thoroughly with the text, you then must decide whether you will have sufficient textual material with which to work if you use a particular methodology. If you are thinking about using a psychoanalytic methodology (Chapter 4), does the text seem to reveal a set of character-level, authorial, or social-psychological tensions? Similarly, if you are considering using a Marxist or materialist methodology (Chapter 3), is there substantial textual material regarding economics and social class with which to work? Sometimes, depending on the assignment or your thesis, you will look well outside the boundaries of the text itself to its reception or social use, so the answer to such questions may not always be immediately clear. Indeed, you may discover relevance as you proceed with your research and writing. But if you find little or no connection between a methodology and a text, then proceed with caution; if, for instance, you can discover no gay- or lesbian-relevant imagery or themes in the set of brief poems you have decided to analyze, think carefully before committing yourself to a long research paper using gay/lesbian/queer methodologies (Chapter 8). There is no surer recipe for disaster than choosing a text, methodology, and topic and then changing them dramatically in the last days or hours before the assignment is due. Careful thought about and logical match-ups between texts and methodologies very early in the critical process will make your life much easier later on.

4 *Understand your methodology's strengths and weaknesses as well as its basic principles.*

There are many misconceptions, stereotypes, and oversimplifications in popular circulation about the methodologies covered in this book. Reader-response analysis (Chapter 2) is often equated with sloppy and impressionistic personal responses. Psychoanalytic analysis (Chapter 4) is often erroneously thought to be a search for phallic symbols in texts. Deconstruction and post-structuralist analysis (Chapter 6) is misunderstood as being completely divorced from practical concerns and political commitments. As you choose and begin to apply a methodology, you must separate hearsay from fact. Furthermore, you should remember that no methodology is perfect; all have both strengths and weaknesses. Freudian-influenced analysis (Chapter 4) may help you analyze with clarity and insight certain familial tensions in a text but may lead to problematic analysis of gender roles in the same text. Gay/lesbian/queer analysis (Chapter 8) of a text may allow compelling insights into the sociosexual tensions in and around a text but may obscure the class or racial tensions that the same text addresses. The methodologies introduced in this book are distinct and memorable because they have distinct, often dramatically different, emphases and presuppositions. They are usually powerful because they narrowly limit their fields of inquiry and their agendas. Read the overview of and key principles underlying your methodology carefully, and then study the application provided and consult works from the annotated bibliography to the extent that time permits. Do not claim a methodological base without a firm grasp of what that claim entails.

5 *Provide ample textual evidence to support analysis and interpretive claims.*

This book is designed for use by students of literature and culture, whose primary task is to interpret a text or set of texts. Given those parameters, a significant principle that underlies all successful analysis is that of providing ample textual evidence. If you followed principle 2 above, you should have the basic material you need to construct a compelling interpretation. But that material should not serve only as background to your own thinking; it must also be woven carefully into your writing, in the form of direct quotations, succinct references to scenes and imagery, and other powerful and pithy pieces of evidence that back up your generalizations and interpretive claims. Although you may move well outside of the text in your research and argument (perhaps into the realm of social history and/or audience responses), understanding the primary text must remain your focus and goal; its centrality should never be lost as your analysis proceeds. If your text does not provide ample evidence to support your claims, then you have probably mischosen a methodology or a topic. But if you have followed the principles above in working toward a final draft, your only task will be choosing judiciously from the ample evidence that you possess, rather than attempting hastily to find evidence that may or may not exist.

6 *Use your methodology consistently as you construct a thesis and organize your analysis.*

Because the methodologies covered in this book are distinct and have underlying principles that may be irreconcilable, you should make your methodology clear to your reader at the start and then use it consistently throughout your analysis. This is not to say that a synthetic methodology, drawing on two or more of the methodologies covered in this book, is impossible or inappropriate, but if you do such synthetic work, be aware of and make your readers aware of the methodological choices that you have made and what problems those choices may generate. And whatever those choices are, retain your focus and purpose: Do not swerve suddenly into class analysis if you have been probing the gender biases of a text unless you have announced that combination of focuses and methodologies early in your essay.

As you probably remember from composition classes, this announcement usually occurs in the introduction to your paper and will most often take the form of a precise thesis statement, that declaration of persuasive intent that controls your essay and anticipates its major point(s). Of course, it is rarely necessary to state simplistically, "I will use a feminist methodology in the following essay," because usually that methodology is implied in the thesis itself, as it draws the reader's attention to the gender belief systems inherent in the text or to your interpretation of the social implications of representations of women in it. And in articulating a clear and persuasive thesis, and then making sure that each paragraph relates to it clearly as you follow a carefully constructed outline or organizational plan, you will make the process of revision relatively easy.

Indeed, I remind students in classes from the freshman through the graduate level that if *they* do not understand the organizational structure of their arguments, how can their readers possibly comprehend it? The very best analysis can go awry for lack of something as simple as an outline. If you are moving between data from the text and data from other sources, decide how best to present such diverse material. Will your analysis move back and forth between text and context, alternating paragraphs on each? Will you divide your essay into very large sections of background information and then application or textual reading? Or will you seamlessly interweave the two throughout your essay, so that readers see connections within each paragraph as you draw out the implications of your research and its relevance to the text at hand?

7 *Always consider your readers and their needs as you write and revise.*

The preceding principle points clearly to your responsibility to your readers as well as to your own argument. Remember that analytical writing builds on a contract that you establish with your readers: that you will give them important information and an enhanced perspective on a text if they will take the time to read your analysis. Do you provide succinct explanations of any confusing or obscure terms? Does your tone remain consistent, so that there is no question about your authority as a persuasive writer? Obviously, all writers have their own styles, but unlike creative writing, successful literary and cultural analysis places the needs of the reader over the writer's need to self-express in an individualistic way. You must seek the proper balance between providing what the reader needs to know and moving your argument forward efficiently and effectively. That balance means keeping the reader's attention by foregrounding the persuasive intent of the analysis and meeting the terms of the contract established through the thesis statement.

If you have followed the principles discussed above, determined a purpose, amassed and judiciously presented evidence, and organized your analysis carefully, the process of revision should be an easy and even enjoyable one. It is your responsibility to deliver to your readers a polished and convincing piece of literary or cultural analysis; decide in advance how you will achieve that level of polish and effectiveness in your final draft. Leave ample time for revision, including time to rethink sections of analysis or to restructure and rearrange for greater clarity and impact. If time permits, show your analysis to friends, classmates, and colleagues during the revision process, and ask for direct feedback about its effective and ineffective aspects. Never waste such an opportunity for insight into your readers' needs by soliciting or allowing only praise or positive feedback. As critics, we should also be open to criticism; our writing should be as available for energetic textual analysis as that of the authors we scrutinize. But this requires time. Build that time for response and revision into your schedule from the very beginning of your work on a project, planning backwards from your due date to give yourself enough time to rethink and rewrite. Working with a calendar and devising a reasonable schedule will allow you to take control of your writing process.

8 *Remember, finally, that no methodology explains a text completely or definitively.*

The generation of literary and cultural analysis can be an exciting and energizing project, but it can also be a daunting one. Yet one of the most fundamental insights of contemporary theory can help reduce the level of stress that such a task often engenders. While it is always your responsibility to generate effective and polished analysis, you are not expected to provide definitive answers or "final" interpretations. Contemporary forms of literary and cultural theory remind us that all texts, including analytical texts, are produced within a context, that they are human creations and therefore always imperfect and incomplete. To state this is neither to diminish the writer's responsibility to the reader nor to excuse offensive or oppressive articulations as simply being "socially produced." We must all take responsibility for how we act toward others and what we write. But if we see our analysis as part of an ongoing intellectual dialogue, as furthering a discussion rather than concluding it, then the pressure that we might feel to produce the supposed "last word" will be eliminated. Yes, your writing must be polished and persuasive, but it will not, indeed it cannot, provide all the answers. While some earlier forms of literary analysis claimed to be definitive, you need only claim to provide insight. If you follow the guidelines above and acquaint yourself thoroughly with the methodology that your analysis depends on, then you will provide that insight. It will be the responsibility of future writers to build on that insight and further the discussion with their own literary and cultural analysis.

Bibliography

Barry, Peter. *Beginning Theory: An Introduction to Literary and Cultural Theory.* Manchester, UK: Manchester University Press, 1995.

This is a helpful guide to contemporary literary and cultural analysis, and it includes coverage of all the fields discussed in this book. Its only omission is of extended applications of the theories it traces. Its general accessibility will make it of use to readers at all levels.

Booker, M. Keith. *A Practical Introduction to Literary Theory and Criticism.* White Plains, NY: Longman, 1996.

While this introduction to theory is not as practical as it claims to be (it is organized in a particularly confusing manner), it does cover most of the fields discussed in this book, with the exception of gay/lesbian/queer analysis. It also offers applications of methodologies, though sometimes to texts with which many readers will be unfamiliar. Its clarity and accessibility, however, will make it of interest to many readers from the beginning through advanced levels.

Cowles, David, ed. *The Critical Experience: Literary Reading, Writing, and Criticism,* 2nd ed. Dubuque, IA: Kendall/Hunt Publishing, 1994.

This is a useful if lengthy introduction to most of the fields of analysis covered in this book. While it contains no primary texts or applications, it does explain terms of analysis and basic methodological concepts. Its clarity and accessibility will make it appropriate for readers at all levels.

Davis, Robert Con, and Ronald Schleifer. *Contemporary Literary Criticism: Literary and Cultural Studies,* 3rd ed. White Plains, NY: Longman, 1994.

This is a solid and popular anthology of primary texts by theorists in most of the fields covered in this book. As with all such anthologies, its general level of difficulty is very high, though readers at both the intermediate and advanced levels will find some of its selections useful.

Eagleton, Terry. *Literary Theory: An Introduction,* 2nd ed. Oxford: Blackwell, 1996.

This second edition of Eagleton's *Literary Theory,* a popular text among advanced undergraduate and graduate students, solves some of the problems of the first edition by providing some discussion of issues of gender. But Eagleton's own bias toward Marxist analysis still comes through, and there is still no attention to gay/lesbian/queer analysis. Depending on one's needs, this book will be appropriate for some readers at the intermediate and advanced levels.

Green, Keith, and Jill LeBihan. *Critical Theory and Practice: A Coursebook*. New York: Routledge, 1996.

This is an interesting overview of some of the methodologies discussed in this book, with particularly good coverage of psychoanalysis and the New Historicism. Other fields are wholly ignored, such as Marxist/materialist, formalist, and gay/lesbian/queer analysis. It is appropriate for intermediate and advanced readers.

Groden, Michael, and Martin Kreiswirth, eds. *The Johns Hopkins Guide to Literary Theory and Criticism*. Baltimore: Johns Hopkins University Press, 1994.

This is a massive dictionary of literary criticism—its genres, theorists, and terms. It contains no primary texts but does include solid entries on most of the fields and theorists discussed in this book. It is designed for both intermediate and advanced readers.

Lentricchia, Frank, and Thomas McLaughlin, eds. *Critical Terms for Literary Study*, 2nd ed. Chicago: University of Chicago Press, 1995.

This is an important and accessible introduction to many of the controversies in and terms of contemporary literary and cultural studies. It contains no primary texts but does offer entries by respected scholars on subjects such as "culture," "canon," "diversity," and "gender." It is appropriate for readers at both the intermediate and advanced levels.

Lynn, Steven. *Texts and Contexts: Writing About Literature with Critical Theory*. New York: HarperCollins, 1994.

This introductory guide covers some, but not all, of the methodologies discussed in this book. Notable omissions are of any sustained reference to Marxist/materialist analysis, gay/lesbian/queer analysis, and issues in race, ethnicity, and post-coloniality. However, its clear discussion of other fields, such as psychoanalysis and feminism, will make it appropriate for interested readers at all levels.

Rivkin, Julie, and Michael Ryan, eds. *Literary Theory: An Anthology*. Oxford: Blackwell, 1998.

This is a superb anthology of primary texts in literary theory since the New Criticism. It is highly recommended for its inclusion of difficult but important works by theorists in all the fields covered in this book, including (notably) the emerging field of queer theory. While readers at all levels will find some of its texts of use, most are appropriate for those at the advanced level.

The New Criticism
and Formalist Analysis

Overview

In these days of politically charged criticism and dense theoretical discussions, is the analysis of literary form anachronistic or irrelevant? Not at all; in fact, it remains fundamental to what we do as critics. Even when we use such basic terms as "short story," "poem," "novel," and "documentary," we are already making significant and value-laden *formal* distinctions. But even though the language of form is fundamental to our very perception of literary and other cultural texts, we often reference formalist concepts and constructs automatically, with little reflection on their history and meaning or on the assumptions we may be bringing to the text at hand. Such reflection, however, is vital for the success of all our critical endeavors. Indeed, one of the most widely acknowledged expectations for all literary and cultural critics today is that they demonstrate self-awareness in their use of language and a clear understanding of the presuppositions on which their methods and concepts depend. The following overview and set of principles are therefore designed to aid students in sorting out their beliefs about textual form and function as they begin to reflect on their assumptions regarding literature's time-bound and/or timeless qualities.

Intense disagreements over aesthetic forms and their possible meanings date back many centuries. While the analysis of literature with a specific focus on its form began with Aristotle, the degree to which formal considerations could be divorced from discussions of literature's social contexts and functions was already subject to debate. Plato, Aristotle's mentor, expressed in his *Republic* profound concern about the potentially harmful effects of poetry and drama on society, because he considered them only misleading imitations of "truth" rather than expressions of it. But Aristotle, in *The Poetics*,

13

approached the issue of aesthetics and aesthetic value quite differently, focusing on the internal elements in literature that are most effective in eliciting an authorially desired and socially desirable response from the audience. Indeed, his delineation of the formal elements that characterize and contribute to the success of epic poetry, tragedy, and comedy has continuing relevance, for, like Aristotle, we still analyze plot and character, rhythm and poetic language, even if, like Plato, we also worry at times about literature's social impact.

While such debates have continued over the intervening millennia, the pervasiveness today of formalist terms and frames of reference is directly attributable to one of the most powerful critical movements of the past century. Perhaps the most influential, and certainly some of the most narrowly focused, proponents of formalism in all of history have been the practitioners of the New Criticism, a movement dating from the 1920s, but one holding sway in many college English departments in the United States well through the mid-twentieth century and continuing to influence critics and readers today. The term *New Criticism* was coined by John Crowe Ransom to capture his and his colleagues' singular and unparalleled critical interest in form and intrinsic meaning and their rejection of criticism's most common subject matter: literature's historical and biographical contexts, its social functions, and other extrinsic uses and implications. A key belief underlying New Critical analysis (one that remains a powerful, and often unquestioned, assumption of many readers and critics today) is that literature expresses "universal" meanings beyond its own time period and cultural context. The New Critics asserted that the sole task of the critic is to explore precisely how, through language and form, those meanings are expressed and powerfully impressed upon readers. This is, of course, a very limited critical task, and the New Criticism, in this strictest sense, is rarely practiced today. But even if the heyday of the New Criticism has passed, its belief that literary texts should be treated with great reverence lingers and its intense interest in form resonates throughout later methodologies.

It is important to remember that the New Criticism has not been the only influential manifestation of formalism in recent years; other varieties of formalism have been more willing to include discussions of culture and society, and they have left their own traces on the critical practices of students and scholars. At roughly the same time that the theoretical foundations for the New Criticism were being laid by Ransom, Cleanth Brooks, and their colleagues in the United States, a similar movement was underway on the other side of the globe. *Russian Formalism* denotes the theories and analyses generated by a group of academics in the Soviet Union in the 1920s; like the New Criticism, it was a response to the common critical practice of interpreting literature with an emphasis on its sociological and historical functions and reflections. As practiced by Victor Shklovsky, Boris Eichenbaum, Roman Jakobson, and others, Russian Formalism emphasized that literary critics need tools and analytical emphases distinct from those of historians, psychologists, and sociologists. In particular, the proponents of Russian Formalism looked to plot structures in novels and to the rhythm, sound, and syntax of poetry as literature's most unique and therefore critically revealing aspects. In its focus at times on the language characterizing literary expression, Russian Formalism is separated only by a murky line from the critical movement known as structuralism, which will be discussed in Chapter 5 of this book; indeed, the two share not only interests but also practitioners. And as with structuralism, Russian Formalism also had an abiding interest in literature's social function, most specifically in the way that aesthetic forms make otherwise ordinary experiences seem new and strange, thereby disrupting the automatism (mechanical nature) of everyday, unthinking perception. A poem about nature, for example, may invite the reader to see the natural world with a fresh perspective, perhaps in isolation from human intervention or with heightened attention to a potentially beneficial effect. This process of "making new and strange" remains important in current analyses of what distinguishes literary expression from other forms of expression; it is a concept students may wish to keep firmly in mind as they begin to choose a text to consider and generate a reading of it.

Indeed, discussions of form and function can go hand in hand, as we have continued to see in recent years. Works of narrative theory, such as those discussed by Wallace Martin in *Recent Theories of Narrative,* have provided insight into the many ways that fictional forms meet the psychological and ideological needs of audiences. The social functions of poetic form have also held continuing interest for scholars such as Antony Easthope and Donald Wesling. Similarly, discussions of form are central to important recent works on film by feminist scholars such as Laura Mulvey and Andrea Weiss. As becomes readily apparent from a perusal of the work of these critics, the analysis of form is central to many of the methodologies discussed in later chapters of this book. While formalist analysis is rarely done in isolation today, form still matters, carrying meaning(s) that may touch on issues of class, gender, race, sexuality, and psychology. In the example of a poem about nature, mentioned above, the poem's line breaks, rhythms, rhymes, and other formal aspects could all reflect or challenge certain traditional cultural associations of, say, "nature" with "the feminine." Careful attention to such aspects of form may enrich one's analysis of almost any text, its audience responses, and its social functions. Indeed, a solid background knowledge of form is considered by most scholars to be an essential foundation for understanding the many uses and meanings of literary and other cultural texts. Yet in examining form and using theories of formalist analysis, critics today will often foreground, or make explicit to their readers, their own assumptions about the relationship between form and social context, whether they are analyzing form in isolation from its roots in social conventions and changing belief systems or with direct reference to context and social effect.

Key Principles

1 *The aesthetic experience is unique, powerful, and significant.*

As discussed in the Introduction, literary and cultural analysis in general explores the complex relationship between the text and its audience. But formalist critics have often focused even more intensely and explicitly than others on the unique nature of aesthetic expression and the precise ways that texts elicit responses. Formalism's strictest practitioners, the New Critics, approached literary texts with unparalleled reverence, because such critics found in literature expressions of "universal" truth and the possibility not only of delight but also of enlightenment. According to such critics, the primary task of the interpreter of literature is to illuminate how such results are achieved and thereby to further the reader's ability to appreciate literature. But it is important to remember that the New Critics always focused on the text itself rather than on its emotional effect (they dismissed the critical preoccupation with readers' responses as the "affective fallacy"), for fundamental to their analysis was the assumption that certain powerful emotions and moments of insight would be common to all perceptive readers of a given text. They emphasized that one of the best ways to cultivate the openness and discernment necessary for such to occur is to attune oneself to literature's formal aspects, to learn how to read it on its own terms. While many later critics disagreed with the New Critics belief in universality and their separation of the formal and the social, few would deny the importance of understanding form and form's impact on an audience. If we are to probe a text's meaning, certainly *how* it conveys those meanings will be of continuing interest to us.

2 *Literature has formal aspects that distinguish it clearly from other types of expression.*

Indeed, although many critics today would disagree with some of the most narrowly formalist assertions expressed in principle 1, most would agree that literature, unlike speeches or persuasive writing, certainly has unique aesthetic qualities that can affect its audience in powerful ways. We might say that literature operates not only on readers' intellects but also on their sensibilities in ways that draw on aesthetic traditions and our associations with them. Underlying even the most politically charged contemporary analysis is the recognition that literature's unique impact is the result of powerful, evocative language presented in ways that reference cultural traditions and that often follow time-tested mechanisms for eliciting certain audience responses. To look only at the implications of *what* is said explicitly in a text without looking at *how* it is said is to miss a significant aspect of a text's meaning.

Thus formalist analysis, or a formalist component to analysis, demands that the reader recognize the constructed nature of the literary work and realize that the construct itself is always meaningful. A stanza break in a poem is hardly arbitrary; it is there to enhance or advance the meaning(s) of the poem. The practitioners of feminist, materialist, psychoanalytic, multicultural, and other types of analysis return often to such issues of form because they recognize that textual meanings and readers' reception of them are affected significantly by how a text appears on the page; how a given form reflects or ignores the rules of "high culture" (or those of a popular genre such as the ballad, spiritual, or folktale); how a certain form has a history of associations with a particular class, ethnic group, or gender; and what expectations the reader brings to the text regarding such formal aspects as linearity of narrative and resolution of conflict. These possibilities are only a very few of the many ways in which a consideration of form can amplify a reading of a text and augment what is revealed through a careful investigation of the denotations and connotations of the words themselves. A discussion of form can in fact empower an intellectually dynamic and theoretically informed discussion of culture and society.

3 *Literature can be usefully subdivided into genres.*

Form has held indisputable significance for both writers and audiences, and much of this significance is genre-specific. Formalist analysis demands a knowledge of the unique qualities of poetry, drama, and fiction, of their internal components, histories, and vocabularies. In conducting formalist analysis of our poem about nature, for example, the critic must be able to discuss meter, rhythm, and other aspects of versification that have led to meaningful distinctions between such nature-associated subgenres of poetry as the pastoral and idyll. Nature poets have worked often with such standardized forms, making generic and formal choices that convey part of the meaning of their work, even if they shape and complicate such traditional forms for their own purposes. And it is clear that one can only recognize the degree to which that individualization of form has occurred if one knows the starting point, or standard, from which the poet has departed. Similarly, fictional forms such as the novel and short story have components that not only provide us with the vocabulary of analysis (plot, theme, characterization, etc.) but that also have histories and norms that provide a rich and significant subtext to the work, discernible only to the knowledgeable reader. While it is impossible here to provide explanations and detailed histories of literary genres and their formal components, students should acquaint themselves, through standard reference works and introductory texts, with the genre-specific vocabulary of literary form and literary analysis.

4 *Literary analysis has its own specific interests, focuses, and, of course, terminology that differentiate it from the fields of history, psychology, and sociology.*

Even if literature allows us considerable insight into personal and cultural histories, into the psychologies of individuals and groups, and into the workings of distant or contemporary societies, it also has unique qualities that demand attention. While literary and cultural analysis may be politically charged, it is not the same as political analysis. If we forget that a poem about nature differs dramatically from a speech or a political tract in its rules of expression and its culturally entrenched and powerful conventions, then we ignore some key aspects of its meaning, target audience, and impact. Few scholars today would deny that history, psychology, and sociology can help us understand the context and meanings of a given text, but ask any social scientist about her or his methodology (which can be based heavily on quantitative research) and you will quickly see how individual disciplines have their own standards and methodological demands. Just as a sociologist may be required to conduct fieldwork and amass statistical data, so, too, is our analysis of literary texts discipline-specific, deploying a vocabulary suited to the nuances and idiosyncrasies, indeed the richness, of our particular subject matter. Our evidence, unlike that of the sociologist, is textual detail as well as (perhaps) sociocultural detail; our language and frames of reference may draw heavily on other fields but also include basic formal terms. At the very least, the vocabulary and methodology of formalist analysis provides a solid base on which to build an interpretation using the theories and emphases explored in later chapters of this book.

5 *Literature has meaning(s) beyond the "intent" and biography of the author.*

One of the most useful and enduring contributions of the New Criticism to contemporary analytical methodologies is its foregrounding of the *intentional fallacy*. This principle asserts that literary critics should not search for ultimate meanings in texts by probing what their creators "intended." Such a search is both futile and unnecessary for reasons that underlie much contemporary critical analysis: (1) Writers do not always understand or consciously plan every aspect of their work—much in artistic creation is unplanned or not consciously intended. (2) Intentions are misleading, since outcomes often diverge from them significantly—what may be true at the beginning of a writing project may or may not be reflected in a work's conclusion or its final draft (as you probably know very well from your own writing). (3) Texts are larger than and bear meanings beyond those of their creators—not only do their audiences participate in the making of meanings but their backgrounds are culturally and aesthetically complex. (4) Even if an "intention" is carried out, the text itself must provide the proof of its own meaning—to try to discover "intent" is unnecessary if the meaning is present in and provable with reference to the text, as it always should be. Similarly, the New Criticism usefully emphasized that biographical contexts for understanding a work are of limited use; biographical "fact" is, itself, unreliable, since it is often a creation and interpretation—and, again, the text itself bears its own meaning. While the New Critical insistence on completely ignoring a writer's biography or explicit statements of "intent" is itself artificial and, in most critics' opinion today, unnecessary, contemporary critics are certainly never bound by such background material or statements. All the methodologies discussed later in this book emphasize that writers are subject to belief systems and forces well beyond their own control and consciousness. In our earlier example of a nature poem, the poet would hardly be aware and in full control of all the prevalent and powerful cultural associations of nature with gender, sexuality, and so forth. "Intent" can be a trap, and most contemporary critics would therefore agree with the New Critics that what is actually present in the work and how it is received and used by the audience is of greater importance than what a writer articulates as a "purpose" or what a biographer may isolate as a simple parallel between a writer's life and literary representations.

6   *Close reading and an attention to form, language, and detail are key to a discussion of literature's qualities, themes, and functions.*

The principles above lead to a recognition that careful examination of and concrete references to the text are of the utmost importance in critical analysis. As we will see throughout this book, literary analysis has its own methodological emphases, and these take us back to the text time and time again. Imagery, characterizations, symbolism, narration, scene breaks, settings, and rhythm are among the many concrete aspects of literature that provide grist for our interpretive mills. Successful literary analysis demands careful and close reading of texts with judicious examples provided to support generalizations and draw conclusions. Pay careful attention to the suggestions in the Introduction about interacting with the text and amassing detail to use in constructing arguments. Even at its most speculative, literary and cultural analysis still must be successfully argued from the text itself, even if you move expeditiously from its form to its social function in your interpretation. To deny or forget your responsibility as a persuasive writer—with textual evidence to back up your claims—is to ensure your failure as a critic. As we explore the provocative principles underlying such methodologies as materialist, feminist, queer, and new historicist analysis, students should remember that in ignoring formal complexities and generic nuances they only impoverish their arguments and risk having their elaborate interpretive structures collapse for want of a solid and secure base.

Bibliography

Aristotle. *Poetics*. Trans. and introduced by James Hutton. New York: Norton, 1982.

> This is a fundamental and still very pertinent work of formalist analysis. Its analytical vocabulary remains that of many critics today, and its enduring insights into the forms of drama and epic poetry and their impact on their audiences cannot be ignored. It is a key text for beginning through advanced readers.

Brooks, Cleanth. *The Well Wrought Urn: Studies in the Structure of Poetry*. New York: Harcourt, Brace & World, 1947.

> This work of highly influential, applied New Critical analysis is still well worth consulting for its demonstration of the practices of close reading. While readers today may disagree with Brooks's conclusions, his ability to construct an interpretation through close examination of the text remains impressive. It is most appropriate for intermediate through advanced readers.

Easthope, Antony. *Poetry as Discourse*. New York: Methuen, 1983.

> This work argues strongly that the form of poetry carries distinct ideological meanings, even when the theories behind its creation work to deny a specific ideological content (which Easthope argues was the case with the Romantics). Its level of difficulty makes this work most appropriate for advanced readers.

Eichenbaum, Boris. "The Theory of the 'Formal Method.'" In *Russian Formalist Criticism: Four Essays*, ed. Lee T. Lemon and Marion J. Reis. Lincoln: University of Nebraska Press, 1965.

This is a key work of basic theory in the Russian Formalist movement. Its succinctness will make it of interest to many, but its level of difficulty renders it most appropriate for advanced readers.

Erlich, Victor. *Russian Formalism: History-Doctrine*. New York: Mouton, 1955.

This overview of the Russian Formalist movement provides both a history and an investigation of its key tenets. Its level of difficulty makes it most appropriate for advanced readers.

Hobsbaum, Philip. *Metre, Rhythm and Verse Form*. New York: Routledge, 1996.

This is a superb overview of the fundamentals of the analysis of poetry. Succinct and clearly expressed, it is useful for readers of all levels.

Levine, George, ed. *Aesthetics and Ideology*. New Brunswick, NJ: Rutgers University Press, 1994.

This collection of essays provides an overview of the contemporary debate over issues of aesthetics and literary form. It argues strongly that formal concerns still demand careful consideration. Its presupposition of previous knowledge of literary theory and its specialized language make it most appropriate for advanced readers.

Martin, Wallace. *Recent Theories of Narrative*. Ithaca, NY: Cornell University Press, 1986.

This work provides a solid overview of twentieth-century theories of fictional form and narrative construction. It will be useful for intermediate to advanced readers, who may also find its extensive bibliography of great value.

Mulvey, Laura. "Visual Pleasure and Narrative Cinema." In *Issues in Feminist Film Criticism*, ed. Patricia Erens. Bloomington: Indiana University Press, 1990.

This very influential work of feminist film theory is highly dependent on a discussion of the narrative form of film. Its level of difficulty makes it most appropriate for advanced readers.

Thompson, Ewa. *Russian Formalism and Anglo-American New Criticism*. The Hague: Mouton, 1970.

Although this work is not as user-friendly as one might hope, it presents a solid overview of convergences and divergences between two literary movements that are still influencing critical practices today. Its level of difficulty makes it most appropriate for advanced readers.

Weiss, Andrea. *Vampires and Violets: Lesbians in Film*. New York: Penguin, 1992.

This book provides a solid example of how discussions of form can be integrated into works of lesbian and gay studies. Its level of difficulty makes it appropriate for intermediate to advanced readers.

Wellek, Rene and Austin Martin. *Theory of Literature.* New York: Harcourt Brace Jovanovich, 1977.

Originally published in 1942, this work no longer represents a reliable overview of all contemporary critical practices. But its last section, on "The Intrinsic Study of Literature," still provides a very useful and accessible overview of the basics of formalism for beginning through advanced readers.

Wesling, Donald. *The Chances of Rhyme: Device and Modernity.* Berkeley: University of California Press, 1980.

This is a superb addition to formalist analysis, and one that does not divorce a discussion of form from one of its historical and social contexts. Its level of difficulty makes it most appropriate for advanced readers, but its insights make it well worth the effort for intermediate readers, too.

Application

Reading Prompts

1. In "Wordsworth and the Paradox of the Imagination" Cleanth Brooks is responding to a long history of Wordsworth criticism. Highlight and mark for future reference how and where he suggests that his reading will differ from previous considerations of Wordsworth's "Intimations."

2. Some aspects of poetic form are of great interest to Brooks; underline or highlight passages that reveal those that intrigue him. After finishing this essay, consider what other aspects of form he de-emphasizes or ignores.

3. Brooks concentrates on poetry here, but his methodology does have implications for the analysis of other genres. As you read, consider how the analysis of a novel or a play might differ from or be similar to Brooks's reading of a poem if one retained his general emphasis on form.

4. As you read, pay careful attention to the quantity and types of evidence that Brooks amasses to support his reading of "Intimations."

5. Mark all explicit and implicit statements of purpose in which Brooks reveals his view of the proper role of the literary critic. Consider what relationship he appears to believe that the literary critic should have with the text and with the author of the text. After finishing this essay, think about whether you agree or disagree with his statements and assumptions.

CLEANTH BROOKS

Wordsworth and the Paradox
of the Imagination

Wordsworth's great "Intimations" ode has been for so long intimately connected with Wordsworth's own autobiography, and indeed, Wordsworth's poems in general have been so consistently interpreted as documents pertaining to that autobiography, that to consider one of his larger poems as an object in itself may actually seem impertinent. Yet to do so for once at least is not to condemn the usual mode of procedure and it may, in fact, have positive advantages.

Wordsworth's spiritual history is admittedly important: it is just possible that it is ultimately the important thing about Wordsworth. And yet the poems are structures in their own right; and, finally, I suppose, Wordsworth's spiritual biography has come to have the importance which it has for us because he is a poet.

At any rate, it may be interesting to see what happens when one considers the "Ode" as a poem, as an independent poetic structure, even to the point of forfeiting the light which his letters, his notes, and his other poems throw on difficult points. (That forfeiture, one may hasten to advise the cautious reader, need not, of course, be permanent.) But to enforce it for the moment will certainly avoid confusion between what the poem "says" and what Wordsworth in general may have meant; and it may actually surprise some readers to see how much the poem, strictly considered in its own right, manages to say, as well as precisely what it says.

If we consider the "Ode" in these terms, several observations emerge. For one thing, the poem will be seen to make more use of paradox than is commonly supposed. Of some of these paradoxes, Wordsworth himself must obviously have been aware; but he was probably not aware, the reader will conjecture, of the extent to which he was employing paradox.

The poem, furthermore, displays a rather consistent symbolism. This may be thought hardly astonishing. What may be more surprising is the fact that the symbols reveal so many ambiguities. In a few cases, this ambiguity, of which Wordsworth, again, was apparently only partially aware, breaks down into outright confusion. Yet much of the ambiguity is rich and meaningful in an Empsonian sense, and it is in terms of this ambiguity that many of the finest effects of the poem are achieved.

There are to be found in the "Ode" several varieties of irony; and some of the themes which Wordsworth treats in the poem are to be successfully related only through irony. Yet the principal defect of the "Ode" results from the fact that Wordsworth will not always accept the full consequences of some of his ironical passages.

Lastly, as may be surmised from what has already been remarked, the "Ode" for all its fine passages, is not entirely successful as a poem. Yet, we shall be able to make our best defense of it in proportion as we recognize and value its use of ambiguous symbol and paradoxical statement. Indeed, it might be maintained that, failing to do this, we shall miss much of its power as poetry and even some of its accuracy of statement.

It is tempting to interpret these propositions as proof of the fact that Wordsworth wrote the "Ode" with the "dark" side of his mind—that the poem welled up from his unconscious and that his conscious tinkering with it which was calculated to blunt and coarsen some of the finest effects was, in this case, held to a minimum. But it hardly becomes a critic who has just proposed to treat the poem strictly as a poem, apart from its reflections of Wordsworth's biography, to rush back into biographical speculation. It is far more important to see whether the generalizations proposed about the nature of the poem are really borne out by the poem itself. This is all the more true when one reflects that to propose to find in the poem ambiguities, ironies, and paradoxes will seem to many a reader an attempt to fit the poem to a Procrustean bed— . . . the bed in which John Donne slept comfortably enough but in which a Romantic poet can hardly be supposed to find any ease.

In reading the poem, I shall emphasize the imagery primarily, and the success or relative failure with which Wordsworth meets in trying to make his images carry and develop his thought. It is only fair to myself to say that I am also interested in many other things, the metrical pattern, for example, though I shall necessarily have to omit detailed consideration of this and many other matters.

In the "Ode" the poet begins by saying that he has lost something. What is it precisely that he has lost? What does the poem itself say? It says that things uncelestial, the earth and every common sight, once seemed apparalled in celestial light. The word "apparelled" seems to me important. The light was like a garment. It could be taken off. It was not natural to the earth; it *has* been taken off. And if the celestial light is a garment, the earth must have been clad with the garment by someone (the garment motif, by the way, is to appear later with regard to the child: "trailing clouds of glory do we come").

The earth, which has had to be apparelled in the garment of light, is counterbalanced by the celestial bodies like the sun, moon, and stars of the next stanza. These are lightbearers capable of trailing clouds of glory themselves, and they clothe the earth in light of various sorts. One is tempted here to say that the poles of the basic comparison are already revealed in these first two stanzas: the common earth on which the glory has to be conferred, and the sun or moon, which confers glory. We can even anticipate the crux of the poem in these terms: has the child been clothed with light? Or does he himself clothe the world about him in light? But more of this later.

This celestial apparel, the garment of light, had, the speaker says, the glory and the freshness of a dream. A dream has an extraordinary kind of vividness often associated with strong emotional coloring. It frequently represents familiar objects, even homely ones, but with the familiarity gone and the objects endowed with strangeness. But the dream is elusive, it cannot be dissected and analyzed. (Even if Wordsworth could have been confronted with Dr. Freud, he would, we may surmise, have hardly missed seeing that Freud's brilliant accounts of dreams resemble science less than they do poems—"Odes on the Intimations of all too human humanity from unconscious recollections of early childhood.") Moreover, the phrase, taken as a whole, suggests that the glory has the unsubstantial quality of a dream. Perhaps this is to overload an otherwise innocent phrase. But I should like to point out as some warrant for this suggestion of unsubstantiality that "dream" is rhymed emphatically with "To me did *seem*," and that it is immediately followed by "It is not now as it hath been of yore." The dream quality, it seems to me, is linked definitely with the transience of the experience. Later in the poem, the dream is to be connected with "visionary gleam," is to be qualified by the adjective "fugitive," and finally is to be associated with "Those shadowy recollections."

The ambiguous character of the child's vision as remembered by the man is implicit, therefore, in the first stanza of the poem. What the speaker has lost, it is suggested, is something which is fleeting, shadowy, and strange, but something which possesses a quality of insight and wholeness which no amount of other perception—least of all patient analysis—will duplicate. It is *visionary;* that is, like a vision, a revelation. But visionary perhaps also suggests something impractical, not completely real. Perhaps most interesting of all, the speaker, a little later in the "Ode," has it fade into the light of common day, which is inimical to both its freshness and its glory. The vision which has been lost is at once more intense and less intense than common daylight.

The second stanza, I think, is very important in defining further the relation of the visionary gleam to the man and to the earth. Ostensibly, this second stanza simply goes on to define further the nature of the thing lost: it is not mere beauty; nature is still beautiful, but a special quality has been lost. Yet the imagery seems to me to be doing something else beneath this surface statement, and something which is very important. In contrast to the earth, we have the rainbow, the moon, the stars, and the sun—all examples of celestial light; and to these we may add the rose by the sort of extension, not too difficult to be sure, by which Cowley treats it as light in his "Hymn to Light." Wordsworth says that the rainbow and the rose are beautiful. We expect him to go on to say the same of the moon. But here, with one of the nicest touches in the poem, he reverses the pattern to say, "The moon doth with delight/ Look round her when the heavens are bare." The moon is treated as if she were the speaker himself in his childhood, seeing the visionary gleam as she looks round her with joy. The poet cannot see the gleam, but he implies that the moon can see it, and suggests how she can: she sheds the gleam herself; she lights up and thus creates her world. This seems to me a hint which Wordsworth is to develop later more explicitly, that it is the child, looking round him with joy, who is at once both the source and the recipient of the vision. In this stanza even the sunshine (though as the source of common day it is to be used later in the poem as the antithesis of the visionary gleam) participates in the glory—"The sunshine is a glorious birth." The word *birth*, by the way, suggests that it is a dawn scene: it is the childhood of the sun's course, not the maturity. Like the moon, the sun joyfully creates its world. The poet is giving us here, it seems to me, some very important preparation for Stanza V, in which he is to say "Our birth is but a sleep and a forgetting:/ The Soul that rises with us, our life's Star,/ Hath had elsewhere its setting . . ." Surely, it is perfectly clear here that the child, coming upon the world, trailing his clouds of glory, is like the sun or moon which brings its radiance with it, moonlight or starlight or dawn light.

I shall not try to prove here that Wordsworth consciously built up the imagery of Stanza II as preparation for Stanza V. In one sense I think the question of whether or not Wordsworth did this consciously is irrelevant. What I am certain of is this: that the lines

> The Moon doth with delight
> Look round her. . . .

strike any sensitive reader as fine to a degree which their value as decoration will not account for. Certainly it is a testimony of many readers that the famous passage "Our birth is but a sleep, etc." has registered with a special impact, with more impact than the mere "beauty" of the images will account for. The relation of both passages to the theme, and their mutual interrelations seem to me one way of accounting for their special force.

This relation of both passages to the theme is so important, however, that I should like for the moment to pass over consideration of Stanzas III and IV in order to pursue further the central symbolism of light as treated in Stanza V. The basic metaphor from line sixty-seven onward has to do with the child's moving away from heaven, his home—the shades of the prison house closing about him—the youth's progress further and further from the day-spring in the east. We should, however, if the figure were worked out with thorough consistency, expect him to arrive at darkness or near darkness, the shades of the prison house having closed round the boy all but completely—the youth having traveled into some darkened and dismal west. Yet the tantalizing ambiguity in the symbol which we have noticed earlier, continues. The climax of the process is not darkness but full daylight: "At length the Man perceives it die away,/ And fade into the light of common day." We have a contrast, then, between prosaic daylight and starlight or dawn light—a contrast between kinds of light, not between light and darkness. There is a further difficulty in the symbolism: the sunlight, which in Stanza II was a glorious birth, has here become the symbol for the prosaic and the common and the mortal.

I point out the ambiguities, not to convict the poet of confusion, but to praise him for his subtlety and accuracy. I suggest that the implied comparison of the child to the sun or the moon is still active here, and that Wordsworth is leaning on his earlier figure more heavily than most of his critics have pointed out, or than, perhaps, he himself realized. If the sun, at his glorious birth, lights up a world with the glory and freshness of a dream, with a light which persists even after he has begun to ascend the sky, yet the sun gradually becomes the destroyer of his earlier world and becomes his own prisoner. Indeed it is very easy to read the whole stanza as based on a submerged metaphor of the sun's progress: the soul is like our life's star, the sun, which has had elsewhere its setting. It rises upon its world, not in utter nakedness. The trailing clouds of glory suggest the sunrise. The youth is like the sun, which, as it travels farther from the east, leaves the glory more and more behind it, and approaches prosaic daylight. But it is the sun itself which projects the prosaic daylight, just as the man projects the common day which surrounds him, and upon which he now looks without joy.

I do not insist that we have to read the stanza as a consistent parallelism between the growing boy and the rising sun. Certainly other metaphors intrude: that of the darkening prison house, for example. But whether or not we bring the dominant symbolism to the surface, there is no question, I think, that it is at work within the stanza. And it *is* a symbolism: we are not permitted to pick up the metaphors when we please and drop them when we please. Light plays throughout the poem, and the "Ode," one must remember, closes with another scene in which sunlight again figures prominently:

> The Clouds that gather round the setting sun
> Do take a sober colouring from an eye
> That hath kept watch o'er man's mortality. . . .

Here, by the way, the hint that it is the child who confers the "gleam" upon the world becomes explicit. The clouds take their sober coloring from the eye. Even if we make "eye" refer to the sun as the eye of day, we have but brought the basic metaphors into closer relationship. If the sun, the eye of heaven, after it has watched over mortality, is sobered, so is the eye of the man who has kept the same watch. The parallel between the sun and the developing child which we noticed in Stanza V is completed.

To some readers, however, the occurrence of the word "shades" may still render such an interpretation bizarre. But such a reader will have to prepare himself to face another even more startling ambiguity in the central symbol. Blindness and darkness in this poem are not the easy and expected antitheses to vision and light. The climax of man's falling away from his source is, as we have seen, not the settling down of complete darkness, but of common day. In Stanza IX when the poet pays his debt of gratitude to the childhood vision he actually associates it with blindness and darkness:

> But for those obstinate questionings
> Of sense and outward things,
> Fallings from us, vanishings;
> Blank misgivings. . . .

> But for those first affections,
> Those shadowy recollections,
>   Which, be they what they may,
> Are yet the fountain light of all our day,
> Are yet a master light of all our seeing. . . .

The supernal light, the master-light of all our seeing, is here made to flow from the shadowy recollections. Even if we argue that "shadowy" means merely "fitful," "fugitive," we shall still find it difficult to discount some connection of the word with shades and darkness. And if we consider the changing points of view in the "Ode," we shall see that it is inevitable that light should shift into dark and dark into light. For the man who has become immersed in the hard, white light of common day, the recollections of childhood are shadowy; just as from the standpoint of the poet, such a man, preoccupied with his analysis and dissection, must appear merely blind.

As a matter of fact, I think we shall have to agree that there is method in Wordsworth's paradoxes: he is trying to state with some sensitiveness the relation between the two modes of perception, that of the analytic reason and that of the synthesizing imagination. They do have their relationships; they are both ways of seeing. The ambiguities which light and darkness take on in this poem are, therefore, not confusions, as it seems to me, but necessary paradoxes.

A further treatment of the relationship in which Wordsworth is certainly making a conscious use of paradox seems to clinch the interpretation given. I refer to the passage in which the child is addressed as

> Thou best Philosopher, who yet dost keep
> Thy heritage, thou Eye among the blind,
> That, deaf and silent, read'st the eternal deep. . . .

> Why with such earnest pains dost thou provoke
> The years to bring the inevitable yoke,
> Thus blindly with thy blessedness at strife?

The child who sees, does not know that he sees, and is not even aware that others are blind. Indeed, he is trying his best (or soon will try his best) to become blind like the others. Yet, in this most extravagant passage in the poem, Wordsworth keeps the balance. In the child we are dealing with the isolated fact of vision.[1] The eye, taken as an organ of sense, is naturally deaf and silent. The child cannot tell what he reads in the eternal deep, nor can he hear the poet's warning that he is actually trying to cast away his vision. If the passage seems the high point of extravagance, it is also the high point of ironic qualification. How blind is he who, possessed of rare sight, *blindly* strives to forfeit it and become blind!

In pursuing the implications of the light-darkness symbolism, however, I do not mean to lose sight of the "Ode" as a rhetorical structure. To this matter—the alternation of mood, the balance of stanza against stanza, the metrical devices by which the poet attempts to point up these contrasts—to this matter, I shall be able to give very little attention. But I do not mean to desert altogether the line of development of the poem. It is high time to turn back to Stanzas III and IV.

With Stanza III the emphasis is shifted from sight to sound. It is a very cunning touch. The poet has lamented the passing of a glory from the earth. But he can, he suggests, at least *hear* the mirth of the blessed creatures for whom the earth still wears that glory. Stanza III is dominated by sound: the birds' songs, the trumpets of the cataracts, echoes, the winds—presumably their sound—one can't *see* them. Even the gamboling of the lambs is associated with a strong auditory image—"As to the tabor's sound." Hearing these sounds, the poet tries to enter into the gaiety of the season. He asks the shepherd boy to shout, and he goes on to say in Stanza IV,

>   Ye blessed Creatures, I have heard the call
>   Ye to each other make. . . .

The effect is that of a blind man trying to enter the joyful dawn world. He can bear the blessed creatures as they rejoice in the world, but he himself is shut out from it. If one argues against this as oversubtle—and perhaps it is—and points out that after the poet says,

>   . . . I have heard the call
>   Ye to each other make

he goes on immediately to say

>   I see
>   The heavens laugh with you in your jubilee,

we are not left entirely without a rejoinder. One can point out that at this point another strong auditory image intervenes again to make sound the dominant sense, not sight. One sees a smile, but laughter is vocal. The heavens are laughing with the children. The poet does in a sense enter into the scene; certainly he is trying very hard to enter into it. But what I notice is that the poet seems to be straining to work up a gaiety that isn't there. If his heart is at the children's festival, it is their festival, after all, not his. I hasten to add that this sense of a somewhat frenetically whipped-up enthusiasm is dramatically quite appropriate. (The metrical situation of the stanza, by the way, would seem to support the view that the strained effect is intentional.[2]) The poet under the influence of the morning scene, feeling the winds that blow "from the fields of sleep," tries to relive the dream. He fails.

But to return to the contrast between sight and sound, the poet should be saying at the climax of his ecstasy,

> I see, I see, with joy I see!

not,

> I hear, I hear, with joy I hear!

Consequently, we are not surprised that the sudden collapse of his afflatus occurs in the very next line, and occurs with the first particular object which is concretely visualized in this stanza:

> —But there's a Tree, of many, one,
> A single Field which I have looked upon . . .

The influences of the May morning will no longer work.

I have already discussed the manner in which the first two stanzas of the "Ode" charge the imagery of the famous fifth stanza. I should like to take a moment to glance at another aspect of this stanza. The poet, in "explaining" the loss of vision, says,

> Our birth is but a sleep and a forgetting. . . .

The connection with

> The glory and the freshness of a dream

of Stanza I is obvious, but I think few have noticed that the expected relation between the two is neatly reversed. Our life's star is rising: it is dawn. We expect the poet to say that the child, in being born, is waking up, deserting sleep and the realm of dream. But instead, our birth, he says, is a sleep and a forgetting. Reality and unreality, learning and forgetting, ironically change places.

Parallel ambiguities are involved in the use of "earth." In general, earth is made to serve as a foil for the celestial light. For example, when the poet writes,

> . . . when meadow, grove, and stream,
> The earth and every common sight,

it is almost as if he had said "even the earth," and this is the implication of "While earth *herself* is adorning," in Stanza IV. Yet, logically and grammatically, we can look back and connect "earth" with "meadow, grove, and stream"—all of which are aspects of earth—just as properly as we can look forward to connect "earth" with "every common sight." The poet himself is willing at times in the poem to treat the earth as the aggregate of all the special aspects of nature, at least of terrestrial nature. This surely is the sense of such a line as

> . . . there hath passed away a glory from the earth

where the emphasis suggests some such statement as: the whole world has lost its glory.

But these somewhat contradictory aspects of the word "earth" overlay a far more fundamental paradox: in general, we think of this poem as a celebration of the influence of nature on the developing mind, and surely, to a large degree, this is true. The poem is filled with references to valleys, mountains, streams, cataracts, meadows, the sea. Yet, though these aspects are so thoroughly interwoven with the spontaneous joy of the child which the poet has himself lost, it is the earth which is responsible for the loss. Stanza VI is concerned with this paradox:

> Earth fills her lap with pleasures of her own. . . .

What are these pleasures? They would seem to be suspiciously like the pleasures which engage the children on this May morning and in which the speaker of the poem regrets that he cannot fully indulge. It is true that the next stanza of the "Ode" does emphasize the fact that the world of human affairs, as the stanza makes clear, is seized upon by the child with joy, and that this is a process which is eminently "natural":

> Fretted by sallies of his mother's kisses,
> With light upon him from his father's eyes!

Earth, "even with something of a Mother's mind," "fills her lap with pleasures."

> Yearnings she hath in her own natural kind.

What are these yearnings but yearnings to involve the child with herself? We can translate "in her own natural kind" as "pertaining to her," "proper to the earth"; yet there is more than a hint that "natural" means "pertaining to nature," and are not the yearnings proper to the earth, *natural* in this sense, anyway?

In trying to make the child forget the unearthly or supernatural glory, the Earth is acting out of kindness. The poet cannot find it in him to blame her. She wants the child to be at home. Here we come close upon a Wordsworthian pun, though doubtless an unpremeditated pun. In calling the Earth "the homely Nurse" there seems a flicker of this suggestion: that Earth wants the child to be at home. Yet "homely" must surely mean also "unattractive, plain."[3] She is the drudging common earth after all, homely, perhaps a little stupid, but sympathetic, and kind. Yet it is precisely this Earth which was once glorious to the poet, "Apparelled in celestial light."

This stanza, though not one of the celebrated stanzas of the poem, is one of the most finely ironical. Its structural significance too is of first importance, and has perhaps in the past been given too little weight. Two of its implications I should like to emphasize. First, the stanza definitely insists that the human soul is not merely natural. We do not of course, as Wordsworth himself suggested, have to take literally the doctrine about pre-existence; but the stanza makes it quite clear, I think, that man's soul brings an alien element into nature, a supernatural element. The child is of royal birth—"that imperial palace whence he came"—the Earth, for all her motherly affection, is only his foster-mother after all. The submerged metaphor at work here is really that of the foundling prince reared by the peasants, though the phrase, "her Inmate Man," suggests an even more sinister relation: "Inmate" can only mean inmate of the prison-house of the preceding stanza.

The second implication is this: since the Earth is really homely, the stanza underlies what has been hinted at earlier: namely, that it is the child himself who confers the radiance on the morning world upon which he looks with delight. The irony is that if the child looks long enough at that world, becomes deeply enough involved in its beauties, the celestial radiance itself disappears.

In some respects, it is a pity that Wordsworth was not content to rely upon this imagery to make his point and that he felt it necessary to include the weak Stanza VII. Presumably, he thought the reader required a more explicit account. Moreover, Wordsworth is obviously trying to establish his own attitude toward the child's insight. In the earlier stanzas, he has attempted to define the quality of the visionary gleam, and to account for its inevitable loss. Now he attempts to establish more definitely his attitude toward the whole experience. One finds him here, as a consequence, no longer trying to recapture the childhood joy or lamenting its loss, but withdrawing to a more objective and neutral position. The function of establishing this attitude is assigned to Stanza VII. The poet's treatment of the child here is tender, but with a hint of amused patronage in the tenderness. There is even a rather timid attempt at humor. But even if we grant Wordsworth's intention, the stanza must still be accounted very weak, and some of the lines are very flat indeed. Moreover, the amused tenderness is pretty thoroughly over-balanced by the great stanza that follows. I am not sure that the poem would not be improved if Stanza VII were omitted.

If Stanza VII patronizes the child, Stanza VIII apparently exalts him. What is the poet's attitude here? Our decision as to what it is—that is, our decision as to what the poem is actually saying here—is crucial for our in-

terpretation of the poem as a whole. For this reason I believe that it is
worth going back over some of the ground already traversed.

Coleridge, one remembers, found the paradoxes which Wordsworth
uses in Stanza VIII too startling. Several years ago, in his *Coleridge on Imagination*, I. A. Richards answered Coleridge's strictures. He replies to one of
Coleridge's objections as follows:

> The syntax is "faulty" only in that the reader may be required to reflect.
> He may have to notice that *eye* is metaphorical already for *philosopher*—that the
> two conjointly then have a meaning that neither would have apart. "An idea in
> the mind is to a Natural Law as the power of seeing is to light," said Coleridge
> himself. As an eye, the philosopher is free from the need to do anything but re-
> spond to the laws of his being. *Deaf* and *silent* extend the metaphor by perfectly
> consentaneous movements. . . . The child will not hear (cannot understand)
> our words; and he will tell us nothing. That which Wordsworth would derive
> from him he cannot give; his silence (as we take it through step after step of in-
> terpretation, up to the point at which it negates the whole *overt* implication of
> the rest of Wordsworth's treatment) can become the most important point in
> the poem. We might look to Lao Tzu to support this: "Who knows speaks not;
> who speaks knows not." But it is enough to quote, from Coleridge himself,
> "the words with which Plotinus supposes NATURE to answer a similar difficulty.
> 'Should anyone interrogate her, how she works, if graciously she vouchsafe to
> listen and speak, she will reply, it behoves thee not to disquiet me with inter-
> rogatories, but to understand in silence even as I am silent, and work without
> words.'"

Before going further with Richards, however, the reader may wonder
how far Wordsworth would be prepared to accept this defense of the lines,
particularly in view of Richards' statement that the child's silence "*can* become the most important point in the poem." *Did* it become the most important part for Wordsworth? And regardless of how we answer that
question, *does* it become such for us? How is it that the child is an eye
among the blind?

Because he "yet [doth] keep/ [His] heritage"; because he still dreams
and remembers, for all that birth is a sleep and a forgetting; because he is
still near to God, who is our home. This, I take it, is what Richards calls the
"*overt* implication of . . . Wordsworth's treatment." But it is not so simple
as this in Wordsworth's poem. We have seen the hints of another interpretation: the suggestion that the child is like the moon which "with delight/
Look[s] round her," and the association of the joyous vision of the child
with the child's own joyous activity, and further, with the joyous activity of
the birds and the lambs. Is the poem theistic or pantheistic? Coleridge was
certainly alive to the difficulties here. He went on to question:

. . . In what sense can the magnificent attributes, above quoted, be appro-
priated to a *child*, which would not make them equally suitable to a *bee*, or a *dog*,
or a *field of corn;* or even to a ship, or to the wind and waves that propel it?

Richards' answer is forthright:

. . . why should Wordsworth deny that, in a much less degree, these attributes are equally suitable to a bee, or a dog, or a field of corn? What else had
he been saying with his

> And let the young lambs bound
> As to the tabor's sound!

And what else is Coleridge himself to say in Appendix B of his *Statesman's
Manual?* "Never can I look and meditate on the vegetable creation without a
feeling similar to that with which we gaze at a beautiful infant. . . ."

Whatever Coleridge was to say later, there can be little doubt as to
what Wordsworth's poem says. The lambs and birds are undoubtedly included, along with the children, in the apostrophe, "Ye blessed Creatures."
It will be difficult, furthermore, to argue that the poet means to exclude the
moon, the stars, and the sun. (If Wordsworth would have excluded the bee
and the dog, the exclusion, we may be sure, would have been made on
other grounds—not philosophical but poetic.) The matter of importance
for the development of the poem is, of course, that the child is father to the
man, to the man Wordsworth, for example, as the birds, the lamb, and the
moon are not. But it is also a point of first importance for the poem that
the child, whatever he is to develop into later, possesses the harmony and apparent joy of all these blessed creatures. It may not be amiss here to remind
ourselves of Coleridge's definition of joy with which Wordsworth himself
must have been familiar: " . . . a consciousness of entire and therefore well
being, when the emotional and intellectual faculties are in equipoise."

Consider, in this general connection, one further item from the poem
itself, the last lines from the famous recovery stanza, Stanza IX:

> Nor all that is at enmity with joy,
> Can utterly abolish or destroy!
>   Hence in a season of calm weather
>   Though inland far we be,
> Our Souls have sight of that immortal sea
>   Which brought us hither,
>   Can in a moment travel thither,
> And see the Children sport upon the shore,
> And hear the mighty waters rolling evermore.

Wordsworth has said that the child as the best philosopher "read'st the eternal deep," and here for the first time in the poem we have the children brought into explicit juxtaposition with the deep. And how, according to the poem, are these best philosophers reading it? By sporting on the shore. They are playing with their little spades and sand-buckets along the beach on which the waves break. This is the only explicit exhibit of their "reading" which the poem gives. It seems to corroborate Richards' interpretation perfectly.

In writing this, I am not trying to provoke a smile at Wordsworth's expense. Far from it. The lines are great poetry. They are great poetry because, although the sea is the sea of eternity, and the mighty waters are rolling evermore, the children are not terrified—are at home—are filled with innocent joy. The children exemplify the attitude toward eternity which the other philosopher, the mature philosopher, wins to with difficulty, if he wins to it at all. For the children are those

> On whom these truths do rest,
> Which we are toiling all our lives to find.

The passage carries with it an ironic shock—the associations of innocence and joy contrasted with the associations of grandeur and terror—but it is the kind of shock which, one is tempted to say, is almost normal in the greatest poetry.

I asked a few moments ago how the child was an "Eye among the blind." The poem seems to imply two different, and perhaps hostile, answers: because the child is from God and still is close to the source of supernal light; *and*, because the child is still close to, and like, the harmonious aspects of nature, just as are the lamb or the bee or the dog. According to the first view, the child is an eye among the blind because his soul is filled with the divine; according to the second, because he is utterly natural. Can these two views be reconciled? And are they reconciled in the poem?

Obviously, the question of whether "divine" and "natural" can be reconciled in the child depends on the senses in which we apply them to the child. What the poem is saying, I take it, is that the child, because he is close to the divine, is utterly natural—natural in the sense that he has the harmony of being, the innocence, and the joy which we associate with the harmonious forms of nature. Undoubtedly Wordsworth found a symbol of divinity in such "beauteous forms" of nature; but the poem rests on something wider than the general context of Wordsworth's poetry: throughout the entire Christian tradition, the lamb, the lilies of the field, etc., have been used as such symbols.

But we may protest further and say that such a reading of "nature" represents a selection, and a loaded selection at that, one which has been made by Wordsworth himself—that there are other accounts of nature which will yield "naturalism" which is hostile to the claims to the divine. It is profitable to raise this question, because an attempt to answer it may provide the most fundamental explanation of all for the ambiguities and paradoxes which fill the "Ode."

Richards says that from "Imagination as a 'fact of mind'" there are "two doctrines which Coleridge (and Wordsworth) at times drew from it as to a life in or behind Nature." The two doctrines he states as follows:

> 1. The mind of the poet at moments, penetrating "the film of familiarity and selfish solicitude," gains an insight into reality, reads Nature as a symbol of something behind or within Nature not ordinarily perceived. [In the "Ode," the child, untarnished by "the film of familiarity and selfish solicitude," sees nature clad in a *celestial* light.]
> 2. The mind of the poet creates a Nature into which his own feelings, his aspirations and apprehensions, are projected. [In the "Ode," the child projects his own joy over nature as the moon projects its light over the bare heavens.]
> In the first doctrine man, through Nature, is linked with something other than himself which he perceives through her. In the second, he makes of her, as with a mirror, a transformed image of his own being.

But Richards interrupts the process of determining which of these doctrines Coleridge held and which, Wordsworth, to raise two questions which he suggests have a prior status: the questions are, namely, "(1) Are these doctrines necessarily in opposition to one another? (2) What is the relation of any such doctrine to the fact of mind from which it derives?" And Richards goes on to argue:

> The Imagination projects the life of the mind not upon Nature . . . [in the sense of the whole] field of the influences from without to which we are subject, but upon a Nature that is already a projection of our sensibility. The deadest Nature that we can conceive is already a Nature of our making. It is a Nature shaped by certain of our needs, and when we "lend to it a life drawn from the human spirit" it is reshaped in accordance with our other needs. [We may interrupt Richards to use Wordsworth's own phrasing from "Tintern Abbey": ". . . all this mighty world/ Of eye, and ear,—both what they half create,/ And what perceive . . ."] But our needs do not originate in us. They come from our relations to Nature . . . [as the whole field of influences from without]. We do not create the food that we eat, or the air that we breathe, or the other people we talk to; we do create, from our relations to them, every image we have "of" them. *Image* here is a betraying and unsatisfactory word; it suggests that these images, with which all that we can know is composed, are in

some way insubstantial or unreal, mere copies of actualities other than themselves—figments. But *figment* and *real* and *substantial* are themselves words with no meaning that is not drawn from our experience. To say of anything that it is a figment seems to presuppose things more real than itself; but there is nothing within our knowledge more real than these images. To say that anything is an image suggests that there is something else to which it corresponds; but here all correspondence is between images. In short, the notion of reality derives from comparison between images, and to apply it as between images and things that are not images is an illegitimate extension which makes nonsense of it.

This deceiving practice is an example of that process of abstraction which makes it almost inevitable that the two doctrines . . . —the projective and the realist doctrines of the life in Nature—should be conceived as contradictory. "If projected, not real; if real, not projected," we shall say, unless we are careful to recall that the meanings of *real* and *projected* derive from the imaginative fact of mind, and that when they are thus put in opposition they are products of abstraction and are useful only for other purposes than the comprehension of the fact of mind.

This is all very well, I can hear someone say; but even if we grant that the realist and projective doctrines are not necessarily in opposition, what warrant have we for believing that *Wordsworth* believed they were not in opposition? In trying to answer this objection, I should agree that merely to point out that both realist and projective doctrines seem to *occur* in the "Ode" is not to give an answer. We can argue for the reconciliation of these doctrines only if we can find where these doctrines impinge upon each other. Where do they meet? That is to say, where is the real center of the poem? What is the poem essentially about?

The poem is about the human heart—its growth, its nature, its development. The poem finds its center in what Richards has called the "fact of imagination." Theology, ethics, education are touched upon. But the emphasis is not upon these: Wordsworth's rather awkward note in which he repudiates any notion of trying to inculcate a belief in pre-existence would support this view. The greatness of the "Ode" lies in the fact that Wordsworth is about the poet's business here, and is not trying to inculcate anything. Instead, he is trying to dramatize the changing interrelations which determine the major imagery. And it is with this theme that the poem closes. Thanks are given, not to God—at least in this poem, not to God—but to

> . . . the human heart by which we live,
> Thanks to its tenderness, its joys, and fears . . .

It is because of the nature of the human heart that the meanest flower can give, if not the joy of the celestial light, something which the poet says is not sorrow and which he implies is deeper than joy: "Thoughts that do often lie too deep for tears."

If the poem is about the synthesizing imagination, that faculty by which, as a later poet puts it,

> Man makes a superhuman
> Mirror-resembling dream

the reason for the major ambiguities is revealed. These basic ambiguities, by the way, assert themselves as the poem ends. Just before he renders thanks to the human heart, you will remember, the poet says that the clouds do not give *to*, but take *from*, the eye their sober coloring. But in the last two lines of the stanza, the flower does not take *from*, but gives *to*, the heart. We can have it either way. Indeed, the poem implies that we must have it *both* ways. And we are dealing with more than optics. What the clouds take from the eye is more than a sober coloring—the soberness is from the mind and heart. By the same token, the flower, though it gives a color—gives more, it gives thought and emotion.

It has not been my purpose to present this statement of the theme as a discovery; it is anything but that. Rather, I have tried to show how the imagery of the poem is functionally related to a theme—not vaguely and loosely related to it—and how it therefore renders that theme powerfully, and even exactly, defining and refining it. But I can make no such claim for such precision in Wordsworth's treatment of the "resolution," the recovery. In a general sense we know what Wordsworth is doing here: the childhood vision is only one aspect of the "primal sympathy"; this vision has been lost—is, as the earlier stanzas show, inevitably lost—but the primal sympathy remains. It is the faculty by which we live. The continuity between child and man is actually unbroken.

But I must confess that I feel the solution is asserted rather than dramatized. Undoubtedly, we can reconstruct from Wordsworth's other writings the relationship between the primal sympathy and the joy, the "High instincts" and the "soothing thoughts," but the relationship is hardly digested into poetry in the "Ode." And some of the difficulties with which we meet in the last stanzas appear to be not enriching ambiguities but distracting confusions: *e.g.*, the years bring the philosophical mind, but the child over which the years are to pass is already the best philosopher. There is "something" that remains alive in our embers, but it is difficult for the reader to define it in relation to what has been lost. If we make a desperate effort to extend the implied metaphor—if we say that the celestial light is the flame which is beautiful but which must inevitably burn itself out—the primal sympathy is the still-glowing coal—we are forced to realize that such extension is overingenious. The metaphor was not meant to bear so much weight. With regard to this matter of imagery, it would be interesting to compare with the "Ode" several poems by Vaughan which embody a theme very closely related to that of the "Ode." And lest this remark seem to hint at an inveterate prejudice in favor of the metaphysicals, I propose another comparison: a comparison with several of Yeats's poem which deal with still another related theme: unity of being and the unifying power of the imagination. Such comparisons, I believe, would illuminate Wordsworth's difficulties and account for some of the "Ode's" defects. Yet, in closing this account of the "Ode," I want to repudiate a possible misapprehension. I do not mean to say that the general drift of the poem does not come through. It does. I do not mean that there is not much greatness in the poem. There is. But there is some vagueness—which is not the same thing as the rich multiplicity of the greatest poetry; and there are some loose ends, and there is at least one rather woeful anticlimax.

But if the type of analysis to which we have subjected the "Ode" is calculated to indicate such deficiencies by demanding a great deal of the imagery, it is only fair to remind the reader that it focuses attention on the brilliance and power of the imagery, a power which is sustained almost throughout the poem, and with which Wordsworth has hardly been sufficiently credited in the past. Even the insistence on paradox does not create the defects in the "Ode"—the defects have been pointed out before—but it may help account for them. Indeed, one can argue that we can perhaps best understand the virtues and the weaknesses of the "Ode" if we see that what Wordsworth wanted to say demanded his use of paradox, that it could only be said powerfully through paradox, and if we remember in what suspicion Wordsworth held this kind of poetic strategy.

NOTES

1.   Cf. I. A. Richards' discussion of this passage in *Coleridge on Imagination*, pp. 133 ff.

2.   I concede that it is quite possible that Wordsworth meant to convey no sense of strain—that the rhythm of the first part of the stanza may have pleased him absolutely and been intended to seem pleasing to others. But the cluster of feminine rimes and the syncopation of the rhythm, apparently meant to connote gaiety, are actually awkward as Wordsworth uses them here.

My heárt is át your féstivál,
Mý head háth its córonál. . . .

Heart and *head* are the points of contrast. Yet the accents awkwardly distinguish between them.

Oh évil dáy! if Í were súllen
While Eárth hersélf is adórning,
   This swéet Máy mórning,
Ánd the children are cúlling . . .

There may be other ways to scan the lines, but I believe that there is no way to read the lines so as to get a quick, gay rhythm. We are to read rapidly lines which are not so constructed as to allow such rapidity with grace. Whatever Wordsworth's intention, the sense of strain fits perfectly the effect which the poem as a whole demands. Unfortunately, some of the quickstep of Stanza VII—

A wedding or a festival,
A mourning or a funeral,

lacks this kind of justification.

   3.   It has been objected that "homely" in British English does not have this sense. Perhaps it does not today, but see Milton's *Comus:*

It is for homely features to keep home,
They had their name thence. . . .

Analysis of Application

Brooks's discussion of "Wordsworth and the Paradox of the Imagination" exemplifies many of the principles discussed in Chapter 1. His is an exercise in very close reading, with the text always taking center stage. Notice that there is no consideration of Wordsworth's life, his historical context, or the sociopolitical implications of the poem under consideration. It is the impact of the poem upon the reader and precisely how that impact is achieved, through language and symbol, that concerns the critic here. In this way Brooks's essay stands as a memorable example of New Critical analysis, even as its attention to detail and nuance makes it useful to critics-in-training today.

   Brooks moves through the poem carefully, asking and answering questions about diction and images as they arise in the critic's mind and as he (in this case) encounters the poem line by line. And the text's generic identity as a poem is never forgotten. Indeed, you will have noticed, no doubt, that Brooks consistently focuses on those aspects of "Intimations" that most clearly identify it as a poem: rhyme, stanza, imagery, and so forth. Of course the purpose of his essay is to reveal the poem's theme, which is an aspect of writing common to all genres, even as the way that theme is expressed is shown to be genre-specific. Nowhere in Brooks's essay would one confuse his discussion of the poem in question with a discussion of a nonliterary form, such as a speech or an advertisement. Brooks is firmly grounded in an aesthetic tradition that goes back as far as Aristotle's *Poetics.*

But even if Brooks's isolation of the poem from sociopolitical concerns and his clear adulation for the author may appear anachronistic to us, what remains impressive and relevant in his essay is his very careful attention to language and detail. Still worth noticing is Brooks's judicious use of direct quotations from the poem, his intense scrutiny of single words, such as "eye" and "shades," and his careful amassing of evidence to support his discussion of paradox. The critic's authority here is therefore unquestionable, even if his own language and use of the first person gives his discussion an informal, at times conversational, tone. His quotation of Coleridge and citation of I. A. Richards demonstrates his knowledge of previous critical work on Wordsworth, even as his departure from those readings is also clearly expressed.

Where Brooks may appear to violate one of the rules of the New Criticism is in his occasional reference to Wordsworth's intent in this poem, although, importantly, that "intent" is never handled as something expressed outside of the poem; rather, it is inherent within the poem, which must always bear and provide proof of its own meanings. Critics today may or may not reference extratextual evidence of a writer's intent, if it exists, but what remains useful about Brooks's handling of intent is his constant reference to the work itself, finding in it ample proof for his interpretation.

Brooks's placing of the poet on a pedestal of sorts may seem antiquated to some critics interested in the social forces producing literary expression, but his respect for the intricacies of poetic expression and the complexity of the text are by no means dated. "Wordsworth and the Paradox of the Imagination" remains a useful model for formalist analysis, for it demonstrates how a critic can take an aesthetic work to which he clearly feels a sense of profound attachment, isolate an aspect of it that he believes requires exploration and interpretation, delineate his purpose and methodology carefully, and then present evidence to support his claims. Brooks's organization is logical and effective, and some of the limitations of his interpretation are mentioned and explained. While his focus may be much narrower than that of some critics today, his sensitivity to genre and form remain impressive.

2

Reader-Response
Analysis

Overview

Unlike many of the other approaches discussed in this book, reader-response analysis has no single set of core practices that can be listed and then committed to memory by students. Rather than a methodology, it is an emphasis—one that must be combined with a methodology before a reading or interpretation can be generated. Even so, it is an emphasis that has become very well-known and that deserves ample consideration here, if for no other reason than that many students who claim to be engaging in reader-response analysis are not engaging in analysis at all, but rather in impressionistic personal reactions. Indeed, *reader-response analysis* is a term more often misused than appropriately used. All of us have impressionistic personal responses to texts, and it is enticing to think that there might be a critical approach that would validate our reactions; after all, such a validation would make hard thought or further exploration wholly unnecessary. But key to our discussion here is the fact that a reaction or initial response does not, by itself, constitute analysis.

Yet complicating any attempt to articulate a precise definition of what *does* constitute reader-response analysis is the fact that most works to date on the subject diverge dramatically in defining the theory involved. While all emphasize the reader's role in the making of textual meaning, their methodologies, practices, and terminologies vary greatly. In scanning the essays included in such groundbreaking collections as Jane Tompkins's *Reader-Response Criticism* and Susan Suleiman and Inge Crosman's *The Reader in the Text*, one notes that essays range from formalist readings to post-structuralist and feminist applications (see Chapters 1, 6, and 7 for discussions of those methodologies). This wide variety has meant that the "reader-response" label is often used very loosely; in fact, it has been rendered, in popular jargon at least, practically meaningless through oversimplification.

Even so, the term "reader-response analysis" is hardly worthless, because it clearly indicates an emphasis on the reader in the process of textual interpretation. This differentiates it most obviously, of course, from the New Criticism (discussed in Chapter 1). The New Criticism implies that the idiosyncracies of the individual reader are wholly inconsequential in textual studies, because meanings are always fixed and inherent in the text, its mode of expression, and its very form; the critic's job is simply to illuminate that intrinsic meaning. But later critics disagreed; working from such methodological bases as Marxism, psychoanalysis, and feminism (see Chapters 3, 4, and 7), they refocused attention on readers, their belief systems, and their active role in creating meaning. This redirection of interest away from the text as an autonomous entity and onto the many ways in which readers interact with texts is superbly traced by Tompkins in her introduction to *Reader-Response Criticism*. That collection also brings together essays by some of the most prominent theorists who have directly addressed the many roles of the reader in the interpretive process: Wolfgang Iser, Stanley Fish, Michael Riffaterre, and Norman Holland. A perusal of their works shows just how diverse the methodologies are that comprise reader-response analysis—but also how rigorous and sophisticated its practitioners are. Further evidence of the same is offered by the essays that make up Suleiman and Crosman's *The Reader in the Text*, whose authors include many of the theorists above, as well as Tzvetan Todorov, Naomi Schor, and Gerald Prince.

Common to all these works is the recognition that whatever meanings an author may intend to communicate through a text and whatever meanings a text may generate in seemingly clear fashion through its language or imagery, it is ultimately the reader who must decode those meanings and whose acceptance of, use of, and response to them may vary widely. Yet, as Steven Mailloux traces in his superb overview of reader-response criticism, *Interpretive Conventions*, critics working in the field disagree widely on precisely how much autonomy the individual reader has from the intentions of the writer; from the words, images, and other component parts of the text itself; and from the social and historical forces surrounding both the reader and the text. Rhetorical critics such as Wayne Booth (whose influential work Suleiman and Mailloux place firmly within the reader-response category) go to great lengths to discuss the powerful effect of the text on the reader, finding within the text an authorial presence that leads the text's rhetorically attuned reader toward an authorially desired interpretation or response. Phenomenological critics such as Wolfgang Iser, on the other hand, are much more interested in the many interpretive choices an individual reader makes as she or he moves through a text. Phenomenological criticism investigates the communication process that occurs between the text and the reader, exploring not only how the text may "suggest" a certain response to readers but also how those suggestions may or may not be accepted. Forms of reader-response analysis that reflect methodologies investigating the sociopolitical uses and implications of texts may focus substantially on how readers respond out of their own idiosyncratic beliefs, knowledge bases, and ethnic, gender, and class backgrounds, among other factors.

In fact, reader-response analysis generally recognizes that even outright "misreadings" often occur—ones that the author never intended and that differ widely from agreed-upon or critically approved responses. To a certain extent, the reader-response approach validates those variant responses as inevitable and even legitimate, in that the reader always has sovereignty over her or his own reading process. But it is important to remember that reader-response *analysis*, the type of work performed by literary and cultural critics and by students reading this book, does not consist simply and solely of articulating those divergent and sometimes intellectually sloppy responses. Reader-response analysis is a rigorous probing of the response process itself, and it has a wide variety of possible *analytical* focuses: on the presuppositions that the reader brings to the text, on the fragile contract of trust established between the writer or narrator and the reader, on the linguistic challenges posed by a text to a reader or set of readers, and so forth. Students who misuse the "reader-response" label often claim that it means "anything goes." Nothing could be further from the truth. For example, a reader certainly has the "right" to be bored by Herman Melville's *Moby Dick*, but a statement of that boredom does not constitute reader-response analysis. The claim that *Moby Dick* is boring, however, may represent the beginning of such analysis if it leads to a sustained and detailed exploration of how and where the contract of believability, moral urgency, and narrative engagement breaks down during the reading process. Such an examination would necessarily involve a close examination of the text of the novel itself and a statement of the precise needs and desires of the reader in question. As with any other form of analysis, unsupported claims and loose generalizations—that the novel is "too long" or that Ahab is not a "realistic" character—are always recipes for disaster in the generation of reader-response analysis.

Thus students should be especially careful if they choose to pursue reader-response analysis, for it is not simply an interpretation of a text, it is always an interpretation of the act of interpretation. Some works of reader-response analysis carefully examine the clues to authorially intended interpretations that the text offers to readers; others probe carefully why readers reject those clues. But all reader-response analysis is meta-theoretical analysis in that it is at least one (very large) analytical step removed from the reader's immediate response to the text. It is an analytical response to the reader's response.

Key Principles

1 *The "meaning" of a text is not wholly intrinsic to the text.*

While many formalist critics, especially practitioners of the New Criticism (see Chapter 1), believe that the text has sole authority in constructing and conveying meaning(s) to the reader, even they have always admitted the possibility of misreadings and flawed interpretations. Of course, such misreadings have no legitimacy and certainly receive no critical attention among the New Critics; by acknowledging such misreadings, however, they implicitly admit that the making of textual meaning always involves multiple parties. While never denying that authors do attempt to convey certain meanings in their texts, reader-response analysis shifts the analytical focus onto the actual receiver of the textual/authorial message, addressing how that message is decoded, interpreted, and used. In this way, it might be considered the mirror image of the New Criticism and, in some ways, its complement. Just as the New Critics theorize about and carefully explore the intrinsic meanings of texts (as well as their powerful conveyance of emotions, themes, and aesthetic values), reader-response critics theorize about and explore with equal care the reader's reception of emotions, themes, and values, as well as how meaning is made through the complex interplay of a text and a reader, both of which have interests, characteristics, and limitations. While the New Critics often assume an "ideal" reader, fully attuned to the complexity, beauty, and power of the text, reader-response critics are often highly attentive to the responses of "real" readers, with all of their inevitable flaws and complexities.

2 *The reading experience may be intensely private and subjective. Carefully and thoroughly investigating the roots of differing, even wildly variant, responses and interpretations can be an important critical exercise.*

If one important goal of literary and cultural analysis is to understand the ways in which texts construct and circulate values and meanings, then certainly all aspects of that construction and circulation bear investigation,

even ones that have little to do with authorial intent or authoritative interpretations and interpretive strategies. Misreadings, wildly subjective responses, and hasty generalizations often occur, and even though these are
hardly appropriate for the classroom or defensible in a research paper, they
may tell us much about how texts are used culturally and how they have a
powerful impact on readers and even groups of nonreaders. After all, a text's
reputation (sometimes arising from many people's hasty readings or commonly accepted, skewed interpretations) may have little to do with its actual
content. The reputation of reader-response analysis itself provides a case in
point; readers with little knowledge of the texts of reader-response critics
sometimes use the category to justify their own hasty, impressionistic work,
for reasons explored briefly in this chapter's overview. The earlier example
of *Moby Dick* is also pertinent. Its reputation among some students as long-
winded and difficult, as "boring" or full of meaningless details, might not
tell us very much about the novel itself, but it could certainly lead to an investigation of a range of responses—perhaps comparing expectations of
today's readers with those of nineteenth-century readers or probing the
uses and misuses of a novel such as *Moby Dick* in high school and/or college
classrooms.

And, of course, misreadings of the reader-response category hardly in-
validate the category itself, since a careful and well-supported investigation
of the range of possible responses to a given text can allow a better understanding of culture and the role of readers in replicating or changing cultural belief systems. Indeed, in moving from a simple expression of a
subjective reading or misreading to an active consideration of how and why
that reading or misreading occurred, one moves from simple response to responsible analysis, which is the goal of all of this book's own readers.

3 *Texts often presuppose an "ideal" reader, while a "real" reader has his or
her own idiosyncratic background, context, expectations, and interpretive
strategies.*

The rhetorical criticism of Wayne Booth carefully examines the ways in
which texts work to convey meanings to their readers. His work opens up a
discussion of reading as a communication process, while his emphasis remains on the author's guiding role in that process. Certainly those of us
who study and write about literary and other cultural texts are concerned
with becoming more careful, informed textual readers and respondents, but
we also realize that innumerable factors may affect the quality of our response to a given text. The conditions under which we read or study a novel
such as *Moby Dick* (perhaps with a headache, perhaps with music playing);

the care with which we attend to the development of its plot or intricate characterizations; the political, religious, and social beliefs we bring with us to the novel (perhaps anti-whaling, perhaps pro-feminist); the experiences we may have had that mirror or differ from those of major characters (perhaps an interest in nautical history, perhaps never even having seen the ocean firsthand); the theories of interpretation we have studied or otherwise been exposed to and internalized—all of these may affect the way in which we interact with the text itself. Reader-response analysis often probes how our individualistic, sometimes wildly variant, interpretations and responses come into being.

Reader-response analysis recognizes that while successful and sophisticated interpretation requires an attention to detail and nuance in texts, not all responses to texts are generated with such care; the communication process may break down or be clouded by any number of factors, as indicated above. You may decide to make it your task, as a reader-response critic, to explore precisely where and how that communication process has been, is, or may become complicated. For example, you might begin by asking who *Moby Dick*'s intended audience appears to be. What is that audience's nationality, ethnicity, gender, sexuality, social class, or age? Where in the novel can you find details or clues that allow you to establish that fact? Then, how might a reader who differs in one or more ways from the novel's intended reader respond individualistically to a characterization, theme, plot development, or use of language in Melville's text? A feminist reader may respond to Melville's lack of female characters very differently from a male reader. Similarly, a gay or lesbian reader may respond to the seeming homoeroticism of the novel in a fashion dramatically different from that of a reader who has little knowledge of gay individuals or issues. To probe such responses is to explore their highly subjective nature. Even "well-intended" messages or themes may be received in ways that vary widely from the author's purpose. Consider, for example, the continuing controversy over the racist language used in texts such as Mark Twain's *Huckleberry Finn*; reader-response analysis could focus directly on how a text's seemingly antiracist message is received as racist or hurtful because of the words used by characters or narrators and on the social context of the readers who receive that message in a fashion very different from its author's intent.

An emphasis on the subjective nature of reading builds on the recognition that texts never exist in vacuums. As readers read and respond to them, they process the language they encounter and look for clues within the text to help them understand and render judgments. But even powerfully expressed themes may not convince a reader who does not recognize or accept all the clues to meaning that the text offers. Readers always interpret and judge textual data with reference to extratextual information and systems of meaning. Reader-response analysis might directly examine any of those factors in a reader's interaction with a text. What belief system might lead a reader to a certain response to a text—horror at the mere idea of whaling, for example, or suspicion of authority figures such as Ahab, or intense interest in adventure narratives? And precisely where outside the text—in other media, historical phenomena, social movements, or political/literary/cultural theories—can you find contextual expressions and explorations of the belief systems that help determine those responses within an individual reader? Indeed, what complex interplay of textual and extratextual forces helps illuminate a given response to a novel such as *Moby Dick*? Because no response exists without a text to help generate it, just as no text exists within a vacuum, practitioners of reader-response analysis often examine both textual and extratextual sources of meaning and information as their analysis proceeds.

4 *The investigations suggested above may lead to research in psychology, social history, gender studies, or other fields.*

Critics interested in reader-response analysis may wish to consult other chapters of this book, for in exploring the complex backgrounds, expectations, and roles of readers as subjective makers of textual meaning, the critic may wish to investigate the powerful social, historical, and psychological forces that affect readers. A successful discussion of those forces demands some understanding of the fields devoted to their study and their methodological norms. While starting with a sophisticated premise and analytical intent is always important for the literary and cultural critic, a successful essay or project depends on a well-chosen and consistently applied methodology or combination of methodologies. Reader-response analysis must be rigorous and well-grounded in appropriate theory and textual evidence. If you decide to proceed with an exploration of the subjective nature of a given response to a text such as *Moby Dick*, you should combine your reading of this chapter with a careful consideration of chapters devoted to gender, sexuality, race, or class, depending on your interests. In combining a reader-response emphasis with attention to the intricacies of the reader's sociocultural position, the critic will often be able to complicate a reading and offer multiple insights into the process of textual communication and interpretation.

5 *As readers proceed through a text, they make choices and engage in interpretive processes that may be traced and analyzed.*

The reader-response emphasis contends that reading is not a simple process of opening oneself up to a text or of passively allowing it complete control over one's consciousness. Certainly readers become aware of and are affected by the words and images they encounter on the page, but they also make choices and engage in active processes of interpretation as they read. An exploration of these moment-by-moment processes may also serve as the basis of reader-response analysis of the phenomenological variety. This form of analysis examines our processing of phenomena, or textual information. In looking carefully at the unfolding of *Moby Dick*'s plot, the development of its characters or themes, or its uses of a symbol or image, the phenomenological critic may wish to examine the many decisions that readers make as they interpret and render judgment. In examining the novel on the level of the sentence, paragraph, or other small unit, a reader-response critic might ask how the individual reader makes sense of it with reference to preceding information or uses it to anticipate later developments or larger themes. The reader's mind is never fixed solely and securely on the present moment in the text; it always moves backwards and forward in time and narrative. What previously encountered plot developments or characterizations resurface as new developments or characterizations occur? How are those used to project into the future? What uncertainties persist or arise as new sentences, paragraphs, or actions are encountered? In focusing so intensely on the microprocess of reading and response, the phenomenological critic often seeks to understand some of the smallest units that comprise the experience of reading, thus helping to illuminate the full impact—indeed, the many sequential and overlapping impacts—that a text may have on the reader. If we think of the New Criticism as the mode of response that most aggressively seeks to understand the unity of the text and the textual experience, this microstudy of the reading process represents the other extreme: the study of the many disruptions, alterations, and variations that characterize an ongoing encounter with the text as many interconnected parts.

6 *The success of reader-response analysis depends largely on the sophistication of the critic's meta-theoretical approach to the reading process and the quality of the evidence presented to support any conclusions or generalizations.*

Here as elsewhere we return inevitably to some of the basic rules of successful writing and critique. The reader-response critic, just as the formalist or Marxist critic, must keep her or his own reader in mind and present the evidence necessary to sway that reader. The critic's thesis, methodology (or synthesis of methodologies), supporting detail, and conclusions must be powerful, appropriate, and crystal clear. Of course, no argument is irrefutable, for as we have seen in this chapter, readers may reject or misunderstand what they read; their biases and hasty or subjective responses may be difficult to challenge (indeed, it is always important to keep this in mind as you consider the advice on and responses to your writing offered by colleagues and friends). We can all learn something from the reader-response approach, for it allows us *as writers* to understand how and why we get such a wide range of responses to our work; furthermore, it challenges us *as readers* to recognize our own hasty and ill-supported reactions. Of course, the possibility of a misreading or ill-considered response is part of the exciting and unpredictable experience of being a writer and critic. Your own responsibility is simply to present your argument as clearly and forcefully as possible.

Bibliography

Bloom, Harold. *A Map of Misreading*. New York: Oxford University Press, 1975.

> This study of "influence" concerns the relationship between writers as readers and the texts that they generate from their readings and misreadings of predecessors. A dense and complex text, it will be of greatest use to advanced readers.

Booth, Wayne C. *The Rhetoric of Fiction*, 2nd ed. Chicago: University of Chicago Press, 1983.

> This classic text of literary theory predates the coining of the term "reader-response criticism" but has had an enduring impact on the field and on literary criticism in general. While Booth focuses largely on the role of the author in conveying meaning, he also discusses the ways in which readers must be molded and their needs addressed. It may be useful for both intermediate and advanced readers.

Fish, Stanley. *Is There a Text in This Class? The Authority of Interpretive Communities*. Cambridge, MA: Harvard University Press, 1980.

> This wide-ranging collection of essays by Fish is one of the most important works in the development of reader-response criticism and remains highly influential. Its conceptual difficulty and diction make it most appropriate for advanced readers.

Freund, Elizabeth. *The Return of the Reader: Reader-Response Criticism*. New York: Methuen, 1987.

> This study is the best single-authored introduction to the field of reader-response criticism. Both accessible and well-written, it is appropriate for intermediate and advanced readers.

Iser, Wolfgang. *The Implied Reader: Patterns of Communication in Prose Fiction from Bunyan to Beckett.* Baltimore: Johns Hopkins University Press, 1974.

This remains one of the most influential primary texts in reader-response analysis of the novel, covering English literature from the seventeenth through the twentieth centuries. Its sophisticated language and conceptual difficulty make it most appropriate for advanced readers.

Mailloux, Steven. *Interpretive Conventions: The Reader in the Study of American Fiction.* Ithaca, NY: Cornell University Press, 1982.

This is an influential and comprehensive introduction to reader-response theories with application directly to the field of American literature. Well-written, though conceptually sophisticated, it is appropriate for intermediate and advanced readers.

Suleiman, Susan R., and Inge Crosman, eds. *The Reader in the Text: Essays on Audience and Interpretation.* Princeton: Princeton University Press, 1980.

This superb collection of essays contains major statements on a wide variety of reader-response methodologies and issues. It is especially useful, however, for Suleiman's clear and comprehensive introduction. While many of its essays demand a substantial background in theory, the introduction is useful for intermediate as well as advanced readers.

Tompkins, Jane P., ed. *Reader-Response Criticism: From Formalism to Post-Structuralism.* Baltimore: Johns Hopkins University Press, 1980.

Much like the Suleiman and Crosman work listed above, this groundbreaking collection of essays provides a comprehensive overview of the theories and variety of reader-response analysis. Its introduction by Tompkins is accessible and highly useful. While it, too, contains some essays that demand a substantial theoretical background, it remains a useful collection for intermediate and advanced readers.

Application

Reading Prompts

1. In his two introductory paragraphs, Iser indicates the central focus of the discussion that follows. Mark or highlight the thesis statement or statements that Iser offers to help his own readers receive and make productive use of his essay.

2. As you read, consider how Iser organizes his discussion. Mark or highlight statements and passages that help him retain the reader's response to Faulkner's novel as his central focus.

3. In his discussion of Benjy, pay close attention to the quantity and types of evidence that Iser provides to support his interpretation of the reader's likely response to this character.

4. In his sections on Quentin and Jason, Iser uses the word "reader" less often than he does in his section on Benjy. Consider how his discussion nevertheless continues to center on the reader's ongoing relationship with Faulkner's narrative.

5. Examine Iser's last sentence and think about how its ambiguity reflects the discussion that precedes it and his overall emphasis on the reader.

WOLFGANG ISER

Perception, Temporality, and Action as Modes of Subjectivity

W. Faulkner: *The Sound and the Fury*

With the exception of Joyce's *Ulysses*, Faulkner's *The Sound and the Fury* (first published in 1929) is probably the most important modern experiment in the use of narrative techniques to give form to individual structures of consciousness. The 'story,' presented from four different points of view, consists of events and impressions connected with the gradual decline of the Compson family in the Deep South. Through the first person narratives of the Compson brothers, this single theme is split into a variety of fragments and facets, and even the final, authorial part does not bring these together in a clearly organized whole. Furthermore, the different accounts—all precisely dated—are not given in chronological order, so that the reader is forced to jump backward and forward in time, thus constantly supplying a background to each individually drawn picture. This even applies when events take on a degree of clarity that was lacking in the beginning as in the third and fourth sections, which offer a partial untangling of the perplexities produced by Benjy and Quentin. Here we have the somewhat extraordinary effect that the unexpected explicitness, contained in Jason's account and that of the author, seems somehow to impoverish the proceedings, for if the reader has taken the trouble to immerse himself in Benjy's erratic perceptions and in Quentin's consciousness, Jason's clearly defined attitude will appear decidedly banal—not least, *because* of its clarity.

As the individual narrative perspectives overshadow one another, there arises between them a sort of no-man's-land of unformulated connections, and it is these that involve the reader directly in the novel. The effect on him has been described by Richard Hughes as follows:

> It is here this curious method is finally justified: for one finds, in a flash, that one knows all about them, that one has understood more of Benjy's sound and fury than one had realized: the whole story becomes actual to one at a single moment. It is impossible to describe the effect produced, because it is unparalleled; the thoughtful reader must find it for himself. It will be seen to be a nat-

ural corollary that one can read this book a second time at least. The essential quality of a book that can be read again and again, it seems to me, is that it shall appear different at every reading—that it shall, in short, be a new book[1]

These different appearances that confront the "thoughtful reader" are evoked by the structure of the text, which we are now going to examine in some detail.

The novel begins with a series of fluctuating impressions of April 7, 1928 which Benjy, an idiot, attempts to hold onto. Benjy differs from most other idiots in literature mainly because he is seen from inside and not from outside. The reader sees the world through his eyes and depends almost exclusively on him for orientation. As a result, the reader's attention is drawn to the peculiar nature of this perception, so that the subject matter seems to be the idiot's experience of life rather than his effect on the intersubjective world; indeed, this could only become the subject if he were seen in the context of normality. This, clearly, is why it is not until the fourth, authorial part of the novel that we are given the familiar picture of the idiot: " . . . the swing door opened and Luster entered, followed by a big man who appeared to have been shaped of some substance whose particles would not or did not cohere to one another or to the frame which supported it. His skin was dead looking and hairless; dropsical too, he moved with a shambling gait like a trained bear. . . . His eyes were clear, of the pale sweet blue of cornflowers, his thick mouth hung open, drooling a little."[2] This description seizes on Benjy's external appearance, projecting it implicitly onto a normal human appearance in order to create the portrait of the idiot out of the differences. The contrast between normality and idiocy is an integral part of this section, which deals with the question of whether Benjy can continue to stay with the family or should be sent to a lunatic asylum.

The implicit criteria of normality are not available, however, when Benjy is viewed from the inside, unless one compares his monologue with psychiatric case histories, which even then will only yield meager results, limited to establishing differences and similarities.[3] The fictional idiot viewed from the outside cannot be regarded merely as a symbol of human deformity, and, equally, the interior monologue cannot be simply a case history and nothing more:—everything depends on the function of the idiot in the context of what is to be presented.

First let us look at the signals the author gives the reader in Benjy's account. The various events, conversations, impressions, and ideas are expressed with precision and a quite undamaged syntax. What is missing, however, is a coherence between the individual sentences, which do not come together to form a larger unit of meaning.[4] The sentences seem to point in various directions without ever accomplishing the perception at which they are aimed. These undeveloped indications produce the impression that a 'plot' is in the process of being formed but is constantly being broken up. This impression is essentially the reader's own contribution, for Benjy himself offers up the fragments of his monologue as if they were part of a self-evident process. Indeed, it is his very passiveness in this respect that activates the reader, for the latter wants to understand why the thirty years of life that Benjy is surveying should dissolve in this way the moment he perceives them.

The author offers another aid by italicizing certain passages of the monologue in order to show differences in time which otherwise would probably not be apparent. But here, too, the clarification seems paradoxically to enhance the confusion. It has been calculated that in Benjy's monologue, 13 scenes from 13 different periods of time have been broken up into 106 fragments,[5] the arbitrary juxtaposition of which shows that for Benjy everything exists on a single time level. Just as the integral sentences serve to accentuate the lack of any integrated content, so do the time divisions show up the absence of any concept of time. Here again there is a definite effect on the reader. Benjy's past appears as a continuous but haphazard movement, brought about by a series of impressions that are specifically though erratically set in time. Some critics have called this movement a 'stream of consciousness',[6] but such a term is misleading, for it implies a direction—a stream flowing from the past into the future. But this is not how events are presented in an interior monologue—on the contrary, one has to reverse the direction of the 'stream', as it is mainly present or future events that affect a character's retrospective perception and so mobilize memories afresh, endowing them with changing relevance.[7]

This is certainly what happens to Benjy,[8] when at the beginning of his monologue he sees some golfers through a hedge.[9] The present sets the past in motion and must inevitably give it a different appearance from before, because it has been aroused by something which did not exist at the time. This is why the interior monologue involves a continual changing of what is remembered. But with Benjy there is no time relation, so that his memories of thirty years and his impressions of April 7, 1928, are all flattened out on a single level. If the author had not indicated which was which, it would be almost impossible to gauge it from the monologue.

As Benjy's perception cannot distinguish between past and present, no one facet of his life is shaped or even influenced by any other. The lack of any such interaction, and the aimlessness with which events are lumped together, endows these events with an extraordinary self-sufficiency. It is as if we were confronted with the 'raw materials'[10] of reality waiting to be put together in a recognizable living form. Now these raw materials do in fact contain the outlines of a story which in the course of the novel is more and more clearly developed. But the result of this development is a gradual diminution of the richness of Benjy's monologue, so that the story as unfolded in the fourth part seems positively trivial.

Thanks to the signals inserted by the author, the reader will gain the impression from Benjy's monologue that he can only observe its reality (and so, at this stage, all reality) as a constant and elusive fragmentation. This effect is achieved in various ways. First and foremost is the fact that this is a form of perception devoid of any active consciousness. Benjy has a minimal, basically sensual ability to differentiate between things and people in his environment. If acts of perception lack coordination, the phenomena perceived will constantly disintegrate; there will be no distance between the observer and the things observed, and this distance is essential if one is to be able to see in the first place. "Perception is precisely that kind of act in which there can be no question of setting the act itself apart from the end to which it is directed. Perception and the percept necessarily have the same existential modality, since perception is inseparable from the consciousness which it has, or rather is, of reaching the thing itself. . . . Vision can be reduced to the mere presumption of seeing only if it is represented as the contemplation of a shifting and anchorless *quale*." [11]

Merleau-Ponty's analysis can be directly applied to Benjy. He is restricted purely and simply to perception and registers only fleeting configurations of people whom he cannot differentiate into characters, despite the many details he gives about them. In fact, paradoxically, they seem undifferentiated precisely because of all these details, for they are given a definite reality which merges into an almost total blur through the welter of unrelated, fugitive information. [12] From this one can infer that Benjy experiences a good deal more than he realizes. But whatever he experiences flashes into and out of existence, because he is totally devoid of the consciousness that is the prerequisite for an overall field of perception which would guarantee a pattern for these experiences. This is why his perceptions merge into one another with such apparent arbitrariness.

This reduction to deintellectualized perception makes the reader feel that there is more in the fragmented figures and situations than Benjy's restricted vision can convey. There is a kind of compulsion for him to work out how things fit together—to gain the privileged overall view which he is normally granted in novels but of which he is deprived by Benjy's first-person narrative. In this way, he is forced to activate his own conscious mind, as it were to compensate for Benjy's lack of consciousness. The result for the reader is that he experiences Benjy's perspective not only from the inside—with Benjy—but also from the outside, as he tries to understand Benjy. It seems as if Benjy's life, as it constantly eludes his grasp through the fleetingness of its perceptions, takes on the unreality of a mirage, though Benjy himself never experiences it as such, for it is the reader alone, who bears the burden of this experience, Benjy having a congenital immunity to such insights.

In actualizing situations of which Benjy himself is not aware, the reader is drawn into the narrative process and provoked into a wide variety of reactions. Whatever these may be (depending on the temperament of the individual reader), he finds himself forced into experiences which are quite unfamiliar to him, and the immediate impact of these experiences is to create tension. But tensions demand to be relieved, and this is what seems to be promised by the monologues of Benjy's brothers. As the idiot's perception was lacking in consciousness—the act which is "by definition, the violent transition from what I have to what I aim to have, from what I am to what I intend to be"[13]—one naturally assumes that an active consciousness will provide all the missing links.

And, indeed, the next monologue does present us with the one character in the novel who in fact has a highly developed, active consciousness. However, our expectations are not to be fulfilled—and if they were, we should probably say that *The Sound and the Fury* was a bad novel, for when tension is relaxed, and the reader's assumptions are confirmed, he will invariably lose interest. This would happen if the subjectivity reduced to mere perception were not to be shown as nothing more than a phantasma without a reality of its own, but instead we are confronted by an extremely conscious subjectivity which, in reflecting upon itself, still does not stabilize its own identity. As a result, the tension that grew out of the Benjy monologue is not resolved, but if anything enhanced.

Quentin's narrative begins with a reflection on time, which provides an indirect link with Benjy's disjointed, timeless world. Here the order of time does, at first sight, appear to offer the most basic guarantee that the rich variety of perceptions can be shaped into a coherent experience through which the self may observe itself. But the question arises as to whether the absence of such a time relation will necessarily prevent the self from, so to speak, objectifying itself. If it does, then time must possess a significance that is independent of subjectivity. Quentin's monologue is therefore concerned with the interdependence of time and subjectivity.

When he wakes up on the morning of June 2, 1910, and looks at his watch, he remembers what his father said to him when he gave him the watch:

It was Grandfather's and when Father gave it to me he said, Quentin, I give you the mausoleum of all hope and desire; it's rather excruciating-ly apt that you will use it to gain the reducto absurdum of all human experience which can fit your individual needs no better than it fitted his or his father's. I give it to you not that you may remember time, but that you might forget it now and then for a moment and not spend all your breath trying to conquer it. Because no battle is ever won he said. They are not even fought. The field only reveals to man his own folly and despair, and victory is an illusion of philosophers and fools.[14]

Time here is seen from different points of view: as the mausoleum of hope it seems to nullify the fulfillment of all desires; as the *reductio ad absurdum* of all human experience it seems to uncover its own futility, which can only be temporarily overcome by pursuing pragmatic aims; as a chance to forget, it offers a brief respite from the need to conquer it; and as a battlefield, it reveals the outcome of all man's dreams and high ideals. If time can have so many meanings, the reason for the diversity must lie not in itself, but in the purposes which are projected onto it. Despite all the close relations between time and human intentions, for the Father it still has the character of an independent entity—a continual provocation to arouse countless forms of reaction from man who suffers under it.

    The ceaseless ticking of the watch seems like a living expression of this independence of time, which can only be measured in mechanical and not in human terms. The regularity of the ticking suggests the consecutiveness through which past and present are linked together: "it can create in the mind unbroken the long diminishing parade of time."[15] If one can only go back far enough, says the Father, one will see Jesus and St. Francis "walking" again.[16] If time is regarded as the keeper of the unlosable, then interest lies not in time itself, but in the events it has contained—in other words, time is a purely external factor. Such conclusions must have seemed dubious to the Father himself, for Quentin recalls two more statements pointing to the division between what time is and what occurs within time: "Father said that. That Christ was not crucified: he was worn away by a minute clicking of little wheels."[17] If time is an independent entity, measurable only as a mechanical process and transcending everything that takes place inside it, this view of the crucifixion is not altogether illogical, for time's independence of life can only be shown by its indifference to life. Finally, Quentin recalls: "Father said that constant speculation regarding the position of mechanical hands on an arbitrary dial which is a symptom of mind-function. Excrement Father said like sweating. And I saying All right."[18] If the hands gliding over the dial determine the activity of the mind, then man is constantly involved in concepts which are called forth by

time itself. Time is the force underlying a movement that is as inescapable
as the functions of one's own body. And yet it is present only as somebody's
concept of it. So much for the Father's views on time, recalled by Quentin
as he wakes up on the last morning of his life.

For Quentin the situation is somewhat different, in that the hands of
the watch have broken off and he feels uneasy at the ticking.[19] Sometimes
he lays it face down, and eventually he decides to take the watch to be repaired.[20] Against the background of he Father's ideas, this decision might
be taken as an incipient allegory, but the desire to have the watch repaired
remains as transient as the Father's view that one must attempt to overcome the vacuity of time through concrete, pragmatic conceptions of it.

The trip to the watchmaker's is synchronized with an interior monologue of Quentin's, in which the division between time, as an independent,
consecutive entity, and the concepts it provokes, is obliterated. As in
Benjy's monologue, the author has inserted a number of clear signals that
reveal three different, interlinking processes. Normal syntax, individual
passages in italics, and in ordinary type without any punctuation indicate
different layers of consciousness is which is reflected Quentin's actualization of his past and present. The passages in italics and those without punctuation deal mainly with his memories of events that took place within the
family circle. The two different modes of presentation are used in accordance with the type and the relevance of the events described: italics generally for unprocessed situations, and unpunctuated monologue for external
events. However, these passages—though clearly distinguished through the
print—often run together and so disrupt the consecutiveness of past and
present. Quentin's journey through the town act as a random inducement
to reinvoke past situations which, in their turn, release reflections which go
far beyond his present situation. This interaction between different levels
reveals a structural pattern of the interior monologue, the beginnings of
which were already apparent in Benjy's section. The present actualizes particular impulses of the past, which appear strange and fragmentary because
they are not remembered as they were, but as they are now under the influence and in the context of the present. This breaking up of the past is a sign
of the inevitable change which it must undergo in the course of its reenact-
ment, for now something is added which did not exist at the time, imposing
an order which discounts the conditions and demolishes the context that
originally prevailed.

In this process, time has a different gestalt from that which Quentin's
Father had apparently given it. No longer is it a constant, independent
force flowing from past to future and collecting en route all the answers to

all the problems it has set; instead it can only take on a form through a self with a present that ceaselessly becomes a past and is replaced by a new, equally transient present. And so time as such is only conceivable in terms of the present working on the past; it is a process of continual, almost kaleidoscopic change, with an unending series of pasts taking shape through each individual present. Whenever something is remembered, it changes according to the circumstances under which it is remembered, but the resultant change in the past becomes a past itself which, in turn, can be remembered and changed again.

The close relations between time and subjectivity shape the structure of Quentin's monologue. The peculiar quality of time is that it constantly forms itself as the self experiences a present which passes but can be actualized anew. The connections between what is and what was are created by the self, which in fact only comes into being because of this very process. But as all experience is constantly exposed to a new present or future, it will constantly be in a state of flux, so that what has been experienced can never be fully understood, and what has been understood can never coincide totally with what constitutes the self.

This state of affairs is indicated by the general lack of coherence in Quentin's monologue. What is communicated first and foremost by the fragmented form is the fact that past and present can never be completely synthesized. Every incipient systematization is refuted by time, which as a new present exposes the ephemeral nature of any such synthesis. But it is only through subjectivity itself that time takes on its form of past, present, and future; the self is not the passive object of this process, but actually conditions it. With which of its states, then, is the self to be identified? Is it that which existed in the circumstances of the past, is it that which it is at this moment in the present, or is it simply that force which constantly creates new connections and time relations but which, at the same time, constantly plunges every one of its visible manifestations into the maelstrom of change? The self is essentially incapable of completion, and this fact accounts both for its inadequacy and its richness. The knowledge that it can never be completely in possession of itself is the hallmark of its consciousness.[21]

Quentin repeatedly describes his attitudes and actions as shadows which he walks into or which hasten on ahead of him.[22] But these shadows are his reality. They incorporate the temporality of subjectivity, which is present in all the experiences of the self, as well as in the changing order which these experiences take on and cast off in the course of time. The self is never fixed, and so none of its manifestations can ever be complete; thus although it alone can constitute its past and its present, there is always a feeling that it is strangely unreal. In the last part of this monologue, Quentin reflects on this phenomenon:

> Sometimes I could put myself to sleep saying that over and over until after the honeysuckle got all mixed up in it the whole thing came to symbolize night and unrest I seemed to be lying neither asleep nor awake looking down a long corridor of grey half-light where all stable things had become shadowy paradoxical all I had done shadows all I had felt suffered taking visible form antic and perverse mocking without relevance inherent themselves with the denial of the significance they should have affirmed thinking I was I was not who was not was not who.[23]

As Quentin realizes that his own life dissolves into shadows and makes a fool of him because he imagined there was substance and meaning in it, the fact becomes apparent that the self cannot comprehend itself as the synthesis of its manifestations. There can be no such thing as a complete survey, and however eager the self might be to experience an apotheosis of its identity, its very consciousness refutes any such restriction. Quentin reflects on this, too: ". . . you are not lying now either but you are still blind to what is in yourself to that part of general truth the sequence of natural events and their causes which shadows every mans brow even benjys you are not thinking of finitude you are contemplating an apotheosis in which a temporary state of mind will become symmetrical above the flesh and aware both of itself and of the flesh."[24] Identity as an apotheosis of the self could only come into being if one of the possible states of that self could be hypostatized. Quentin also mentions the reason for this desire—to ward off finitude. But in Quentin's monologue, the self is reflected precisely in the consciousness of its own finitude. What, then, is this identity? According to what may be gauged from Quentin's monologue, it is the constant overlapping of temporal horizons opened up by the self, the intersection of attitudes and actions, and the potentiality of situations.

The effects of this condition are illustrated by two episodes which Quentin describes on the last day of his life. One records his reaction when an attempt is made to trace his conduct back to a particular motive; the other shows what happens when one acts in the present according to ideas that were only valid in the circumstances of the past.

When Quentin is walking through the suburbs of Boston, he is followed by a little girl.[25] He wants to get rid of her and decides to take her home, but the girl does not know where she lives, and so the two of them wander through the streets, aimlessly and yet with a specific aim in mind. The desire to get rid of the child awakens in Quentin the memory of how he once used to worry about his sister Caddy; at that time he wanted to win Caddy's love, and now he wants to be free of the child. These two contrasting desires change the direction of the past and shed new light on the present. The dumb persistence of the child and the painful relationship with the sister run into one another, creating a new situation, of which the past and present situations become mere shadows. Through the interplay of possibilities, what was real and what is real now takes on an element of unreality, and yet the thoughts now preoccupying Quentin come directly out of his past and his present. And so life can be marshalled into ever new orders—but at the cost of its own factualness, which becomes increasingly shadowy. When finally Quentin is found by the girl's brother, taken to the sheriff, and accused of wicked intentions, he reacts with wild laughter,[26] because he can only regard as absurd the reduction of his various thoughts to a single motive—especially of this nature; it is in fact his very lack of motivation that enables him to become involved in those processes of consciousness which show him his own constant movement between the possible future, present, and past.

But it is also absurd for Quentin to act in the present in a way that, at best, would have suited a past situation. This is what happens in the second episode. In a state of trance, Quentin gives a beating to his friend Gerald.[27] The fight starts because of a quite casual question, but one which weighs heavily on Quentin's personal existence: namely, having a sister.[28] This touches Quentin on a very sore spot, and suddenly Gerald appears to be his rival for Caddy's love, so that he takes a belated revenge on him. But by letting himself be taken over by motivations of the past, Quentin is behaving absurdly in the present. During the fight, his interior monologue increases in pace, while images of the past appear to him in such close-up proximity that they become blurred and distorted. Real events and mere imaginings become interchangeable, so that the total synchronization of past and present is possible only as a total unreality. Here again is confirmation of Quentin's basic experience: he cannot be contained in any of his own manifestations of himself, but at the same time his only point of reference is whatever of him has been actualized.

Each shadow-like gestalt of his life is the product of the unfathomable base, and shadow and base communicate themselves in time, which is both the producer and the product of the self. "It is true that I find, through time, later experiences interlocking with earlier ones and carrying them further, but nowhere do I enjoy absolute possession of myself by myself, since the hollow void of the future is for ever being refilled with a fresh present. There is no related object without relation and without subject, no unity without unification, but every synthesis is both exploded and rebuilt by time which, with one and the same process, calls it into question and confirms it because it produces a new present which retains the past.[29]

The Quentin monologue does not fulfill the expectation, arising out of the first part of the novel, that an active consciousness might bring about an integration between self and the world. Although the monologue *is* characterized by a higher level of consciousness, this only serves to divulge the ambiguity of the self, which is both the basis and the shadow of itself. This condition is made actual by the temporality of the self.

After the Quentin monologue, there remains little more than one's curiosity as to how the fragments of the story will be put together; and precisely at this moment, when total comprehension seems to be out of the question, the Jason monologue provides the reader with the privilege of overall vision that has been withheld from him till now. Typical of Jason is the decisiveness of his actions, which at first sight might be taken for the long awaited solution to the problems of the self. But the nonalignment of the first two monologues has already precluded the idea that they are in any way complementary, and so the apparent implication that the answer lies in action must clearly be treated with the utmost caution. Although the monologues both of Benjy and of Quentin eluded the reader's own everyday experience, they still influence his observation once he has regained a degree of detachment from the proceedings. Now that he is confronted by an apparently straightforward text, he will be concerned less with the 'solution' than with the conditions that give rise to such decisiveness. And so the potential experiences of the first two monologues serve to sharpen the reader's critical eye, creating a new background against which he will judge Jason's clear-cut actions.

The Jason monologue is simple enough to understand: the events he describes are coherent and the connections between them are clearly formulated. This clarity, however, is by no means identical with a greater insight or a more penetrating vision of the events—on the contrary: the very coherence of the Jason account strikingly diminishes the richness of the world contained in the Benjy and Quentin sections. For Jason things arrange themselves in accordance with his ideas; he has to provide for the Compson family, and for this reason alone he is pragmatic. But this fact is not enough to explain the attitude to the world which gives rise to the clarity of his monologue. Unlike Quentin, he lacks the capacity to reflect on things. This is particularly apparent when he tries to corroborate his own standpoint. Whenever he describes critical situations in which he has come across opposition to his views, he simply repeats the conversation that took place at the time, assuming that this will give weight to his opinion. A feature of primitive narration is the repetition of one's own words to indicate insistence on the rightness of what has been said. To find other means of corroboration, the speaker must look beyond himself, so that he can view moments of crisis from a different standpoint. But here the mode of narration is frequently that of the interior monologue, and even when it is a straightforward first-person singular account, Jason remains his own referee. His protestations of the rightness of his opinions suggest the underlying tensions between him and the world around him, but Jason is never conscious of the reasons for these tensions, although one would have expected him to be, in view of all the opposition he meets. For him, the world remains identical to his conceptions of it. This is the key to the decisiveness of his actions as well as to the ambiguity of that decisiveness. If, against the background of the Quentin monologue, one might be tempted to see action as the way out of the "pale cast of thought," Jason's monologue reveals the consequences that arise from the inevitable limitations of the person acting. In this connection, there is a revealing remark of Quentin's which deals precisely with the preconditions of action. On his way through Boston he comes across a group of boys who have spotted a trout in a pool and are already engaged in a lively discussion about what they will buy with the proceeds of their as yet uncaught catch. Quentin says: "They all talked at once, their voices insistent and contradictory and impatient, making of unreality a possibility, then a probability, then an incontrovertible fact, as people will when their desires become words."[30]

Now Jason's intention is to cheat his niece, who is a member of his household, of the money her mother is sending her.[31] This intention and the fulfillment of it are the focal point of his whole narrative. This is the main motive for his actions and accounts for the decisiveness of his conduct, which in turn accounts for the coherence of his narrative. As his wishes become "incontrovertible facts," the gap between himself and the world seems to have disappeared. But such "incontrovertible facts" contain a strong element of illusion, which is conveyed in two ways by Jason's monologue. First, he is blind to himself, because through his inability to achieve any critical detachment from himself he is unable to recognize himself in the mirror of his own judgments: he hates frauds, and is himself one; he cheats his niece because of her immoral conduct and behaves with equal immorality; the great schism between his judgment of others and his judgment of himself shows just how illusory his conduct is. Second, Jason finds that the world around him does not arrange itself according to his ideas after all. And so his attitude becomes all the more decisive, but only with the result that he proceeds more and more to lose control of his surroundings. In the course of his account, he becomes increasingly irritated, because he sees himself entangled through his own actions in situations where he is forced to depend on others. And the more firmly he acts, the more uncontrollable become these situations, which then, naturally, push him into further firm actions. It is precisely because Jason identifies himself with his ideas and his ideas with the world that he simply cannot bear opposition. But in trying to overcome opposition, he merely increases the scope of the uncontrollable. All this hot-headed action and increasing lust for power implies that mediation between self and world is Utopian, and this element emerges in proportion to the efforts made to produce such a mediation. Jason's attempts to bring his surroundings totally into line with himself compel him to try and control them; in doing so, he himself causes their uncontrollability.

Faulkner's novel ends with an authorial account of the day after the one described by Benjy and Jason. The Compson household is viewed from an external, neutral standpoint, focused principally on the negress Dilsey. In his appendix, Faulkner says of her: "DILSEY. They endured."[32] With these words, the author links the last section of his book with a central feature of his philosophy. "Endure" is an ambiguous word, with connotations both of suffering and of survival,[33] and it refers to that experience of the world that precedes all processes of reflection and can never be comprehensively grasped *by* reflection. Here we have in the last part of the novel a peculiar extension of the previous parts: against this background, the earlier, reduced forms of subjectivity are seen as processed modes of experiencing and comprehending the world. But at the same time they expose the unprocessed core on which they feed and which for them "constitutes . . . a kind of original past, a past which has never been a present."[34] This interaction between the processed and the unprocessed worlds is brought out in two ways. In the fourth part, there is the change in narrative perspective, which releases the world of the Compson brothers from the restrictions of the first-person view, and so endows it with an expansibility which none of the interior monologues can capture or even approach. But the interaction is also reflected within the monologues themselves, which take on a new dimension when viewed in this light. The images of reduced subjectivity which they provide do show certain basic features of subjectivity that are essential to an actualization of self and world; but in the course of this actualization, during which the self enters into a relationship with itself or with the world, the element of breakdown becomes apparent. Benjy is subjectivity reduced to the senses. It retains nothing but perception as a minimal distinction between itself and the world, and its unstable grasp lets slip whatever it tries to hold onto. The life of this self seems to be in a constant state of dynamic fragmen-

tation. Quentin is subjectivity reduced to its consciousness, which can only divulge the ambiguity of its temporality. As a potential of situations it is present in all its manifestations, but can only unfold itself as a spectrum of shadows because its existence in the here-and-now precludes its total existence in the there-and-then. And, finally, Jason is subjectivity reduced to action and dominance, which in its commitment to the pursuit of its aims brings about the dynamic uncontrollability of its surroundings.

By means of these different forms of reduction, the world of the Compson brothers is given different patterns, and these differences convey both the comprehension and the breakdown of the patterns. But it is the breakdown that divulges the unprocessed basis of experience—a basis that can only be communicated in this way because otherwise it could be misconstrued as an illustration of something else. And so out of the reduced forms of the self, and out of the breakdown of their respective patterns, there emerge—albeit obliquely—the unplumbed and unplumbable depths of the self, full of sound and fury, signifying . . . something.

NOTES

1.   R. Hughes, "Introduction," William Faulkner, *The Sound and the Fury* (Penguin Books) (Harmondsworth, 1964), p. 8. There is not space enough here for a discussion of the literature on Faulkner. A critical account of the important works is given in his introduction by M. Christadler, *Natur und Geschichte im Werk William Faulkners* (Beihefte zum Jahrbuch fur Amerikastudien, 8) (Heidelberg, 1962). The main trends in Faulkner criticism are shown by H. Straumann in his essay "The Early Reputation of Faulkner's Work in Europe: A Tentative Appraisal," in *English Studies Today* (4th Series) (Rome, 1966), pp. 443–59.

2.   Faulkner, *The Sound and the Fury.* p. 244.

3.   See, e.g., G. Irle, *Der psychiatrische Roman* (Stuttgart, 1965), pp. 114–24.

4.   See also O. W. Vickery's interesting essay "Language as Theme and Technique," *in Modern American Fiction, Essays in Criticism*, ed. A. W. Litz (New York, 1963), pp. 179 ff.

5.   See G. R. Stewart and J. M. Backus, "'Each in its Ordered Place': Structure and Narrative in 'Benjy's Section' of *The Sound and the Fury,*" *American Literature* 29 (1958): 440–56.

6.   See, e.g., R. Humphrey's view of Faulkner in *Stream of Consciousness in the Modern Novel* (Berkeley and Los Angeles, 1959). In his essay "The Form and Function of Stream of Consciousness in William Faulkner's *The Sound and the Fury,*" *University of Kansas City Review* 19 (1952): 34–40, Humphrey discusses only the meaning of the symbols which determine the structure of the stream of consciousness.

7.   See the discussion on time perception in M. Merleau-Ponty, *Phenomenology of Perception*, transl. Colin Smith (New York, 1962), pp. 411 ff.

8.   Re the fascination that idiocy had for Faulkner, see Christadler, *Natur und Geschichte*, pp. 69 f.

9.   See Faulkner, *The Sound and the Fury*, pp. 11 ff. Re the form of the 'incidental' opening of novels, see R. M. Jordan, "The Limits of Illusion: Faulkner, Fielding, and Chaucer," *Criticism* 2 (1960): 284 f.

10.   See also J. Peper, *Bewusstseinslagen des Erzählens und erzählte Wirklichkeiten* (Studien zur amerikanischen Literatur und Geschichte, III) (Leiden, 1966), p. 129, and the literature he deals with. See also Jordan, "Limits of Illusion," pp. 286 f.

11.   Merleau-Ponty, *Phenomenology*, pp. 374 f.

12.   Only the relationship with Caddy, Benjy's sister, has any clear definition, as compared with relationships with the rest of the Compson household. Benjy continually speaks of the fact that Caddy smells of trees, but the monotonous repetition of this observation merely indicates his state of excitation and so conceals the individuality of Caddy, who obviously remains in a state of continual movement within Benjy's imagination. And so for Benjy, people seem to vary in importance. But as he cannot distinguish their individuality, the reader can get nothing but a blurred impression of them. See O. W. Vickery, *The Novels of William Faulkner: A Critical Interpretation* (Baton Rouge, 1961), p. 31.

13.   Merleau-Ponty, *Phenomenology*, p. 382. See also I. E. Bowling. "Faulkner: Technique of *The Sound and the Fury*," *Kenyon Review* 10 (1948): 558.

14.   Faulkner, *The Sound and the Fury*, p. 73.

15.   Ibid. J. Onimus, "L'Expression du temps dans le roman contemporain," *Revue de Littérature Comparée* 28 (1954): 314, regards the impossibility of returning across time to the origin as a central problem in Faulkner.

16.   Faulkner, *The Sound and the Fury*, p. 73.

17.   Ibid., p. 74.

18.   Ibid.

19.   See ibid., pp. 76 f., 79, 80 f., 155, and 157. See also P. Lowrey, "Concepts of Time in *The Sound and the Fury*." in *English Institute Essays* (1952), ed. A. S. Downer (New York, 1954), p. 70.

20.   See Faulkner, *The Sound and the Fury*, p. 79.

21.   This problem is viewed somewhat differently by H. Meyerhoff, *Time in Literature* (Berkeley and Los Angeles, 1960), pp. 26–54. Although Meyerhoff's discussion "Of Time and the Self" does not refer specifically to Faulkner but draws its examples from Proust, Woolf, and Joyce, he holds fast to the old image of the flowing stream of time: "It is the 'stream of consciousness' which serves to clarify or render intelligible both the element of duration in time and the aspect of an enduring self. The technique is designed to give some kind of visible, sensible impression of how it is meaningful and intelligible to think of the self as a continuing unit despite the most perplexing and chaotic manifold of immediate experience. The continuity of the 'river' of time thus corresponds to the continuity of the 'stream' of consciousness within the self. In other words, the same symbol, 'riverrun,' expresses the same unity of interpenetration within time and the self. More specifically, this

aspect of the self is conveyed by the effect of the associative technique, or the 'logic of images,' operating within the framework of the stream of consciousness. For what binds the chaotic pieces floating through the daydreams and fantasies of an individual into some kind of unity is that they make 'sense'—sense defined in terms of significant, associative images—only if they are referred to or seen within the perspective of the *same* self" (p. 37). The old image of the flowing river of time is offered as an analogy to the self, so that time can be envisaged as a duration and the self as the associative chain stretching out in this duration in order for its continuity to be conceivable. However, this category no longer applies to Faulkner's time consciousness (i.e., the temporality of the self), for the self cannot be actualized through the succession of its remembered forms. It is not surprising, then, that Proust provides the main evidence for Meyerhoff's conception of time and self. As we see in Faulkner, the self as a temporal phenomenon cannot ensure its own identity through memory, but for Meyerhoff it is memory that provides the basis for the ego's self-actualization in its imaginative form. "All psychological theories since have emphasized the integral relationship between memory and the self. The past, as we have seen, differs from the future, among other things in that it leaves records, whereas the future does not. And the mind is a recording instrument of peculiar sensitivity and complexity: I know who I am by virtue of the records and relations constituting the memory which I call my own, and which differs from the memory structure of others" (p. 43). One must see Faulkner's conception of time against this generally accepted background in order to realize the possibilities inherent in it. The temporality of the self cannot be properly grasped either through the image of the river of time or through the accumulating activities of memory. M. Le Breton, "Temps et Personne chez William Faulkner," *Journal de Psychologie Normale et Pathologique* 44 (1951): 344–54, imposes on Benjy and Quentin's behavior a normative concept of identity which is irrelevant to them (p. 346); but Le Breton rightly claims that time is Quentin's master—"un maître despotique" (see pp. 353 f.). We need not concern ourselves here with Sartre's critique of Faulkner's concept of time; see Peper, *Bewusstseinslagen des Erzählens.* pp. 135 ff. and II. Straumann, "Das Zeitproblem im englischen und amerikanischen Roman: Sterne, Joyce, Faulkner und Wilder," in *Das Zeitproblem im 20. Jahrhundert.* ed. R. W. Meyer (Berne, 1966), p. 156. Common ground between Faulkner and Sartre is pointed out by J. K. Simon, "Faulkner and Sartre: Metamorphosis and the Obscene," *Comparative Literature* 15 (1963): 216–25.

22.   See Faulkner, *The Sound and the Fury*, pp. 94, 104, 111, 122, and 154. Re 'shadow' as a key word in *The Sound and the Fury*, see K. G. Gibbons, "Quentin's Shadow," *Literature and Psychology* 12 (1962): 16–24, where the 'shadow' is given a completely psychological interpretation. A much more discerning interpretation of the shadow motif is offered by Vickery, *Novels of Faulkner*, p. 41.

23.   Faulkner, *The Sound and the Fury*, p. 154.

24.   Ibid., p. 160. See also P. Swiggart, *The Art of Faulkner's Novels* (Austin, 1962), p. 95.

25.   See Faulkner, *The Sound and the Fury*, pp. 115 ff.

26.   Ibid., pp. 128 and 134. See also Vickery, *Novels of Faulkner*, p. 37.

27.   See Faulkner, *The Sound and the Fury*, pp. 136 ff.

28.   Ibid., p. 151.

29.   Merleau-Ponty, *Phenomenology*, p. 240.

30.   Faulkner, *The Sound and the Fury*, p. 109.

3l.   See ibid., pp. 187, 189, and esp. 194 ff. Re the view of Jason as the only 'healthy' Compson, and his ironic position in relation to his 'sick' brothers, see C. Brooks, *The Hidden God* (New Haven and London, 1963), p. 41. There is a somewhat far-fetched allegorical interpretation of Jason by C. Collins, "The Interior Monologues of *The Sound and the Fury*," in *English Institute Essays* (1952), ed. A. S. Downer (New York, 1954), p. 34: Collins sees him as the 'poor player' in that same speech of Macbeth's. The relations between the individual characters are viewed more cautiously by L. Thompson, "Mirror Analogues in *The Sound and the Fury*." in *William Faulkner, Three Decades of Criticism*, ed. F. J. Hoffman and O. W. Vickery (East Lansing, 1960), pp. 211–25.

32.   William Faulkner, *The Sound and the Fury* (Vintage Book) (New York, no date), p. 22.

33.   See Peper, *Bewusstseinslagen des Erzählens*, pp. 160 ff.; see also A. Kazin, "Faulkner in His Fury," in *Modern American Fiction, Essays in Criticism*, ed. A. W. Litz (New York, 1963), p. 177, and Christadler, *Natur und Geschichte*, pp. 55 f., 62, and 177 f.

34.   Merleau-Ponty, *Phenomenology*, p. 242; see also the context in which this is discussed.

Analysis of Application

Iser's investigation of Faulkner's *The Sound and the Fury* has as its central focus the impact on the reader of the various first-person narratives that comprise the novel—a reflection of principle 5 in the key points section. It does not exemplify all the preceding four principles; indeed, it cannot do so, because reader-response analysis is not a unified methodology but rather (as stated in the overview) an "emphasis" that may take any of a number of forms. Yet Iser's phenomenological essay stands as a model application in its attention to textual detail and its investigation of the cumulative effects of the novel's four sections on the reader.

Iser focuses on the communication process between text/author and reader throughout his essay. He moves through the novel in the same sequence readers do, discussing each section as it occurs. Much of his commentary examines the Benjy and Quentin sections of the novel because they are the most difficult for readers to process, given our common presuppositions about time and "normality." In his discussion of Benjy, Iser draws important parallels between Benjy's perception of the world around him and the reader's reception of that perception, for the two are largely co-extensive in that both consist of the fragmented information on the page before us. However, Iser also distinguishes the reader's struggle to make sense of this information from the character's existence in a chaos of perception. In this way, Iser reveals the tension that the first section of *The Sound and the Fury* creates in the reader, one that will be exacerbated and relieved in succeeding sections of the novel.

As Iser discusses the Quentin, Jason, and (briefly) Dilsey sections of the novel, he retains his focus on how the reader responds to the text, drawing on the knowledge acquired in the preceding encounter with Benjy. Iser uses direct and indirect quotations from the novel to support his generalizations, teasing out the novel's effects on the reader by examining exemplary passages and scenes. Throughout, Iser foregrounds the reader's expectations and how the novel meets or thwarts them, both finding in the Quentin and Benjy sections reflections of temporality (existence in time) and examining the reader's own processing of the text and likely reflections on temporality. In this way Iser sets up his reading of the seemingly straightforward Jason section, which he suggests exacerbates the reader's frustrations because Jason is ultimately so unreflective. Iser suggests that throughout the novel, indeed, up to its very conclusion, Faulkner thwarts the reader's desire for authoritative explanation.

Iser's several quotations of Merleau-Ponty's *Phenomenology* are important, because they signal his own reader-response interests. Some forms of reader-response analysis focus on the reader's cultural background or idiosyncratic reading experience, but those are not Iser's concerns here. Instead, he examines how the novel's own representations of "perception" through its first-person narratives have an impact on the reader's perception but lead also to forms of consciousness that are peculiar to the reader. Rather than examining what the novel "means," Iser is much more interested in how the reader struggles to make meaning. Unlike some other reader-response critics, Iser does not differentiate among different readers; instead, he examines what he believes to be the cumulative effect of the novel on any reader, arguing, in effect, that his own "reading," or interpretation, is legitimate because it is provable. This is all that we as readers of criticism can ask of critics—that they support their analysis and offer a new and useful perspective on the text at hand. Indeed, Iser offers even more than that in his conclusion, directing our attention to the novel's own revelation of the idiosyncracy and reductive nature of "selfhood" itself and thereby suggesting that all perceptions, including those of all readers, are always partial and partisan.

Marxist and Materialist Analysis

Overview

While the international currency of Marxism as a rigidly defined political movement has waned in recent years, Marxist-influenced analysis of literature is still practiced widely, both as a distinct methodology and in combination with methodologies emphasizing issues of gender, sexuality, and/or race (discussed in Chapters 7, 8, and 9). In all of these manifestations, and in clear contrast to the practices of formalism discussed in Chapter 1, Marxist and materialist analysis is rooted in historical research and changing social contexts for understanding literary and other cultural texts. Yet at the same time, wide differences of opinion exist about the application of Marxist and materialist theories. Methodological purists would insist that any deviation from Marx's specific theories of class and cultural production represents a corruption of the only tool that we have to effect profound social change. Other critics, however, would suggest that attention to material conditions (those of economic situation and historical circumstances) and ideology (the belief systems accounting for and justifying those conditions) can augment almost any reading and that Marxist theories represent one important tool among many that allow insight into the complex workings of culture and the diverse uses and meanings of texts.

While Marxism obviously takes its name from Karl Marx (1818–1883), the nineteenth-century German philosopher and social critic, the Marxist and materialist study of aesthetics has had diverse proponents (many of whom have disagreed with each other on key concepts), as well as a host of subcategories and emphases. While the following discussion usually combines Marxist and materialist analysis, the former is best understood as work clearly following and referencing the specific social theories of Marx and the latter as a broader interest in class and economic conditions that may or may not invoke Marx directly. But certain concepts and analytical tools provide both an overall unity to this methodological genre and compelling evidence that Marx changed forever the way we understand social organization and representation. According to Marx, society is stratified into three primary classes—the aristocracy, the bourgeoisie, and the proletariat—each with a different worldview and set of interests. The aristocracy is the traditional class of nobles, those individuals who for many centuries held extraordinary power over others and enjoyed equally extraordinary privileges because of their ownership of land, their control of political structures ranging from kingships to local feudal positions, and their proprietorship over the bodies and labor of their subjects. The members of this class are very few in number, and both their political and economic power has diminished considerably as the Western world has moved to post-feudal forms of social organization. In the past three centuries, far greater socioeconomic power has accrued to the bourgeoisie, those individuals who have accumulated wealth and influence through their control of factories, businesses, and other highly profitable enterprises. Yet oppression has by no means diminished with this change, because under capitalism—the competitive economic system emphasizing self-motivated acquisition—the bourgeoisie have continued the aristocratic tradition of exploiting the labor of others and ensuring their own wealth through practically every means possible. Those whom they exploit, but also depend on, are the proletariat, the working class, who sell their labor and bodies but control none of the institutions or structures that generate the great wealth of the bourgeoisie.

While one can make fine distinctions within this class structure (and certainly vague terms such as "upper class" and "lower class" have boundaries that are open to debate), the categories named above have served as a basis for much Marxist and materialist analysis. And the word "materialism" needs some explanation, because underlying all such analysis is the belief that material conditions—those components of daily life related directly to one's economic existence, such as housing, work environment, and access to education and health care—not only leave indelible marks on literary and other cultural texts but also are key to understanding their reception and function. To see how this occurs, we should consider one of the most important concepts in Marxist and materialist theory (and one that resonates throughout much contemporary critical analysis): ideology. This concept helps us connect the material and immaterial components of social existence. Although different theorists define the term with varying inflections, most crucial for our purposes here is a basic understanding of "ideology" as those belief systems that underlie our actions and material lives, beliefs that are rarely reflected on and that structure our world in ways that produce and reproduce social relationships. In both its common and critical usages, "ideology" is a slippery term, sometimes used broadly (as in "bourgeois ideology") and at other times, narrowly (as in "the ideology equating new car ownership with success in life"). Yet, as Louis Althusser argues in "Ideology and Ideological State Apparatuses," ideologies create social roles and make them appear "natural," and in forming our consciousness of those roles, they justify and perpetuate the economic relationships in which people exist. And those ideologies are themselves perpetuated and transmitted through literary, political, and religious texts, through the media, through the educational system, and so forth, all of which offer rich opportunities for analysis by class-conscious, politically attuned cultural critics. If we remember that ideologies are beliefs that are shared by large groups of people and that ultimately account for their actions, then we can understand why many critics work so hard to expose and challenge oppressive ideologies in their interpretations of texts. Ultimately, they want to improve the material existence of oppressed peoples by revealing the belief systems responsible for that oppression.

Those ideology-revealing interpretations can emphasize any of a number of specific materialist concerns, though always with an eye toward concrete economic and historical conditions. For example, we might briefly consider the diverse ways a common plot—such as the differing fates and fortunes of the members of a working-class family—might be represented and interpreted with some form of attention to class issues. As we trace some of the basic principles of Marxist and materialist social theory, we shall see how Marxist and materialist textual analysis can explore a wide range of issues and social forces inside and/or outside of the boundaries of such texts as Charles Dickens's *Great Expectations*, John Steinbeck's *The Grapes of Wrath*, and Alice Walker's short story "Everyday Use." For purposes of clarity, the principles below examine Marxist and materialist methodologies in isolation; but, as mentioned above, such analysis is often combined with other methodologies to enrich our understanding of texts. Thus one finds materialist feminists and post-colonial and queer critics whose work is heavily dependent on Marxist and materialist theories. Certainly Walker's "Everyday Use" demands an attention to race and gender, as well as class, issues. But all critics working with Marxist and materialist theories, either alone or in combination with other approaches, are motivated by a sense of political and economic urgency; they attempt in various ways to reveal how our unwitting participation in class-based ideologies has both concrete and more diffuse effects on the quality of human life, and they explore precisely how that participation is effected and maintained through textual production, representation, and reception.

Key Principles

1 *An attention to the material conditions of life and a critical engagement with our attitudes about those conditions are essential for achieving positive social change.*

Fundamental to Marxist and materialist analysis is the belief that an attention to economic conditions is essential for understanding human attitudes and actions, past and present, as well as key to creating a more equitable future. It is a testament to Marx's profound and lasting influence on our understanding of social organization that at least nascent forms of class consciousness are quite common today. Most of us (perhaps all but the very wealthiest of us) are aware that certain material realities help determine the quality of our lives and the opportunities available to us. Clothing, housing, food, education, and so forth, can be very costly, and while some individuals enjoy many luxuries, others cannot afford even basic necessities. Outrage at such gross economic inequities and a desire to improve the material conditions of the world's poor have motivated Marxist social commentary for more than a century. But attitudes must be critically engaged as well, for beyond the issue of whether or not a person can afford basic clothing, for example, it is clear that social meaning is attributed to, for example, brands of clothing and that people are judged on the basis of how current and stylish their clothes are. Thus Marxist and materialist critics focus not only on the bare facts and figures related to an individual's economic status but also on the wide variety of social meanings attributed to that status and to the goods and services that an individual purchases or aspires to purchase. An important concept in Marxist analysis is that of the "commodity fetish," which refers most specifically to our attribution of intrinsic value to commodities without recognition of the labor that produced them. But the term "fetish" can also point to the magical qualities associated with buying or owning a particular commodity—how we invest a purchase or possession with the power to make us happy, secure, or complete. In doing so, we sometimes come to value commodities even more highly than other human beings. Certainly this is one of the key issues explored by Walker in "Everyday Use," in which one daughter, representing a new generation and set of material concerns, values a family quilt in ways very different from her sister and mother, who still see in it the loving work of beloved grandmother. Of course, the story prods its readers into contemplating their own value systems; indeed, Marxist and materialist critics commonly suggest that by becoming conscious of the many ways in which our lives are affected by material realities, anxieties, and aspirations, we are better able to change them, to sort out what is truly important from what is selfish and hollow, and, ultimately, to make the world a less oppressive place.

2 *The traditional social structure of classes, within and around texts, is built on the oppression of workers.*

Key to Marxist and materialist analysis is the recognition that a relatively small number of people possess far too much wealth in our world, that given the resources theoretically available to all, too many individuals are hungry, are in need of health care and education, and are unemployed or underpaid for the hard work that they perform. Marxist commentators assert that the aristocracy in the past and the bourgeoisie today can afford so many luxuries because the proletariat is kept in poverty and that capitalism—the relentless pursuit of self-interest—is largely to blame. It is morally unacceptable, they insist, that corporate executives today earn millions of dollars a year but that some of these executives' own gardeners and housekeepers (who may work even more hours a day than their employers) earn wages that are so low they cannot pay for their children's education or for basic health care. Marxist and materialist critics explore the reasons behind such gross economic disparities, their changing historical nature, and the many ways in which class systems perpetuate themselves through institutions, laws, and other social structures. Some works focus on the world class structure; others focus more intensely on the class structure of a nation or community as it functions now or at some time in the past. Literary engagements with such issues vary similarly, of course. In Steinbeck's *The Grapes of Wrath*, for example, the reader finds a compelling portrait of a specific time, place, and people: an exploration of the fates of a 1930s "dust bowl" family—the Joads—who are virtually destroyed by poverty and social institutions that are either indifferent or hostile to them. In analyzing the social dynamics of the Great Depression or the texts that fictionally represent it, Marxist and materialist scholars always ask why and how oppressive social systems operate as they explore avenues for changing them.

3 *Social classes, within and around texts, ultimately have conflicting interests, even if they share certain beliefs at the present time.*

Class conflict is necessary and inevitable from a Marxist standpoint, even if individuals have been taught to accept the status quo. Of course, dominant groups invariably have a rationale to justify their positions of power. The theoretician Antonio Gramsci used the term "hegemony" to describe how powerful social groups "naturalize" their domination of others.

Unlike "ideology," which refers to a specific set of beliefs, "hegemony" refers to the system of interlocked institutions, practices, worldviews, expectations, hopes, and fears, as well as specific ideologies, that makes the status quo and the stratification of power and economic resources within that status quo seem natural and unchallengeable. Thus the aristocracy and, later, the bourgeoisie have not only acquired the power to exploit the labor of the proletariat, they also assert that they have the right, even the duty, to do so. Indeed, this is a belief shared by many members of the proletariat, who have been taught to devalue themselves and may even believe that they deserve the conditions they live in. Therefore the first step toward changing the status quo is consciousness-raising. By understanding the dynamics of economic oppression and the dependence of the wealthy on the labor of the proletariat, the working class will become able to redefine their worldview and organize in ways that allow them effectively to demand a share of the world's wealth that is proportionate with their numbers. And certainly our understanding of this process of consciousness-raising could be key to our interpretation of Steinbeck's "radicalizing" of Tom Joad at the end of *The Grapes of Wrath*. But even as we discover and appreciate such acts of politicization and the dawning of class awareness, we should also remember that hegemonic forces are resilient and that the proletarian struggle toward self-awareness and effective social mobilization has been far from uniformly successful. Thus many works of Marxist and materialist analysis examine in great detail the wide variety of strategies used by the aristocracy and bourgeoisie to promote their own interests as natural and unchallengeable, exploring carefully the degree to which the proletariat at a given time and place resist or accept hegemonic definitions and institutions.

4   *Literary and other cultural texts are ideological in background, form, and function.*

Literary and other cultural texts help form our worldview, playing an important role in the ways that classes regard themselves and others. Thus we might say that Marxist and materialist critics (unlike practitioners of strictly formalist methodologies) focus specifically on the political and sociological power of texts as those texts reflect preexisting belief systems and contribute to either their continuation or their metamorphosis. Of course, any text may reflect numerous ideologies simultaneously, ones of gender, race, sexuality, nationhood, and class, for example; indeed, conflicting ideologies may coexist within a text, which may reveal implicit contradictions and will certainly contain explicit disagreements among characters. Such is obviously the case in Walker's story, which clearly shows overt tensions surrounding ethnic heritage, generational attitudes, and gender roles, as well as class and social position. But even if a text or author seems or claims to be wholly unconcerned with issues of social class, Marxist and materialist critics never see literature and other forms of cultural expression as being outside of ideology or transcending class concerns; simply put, texts always have ideological implications.

5 *The production and consumption of texts reflect class ideologies.*

Texts are human creations, revealing many of the faults, fears, attributes, and attitudes of their creators; obviously those creators always belong to a specific economic class and would reflect, in the opinion of Marxist and materialist critics, the interests of that class. In the past three centuries, it has most often been the interests of the bourgeoisie that have had an impact on textual production, for they not only have had the resources (time, education level, etc.) to produce texts but have also dominated the publishing industry and other channels for disseminating "culture." Yet production is only one part of the "economy" of texts, for reading texts, as well as interacting with them in other ways, is also a privilege enjoyed by those with sufficient education, time, and income; thus the bourgeoisie have also been the primary audience for literary and other cultural texts. These realities have led to sustained investigations of precisely what a bourgeois audience expects in texts and how they are marketed to that audience. But even though the production and consumption of texts so clearly reflect aspects of social class, Marxist and materialist critics have disagreed on some issues. These include the extent to which writers or texts can distance themselves from a given class background or set of hegemonic interests. Can a bourgeois writer represent the interests of the proletariat in anything other than heavily biased ways? Does a writer who emerges from the proletariat but who then enjoys financial success as an artist lose all touch with the struggles of the oppressed? Can a traditional form—such as the sonnet or the novel—ever serve the interests of the oppressed, or are new forms necessary for proletarian self-representation? All these issues could be investigated vis-à-vis texts such as Dickens's *Great Expectations*, for as we well know, Dickens came from the lower classes and continued to explore their interests in many of his novels, long after he came to enjoy enormous popularity and class privilege. As always, investigations of these or similar topics would carefully examine the specific historical circumstances surrounding the creation or reception of a text, as well as the precise aspects of the class structure at that time and place.

6 *Representations within texts reflect class ideologies.*

A related form of Marxist and materialist analysis focuses on the material conditions and class ideologies present within the boundaries of the text itself. To see how characters' lives and perspectives on the world are informed by their class backgrounds or the class-relevant themes of the text in which they appear is to help illuminate how literary and other cultural texts help support or alter the status quo. Some texts address class issues explicitly, portraying the impoverished living conditions of the poor or the remiss attitudes of the wealthy. Others seem to ignore class issues altogether, but they always reflect class ideologies in their settings, characterizations, and thematic communications to their audience. Indeed, what is ignored is often as important as what is said explicitly, and Marxist and materialist critics have often explored how many aristocratic or bourgeois characters function in ignorance of the workers who must labor relentlessly to support upper-class privileges. Furthermore, when characters change positions in the class hierarchy—perhaps entering the bourgeoisie through good fortune or by working within the system—it is often productive to examine how their perspectives on the world change, how their sympathies metamorphose, and how their interactions with other characters reflect old or new class interests. Indeed, these specific issues and tensions are in the foreground of both "Everyday Use" and *Great Expectations,* as certain members of a younger generation in both texts leave behind their childhood systems of value but encounter family members who still adhere to those old values and worldviews. Of course, some texts, such as these two, will obviously lend themselves more readily to class analysis than others, but few will fail to provide some material on which to base a discussion of class ideologies. The class-interested critic will first establish the class identity of the text's major and minor characters and then investigate how those identities help account for attitudes, actions, hopes, and fears—in sum, how they contribute to the explicit or implicit themes and messages of the text.

7 *The production, consumption, and content of literary and cultural criticism is also ideological in nature.*

What is true for literary and other cultural texts is also true for literary and cultural criticism. The same class-informed perspectives on the production, circulation, and content of a novel, for instance, can be brought to bear on a work of criticism, for it, too, is a text. Marxist and materialist analysis demands self-awareness on the part of the critic, the acknowledgment that critics, too, are members of a class-stratified society and that our choice of texts, our approach to them, and the meanings we find in them are all affected by our class backgrounds and material existences. Unlike formalist methodologies, which cast the critic as exterior to and an objective evaluator of literary or other cultural texts, Marxist and materialist method-

ologies see critics as always subject to and their writings pervaded by the very same ideologies found throughout all other forms of human expression. Again, what is not said is often as important as what is stated explicitly. Thus critics who completely ignore issues of class and material existence are sometimes perceived by Marxist and materialist commentators as in collusion with the prevailing economic system. On the other hand, those who address issues of class with sensitivity can help raise the awareness of their readers and thereby perform a significant social task. Indeed, even a cursory examination of the sometimes heated discussions among critical respondents to the works of Dickens, Steinbeck, and contemporary writers such as Alice Walker reveals the passion and social commitment that Marxist and materialist critics often bring to their analysis of both literary and critical texts.

8 *A key role of the critic is to elucidate textual and extratextual ideologies and thereby to further class awareness and positive social change.*

Marxist and materialist critics build on the insights into class and ideology explored above as they construct powerful interventions into current critical and social debates. Indeed, teaching and consciousness-raising have always been important components of Marxist and materialist theories of social progress; literary and cultural critics, though their writing, can participate in the process of helping people to become aware of class inequities in the past and present and to see how such inequities can be challenged and transformed in the future. As we shall see in later chapters, this sense of social activism and political purpose is common to many contemporary critical methodologies. While they may disagree on priorities and interpretations, practitioners of feminist, post-colonial, and queer analysis, and those attentive to issues of race, class, and material conditions, share a sense of commitment to social relevance, as they work to illuminate the ways that texts help organize our society and explore how such texts influence our perceptions of ourselves and others.

Bibliography

Althusser, Louis. "Ideology and Ideological State Apparatuses." In *Lenin and Philosophy and other Essays*, trans. Ben Brewster. New York: Monthly Review Press, 1971.

This important essay contains Althusser's theory of how human consciousness is shaped by socioeconomic ideologies and the social institutions that transmit them. Its conceptual sophistication and many references to preceding theories will make it of interest primarily to intermediate and advanced readers.

Eagleton, Terry. *Marxism and Literary Criticism*. Berkeley: University of California Press, 1976.

This brief book introduces some of the important concepts and theorists in Marxist literary studies. While it is by no means comprehensive, it represents a solid introduction for intermediate and advanced readers.

Eagleton, Terry, and Drew Milne, eds. *Marxist Literary Theory*. Cambridge, MA: Blackwell, 1996.

This lengthy and substantial collection of theoretical texts and applied analysis is noteworthy for its breadth and historical comprehensiveness and particularly commendable for its inclusion of some of Marx's own statements about literature and culture. Its introductions by Eagleton and Milne provide useful overviews of Marxist concepts and controversies. This collection's specialized language and assumption of previous theoretical knowledge will make it of greatest interest to advanced readers.

Elster, Jon. *Making Sense of Marx*. New York: Cambridge University Press, 1985.

For readers interested in Marx's specific theories of social organization and transformation, this book provides a thorough and relatively accessible overview. Its conceptual sophistication will be make most appropriate for intermediate and advanced readers.

Hawkes, David. *Ideology*. New York: Routledge, 1996.

This brief and accessible overview covers one of the most important concepts in Marxist and materialist analysis, tracing the concept of "ideology" from its origins in classical writing to its revision by theorists in recent years. Its clarity and use of timely examples make it of interest to all readers.

Jameson, Fredric. *The Political Unconscious: Narrative as a Socially Symbolic Act*. Ithaca, NY: Cornell University Press, 1981.

This is perhaps the most important recent work of Marxist-influenced theory and applied criticism. Its language and presupposition of theoretical knowledge render it very difficult, but it has been highly influential in its tracing of the political context and content of fictional works. It is most appropriate for advanced readers.

Marx, Karl, and Frederich Engels. *Marx and Engels on Literature and Art*, ed. Lee Braxadall and Stefan Morawski. St. Louis: Telos Press, 1973.

This work contains selections of the writings of Karl Marx and his fellow theorist Frederich Engels, focusing specifically on those dealing with literature and art. As with all primary texts by Marx, its language and conceptual sophistication render it most appropriate for advanced readers.

Nelson, Cary, and Lawrence Grossberg, eds. *Marxism and the Interpretation of Culture*. Urbana: University of Illinois Press, 1988.

This weighty book, developed from papers delivered at a conference of critics and theorists in 1983, covers a variety of topics and controversies in contemporary Marxist theory and interpretation. It is noteworthy for its inclusion of dialogues concerning many of the papers that it reprints. Its level of difficulty makes it most appropriate for advanced readers.

Williams, Raymond. *Marxism and Literature*. Oxford: Oxford University Press, 1977.

This book explains with clarity and precision the major concepts underlying the Marxist approach to literary creation, representation, and criticism. While it contains few examples of applied analysis, its comprehensiveness and user-friendly organization and language will make it of great interest to intermediate and advanced readers.

Application

Reading Prompts

1. In his introductory paragraph, Ahearn isolates an erroneous conception underlying previous criticism of *Pride and Prejudice* (and *Madame Bovary*). Mark or highlight those statements in which he reveals how his own analysis will differ.
2. Flag or mark those passages that reveal how Ahearn's analysis of Austen's novel draws on historical research, thereby interpreting the novel with reference to a very specific time in British history.
3. Consider how Ahearn differentiates among the class identities of Lady Catherine, Darcy, and Elizabeth. Mark all statements in which he specifies those identities.
4. Pay careful attention to the many different ideologies—of paternal roles, marriage, property, and so forth—that Ahearn reveals in the novel. As you read, consider how they are linked in and through his analysis.
5. Notice Ahearn's particular interest in Austen's use of London in the novel. Mark or highlight those passages that illuminate why and how that usage reveals the belief systems of a specific time, place, and set of class interests.

EDWARD AHEARN

From *Radical Jane and the Other Emma*

Austen and Flaubert may seem so different that it is salutary to view them together in Marx's terms. *Pride and Prejudice* and *Madame Bovary* frame the period of the onset of the bourgeois order to the point that they seem to follow directly one upon the other, Austen's book concluding with an anticipation of the end of the Napoleonic Wars (when Wickham and Lydia are sent home), Flaubert's opening with a reference to 1812 (when Charles Bovary's corrupt father is forced to retire from the imperial army).[1] Published in 1813, *Pride and Prejudice* (on superficial reading) seems to depict a world as yet untouched by the urban industrial system, whereas *Madame Bovary* (1856–57), although situated *en province*, clearly supposes that system. In this respect, Marx's thought helps correct a misconception about both works—that they are not very historically pointed. On the contrary, in various ways together they suggest the transformations of modes of production and hence human relations that Marx delineated: the gradual diminishment of the power of landed wealth, despite the continuing importance of the aristocracy; the development of massive cities, industrial production, and commodities and the creation of needs for them; the accumulation of wealth in the form of capital; new relations among the classes and increasing alienation among individuals, including vicious economic struggle and the unhappiness of women in what Marx and Engels sneeringly called "bourgeois marriage."

Not only are these thematic convergences, as well as the significant differences in Austen's and Flaubert's handling of marriage, sexuality, money, class, country, and city, and so on, historically resonant. Marx's ideas also help us to relate, hence understand in more coherent fashion, features of the writing of these novelists that have been noted, although sometimes as isolated or idiosyncratic. These include the informing obsession with marriage as the increasingly problematic locus of a woman's happiness and the related conflict of romance and realism and distrust of the language of passion, particularly in connection with the special kinds of irony that both writers notably, and sometimes viciously, deploy. Flaubert the misanthropist is a familiar stereotype, but many readers of Austen may have wondered aloud if she was a nasty person. More important than such personalized reactions is the growing awareness of the subversive quality of Austen's writing, produced by "the notorious instability of her novelistic irony."[2] This sounds like Jonathan Culler on Flaubert, and one almost awaits an *Austen: The Uses of Uncertainty*, with the difference that recent Austen criticism, as has long been the case for Flaubert, relates such narrative ambiguity to the complex class situation in which she lived her life and which her novels evoke.

Class identity and aspiration, and the effort to surmount them in the interest of superior insight, can also be explored in Austen's and Flaubert's practice of counterpointing subjective and omniscient voices. Moreover, irony needs to be related to the question of plots and endings as essentially comic or pessimistic. The marriages at the end of *Pride and Prejudice* and the bleak conclusion of *Madame Bovary* have to be seen together, not so much as expressing individual authorial psychology but as mobilizing or deflating, at the onset and end of a historical period of intense class conflict, the impulses of what Jameson has aptly called the political unconscious.

> And now nothing remains for me but to assure you in the most animated language of the violence of my affection. To fortune I am perfectly indifferent, and shall make no demand of that nature on your father, since I am well aware that it could not be complied with; and that one thousand pounds in the 4 per cents, which will not be yours till after your mother's decrease, is all that you may ever be entitled to. (75)

Despite its comic touch (here evident in Collins's absurd proposal to Elizabeth) and satisfying outcome, *Pride and Prejudice* is scandalous in its presentation of marriage as the key to survival—survival in crude financial terms, in terms of the quality of life, in terms finally of life itself. Collins's hypocritical indifference to fortune, characteristic of so many in the book, recalls the opening sentences' presentation of marriage in relation to possession, fortune, property. His research on how much Elizabeth will inherit parallels the insistence throughout on specifying how much everyone is worth. Bingley has four or five thousand pounds a year, Darcy ten thousand, and their sisters have inherited twenty thousand and thirty thousand, respectively. In contrast, Mrs. Bennet has inherited but four thousand, and her husband's yearly income, in addition to the problem of the entail, is only two thousand—which explains the pressing economic aspect of the Bennet sisters' marriage search. As Collins points out to Elizabeth when she refuses him, she may never get a better offer. Such logic underlies Mrs. Bennet's comic pursuit of sons-in-law, Charlotte's "disinterested desire of an establishment' (85), and Fitzwilliams's complaint: "Younger sons cannot marry where they like" (127). Carried to an extreme, it contemplates property as more important than the lives of others—witness Bennet's joke about Collins's possession of his estate after his death, Collins's "mortifying" appreciation of his future property (45), Lady Lucas's calculating "with more interest than . . . ever . . . before, how many years longer Mr. Bennet was likely to live" (86)—where the much remarked financial vocabulary reinforces the inhumanity of the thought.[3] Finally, Collins's egregiously mechanical reference to libidinal emotion and expression indicates the threat to the erotic that is posed by the economic.

The Wickham-Lydia affair is the unhappiest instance of the difficult conjunction of love, marriage, and money, exposing not only their defects but also those of Mr. Bennet, who is criticized for not having provided for Lydia: "Had he done his duty . . . Lydia need not have been indebted to her uncle, for whatever of honour or credit could now be purchased for her. The satisfaction of prevailing on one of the most worthless young men in Great Britain to be her husband, might then have rested in its proper place" (211). This judgment fittingly adopts the accents almost of Bennet's own irony, as when he remarks that Wickham is a "pleasant fellow, and would jilt [Elizabeth] creditably," adding later, "He simpers, and smirks, and makes love to us all. . . . I defy even Sir William Lucas himself, to produce a more valuable son-in-law" (96, 226). Even as Bennet is criticized for financial irresponsibility, the contamination of the sexual by the monetary is again stressed in the vocabulary of debt, credit, purchase, worth, particularly in the sarcastic reference to Wickham's "value" in "making love"—the only use of the phrase that I find in the book. (Moreover, although Bennet supposedly is not sharp on money matters, even he is not beyond profiting from the generosity of Gardiner and Darcy in buying Lydia's marriage—"It will save me a world of trouble and economy" [260].)

As for Lydia and Wickham themselves, they are more troubling if we allow ourselves to experience a certain compassion for them as casualties of the marriage-money system, which the novel, despite its criticism of them, does not preclude. Lydia's compulsion to marry is shared by all at the end, even by Elizabeth: "And they *must* marry! Yet he is *such* a man!" (208). Such a man indeed: Wickham pursues in illegitimate ways what most everyone else is after. In view of parallels and contrasts among Collins, Wickham, and Darcy (Collins succeeds in areas for which Wickham was first destined, Collins was mistreated by his father whereas Wickham was favored by Darcy's father), moreover, we may feel that Darcy and Wickham are a bit too close for comfort and may trace in the latter's bitterness more than a hint of class *ressentiment*. Lydia's pathetic letter provides ammunition for such an interpretation: "It is a great comfort to have you so rich, and when you have nothing else to do, I hope you will think of us" (267).

Against this radical delineation of economic struggle and the difficulties of sexual love, it is the major thrust of the novel to delay, then bring about, the "good" marriages. All are assured about the personal suitability of Bingley and Jane, who also promises to be financially responsible: "Imprudence or thoughtlessness in money matters, would be unpardonable in *me*" (239). And the much more important marriage, that of the heroine, is slowly worked out through the plot, until Elizabeth recognizes that Darcy is "exactly the man, who, in disposition and talents, would most suit her" (214).

This suitability is conditioned by Darcy's great wealth, as those critics have recognized who stress that she is not being completely "unserious" in dating her change of heart from her first seeing "his beautiful grounds at Pemberley" (258). In that scene she is *immediately* moved by an attraction to possession: "'And of this place,' thought she, 'I might have been mistress! With these rooms I might now have been familiarly acquainted! Instead of viewing them as a stranger, I might have rejoiced in them as my own'" (167). This is uncomfortably reminiscent of the book's opening lines and even of Collins's avidity: "The hall, the dining-room, and all its furniture were examined and praised; and his commendation of every thing would have touched Mrs. Bennet's heart, but for the mortifying supposition of his viewing it all as his own future property" (45).

But Elizabeth is a sympathetic character who tries—on the whole if not always successfully—to combine financial realism, genuine affection, and respect for persons. Attracted to Wickham, who however is wooing Miss King's ten thousand pounds, she wonders, "Where does discretion end, and avarice begin" (106), and ruefully admits that "handsome young men must have something to live on, as well as the plain" (104). But when Lydia later makes a denigrating remark about Miss King, Elizabeth has the surprising self-discovery that "the coarseness of the *sentiment* was little other than her own breast had formerly harboured and fancied liberal!" (151). Concerning Fitzwilliam, moreover, she is less self-aware and thoughtful. To his remark about younger sons quoted earlier, she makes the "lively," and justified, but somewhat cruel response: "And pray, what is the usual price of an Earl's younger son? Unless the elder brother is very sickly, I suppose you would not ask above fifty thousand pounds" (127). And once Darcy makes his first proposal and writes his letter, Fitzwilliam quickly fades as a source of interest: "Colonel Fitzwilliam had made it clear that he had no intentions at all" (130); "Elizabeth could but just *affect* concern in missing him; she really rejoiced at it. Colonel Fitzwilliam was no longer an object. She could think only of her letter" (144–45).

We may read in this youthful thoughtlessness, but also evidence of the tendency to give persons consideration only to the extent that they can be viewed as financially suitable marriage partners. Earlier we learned that in her mother's mind Elizabeth rated only a husband of the Collins sort: "Elizabeth was the least dear to her of all her children; and though the man and the match were quite good enough for *her*, the worth of each was eclipsed by Mr. Bingley and Netherfield" (73). In Elizabeth's self-absorbed marital shorthand, something of the same treatment is given to Fitzwilliam, who has "no intentions," who besides Darcy is "no longer an object," and who indeed from this point on is "eclipsed" from the novel.

Marriage and property, objects to own, objects of desire: at every point *Pride and Prejudice* reveals a problematic relation between ownership and love. Austen's frequently remarked distrust of romantic infatuation and its effusive mode of expression is visible in the satire of Collins, the criticism of Lydia and her father, and particularly in the lesson for Elizabeth of the danger of her attraction to Wickham. Mrs. Gardiner calls her use of the phrase "violently in love" hackneyed (97), and she herself adopts an ironic tone in relating to her aunt the realization that she had not felt a "pure and elevating passion" for Wickham (104). Moreover, in feeling as well as expression, Elizabeth is reflective rather than passionate in her responses not only to Wickham and Fitzwilliam but especially to Darcy. This is not to say that she lacks desire. Rather, as already intimated, the strong emotion of sexual love, revealed through blushing and related physical and emotional reactions and rarely if ever verbalized, is mediated—for her and for the reader—by property, specifically Darcy's.

Her cool response to Darcy is noted, and justified. Recognizing his "ardent love," she in contrast is aware of respect, gratitude, and power over him (181, 189). Under the blow of Lydia's flight, she realizes that she "could have loved him," and this is legitimated by a supposition that relates narrator and reader: "If gratitude and esteem are good foundations of affection, Elizabeth's change of sentiment will be neither improbable nor faulty." A further supposition, to the effect that a love-at-first-sight scenario might be more "interesting," is expressed ironically—the narrator seems to be chastening our romantic tendencies (190–91). Even near the end, Elizabeth "rather *knew* that she was happy, than *felt* herself to be so" (257).

But powerful emotion is not lacking. In the first proposal Darcy says his feelings "will not be repressed," adding, "You must allow me to tell you how ardently I admire and love you" (130). Austen does not allow him to tell any more in his own words; the rest comes to us through Elizabeth's reaction, indignation, which he rapidly comes to share. But when he seeks her out again, the responses that earlier expressed anger now have a different meaning: "The colour which had been driven from her face, returned for half a minute with an additional glow, and a smile of delight added lustre to her eyes" (229). Signs of emotion in eye and cheek, combined with reticence of expression, also characterize the second proposal:

> Elizabeth feeling all the more than common awkwardness and anxiety of his situation, now forced herself to speak; and immediately, though not very fluently, gave him to understand, that her sentiments had undergone so material a change, since the period to which he alluded, as to make her receive with gratitude and pleasure, his present assurances. The happiness which this reply produced, was such as he had probably never felt before; and he expressed himself on the occasion as sensibly and as warmly as a man violently in love can be supposed to do. Had Elizabeth been able to encounter his eye, she might have seen how well the expression of heart-felt delight, diffused over his face, became him; but, though she could not look, she could listen, and he told her of feeling, which, in proving of what importance she was to him, made his affection every moment more valuable (252).

The speech of neither is quoted, as again the narrator mobilizes our imagination, with a "probably" and an invitation to "suppose" what a man "violently in love" might say. Elizabeth's reactions continue to be expressed in terms of gratitude, pleasure and value, but of Darcy the narrator uses the phrase that earlier her aunt called hackneyed. The index of the real "violence" of his love is there, though, in the "expression of heart-felt delight, diffused over his face."

The passionate eye, color diffused over the face, like Elizabeth's eyes and complexion, which first attracted Darcy—these are the signals in the novel's discrete code of bodily energy. Elizabeth's inability to raise her eyes is equally expressive. She listens nonetheless to the language of love; while hers in not "fluent," his is both "sensible" and "warm." But as noted, neither is given directly—verbal revelations of love are even rarer than bodily ones. The latter, degraded in Lydia's vulgar energy, are "displayed" innocently only in the Gardiner children on the return of their parents: "The joyful surprise that lighted up their faces, and displayed itself over their whole bodies, in a variety of capers and frisks, was the first pleasing earnest of their welcome" (195). And the former, verbal communication of desire and gratification, is given fullest expression in Elizabeth's reaction—not to Darcy's person but to his estate.

From early on Elizabeth has been attracted to Pemberley as the model of the great country house (25), as opposed to the dwellings of others: the vulgar furnishings of the Philipses, the crowded house at Hunsford, the Bennet property so impertinently evaluated by Lady Catherine, even Rosings, by which Elizabeth is "but slightly affected" despite Collins's expectation of "raptures" (111). The raptures will be reserved for Pemberley.

By the time of her visit, Pemberley has been invested with feelings of desire and loss. It is after Darcy's letter and the frustration of Elizabeth's attraction to Wickham, and after her remark about men which Mrs. Gardiner says "savours strongly of disappointment," that the trip, first planned as a tour of the Lakes District, is proposed. Elizabeth responds with a satirical but compensating burst of ecstatic language, foreseeing "delight," "felicity," "life and vigour," "transport." She laughingly displaces such emotion from the men who have disappointed her to sublime nature: "What are men to rocks and mountains?" And she mocks the conventions of nature description, intending to remember clearly what she sees so that her "effusions" will be bearable (107). There is then a further process of expectation, frustration, and substitution, as the trip on which Elizabeth "had set her heart" is shortened. In Derbyshire rather than at the Lakes, her "alarms" over encountering Darcy are "removed," and she feels she can indulge the "curiosity" of seeing his house in his absence (164–66).

Her parodic project for an orderly but excited evocation of sublime nature becomes, in the narrative handling of her visit, a systematic and rapturous description of Darcy's estate (166–77). Meticulous organization is apparent in the progression of the travelers (and reader): the arrival in the park, which is traversed from "one of its lowest points" to an "eminence, where . . . the eye was instantly caught by Pemberley house"; then the descent to the house, whose rooms and floors are visited in systematic fashion. The subsequent tour with the gardener (Elizabeth has all along been with the Gardiners) is preceded by the appearance of Darcy, whom they meet twice (as there are two portraits and more than one gardener). To be sure, the visit has presaged Darcy's arrival, and the meeting between him and the Gardiners serves powerfully to draw him and Elizabeth together.

Like Elizabeth's idea for a description of the lakes, the Pemberley chapter is also an "effusion," accumulating expressions of emotional response. This is natural in the meetings with Darcy, which produce flushes and silences, reactions of "surprise," "wonder," and so on; it is also natural before Darcy's arrival, as Elizabeth blushes about the first portrait, pays "keenest" attention to Mrs. Reynolds, and goes "in quest" of the second portrait. But her heightened state, her emotions of anticipation and gratification, are stressed from the beginning and are first directed toward Pemberley: "Elizabeth, as they drove along, watched for the first appearance of Pemberley Woods with some perturbation; and when at length they turned in at the lodge, her spirits were in a high flutter"; "Elizabeth's mind was too full for conversation, but she saw and admired every remarkable spot and point of view"; "Elizabeth was delighted"; "Elizabeth . . . went to a window to enjoy its prospect. . . . she looked on the whole scene . . . with delight."

The vocabulary of pleasurable response is matched by descriptive praise, a panegyric to Darcy's estate, which is characterized by magnitude and quality. The park is "very large," with a "great variety of ground" and "a beautiful wood, stretching over a wide extent." Elizabeth admires the "remarkable" views as they ascend "for half a mile." From within, "every disposition of the ground was good"; rooms and furnishing are "large, well-proportioned . . . handsomely fitted up," "lofty," filled with "real elegance." The grounds as seen later are "beautiful," "nobler," "finer," with "many charming views of the valley, the opposite hills, with the long range of woods overspreading many." To the visitors' question about touring the whole, the gardener answers triumphantly that it is "ten miles round."

Nowhere else in the novel is there such a passage of laudatory description;[4] for Elizabeth, and for the reader, Pemberley is a magnificent object of attraction. The word *object*, earlier designating a man of marriageable potential, now refers to things, not artifacts but aspects of nature visible from Darcy's house: "The hill, crowned with wood, from which they had descended . . . was a beautiful object"; "As they passed into other rooms, these objects were taking different positions; but from every window there were beauties to be seen."

As the double meaning of *object* suggests, the scenery may be charged with desire. During the tour of the grounds, near the narrowing path, Elizabeth "longed to explore its windings." Shortly before, she could think only of where Darcy was and "longed to know what . . . was passing in his mind." Even before his arrival, Darcy's house is described in this way: "It was a large, handsome, stone building, standing well on rising ground, and backed by a ridge of high woody hills, and in front, a stream of some natural importance was swelled into greater, but without any artificial appearance." The last note leads to appreciation of the relation of nature and art in Darcy's estate, to the admiration of all, and to the attraction to ownership mentioned earlier: "They were all of them warm in their admiration; and at that moment she felt, that to be mistress of Pemberley might be something!"

Much in the sentences quoted evokes Pemberley in a straightforward manner. But the libidinal dimension, while light, is unmistakable—the longing to explore narrow windings, the delight in standing and rising, in the high back and swelling front. In the last passage cited, the sexual overtones lead rapidly to Elizabeth's desire for ownership. (Note that Darcy is more than once referred to as Pemberley's owner or proprietor, especially in his abrupt appearance: with Gardiner "conjecturing as to the date of the building, the owner of it himself suddenly came forward".) A quite "warm" libidinal notion thus eventuates in a very warm desire for possession.

Fredric Jameson has brilliantly shown how the description of the house and grounds of an unattractive old maid in a Balzac story is charged with an almost sexual intensity and builds an argument about the desire to possess property through marriage as representing the "political unconscious" of postrevolutionary France, an unrealizable urge to roll back history and overcome class conflict. Neither Darcy nor Elizabeth is unattractive, and Austen's novel is a more uncensored expression, at a slightly earlier time and in a different national context, of the urge to class reconciliation. The Pemberley chapter, the turning point that leads to Elizabeth's marriage, is crucial in this regard, since it is by far the most ardent piece of writing in the book, the passage in which language most intensely "makes love" with its "object." This remark is relevant for the protagonist but also for Austen's readership (then and now) in its response to the narrative tissue of the work. The chapter is an unprecedented *textual* investment of desire, an expression in a discreetly libidinal register of the fascination of magnificent property, wealth, and power.

The class dimensions of Elizabeth's marriage have attracted attention by critics who have come to see Austen's fiction as "the very evidence of social history."[5] Of punctual historical detail there is indeed little. Rather, the indication at the end that Lydia and Wickham remain unsettled "even when the restoration of peace dismissed them to a home" (267) has a deeper sociohistorical significance. Although shadowed by undesirable elements, the marriage of Elizabeth and Darcy is seen (or wished) to coincide with the peaceful resolution of a period of international turbulence that had shaken the social world of Austen's England.

That world includes aristocracy (Lady Catherine, Darcy), gentry (Bennet), a "pseudogentry" of clergy, lawyers, and businessmen (Lucas, the Philipses, Collins, and—unsuccessfully—Wickham), and an urban-based commercial class (the Gardiners). Mobility within this framework is remarkable and accounts for many of the work's strains and satisfactions—Bennet's and Lydia's inferior marriages, the social ascension capped by Bingley's purchase of an estate at the end, the Gardiners' association with Darcy, the elder Bennet sisters' marriage into vastly superior status. Satire of pseudogentry and rigid aristocracy in the figures of Lucas, Mrs. Bennet, and Lady Catherine is clear. But Darcy overcomes such limitations. That he is early on attracted to Elizabeth, defending himself only through "the inferiority of her connections" (35), indicates the extent to which the narrative *retard* derives from the dynamics of class. Further, since Lady Catherine's project of uniting two noble families fails, and since the daughters of these families are presented as sickly or unnaturally shy, whereas Darcy benefits from the lively Elizabeth, it is hard not to see their marriage as a

historical allegory with overtones of class stagnation, mobility, and reconciliation. By her arrogance Lady Catherine precipitates Darcy's second proposal, and her "infinite use" in that regard is noted (263). But even more
"useful" are the Gardiners, who in the last lines of the book deserve Elizabeth's and Darcy's gratitude for bringing them together.

The splendid marriage of an attractive young woman of the middle
classes to the scion of a rich, ancient, and powerful family thus occurs
through the agency (negative) of an inflexible aristocracy and (positive) of a
new commercial class, urbane in all the senses of the word. The role of the
Gardiners, their identification with the economic activity of the city, and
the meanings suggested by their name as well as that of Lady Catherine un-
balance somewhat the comfortable setting of the great country estate that
Elizabeth inhabits at novel's end. This adds to our sense of discrepancies
and fissures that the book strives to contain.[6]

Through centered in the country and the lives of the landed classes,
Pride and Prejudice insistently signals the importance of London. A suggestive nomenclature of distance, proximity, and value is stressed in the
country-urban theme—Netherfield, Longbourn, Hunsford, Rosings,
Pemberley, Grosvenor Street, Cheapside, Gracecourt Street. The geography underlines discussion of country and city: Miss Bingley's criticism of
Elizabeth's "country town" ways (24) and her wish to bring in a London
doctor for Jane (shades of Flaubert); Lady Catherine on London's cultural
and educational attractions; Darcy's complaint about the country's "confined and unvarying society" (29), his claim that the fifty miles between
Hunsford and Lucas Lodge is "a *very* easy distance." Elizabeth responds
that this judgment reflects his wealth (it also reflects the importance in the
period of improved transport throughout the country and between country
and city). Darcy accuses her of provincialism, then reveals his admiration:
"*You* cannot have a right to such very strong local attachment. *You* cannot
always have been at Longbourn" (123–24). And we have read that Elizabeth
and Jane "had frequently been staying . . . in town" with their aunt (97).

The role of London and the Gardiners in making Elizabeth and Jane
finer than their sisters (hence worthy of superior marriages) fits with another aspect—that the three marriages of the Bennet sisters are strongly associated with movement to or through "town." Before Mrs. Bennet and her
daughters lay eyes on Bingley, he is "obliged to be in town"—"gone to
London" to get a party for the ball, among whom is Darcy (5–6). Afterwards his projected short trip becomes instead a departure by his whole
party "on their way to town" (81), a fact confirmed by two letters about the
London season from Miss Bingley. Jane goes to London but does not meet
Bingley, even as Elizabeth's discussions with her aunt there do not resolve

her confusion over marriage and money. Darcy's letter after his first proposal recapitulates all concerning Bingley, including the plan to get him
away to London. Bingley finally proposes while Darcy stays away in the city
(having confessed his role to Bingley "on the evening before . . . going to
London" [256]).

Wickham too arrives "from town," with Denny, "concerning whose return from London Lydia came to inquire" (50). He disappoints Elizabeth
by not attending Bingley's ball, pretexting business in London. Later, the
fact that he and Lydia have gone to London is the first indication that they
do not plan marriage. We then learn of Bennet's search for them there, his
return to Longbourn (at the same time that Mrs. Gardiner returns to the
capital), Gardiner's efforts and finally Darcy's success in locating them and
imposing marriage, which occasions a flurry of movement between Pemberley and London: "When all this was resolved on, he returned again to
his friends, who were still staying at Pemberley; but it was agreed that he
should be in London once more when the wedding took place, and all
money matters were then to receive the last finish"—before he was to
"leave town again" (222–23).

Here Darcy's trips between country estate and London accentuate the
money-marriage (and now -city) nexus. And so many iterations of the significance of going to or leaving London! But such is also the case for the
central marriage, influenced by the Gardiners and Lady Catherine, in both
cases with pointed reference to London. Why is Elizabeth's trip shortened?
Because her uncle is "prevented by business from setting out till a fortnight
later in July, and must be in London again within a month" (164). And after
the confrontation with Elizabeth, Lady Catherine returns home through
London, causing Elizabeth to worry that Darcy "would return no more.
Lady Catherine might see him in her way through town; and his engagement . . . of coming again to Netherfield must give way" (248). But she
soon learns that she owes her happiness to the provocation of Lady Catherine, "who *did* call on him in her return through London" (253)!

What all of this shows is a structure that cannot be accidental: though
largely "about" the landed classes, the novel keeps calling our attention to
London, where other forces—undescribed but evidently determining, even
in the countryside—are at work.[7] This is a literary equivalent to Marx's arguments about country and city and to the concept of the historical opposition, persistence, and coexistence of competing modes of production. In
Marx's terms, the urban capitalist mode of production, despite the persistence of earlier forms, is already achieving a position of dominance, but
such characters as Lady Catherine and Mr. Bennet do not know that—although, in some profound way, their creator does. We can appreciate this

further by examining the Gardiners, Lady Catherine, and Darcy in terms of the city-country dialectic and related social and economic elements.

Lady Catherine's adherence to aristocratic forms is flagrant, and most extreme in her argument with Elizabeth. Her assumption that the assertion of noble prerogatives will win the argument is countered by Elizabeth's self-assurance in being "a gentleman's daughter," which provides a readerly satisfaction based in class identity and antagonism and which reduces Lady Catherine to repeating the code words for noble values in an almost incantatory way: "You have no regard, then, for the honour and credit of my nephew!"; "You refuse to obey the claims of duty, honour, and gratitude" (245–7). But the mere expression of such values is inefficacious, we might say, in changed historical circumstances.

Yet at Rosings Lady Catherine operates in a resolutely feudal way. Elizabeth observes that

> though this great lady was not in the commission of the peace for the county, she was a most active magistrate in her own parish, the minutest concerns of which were carried to her by Mr. Collins; and whenever any of the cottagers were disposed to be quarrelsome, discontented or too poor, she sallied forth into the village to settle their differences, silence their complaints, and scold them into harmony and plenty. (117)

In addition to Elizabeth's insightfulness (how different, we shall see, from Emma Bovary), we note the interactions among aristocracy, subordinate clergy, and cottagers and the unmasking of the economic nature of the relations of superiority and inferiority in the discordant series "quarrelsome, discontented . . . poor" and "settle . . . differences, silence . . . complaints, . . . scold . . . into harmony and plenty."

In the context of our earlier discussion of the implications of certain names, we should consider Lady Catherine's, which like Darcy's, suggests ancient French lineage. To be named de Bourg(h) while asserting claims to aristocracy, however, is to be caught in a historical paradox, since the word in medieval French designated a fortified town, whose inhabitants, possessors of a special status, existed in contradistinction to the landed nobility. The adjective deriving from the word is of course *bourgeois*. Lady Catherine is not only an anachronism; her name, associated with the origins of the modern European city and of the bourgeoisie, belies the purity of class hierarchies to which she is devoted. Perhaps this fits with her house, described as a "handsome modern building" (109), and with her ultimate reconciliation to Darcy's marriage despite the "pollution" of Pemberley by Elizabeth's city relatives (268).[8]

If Lady Catherine is a negative and contradictory figure, the Gardiners, unambiguously associated with the city, are presented in celebratory fashion.

Their role is important and is developed with systematic care. We learn at first only that Mrs. Bennet has "a brother settled in London in a re-spectable line of trade" (18); Mrs. Hurst reveals that he lives in Cheapside (Miss Bingley appropriately exclaiming, "That is capital" [24]); later Mrs. Bennet mentions his name (30). In volume 2, we meet him and his wife and learn of their estimable qualities and their influence on Elizabeth and Jane. In the final volume their role becomes major. They contribute much to the union of Darcy and Elizabeth, and in the Wickham-Lydia affair Gardiner shows himself to be generous and at ease in the city—as opposed to Mr. Bennet. Again in opposition to Bennet, the Gardiners' family life is high-lighted, particularly through the happiness of their children. If Elizabeth's marriage to the family-oriented Darcy is meant to repair some of the dam-age done by the Bennets' deficiencies, the Gardiners contribute much to this rehabilitation.

These positive qualities are implicit in the first description of the Gardiners early in volume 2:

> Mr. Gardiner was a sensible, gentlemanlike man, greatly superior to his sister as well by nature as education. The Netherfield ladies would have had diffi-culty in believing that a man who lived by trade, and within view of his own warehouses, could have been so well bred and agreeable. Mrs. Gardiner, who was several years younger than Mrs. Bennet and Mrs. Philips, was an amiable, intelligent, elegant woman. (96–97)

The Gardiners' superiority in nature and education is not unconnected with their name, which tells us briefly about them what Darcy's estate reveals in a magnified way about him. Of course modifications of the natural include not only gardens and estates but cities, where they are often monstrous. Pub-lished two decades after Blake's "London," the novel depicts none of that, just as the glowing picture of the city businessman is hardly predictive for later fiction. Here however the message is clear: the Netherfield ladies, and Darcy, and the reader, are to recognize that urban commercial activity is not incompatible with "well bred" intelligence and elegance.

But this recognition is also postponed. Despite the visits to town in vol-ume 2, no contact is made there with Bingley or Darcy, because, as Mrs. Gardiner explains, city geography also inscribes social differences: "We live in so different a part of town, all our connections are so different" (98). How satisfying, then, in class terms, is the concluding paragraph of the novel: "With the Gardiners, they were always on the most intimate terms. Darcy, as well as Elizabeth, really loved them; and they were both ever sen-sible of the warmest gratitude towards the persons who, by bringing her into Debyshire, had been the means of uniting them" (268). This circle of intimacy, warmth, love, gratitude, and unity projects a societal wish fulfillment of large proportions, a political (not sub- but) superconscious, since all is so clearly delineated.

But the union between Elizabeth and Darcy is the important one. Darcy and what he has—ten thousand per annum, a great uncle who is a judge and an uncle who is a lord, patronage in the church, a house in town, a magnificent family library, as well as Pemberley—are the supreme objects of desire. Again Collins is close to the mark in the worldly judgment that Darcy has "every thing the heart of mortal can most desire,—splendid property, noble kindred, and extensive patronage" (250). Darcy's wealth and its source (only property?), his noble family, and what results from these, his power (in Collins's ecclesiastical terms, patronage), all need to be examined.

Darcy's influence over others is great; he is so wealthy that he exercises a fascination, whether that fascination is experienced as positive or negative. His control over Bingley may not appear malignant, since it contributes so much to the plot and since Elizabeth is able to tease him about it at the end. No harm done either when he gets permission to marry Elizabeth before her father is assured that she loves him: "He is the kind of man . . . to whom I should never dare refuse any thing, which he condescended to ask" (260). His obstinacy (Mrs. Gardiner's word) in settling the Wickham affair makes Elizabeth proud of him (222, 224); ironically it also illustrates what Wickham has complained about all along—Darcy's power to impose his desires. With an ax to grind, too, Fitzwilliam presents a similar if more balanced view: "I am at his disposal. He arranges the business just as he pleases"; "He likes to have his own way very well. . . . But so we all do. It is only that he has better means of having it than many others, because he is rich, and many others are poor" (126). Finally, the fascination Darcy exercises is evident in the scenes in which others attempt to interpret his silent face, culminating in Elizabeth's contemplation of his portrait: "As a brother, a landlord, a master, she considered how many people's happiness were in his guardianship!— How much of pleasure or pain it was in his power to bestow!—How much of good or evil must be done by him!" (170–71).

Elizabeth is overwhelmed here by the sheer extent of Darcy's power, which according to Mrs. Reynolds and what the Gardiners later discover is indeed used as generous "guardianship" and which derives from inherited landed wealth. Note that she had earlier heard from Wickham an identical, but negatively colored, description of Darcy's uses of his wealth as based in pride:

It has often led him to be liberal and generous,—to give his money freely, to display hospitality, to assist his tenants, and relieve the poor. Family pride, and *filial* pride, for he is very proud of what his father was, have done this. Not to appear to disgrace his family, to degenerate from the popular qualities, or lose the influence of the Pemberley House, is a powerful motive. He has also *brotherly* pride, which with *some* brotherly affection, makes him a very kind and careful guardian of his sister. (57)

Wickham's dishonesty is clear; so also is the contrast between Darcy and Lady Catherine and the softening of his arrogance by the end. But Wickham's analysis is not incorrect. Darcy's generosity is possible only because he has immense wealth, whereas others do not; his generosity, moreover, is a means of perpetuating that relationship of superiority and subservience. Darcy exercises magnanimously the power that Elizabeth unmasks in the case of his aunt, though not in that of her future husband. Wickham, a love temptation for Elizabeth, may also be seen—in a novel whose conclusion projects the union of the dominant classes—as an oppositional voice, discredited but not altogether silenced.

Austen hints that Darcy's wealth may not be exclusively of the landed kind. Lucas immediately sniffs out that he has a house in town, where his sister lives; Elizabeth later meets her London companion (17, 57, 182). Darcy himself spends more time there than anyone else but his sister and the Gardiners, for example the ten days during which Bingley proposes to Jane (236). In handling the Wickham-Lydia matter he functions more effectively there even than Gardiner. Perhaps some of those business letters that Miss Bingley would find "odious" to write concern interests "in town" (32)?

This conjecture may gather support from an important passage that to my knowledge has not drawn commentary, the late revelation by Lady Catherine about Darcy's (and her daughter's) lineage: "My daughter and my nephew are formed for each other. They are descended on the maternal side, from the same noble line; and, on the father's, from respectable, honourable, and ancient, though untitled families. Their fortune on both sides is splendid. They are destined for each other by the voice of every member of their respective houses" (245). Lady Catherine's vocabulary of aristocracy is still in evidence. The verbiage cannot hide the fact that neither Darcy nor her daughter comes from absolutely noble lineage; aristocracy in the novel as in history turns out to be a pseudoconcept. There have been in her generation two marriages with "untitled families," with another kind of wealth, presumably commercial in origin. The lateness of the revelation, just before the union of Darcy and Elizabeth, is suggestive; it is as if, before a new fusion of social elements can occur, an earlier one must be admitted.

Admitted—but not foregrounded, in contrast to the narrator's early detailing of Bingley's economic and social background. Bingley's father did not marry into nobility and did not purchase an estate, but we are not told if Pemberley has been in Lady Catherine's family for generations or if Darcy's father purchased it. Either way, the traditional mode of life that reigns there has been infused with wealth deriving from another economic mode. And Darcy himself may easily be thought of as the "protocapitalist,"[9] whose business in the city is not narrated but whose power exercises a discreetly sexual fascination, at a time when the countryside is only beginning to be marginalized and the new economic forces seem to contribute smoothly to the maintenance of the marvelous "aristocratic" world of Pemberley. . . .

NOTES

1.   See R. W. Chapman on Austen's use of the 1811–12 calendar, militia in Brighton in 1793, 1794, 1795, and 1803–14, Peace of Amiens (1802), or anticipation of that which ended the Napoleonic Wars ("The Composition of *Pride and Prejudice*," reprinted in the edition cited here, ed. Donald J. Gray [New York: Norton, 1966], 287–93); also Warren Roberts, *Jane Austen and the French Revolution* (New York: St. Martin's Press, 1979); and Christopher Kent, "'Real Solemn History' and Social History," in *Jane Austen in a Social Context*, ed. David Monaghan (Totowa, N.J.: Barnes and Noble, 1981), 86–104.

2.   Mary Poovey, *The Proper Lady and the Woman Writer: Ideology as Style in the Works of Mary Wollstonecraft, Mary Shelley, and Jane Austen* (Chicago: University of Chicago Press, 1984), 172–83, esp. 173. See also David Monaghan's introduction to *Jane Austen in a Social Context*; Karen Newman, "Can This Marriage Be Saved: Jane Austen Makes Sense of an Ending," *ELH* 50 (1983): 693–710; Judith Lowder Newton, *Women, Power, and Subversion: Social Strategies in British Fiction, 1778–1860* (Athens: University of Georgia Press, 1981); Julia Prewitt Brown, *Jane Austen's Novels: Social Change and Literary Form* (Cambridge, Mass.: Harvard University Press, 1979); Tony Tanner, *Jane Austen* (Cambridge, Mass.: Harvard University Press, 1986). For the conservative stance in the ideological battleground of Austen criticism, see Marilyn Butler, *Jane Austen and the War of Ideas* (Oxford: Clarendon Press, 1975); Alistair Duckworth, *The Improvement of the Estate: A Study of Jane Austen's Novels* (Baltimore: John Hopkins University Press, 1971). See also Duckworth's impartial "Jane Austen and the Conflict of Interpretations," in *Jane Austen: New Perspectives*, ed. Janet Todd (New York: Holmes and Meier, 1983), 39–52; and Jonathan Culler, *Flaubert: The Uses of Uncertainty* (Ithaca: Cornell University Press, 1974).

3.   See esp. Dorothy Van Ghent, "On *Pride and Prejudice*," reprinted in the Norton edition, 362–73; also Igor Webb, *From Custom to Capital: The English Novel and the Industrial Revolution* (Ithaca: Cornell University Press, 1981).

4.   This despite Van Ghent's accurate qualification of the book's "general-ized" descriptive language ("On *Pride and Prejudice*").

5.   Kent, "'Real Solemn History,'" 102. For what follows see Terry Lovell, "Jane Austen and the Gentry: A Study in Literature and Ideology," in *The Sociology of Literature: Applied Studies*, ed. Diana Laureson (Hanley, England: Wood Mitchell, 1978), esp. 20–21; David Monaghan, *Jane Austen, Structure and Social Vision* (New York: Barnes and Noble, 1980); and David Spring, "Interpreters of Jane Austen's Social World," in Todd, *Jane Austen*, 53–72.

6.   See Poovey, *Proper Lady*, 201–7, 243; Newton, *Women, Power*, 83–85; and esp. Newman, "Can This Marriage Be Saved," 704, 708.

7.   This has not been much recognized, even by Williams, *Country and City*, 112–18, 166. In addition to Gardiner's London business, Elizabeth's meeting with Darcy occurs because of his landed property affairs, "business with his steward" (174). Different modes of production conflict and intersect around Elizabeth's marriage.

8.   On the rise of the bourgeoisie and the conflict of codes of values, see *GI*, 153, 173, 179. Austen also shows finesse concerning contradictions of money and class by having Miss Bingley, whose money comes from "trade" but who wanted to marry Darcy, submit to his marriage in feudal fashion, paying off "every arrear of civility" to Elizabeth (9, 267). The possible double meaning of her use of *capital* cited below is unique; elsewhere the word means "of highest quality."

9.   Readers of *The Political Unconscious* will recognize the treatment of Heath-cliff in *Wuthering Heights* (128).

Analysis of Application

Edward Ahearn's "Radical Jane and the Other Emma" opens by briefly ex-ploring the socioeconomic conditions and historical circumstances that ac-count for differences between Jane Austen's *Pride and Prejudice* and Flaubert's *Madame Bovary*, using Marxist theory to suggest that the two novels, separated by fifty or so years, reveal profound changes in British so-ciety. The section of Ahearn's analysis reprinted here is that devoted to a close reading of Austen's work, in which he examines the "presentation of marriage as the key to survival—survival in crude financial terms, in terms of the quality of life, in terms finally of life itself" and relates those thematic concerns to the economic uncertainties and changing class ideologies of the first years of the nineteenth century.

Ahearn suggests that Austen's novel is one pervaded by thinly veiled forms of economic struggle, with the search for a spouse often expressed as a search for security and property. Ahearn's analysis exemplifies the Marxist notion that class ideologies are key to understanding human motivations and interactions, and that material concerns often override other forms of valuation. In the close reading of Elizabeth's reactions to Darcy's Pember-

ley estate, Ahearn demonstrates the degree to which her reactions to Darcy himself are expressed in terms of objectification of and appreciation for his property.

But Ahearn also teases out other materialist concerns from the novel. His exploration of the centrality of London in the book—and that commercial center's challenge to the traditional, rural power of the aristocracy and exemplification of the new economic sway of the bourgeoisie—foregrounds the historical specificity of the novel. The waning social prominence of the landed gentry and the emerging dominance of the urban capitalists are part of the undercurrent of tension that the novel's marriages will help alleviate. Ahearn is particularly intriguing in his reading of Darcy not as a representative of that moribund aristocratic class but instead as a hybrid of sorts, one who is able to bridge the country and the city and whose economic power looks forward to that of the great industrialists of the mid-nineteenth century. Ahearn terms him a "protocapitalist," whose centrality in the novel is an appropriate emblem of the great economic shifts that were going on around Austen at the time of the writing of *Pride and Prejudice*.

Ahearn's essay exemplifies an important type of Marxist/materialist analysis, one that seeks to reveal the class tensions and motivations underlying a work's plot, themes, and characterizations. In exploring the class ideologies of *Pride and Prejudice*, Ahearn helps the reader understand how the novel coheres and accounts for some of its unique qualities as a work of fiction, but he also uses the novel as part of an exploration of sociopolitical forces at play at the time of its writing. In this way, Marxist analysis is interdisciplinary, for unlike the New Criticism's emphasis on the intrinsic meanings of a text, Marxist analysis often draws on social and economic history, on sociology and political science, as it traces the ways that texts can temporarily assuage the fears and anxieties of the reader by rendering fictional solutions to profound social problems and imminent economic crises. Though Ahearn, in the section reprinted here, does not examine the effect of Austen's novel on its readership, he implies that *Pride and Prejudice* does little to challenge the status quo, that it reflects and is therefore complicit in the great economic changes that were occurring in Britain in the early nineteenth century. His role as a critic is to illuminate those changes and tease out the ways that the novel reproduces the ideologies of its day.

Psychoanalytic Analysis

Overview

Of the many genres of analysis covered in this book, psychoanalytic critique is certainly one of the most popular among and familiar to students. Not only is its terminology recognized and used widely, but also the field on which it draws—psychology—centers famously on the interpretation of stories and character, making the connection to literary and cultural analysis a logical one. Furthermore, it is a field on which other critical methodologies have often drawn; forms of psychoanalytic analysis have played key roles in the development of feminist, gay/lesbian/queer, and New Historicist responses to literary and other cultural texts. But the popularity and familiarity of psychoanalytic methodologies carry with them a certain danger, for too often psychoanalytic terms are used very imprecisely, even erroneously. While the following chapter explores psychoanalytic critique and the work of some of its most important theorists in a necessarily brief fashion, students are urged to consult more advanced works as they explore the complex terminology of psychoanalytic theory and construct their own psychoanalytic interpretations of texts.

Many of the central concepts and procedures of modern psychoanalytic critique derive from the work of Sigmund Freud (1856–1939), who synthesized, worked to regularize, and dramatically augmented the theories of previous interpreters of the human mind. Freud effectively transplanted the concerns of psychology from the domain of philosophers to that of scientists and physicians, changing forever the very frames of reference we use in discussing selfhood. Among Freud's many insights and innovations was his refinement of the concept of the "unconscious" to help isolate those hidden forces, desires, and fears that exert influence over us in ways beyond our knowledge and control. The concept of the "unconscious" lends itself to a wide variety of interpretive acts, and following the lead of Freud, some

psychoanalysts and therapists today cast themselves as "readers" of their pa-
tients' lives and stories, working to uncover hidden causes for sometimes
puzzling behavior. While such an authoritative interpretive stance vis-à-vis
human subjects has always carried with it the risk of harmful misreadings
(and even malpractice), the misuses and abuses of psychoanalytic theories
should not blind us to the continuing utility of many Freudian and post-
Freudian concepts in the analysis of literature and culture. Here, as elsewhere, we should remember that theories of human behavior, of social and
textual organization, and of the many ways by which cultural meanings are
made and conveyed are inevitably incomplete; although they can be very
useful in appropriately and precisely defined critical projects, they demand
critical scrutiny.

Indeed, only the most dogmatic of commentators would consider
Freudian theory, for example, as either wholly accurate or thoroughly discredited. To be sure, Freudian notions of gender development and sexual
"normality" have been subject to voluminous criticism. The Freudian construction of women as "castrated," inferior versions of men clearly reflects
oppressive nineteenth-century belief systems. In fact, some of the keenest
articulations of feminist literary and cultural critique (explored in Chapter
7) are framed as responses to Freud and others who have used men's experiences and bodies as the norms by which women are judged and always
found lacking. Similarly, gay/lesbian/queer critics (discussed in Chapter 8)
have offered insightful responses to Freud's rigid equation of heterosexuality with normality. Yet as such commentators often readily admit, Freud,
even at his most biased, allows us remarkable insight into a mindset that
dominated the medical establishment for many years and that has left indelible marks on literary and other cultural texts. And even more important
to remember is that some of Freud's theories—especially those concerning
generational conflict between children and parents and the lasting effects of
childhood trauma—have not been discredited and are of continuing use to
both therapists and critics.

And as much as we equate modern psychoanalysis with Freud, he is not
the only theorist whose work is relevant to psychoanalytic interpretations of
literature, art, and culture. Karen Horney, Nancy Chodorow, and Luce Irigaray are among the many feminist theorists whose works may be consulted
for compelling insights into human behavior and psychology. Furthermore,
the work of group and social psychologists such as Elias Canetti and Erich
Fromm have often been very useful for cultural critics. But without a doubt,
the most influential recent theorist of human consciousness and behavior is
Jacques Lacan (1901–1981), whose modifications of Freud are widely used
in literary and cultural criticism today. While Lacan's responses to Freud

are numerous and complex, perhaps his most significant revision is to Freud's approach to early childhood development. Lacan focuses specifically on the child's entrance into the "symbolic order" as the key to understanding the roots of adult personality and behavior. The symbolic order comprises structures of language, rules of social organization, and interpersonal limits on behavior and desire, the imposition of which mark the child's passage into subjectivity, or differentiated selfhood. Lacan's theories build on the recognition that the beliefs, biases, and gender differentiations of the surrounding culture are actually instilled in the child, that they are culturally specific and conveyed rather than "natural" in the transcendental sense that they often appear to be for Freud. Lacan's theories have thus been embraced by some feminist and queer critics, whose applications of and responses to his theories are often densely theoretical but also highly rewarding. Indeed, Lacan's and Freud's perspectives on culture and the development of personality are the subject of many useful books and articles, from introductory through advanced levels, which students may wish to consult often as they construct their own supple applications of psychoanalytic theory.

Key Principles

1 *Human activity is not reducible to conscious intent.*

While court systems in this country and elsewhere continue to debate the question of exactly when individuals should be held responsible for their actions, it is clear that no one is fully self-aware and in control of all of the fears, desires, and conflicting emotions that can propel actions. Human behavior is often something of puzzle, requiring concerted acts of investigation to discover root causes and multiple effects. We might take as a touchstone example here a violent act such as murder; in a hearing or trial, a court-appointed psychiatrist would carefully and slowly piece together the evidence needed to decide whether a defendant is competent to stand trial, in the process probing the many psychological factors that may have motivated such an extreme act of violence. Indeed, the role of interpreter of the human mind—which is assumed by the psychiatrist, therapist, or psychoanalyst—is quite similar to that of the literary and cultural critic, for both analyze narrative and other forms of textual data and trace hidden sources for sometimes surprising surface behaviors.

2 *While biology may have some part to play in the development of human psychology, environment also has an important role.*

Precisely where human fears, desires, and emotions originate is a subject of considerable controversy. Current research into the physiology of the brain and possible genetic links to mental disorders suggest that part of the puzzle of human behavior may be understood through biology and biochemistry; indeed, genetics may help us account for violent acts and violence-prone personalities. But certainly environment also plays a major role in the wide and dramatic psychological variations that exist among individuals. The primary task of the psychoanalyst is to discover the precise impact on the psyche of environmental factors such as familial dynamics, personal misfortunes, and social crises, as well as to probe the effects of stress and the influences on the individual of the many interpersonal relationships that develop over a lifetime. Yet at the same time, human psychology is never reducible to simple formulas, for as most of us know well, people can respond very differently to similar situations or even practically identical traumas. Interpretation must always be suspended until sufficient pertinent data are collected and then analyzed carefully. First-person narratives, in particular, demand critical scrutiny. Individuals often forget some of the most significant occurrences in their lives and even lie (to themselves as well as to others) about fears and desires. Psychoanalysts must accumulate and carefully judge their data and follow up all leads to what may be very well hidden or even multiple causes for behaviors or ingrained character traits. At the start of their analysis—of the psychological causes for an act of extreme violence, in our example here—psychoanalytic interpreters may wish to ask very wide-ranging questions. When did a specific behavior or trait—perhaps angry or violent interactions with others—first manifest itself? What were the circumstances—familial, interpersonal, or otherwise—immediately surrounding or preceding its appearance? What distant memories or dynamics, even from very early childhood or young adulthood (which may appear inconsequential at first glance), could conceivably bear on, anticipate, or otherwise relate to the development of adult violent behavior? These and other questions may also allow the psychoanalytic interpreter to expand outward from the individual in question to that individual's social and familial context (and, of course, interaction with that context) as pieces to the puzzle of behavior are slowly put together.

3 *Individuals move through developmental stages early in life, and traumas or experiences during that process may have a lasting effect on personality.*

While Freud and Lacan both emphasized the lasting impact of the developmental process that occurs during infancy, childhood, and adolescence, the two theorists differed significantly on the precise definitions, parameters, and component parts of the process itself. Freud's model centers on the importance of the child's experience of various body parts as they are found to give pleasure and as they indicate the degree of separation from the mother. Infants and very young children move from an oral phase, in which they are still connected to the mother's body, through an anal phase of separation and corresponding control over bowel functions, to a phallic phase involving the discovery of pleasure through genital manipulation. But healthy adult personality and sexuality are only achieved, according to Freud, after the child also successfully negotiates the various rivalries involving parents of the same and opposite sex. For boys, this means moving through the Oedipus complex and resolving the fears of castration that follow upon discovering the mother's lack of a penis. For girls, this centers on resolving the rivalry with the mother for the father's attention and then coming to identify with the mother. Of course, as many feminist commentators (such as Luce Irigaray) have pointed out, Freud's work is male-centered (phallocentric) and his theories depend on the unquestioned significance of the penis, which is considered the marker of ultimate value, one the girl lacks and the possession of which she will ("naturally," in Freud's opinion) envy.

Lacan's theories of childhood development differ considerably, centering instead on the child's acquisition of language and cultural norms. Like Freud, Lacan invests with great significance the child's process of separation from the mother, which, Lacan suggests, centers on the dawning of self-awareness in what he called the "mirror stage," when the child becomes aware of itself as a distinct being; indeed, for a while this mirrored being and the world that surrounds it seem completely under the child's control (as the image in a mirror is under control). But as development proceeds, such control is discovered to be illusory, especially as the child encounters language and social signification, which Lacan calls the "symbolic order." Through language the child is placed in gender categories, encounters the uncontrollableness of the social world, and discovers the complex negotiations that are involved in the expression and meeting of desires. While Freud suggested an inherent unity to the healthy adult's psychology, Lacan recognized that social and psychological existence is always plagued by fragmentations and imperfect resolutions (for this reason, his theories have often been adopted by post-structuralist critics, whose work is discussed in Chapter 6). But key to both Lacan's and Freud's theories is the recognition that obstacles and traumas can occur at any point in these early developmental stages, ones that can arrest development or lead to infantile, childish, or even violent and otherwise extreme behavior in individuals who have achieved biological maturity.

4 *The psychology of authors has an impact on literary and other forms of cultural representation.*

The theories described briefly above can influence our understanding of literary and other cultural texts in numerous ways. One of the simplest is to see literary and cultural expression as a reflection of the psychology of the creator of the text. This can be as elementary as attempting to discover unresolved conflicts in a literary text that relate to the author's own biography or as complex as looking for broad social-psychological "norms" in a text that reflect the author's social experience and cultural context. Of course, narrowly biographical forms of criticism are often subject to the same charges of oversimplification and misdiagnosis that are leveled at some psychoanalysts; the reading of a biography or set of extratextual documents (such as letters or essays) rarely, if ever, gives a critic enough information to render a decision about an author's degree of psychological health. But certainly a writer or artist's life story and context can be sources of valuable information about the creation of a text. In particular, it is often useful to place a text in broad social currents of fear, desire, gender formation, and so forth, that an author wittingly or unwittingly reflects. How were the author's experiences unique or commonplace, given her or his class, ethnic, and gender background? What were the child-rearing and familial norms of the age, and how do these relate to commonplace fears and desires? And, finally, how do these currents manifest themselves in plot developments, characterizations, themes, and other textual details? Thus, for example, in analyzing a novel in which a murder occurs, such as Dostoevsky's *Crime and Punishment*, the interpreter might wish to examine the author's belief system and interaction with a philosophical and historical context—including contemporary psychological theories—to probe the novel's place in a history of beliefs regarding the human mind, guilt, and punishment. In seeing psychological undercurrents in texts as historically and culturally specific, we open up their complexity and can come to understand them as rich human documents rather than lifeless artifacts or simple case histories for quick diagnosis.

5 *Characters in texts may also have a complex psychology.*

The rich interplay between the psychological undercurrents of the text and the historical context from which it originated may be quite evident in the development and nuances of specific characterizations. Complexly drawn characters often have a psychology that is well worth exploring at length. Both Freudian and Lacanian theory urge us to examine the familial interactions of an individual during childhood and adolescence to understand more fully her or his behaviors, fears, and desires during adulthood. To probe how an individual first acquires a sense of self separate from parents is to see the foundations of that individual's later sense of autonomy and responsibility vis-à-vis others. But even if a text offers few clues about the specifics of a character's early life, it may be possible to speculate on possible causes for manifest behavior by carefully examining the expression of that behavior and then relating it to other social relationships or interpersonal tensions that are either explicit or implicit in the text. In probing the actions of a character such as the murderer Raskolnikov in *Crime and Punishment*, in exploring his "deviance" from accepted social norms, his insecurities and unresolved interpersonal conflicts, you as an interpreter of that behavior and personality have many possible avenues for analysis. Using Freudian, Lacanian, or other psychological theory, you might relate such a character's violent behavior to problematic interactions with parents or even parental figures (if little is actually know about the character's parents), siblings, or peers, or you might explore that character's social context to see how it defines deviance (either justly or unjustly in your opinion) and how the character is implicitly or explicitly judged (or even self-judges) by those sometimes well-hidden norms. Symbols, colors, imagery, and other textual details may provide clues to the unexpressed but still powerful tensions or other forces underlying a character's actions or pervading his or her milieu.

6   *Literary and other cultural texts may have a psychological impact on readers or meet a psychological need in them.*

One of the most interesting avenues for investigation into the interplay of textuality and psychology concerns the relationship between the reader and the text. Theorists such as Peter Brooks and Norman Holland have explored how narrative forms meet readers' deep-seated psychological needs for control and gratification. Indeed, what effect does the psychological torment and confession of Raskolnikov have on readers of *Crime and Punishment?* Certainly a carefully crafted plot, with complications resolved and villains punished by narrative's end, can temporarily assuage a sense of helplessness in the modern reader, who may be confronted daily with aspects of existence that are chaotic or threatening. The social-psychological function of texts was recognized as far back as Aristotle (discussed in Chapter 1), who found in the unfolding and resolution of tragic drama a process of social and individual purgation, which he termed "catharsis." The reader, through pitying the tragic hero and reacting fearfully to the actions on stage, is purified and uplifted. Other genres and processes of character development and/or textual organization provide equally appropriate subject matter for explorations of how readers' needs are met through literary and other forms of cultural representation. Tania Modleski, for example, has examined the role that romance narratives have played in the formation and maintenance of women's consciousness. Yet another provocative field of inquiry, and one still barely explored, is the relationship between texts and larger mass-psychological forces, such as xenophobia and scapegoating. If a violent character—such as Raskolnikov—self-defines or is perceived as an "outsider" figure (perhaps in terms of philosophical belief or, more overtly, race, ethnicity, sexuality, or religion), how does the punishment or explicit designation of such a figure as an outcast or pariah meet broad social needs or help assuage society's fears and anxieties? The work of social psychologists such as Elias Canetti and Erich Fromm may help you explore how texts inflame or modify social tensions and belief systems; such linkages could be the starting point for innovative cultural criticism.

7　*It is unlikely that any one theory can ever fully capture the complexity of human psychology and development, which can vary widely across cultures, classes, genders, sexual orientations, and familial and other personal contexts.*

Yet it is important to remember that theories of human development and diversity are always partial and imperfect. No definitive, comprehensive, and final reading of a complex, multilayered text such as *Crime and Punishment* (or of human behavior!) is possible through the lens of a single psychological theory. Certainly, very narrowly defined forms of traditional Freudian theory hardly explain adequately the formation of and proper social response to gay and lesbian identity, for example. "Castration anxiety" (the fear of losing the power that the possession of a penis provides) would not be a very useful concept in examining a matriarchal society. Lacanian theory, with its emphasis on the mirror stage, would be of similarly limited use in considerations of blind culture. Theories are best applied to those specific cultures and contexts from which they originate, and even then this should be done with care and sensitivity. While the broadest parameters of human existence are similar across time and geographic setting—birth, development, maturity, and death—the familial and social forces acting on developmental processes and the languages and social constructs through which meaning is made certainly vary widely. The analytical tools that we may use to generate insights into *Crime and Punishment* might be far less useful or credible in analyzing African folktales or Native American creation myths. This need for cultural specificity places a clear and continuing burden on the literary and cultural critic, who must understand the many limitations, as well as potentials, of the theory being deployed.

8 *Thus the literary and cultural critic, like the psychoanalyst, must be very careful to avoid "imposing" meanings on a given story or text.*

The above discussion leads to some simple reminders: that ample and compelling evidence must be offered for any psychological conclusion drawn, and that it is never acceptable to impose a theory on a text without attention to complications and conflicting data. A final example is worth mentioning here, for perhaps the most famous case in which a reading was imposed in such an authoritarian fashion comes from Freud's own case files. "Dora" (the pseudonym Freud gave her) was a young patient who suffered from clear symptoms of trauma. But rather than accepting and sensitively exploring Dora's own tale of sexual assault by one of her father's friends, Freud constructed an elaborate interpretation of Dora's supposed sexual desire for her father and possible homosexual tendencies. He ignored her attempts to provide him with alternate readings and important additional information, and she finally left his "care," feeling completely unaided by his treatment of her. Her case remains an important one, though hardly for the reasons that Freud would have imagined, because it is one of the clearest examples of what *not* to do in psychoanalytic interpretation. Of course, individuals' own narratives are often untrustworthy, but the presuppositions, personal narratives, and interpretive processes that analysts bring to their texts also demand skepticism. As we have seen in the decades of commentary by feminist and other critics on the biases of some psychoanalytic theories, authoritarian interpretations will be judged harshly and finally dismissed by readers and critics. In any form of analysis—psychoanalytic, Marxist, formalist, or other—it is best to anticipate and work to address and minimize your own reader's skeptical reactions to the interpretation you will offer.

Bibliography

Bracher, Mark. *Lacan, Discourse, and Social Change: A Psychoanalytic Cultural Criticism.* Ithaca, NY: Cornell University Press, 1993.

This book argues that Lacanian theory has numerous implications for socially engaged cultural criticism and that psychoanalytic critique can help further progressive social movements. Its clarity and detailed explanations make it appropriate for both intermediate and advanced readers.

Brooks, Peter. *Psychoanalysis and Storytelling*. Cambridge, MA: Blackwell, 1994.

> This brief introduction to the field of psychoanalytic literary criticism centers mostly on Freudian concepts, though Lacan is mentioned occasionally. While far from comprehensive, it may be of use to both intermediate and advanced readers.

Canetti, Elias. *Crowds and Power*. New York: Farrar Straus Giroux, 1984.

> Canetti is an important and accessible recent theorist of group psychology. His ideas on mass movements and the dynamics of crowds may be of use to both intermediate and advanced readers.

Chodorow, Nancy. *The Reproduction of Mothering: Psychoanalysis and the Sociology of Gender*. Berkeley: University of California Press, 1978.

> This influential work of feminist theory both uses and responds to Freud's insights into gender development and familial dynamics. Its useful overviews of Freudian concepts and general level of accessibility will make it of interest to both intermediate and advanced readers.

Felman, Shoshana. *Jacques Lacan and the Adventure of Insight: Psychoanalysis in Contemporary Culture*. Cambridge, MA: Harvard University Press, 1987.

> This solid introduction to the theories of Jacques Lacan examines the usefulness of his work in both criticism and pedagogy. Its relative accessibility makes it appropriate for both intermediate and advanced readers.

Freud, Sigmund. *The Standard Edition of the Complete Psychological Works of Sigmund Freud*. 24 vols. New York: Norton, 1989.

> Many selections of Freud's work are in print but this standard edition, available in paperback, offers complete reprintings of all Freud's major papers, lectures, and books. While Freudian concepts are often complex, his general clarity of expression makes his works accessible to both intermediate and advanced readers.

Fromm, Erich. *Escape from Freedom*. New York: Avon, 1965.

> Fromm is one of the most popular and influential recent theorists of the psychology of fascism and group conformity. This influential book is highly accessible and may be of use to beginning, intermediate, and advanced readers.

Gallop, Jane. *Reading Lacan*. Ithaca, NY: Cornell University Press, 1985.

> While Lacan can be dauntingly complex, Gallop provides a comprehensive introduction and response to his theories that is well written and has been very influential. Its diction and theoretical density will make it of greatest interest to advanced readers.

Gallop, Jane. *Thinking Through the Body*. New York: Columbia University Press, 1988.

This, too, is an intriguing work on Freudian and Lacanian theories, written from a feminist perspective. Its conceptual difficulty and presumption of prior theoretical knowledge will make it of greatest interest to advanced readers.

Horney, Karen. *Feminine Psychology*. New York: Norton, 1967.

Horney is an important respondent to Freudian theories of gender development and an influential theorist in her own right. The clarity and accessibility of this book will make it of interest to both intermediate and advanced readers.

Irigaray, Luce. *Speculum of the Other Woman*, trans. Gillian C. Gill. Ithaca, NY: Cornell University Press, 1985.

Irigaray, Luce. *This Sex Which Is Not One*, trans. Catherine Porter. Ithaca, NY: Cornell University Press, 1985.

These two works by a leading French feminist theorist provide exciting, if sometimes very complex, responses to the theories of Freud and Lacan. Their experimental format and dense theoretical language will make them of greatest interest to advanced readers.

Mellard, James M. *Using Lacan, Reading Fiction*. Urbana: University of Illinois Press, 1991.

This introduction to Lacanian literary criticism is noteworthy because it also contains extended applications of the principles it covers in readings of Hawthorne, James, and Woolf. Its first chapter covers many of Lacan's theories and their relevance to literature. Its diction and theory base make it appropriate for intermediate and advanced readers.

Modleski, Tania. *Loving with a Vengeance: Mass-Produced Fantasies for Women*. New York: Methuen, 1982.

This important work of feminist analysis of popular culture is both intriguing and enjoyable to read. Its revision of standard concepts of women's psychological responses to fiction has made it highly influential. Its simultaneous sophistication and clarity will make it of interest to both intermediate and advanced readers.

Skura, Meredith. *The Literary Use of the Psychoanalytic Process*. New Haven, CT: Yale University Press, 1981.

This is a very practical overview of relevant theories and processes of psychoanalytic literary criticism. Its clarity and accessibility will make it of interest to intermediate and advanced readers.

Wright, Elizabeth. *Psychoanalytic Criticism: Theory in Practice*. New York: Methuen, 1984.

This is a very solid introduction to the field of psychoanalytic critic and the major theories underlying it. It relative accessibility and user-friendly explanations will make it of interest to intermediate and advanced readers.

Application

Reading Prompts

1. Highlight statements in which Kahn reveals her critical interests and objectives, in particular how her analysis will draw on Freud but also differ from previous criticism using Freud's theories.
2. Mark passages in which Kahn makes credible her use of the word "hysteria" (a word commonly associated only with women) to diagnose Lear's state of mind.
3. According to Kahn, Lear demands a significant role reversal in his relationship with his daughters. Mark passages in which she explores why he demands that reversal.
4. Notice how and where Kahn augments her application of psychoanalytic theory with concrete historical data, thereby rendering less problematic the anachronistic use of Freud to analyze an Elizabethan text.
5. Pay careful attention to Kahn's analysis of the forms of realization that King Lear comes to by the end of the play, in particular what she indicates is achieved and not achieved in the play's final scene.

Coppélia Kahn

The Absent Mother in King Lear

Fleeing Goneril's "sharp-tooth'd unkindness," Lear arrives at Gloucester's house in search of Regan, still hoping that she will be "kind and
comfortable," although she was inexplicably not at home when he called
before. He finds his messenger in the stocks, a humiliation that he rightly
takes as directed at him personally. At first he simply denies what Kent tells
him, that Regan and her husband did indeed commit this outrage. Then he
seeks to understand how, or why. Kent recounts the studied rudeness, the
successive insults, the final shaming, that he has endured.

For a moment, Lear can no longer deny or rationalize; he can only
feel—feel a tumult of wounded pride, shame, anger, and loss, which he expresses in a striking image:

> O! how this mother swells upward toward my heart!
> *Hysterica passio!* down, thou climbing sorrow!
> Thy element's below.

(2.4.56–58)[1]

By calling his sorrow hysterical, Lear decisively characterizes it as feminine,
in accordance with a tradition stretching back to 1900 B.C. when an Egypt-
ian papyrus first described the malady. Fifteen hundred years later in the
writings of Hippocrates, it was named, and its name succinctly conveyed its
etiology. It was the disease of the *hyster*, the womb. From ancient times
through the nineteenth century, women suffering variously from choking,
feelings of suffocation, partial paralysis, convulsions similar to those of
epilepsy, aphasia, numbness, and lethargy were said to be ill of hysteria,
caused by wandering womb. What sent the womb on its errant path
through the female body, people thought, was either lack of sexual intercourse or retention of menstrual blood. In both cases, the same prescription
obtained: the patient should get married. A husband would keep that wandering womb where it belonged. If the afflicted already had a husband, con-
coctions either noxious or pleasant were applied to force or entice the
recalcitrant womb to its proper location.[2]

In Shakespeare's time, hysteria was also called, appropriately, "the
mother." Although Shakespeare may well have consulted a treatise by Edward Jordan called *A Brief Discourse of a Disease Called the Suffocation of the*

Mother, published in 1603, like anyone in his culture he would have understood "the mother" in the context of notions about women. For hysteria is
a vivid metaphor of woman in general, as she was regarded then and later, a
creature destined for the strenuous bodily labors of childbearing and childrearing but nonetheless physically weaker than man. Moreover, she was,
like Eve, temperamentally and morally infirm:—skittish, prone to err in all
senses. Woman's womb, her justification and her glory, was also the sign
and source of her weakness as a creature of the flesh rather than the mind
or spirit. The very diversity of symptoms clustering under the name of hysteria bespeaks the capricious nature of woman. And the remedy—a husband
and regular sexual intercourse—declares the necessity for male control of
this volatile female element.[3]

Psychoanalysis was born, one might say, from the wandering womb of
hysteria. Anna O., the star of *Studies in Hysteria*, published by Freud and
Joseph Breuer in 1895, was its midwife. It was she who named psychoanalysis "the talking cure" and in a sense even discovered it. Afflicted with a veritable museum of hysterical symptoms, when Breuer visited her she
spontaneously sank into a rapt, semiconscious state in which she insisted on
talking about what bothered her, thus showing the way to free association
as the distinctly psychoanalytic technique of treating mental disorders. For
psychoanalysis and hysteria both, the discovery that its strangely disparate
physical symptoms were in fact symbolic representations of unconscious
mental conflict constituted a crucial breakthrough. Relocating the cause of
hysteria in the head instead of in the womb, Breuer and Freud were able to
make sense of it, treat it, and, to an extent, cure it. Yet, in the Viennese
women they treated, we can see that hysteria does indeed come from the
womb—if we understand the womb as a metaphor for feelings and needs
associated with women. As Dianne Hunter suggests, what Anna O. talked
out was her specifically *female* subjectivity.[4] She expressed through the body
language of her paralyzed arm, her squint, and her speech disorders the effects on her as a woman of life in a father-dominated family and a male-
dominated world that suppressed the female voice. The matrix of her
disease was both sexual and social: the patriarchal family.

Because the family is both the first scene of individual development and
the primary agent of socialization, it functions as a link between psychic
and social structures and as the crucible in which gender identity is formed.
From being mothered and fathered, we learn to be ourselves as men and
women. The anthropologist Gayle Rubin describes psychoanalysis as "a
theory of sexuality in human society . . . a description of the mechanisms by
which the sexes are divided and deformed, or how bisexual androgynous

infants are transformed into boys and girls . . . a feminist theory manqué."[5] A great Shakespearean critic, C. L. Barber, calls psychoanalysis "a sociology of love and worship within the family."[6] Freud, of course, viewed this family drama from the standpoint of a son; he conceived the development of gender as governed primarily by relationship with the father. Because Freud grounds sexual differentiation in the cultural primacy of the phallus, within the context of a family structure that mirrors the psychological organization of patriarchal society, he enables us to deconstruct the modes of feeling, the institutions, and the social codes in which much if not most of English literature is embedded.

But to use one of Freud's favorite metaphors, to excavate patriarchal sensibility in literature, we must sift through more than one layer. In the history of psychoanalysis, the discovery of the Oedipus complex precedes the discovery of pre-oedipal experience, reversing the sequence of development in the individual. Similarly, patriarchal structures loom obviously on the surface of many texts, structures of authority, control, force, logic, linearity, misogyny, male superiority. But beneath them, as in a palimpsest, we can find what I call "the maternal subtext," the imprint of mothering on the male psyche, the psychological presence of the mother whether or not mothers are literally represented as characters.[7] In this reading of *King Lear*, I try, like an archaeologist, to uncover the hidden mother in the hero's inner world.

Now, it is interesting that there is no literal mother in *King Lear*. The earlier anonymous play that is one of Shakespeare's main sources opens with a speech by the hero lamenting the death of his "dearest Queen."[8] But Shakespeare, who follows the play closely in many respects, refers only once in passing to this queen. In the crucial cataclysmic first scene of his play, from which all its later action evolves, we are shown only fathers and their godlike capacity to make or mar their children. Through this conspicuous omission the play articulates a patriarchal conception of the family in which children owe their existence to their fathers alone; the mother's role in procreation is eclipsed by the father's, which is used to affirm male prerogative and male power.[9] The aristocratic patriarchal families headed by Gloucester and Lear have, actually and effectively, no mothers. The only source of love, power, and authority is the father—an awesome, demanding presence.

But what the play depicts, of course, is the failure of that presence: the failure of a father's power to command love in a patriarchal world and the emotional penalty he pays for wielding power.[10] Lear's very insistence on paternal power, in fact, belies its shakiness; similarly, the absence of the mother points to her hidden presence, as the lines with which I began might indicate. When Lear begins to feel the loss of Cordelia, to be wounded by

her sisters, and to recognize his own vulnerability, he calls his state of mind *hysteria*, "the mother," which I interpret as his repressed identification with the mother. Women and the needs and traits associated with them are supposed to stay in their element, as Lear says, "below"—denigrated, silenced, denied. In this patriarchal world, masculine identity depends on repressing the vulnerability, dependency, and capacity for feeling which are called "feminine."

Recent historical studies of the Elizabethan family, its social structure and emotional dynamics, when considered in the light of psychoanalytic theory, provide a backdrop against which Lear's family drama takes on new meaning as a tragedy of masculinity.[11] Recently, several authors have analyzed mothering—the traditional division of roles within the family that makes the woman primarily responsible for rearing as well as bearing the children—as a social institution sustained by patriarchy, which in turn reinforces it.[12] Notably, Nancy Chodorow offers an incisive critique of the psychoanalytic conception of how the early mother-child relationship shapes the child's sense of maleness or femaleness. She argues that the basic masculine sense of self is formed through a denial of the male's initial connection with femininity, a denial that taints the male's attitudes toward women and impairs his capacity for affiliation in general. My interpretation of *Lear* comes out of the feminist re-examination of the mothering role now being carried on in many fields, but it is particularly indebted to Nancy Chodorow's analysis.

According to her account, women as mothers produce daughters with mothering capacities and the desire to mother, which itself grows out of the mother-daughter relationship. They also produce sons whose nurturant capacities and needs are curtailed in order to prepare them to be fathers. A focus on the primacy of the mother's role in ego-formation is not in itself new. It follows upon the attempts of theorists such as Melanie Klein, Michael and Alice Balint, John Bowlby, and Margaret Mahler to cast light on that dim psychic region which Freud likened to the Minoan civilization preceding the Greek, "grey with age, and shadowy and almost impossible to revivify."[13] Chodorow's account of the mother-child relationship, however, challenges the mainstream of psychoanalytic assumptions concerning the role of gender and family in the formation of the child's ego and sexual identity.

Because I find family relationships and gender identity central to Shakespeare's imagination, the most valuable aspect of Chodorow's work for me is its comparative perspective on the development of gender in the sexes. For both, the mother's rather than the father's role is the important one, as crucial to the child's individuation (development of a sense of self) as to the child's

sense of gender. It is only for the purpose of analysis, however, that the two facts of identity can be separated. Both sexes begin to develop a sense of self in relation to a mother-woman. But a girl's sense of femaleness arises *through* her infantile union with the mother and later identification with her, while a boy's sense of maleness arises *in opposition* to those primitive forms of oneness. According to Robert Stoller, whose work supports Chodorow's argument, "Developing indissoluble links with mother's femaleness and femininity in the normal mother-infant symbiosis can only augment a girl's identity," while for a boy, "the whole process of becoming masculine . . . is endangered by the primary, profound, primal oneness with mother."[14] A girl's gender identity is reinforced but a boy's is threatened by union and identification with the same powerful female being. Thus, as Chodorow argues, the masculine personality tends to be formed through denial of connection with femininity; certain activities must be defined as masculine and superior to the maternal world of childhood, and women's activities must, correspondingly, be denigrated. The process of differentiation is inscribed in patriarchal ideology, which polarizes male and female social roles and behavior.[15]

The imprint of mothering on the male psyche, the psychological presence of the mother in men whether or not mothers are represented in the texts they write or in which they appear as characters, can be found throughout the literary canon. But it is Shakespeare who renders the dilemmas of manhood most compellingly and with the greatest insight, partly because he wrote at a certain historical moment. As part of a wide-ranging argument for the role of the nuclear family in shaping what he calls "affective individualism," Lawrence Stone holds that the family of Shakespeare's day saw a striking increase in the father's power over his wife and children. Stone's ambitious thesis has been strenuously criticized, but his description of the Elizabethan family itself, if not his notion of its place in the development of affective individualism, holds true.[16]

Stone sums up the mode of the father's dominance thus:

> This sixteenth-century aristocratic family was patrilinear, primogenitural, and patriarchal: patrilinear in that it was the male line whose ancestry was traced so diligently by the genealogists and heralds, and in almost all cases via the male line that titles were inherited; primogenitural in that most of the property went to the eldest son, the younger brothers being dispatched into the world with little more than a modest annuity or life interest in a small estate to keep them afloat; and patriarchal in that the husband and father lorded it over his wife and children with the quasi-absolute authority of a despot.[17]

Patriarchy, articulated through the family, was considered the natural order of things.[18] But like other kinds of "natural order," it was subject to historical change. According to Stone, between 1580 and 1640 two forces, one political and one religious, converged to heighten paternal power in the family. As the Tudor-Stuart state consolidated, it tried to undercut ancient baronial loyalty to the family line in order to replace it with loyalty to the crown. As part of the same campaign, the state also encouraged obedience to the *paterfamilias* in the home, according to the traditional analogy between state and family, king and father. James I stated, "Kings are compared to fathers in families: for a king is truly *parens patriae*, the politic father of his people."[19] The state thus had a direct interest in reinforcing patriarchy in the home.

Concurrently, Puritan fundamentalism—the literal interpretation of Mosaic law in its original patriarchal context—reinforced patriarchal elements in Christian doctrine and practice as well. As the head of the household, the father took over many of the priest's functions, leading his extended family of dependents in daily prayers, questioning them as to the state of their souls, giving or withholding his blessing on their undertakings. Although Protestant divines argued for the spiritual equality of women, deplored the double standard, and exalted the married state for both sexes, at the same time they zealously advocated the subjection of wives to their husbands on the scriptural grounds that the husband "beareth the image of God." Heaven and home were both patriarchal. The Homily on the State of Matrimony, one of the sermons issued by the crown to be read in church weekly, quotes and explicates the Pauline admonition, "Let women be subject to their husbands, as to the Lord; for the husband is the head of the woman, as Christ is the head of the church."[20] In effect, a woman's subjection to her husband's will was the measure of his patriarchal authority and thus of his manliness.

The division of parental roles in childrearing made children similarly subject to the father's will. In his study of Puritan attitudes toward authority and feeling, David Leverenz finds an emphasis on the mother's role as tender nurturer of young children, as against the father's role as disciplinarian and spiritual guide for older children. Mothers are encouraged to love their children in their early years but enjoined to withdraw their affections "at just about the time the father's instructional role becomes primary." Thus the breaking of the will is accomplished by the father, rather than by both parents equally. This division of duties, Leverenz holds, fostered a pervasive polarity, involving "associations of feared aspects of oneself with weakness and women, emphasis on male restraint and the male mind's governance of female emotions, the separation of 'head' from 'body,' . . . a language of male anxiety, rather than of female deficiency."[21]

A close look at the first scene in *King Lear* reveals much about lordliness and the male anxiety accompanying it. The court is gathered to watch Lear divide his kingdom and divest himself of its rule, but those purposes are actually only accessory to another that touches him more nearly: giving away his youngest daughter in marriage. While France and Burgundy wait in the wings, Cordelia, for whose hand they compete, also competes for the dowry without which she cannot marry. As Lynda Boose shows, this opening scene is a variant of the wedding ceremony, which dramatizes the bond between father and daughter even as it marks the severance of that bond. There is no part in the ritual for the bride's mother; rather, the bride's father hands her directly to her husband. Thus the ritual articulates the father's dominance both as procreator and as authority figure, to the eclipse of the mother in either capacity. At the same time, the father symbolically certifies the daughter's virginity. Thus the ceremony alludes to the incest taboo and raises a question about Lear's "darker purpose" in giving Cordelia away.[22]

In view of the ways that Lear tries to manipulate this ritual so as to keep his hold on Cordelia at the same time that he is ostensibly giving her away, we might suppose that the emotional crisis precipitating the tragic action is Lear's frustrated incestuous desire for his daughter. For in the course of winning her dowry, Cordelia is supposed to show that she loves her father not only more than her sisters do but, as she rightly sees, more than she loves her future husband; similarly, when Lear disowns and disinherits Cordelia, he thinks he has rendered her, dowered only with his curse, unfit to marry—and thus unable to leave paternal protection. In contrast, however, I want to argue that the socially-ordained, developmentally appropriate surrender of Cordelia as daughter-wife—the renunciation of her as incestuous object—awakens a deeper emotional need in Lear: the need for Cordelia as daughter-mother.

The play's beginning, as I have said, is marked by the omnipotent presence of the father and the absence of the mother. Yet in Lear's scheme for parceling out his kingdom, we can discern a child's image of being mothered. He wants two mutually exclusive things at once: to have absolute control over those closest to him and to be absolutely dependent on them. We can recognize in this stance the outlines of a child's pre-oedipal experience of himself and his mother as an undifferentiated dual unity, in which the child perceives his mother not as a separate person but as an agency of himself, who provides for his needs. She and her breast are a part of him, at his command.[23] In Freud's unforgettable phrase, he is "his majesty, the baby."[24]

As man, father, and ruler, Lear has habitually suppressed any needs for love, which in his patriarchal world would normally be satisfied by a mother or mothering woman. With age and loss of vigor, and as Freud suggests in "The Theme of the Three Caskets," with the prospect of return to mother earth, Lear feels those needs again and hints at them in his desire to "crawl" like a baby "toward death."[25] Significantly, he confesses them in these phrases the moment after he curses Cordelia for her silence, the moment in which he denies them most strongly. He says, "I lov'd her most, and thought to set my rest / On her kind nursery" (1.1.123–24).

When his other two daughters prove to be bad mothers and don't satisfy his needs for "nursery," Lear is seized by "the mother"—a searing sense of loss at the deprivation of the mother's presence. It assaults him in various ways—in the desire to weep, to mourn the enormous loss, and the equally strong desire to hold back the tears and, instead, accuse, arraign, convict, punish, and humiliate those who have made him realize his vulnerability and dependency. Thus the mother, revealed in Lear's response to his daughters' brutality toward him, makes her re-entry into the patriarchal world from which she had seemingly been excluded. The repressed mother returns specifically in Lear's wrathful projections onto the world about him of a symbiotic relationship with his daughters that recapitulates his pre-oedipal relationship with the mother. In a striking series of images in which parent-child, father-daughter, and husband-wife relationships are reversed and confounded, Lear re-enacts a childlike rage against the absent or rejecting mother as figured in his daughters.

Here I want to interject a speculation inspired by Stone's discussion of the custom of farming children out to wet nurses from birth until they were twelve to eighteen months old; at that time they were restored to the arms of their natural mother, who was by then a stranger to them.[26] Many if not most people in the gentry or aristocracy of Shakespeare's day must have suffered the severe trauma of maternal deprivation brought on by the departure of the wet nurse. We know the effects of such a trauma from the writings of John Bowlby: a tendency to make excessive demands on others, anxiety and anger when these demands are not met, and a blocked capacity for intimacy.[27] Lear responds to the loss of Cordelia, the "nurse" he rejects after she seems to reject him, by demanding hospitality for his hundred knights, by raging at Goneril and Regan when they refuse him courtesy and sympathy, and by rejecting human society when he stalks off to the heath. After the division of the kingdom, he re-enters the play in the fourth scene with this revealing peremptory demand: "Let me not stay a jot for dinner; go, get it ready" (1.4.9–10): he wants food, from a maternal woman. I believe that Lear's madness is essentially his rage at being deprived of the maternal presence. It is tantalizing, although I can imagine no way of proving it, to view this rage as part of the social pathology of wet-nursing in the ruling classes.

The play is full of oral rage: it abounds in fantasies of biting and devouring, and more specifically, fantasies of parents eating children and children eating parents. The idea is first brought up by Lear when he denies his "propinquity and property of blood" with Cordelia; that is, he denies that he begot her, that he is her father, as he also denies paternity of Regan and Goneril later. He assures her,

> The barbarous Scythian,
> Or he that makes his generation messes
> To gorge his appetite, shall to my bosom
> Be as well neighbour'd, pitied, and reliev'd,
> As thou my sometime daughter.

> (1.1.116–20)

The savagery of the image is shocking; it indicates Lear's first step toward the primitive, infantile modes of thinking to which he surrenders in his madness. When Cordelia doesn't feed him with love, he thinks angrily of eating *her*. Lear again voices this complex conjunction of ideas about maternal nurture, maternal aggression, and aggression against the mother when he looks at Edgar's mutilated body, bleeding from its many wounds, and remarks.

> Is it the fashion, that discarded fathers
> Should have thus little mercy on their flesh?
> Judicious punishment! 'twas this flesh begot
> Those pelican daughters.

> (3.4.72–75)

Lear seems to think that Edgar first transgressed against his father by "discarding" him as Regan and Goneril discarded Lear, and that Edgar's father then got back at his child, his "flesh," *in* the flesh, as Lear would like to do. But this fantasy of revenge calls forth an answering fantasy of punishment against his own flesh—a punishment he deserves for begetting children in the first place. The image of the pelican may have been suggested to Shakespeare by this passage in a contemporary text, which I will quote because it elucidates both the reciprocating spiral of aggression and revenge and the close identification between parent and child, which possesses Lear's mind:

> The Pellican loueth too much her children. For when the children be haught, and begin to waxe hoare, they smite the father and mother in the face, wherefore the mother smiteth them againe and slaieth them. And the thirde daye the mother smiteth her selfe in her side that the bloud runneth out, and sheddeth that hot bloud upon the bodies of her children. And by virtue of the bloud the birdes that were before dead, quicken againe[28]

The children strike their parents, the mother retaliates, then wounds herself that the children may nurse on her blood. "Is't not," Lear asks, "as this mouth should tear this hand / For lifting food to 't?" (3.4.15–16) referring to "filial ingratitude." His daughters are the mouths he fed, which now tear their father's generous hand; but at the same time, he is the needy mouth that would turn against those daughters for refusing to feed him on demand. Lear's rage at not being fed by the daughters whom, pelican-like, he has nurtured, fills the play. It is mirrored in Albany's vision of all humanity preying upon itself, like monsters of the deep (4.2.46–49), a vision inspired by the reality of Goneril turning her father out in the storm and shortly confirmed by the more gruesome reality of Regan and Cornwall tearing out another father's eyes.

Bound up with this mixture of love and hate, nurture and aggression, is Lear's deep sense of identification with his daughters as born of his flesh. When Goneril bids him return to Regan's house rather than disrupt her own, his first thought is absolute separation from her, like his banishment of Cordelia: "We'll no more meet, no more see one another." But immediately he remembers the filial bond, for him a carnal as much as a moral bond:

> But yet thou art my flesh, my blood, my daughter;
> Or rather a disease that's in my flesh,
> Which I must needs call mine: thou art a boil,
> A plague-sore, or embossed carbuncle,
> In my corrupted blood.
>
> > (2.4.223–27)

Gloucester echoes the same thought when he says wryly to Lear on the heath, "Our flesh and blood, my lord, is grown so vile, / That it doth hate what gets it" (3.4.149–50).

Children are products of an act that, in Elizabethan lore, was regarded as the mingling of bloods. In the metaphor of Genesis, repeated in the Anglican wedding service, man and wife become "one flesh." With regard to mother and child, however, the fleshly bond is not metaphorical but literal. Lear (like Gloucester) ignores the mother-child fleshly bond and insists that his children are, simply, *his* "flesh and blood." In the pelican image, he assimilates maternal functions to himself, as though Goneril and Regan hadn't been born of woman. Like Prospero, he alludes only once to his wife, and then in the context of adultery. When Regan says she is glad to see her father, he replies

> if thou shouldst not be glad
> I would divorce me from thy mother's tomb,
> Sepulchring an adultress.
>
> > (2.4.131–33)

These lines imply, first, that Lear alone as progenitor endowed Regan with her moral nature, and second, that if that nature isn't good, she had some other father. In either case, her mother's only contribution was in the choice of a sexual partner. Thus Lear makes use of patriarchal ideology to serve his defensive needs: he denies his debt to a mother by denying that his daughters have any debt to her, either.

Lear's agonizing consciousness that he did indeed produce such monstrous children, however, persists despite this denial and leads him to project his loathing toward the procreative act onto his daughters, in a searing indictment of women's sexuality:

> The fitchew nor the soiled horse goes to 't
> With a more riotous appetite.
> Down from the waist they are centaurs,
> Though women all above:
> But to the girdle to the Gods inherit
> Beneath is all the fiend's: there's hell, there's darkness,
> There is the sulphurous pit—burning, scalding,
> Stench, consumption; fie, fie, fie! pah, pah!
>
>   (4.6.124–31)

Even if he did beget these daughters, Lear implies, he's not answerable for their unkindness, because they are, after all, women—and women are tainted, rather than empowered as men are, by their sexual capacities. Thus he presses into service another aspect of patriarchal ideology, its misogyny, to separate himself from any feminine presence.

To return for a moment to the social dimensions of Lear's inner turmoil, it is important here that generational conflicts entwine with and intensify gender conflicts. Lear and his daughters, Gloucester and his sons are pitted against one another because the younger generation perceives the authority of the elder as "the oppression of aged tyranny" (1.2.47–52). Stephen Greenblatt remarks that this period has "a deep gerontological bias," revealed in numerous claims that "by the will of God and the natural order of things, authority belonged to the old." At the same time, however, sermons, moral writings, and folk tales of the kind on which *King Lear* is based voice the fear that if parents hand over their wealth or their authority to their children, those children will turn against them.[29] The common legal practice of drawing up maintenance agreements testifies that this fear had some basis in actual experience. In such contracts, children to whom parents deeded farm or workshop were legally bound to supply food, clothing, and shelter to their parents, even to the precise number of bushels of grain or yards of cloth. Thus the law put teeth into what was supposed to be natural kindness. Lear's contest of love in the first scene functions as a maintenance agreement in that he tries to bind his daughters, by giving them their inheritance while he is still alive, into caring for him. This generational bargain is then complicated by the demands proper to gender as well—the father's emotional demand that his daughters be his mothers and perform the tasks of nurture proper to females.

Regan and Goneril betray and disappoint Lear by not being mothers to him, but in a deeper, broader sense, they shame him by bringing out the woman in him. In the following speech, Shakespeare takes us close to the nerve and bone of Lear's shame at being reduced to an impotence he considers womanish:

> You see me here, you Gods, a poor old man,
> As full of grief as age; wretched in both!
> If it be you that stirs these daughters' hearts
> Against their father, fool me not so much
> To bear it tamely; touch me with noble anger,
> And let not women's weapons, water-drops,
> Stain my man's cheeks! No, you unnatural hags,
> I will have such revenges on you both
> That all the world shall—I will do such things,
> What they are, yet I know not, but they shall be
> The terrors of the earth. You think I'll weep;
> No, I'll not weep;
> I have full cause of weeping, but this heart
> Shall break into a hundred thousand flaws
> Or ere I'll weep.

> (2.4.274–88)

He calls his tears "women's weapons" not only as a way of deprecating women for using emotion to manipulate men but also because he feels deeply threatened by his own feelings. Marianne Novy has argued that Lawrence Stone, in calling attention to the "distance, manipulation, and deference" that characterized the Elizabethan family, identified "a cultural ideal of Elizabethan society . . . a personality type that on the one hand kept feelings of attachment and grief under strict control, but on the other was more ready to express feelings of anger." "The model," she comments, "was primarily a masculine ideal."[30] In agreeing, I would suggest that this masculine ideal was produced by the extreme sexual division of labor within the patriarchal family, which made women at once the source and the focus of a child's earliest and most unmanageable feelings.

Despite a lifetime of strenuous defense against admitting feeling and the power of feminine presence into his world, defense fostered at every turn prevailing social arrangements, Lear manages to let them in. He learns to weep and, though his tears scald and burn like molten lead, they are no longer "women's weapons" against which he must defend himself. I will conclude this reading of the play by tracing, briefly, Lear's progress toward acceptance of the woman in himself, a progress punctuated by his hysterical projections of rage at being deprived of maternal nurture. In the passage that I just quoted, as he turns toward the heath, Lear prays that anger may keep him from crying, from becoming like a woman. He also, in effect, tells us one way to read the storm—as a metaphor for his internal emotional process: "I have full cause of weeping, but this heart / Shall break into a hundred thousand flaws / Or ere I'll weep" (2.4.286–88). Shakespeare portrays the storm as the breaking open of something enclosed, a break that lets out a flood of rain; it thus resembles Lear's heart cracking, letting out the hungry, mother-identified part of him in a flood of tears. Lear exhorts the winds to crack their cheeks and the thunder to crack Nature's moulds and spill their seeds; he envisions "close pent-up guilts" riven from "their concealing continents" (3.2.1–9, 49–59). He wants the whole world struck flat and cleft open, so that the bowels of sympathy may flow. What spills out of Lear at first is a flood of persecutory fantasies. He sees everyone in his own image, as either subjects or agents of persecution. Only daughters like his, he thinks, could have reduced Poor Tom to naked misery; Poor Tom and the Fool are, like him, stern judges bringing his daughters to trial. Gloucester is "Goneril, with a white beard," and then, someone who might weep along with Lear although he has only the case of eyes.

Before Shakespeare allows Lear to feel the weeping woman in himself or to face his need for Cordelia and his guilt for the wrong he did her, he evokes and excoriates a world full of viperish women. Interwoven with Lear's indictments of women during acts 3 and 4 are the imaginary lustful mistresses of Poor Tom's sophisticated past, the wearers of plackets and rustling silks, as well as the real Regan tearing out Gloucester's eyes, and the real Goneril, stealthy and lustful, seducing Edmund and sloughing off Albany. It is as though Shakespeare as well as his hero must dredge up everything horrible that might be imagined of women and denounce it before he can confront the good woman, the one and only good woman, Cordelia.

Cordelia's goodness is as absolute and inexplicable as her sisters' reprovable badness, as much an archetype of infantile fantasy as they are. When she re-enters the play, she is described as crying with pity for her father's sufferings, yet in her tears she is still "queen over her passion."

Whereas Lear thought weeping an ignoble surrender of his masculine authority, Cordelia conceives her tears as a source of power:

> All blest secrets,
> All you unpublished virtues of the earth,
> Spring with my tears; be aidant and remediate
> In the good man's distress!
>
> (4.4.15–18)

In these scenes Cordelia becomes, now in a benign sense, that daughter-mother Lear wanted her to be. Like the Virgin Mary, she intercedes magically, her empathy and pity coaxing mercy from nature. Yet finally, as the Doctor's words imply, she can only be "the foster-nurse" of Lear's repose.[31]

Lear runs from the attendants Cordelia sends to rescue him, who appear just after he poignantly evokes the crying infant as a common denominator of humanity:

> Thou must be patient; we came crying hither.
> Thou know'st, the first time that we smell the air
> We wawl and cry . . .
> When we are born, we cry that we are come
> To this great stage of fools.
>
> (4.6.178–80, 182–83)

Here he comes closest to admitting his vulnerability, but he must immediately defend against it and see the proffered help as a threat. Stanley Cavell has argued that the reluctance to be recognized by those whom they love most, which characterizes Lear, Kent, Edgar and Gloucester, lies at the heart of this play; he holds that they are reluctant because they feel that their love bespeaks a demeaning dependency.[32] I agree—and I regard that embarrassed shrinking from recognition as part of a masculine identity crisis in a culture that dichotomized power as masculine and feeling as feminine.

And so Lear exits running in this scene, asserting his kingship ("Come, come, I am a king") but behaving like a mischievous child who makes his mother run after him ("Come, and you get it, you shall get it by running," 4.6.199, 201–202). When he reappears, he is as helpless as a child, sleeping and carried in by servants. He awakes in the belief that he has died and been reborn into an afterlife, and he talks about tears to Cordelia:

> Thou art a soul in bliss, but I am bound
> Upon a wheel of fire, that mine own tears
> Do scald like molten lead.
>
> (4.7.45–47)

These are the tears of ashamed self-knowledge, manly tears caused by a re-alization of what his original childish demands on his daughters had led to. In this scene, which I want to compare with the next scene with Cordelia, Lear comes closer than he ever does later to a mature acceptance of his human dependency. He asserts his manhood, and admits Cordelia's sepa-rateness from him at the same time that he confesses his need for her: he can say "I am a very fond foolish old man" and yet also declare, "For (as I am a man) I think this lady / To be my child Cordelia" (4.7.59, 69). I want to pause at those three words "man," "lady," and "child." Lear acknowl-edges his manhood and his daughter's womanhood in the same line and the same breath. He can stop imagining her as the maternal woman that he yearned for and accept his separateness from her. Yet he also calls her his child, acknowledging the bond of paternity that he denied in the first act. He need not be threatened by her autonomy as a person nor obsessed by the fleshly tie between them as parent and child.

Lear's struggle to discover or create a new mode of being based on his love for Cordelia continues to his last breath. Imagining their life together in prison, he transcends the rigid structure of command and obedience that once framed his world:

> Come, let's away to prison:
> We two alone will sing like birds i' th' cage;
> When thou dost ask me blessing, I'll kneel down
> And ask of thee forgiveness. So we'll live,
> And pray, and sing, and tell old tales, and laugh at gilded
>   butterflies . . .

$$(5.3.8–11)$$

Parent and child are equal, the gestures of deference that ordinarily denote patriarchal authority now transformed into signs of reciprocal love. More-over, Lear now views all power from a quasi-divine perspective that charm-ingly deflates pretension or ambition as mere toys, while nevertheless carrying a certain grandeur of its own. On the other hand, Lear's character-istically fierce defensiveness continues to shape his fantasy, which is pro-voked by Cordelia's request that they confront their enemies: "Shall we not see these daughters and these sisters?" The prospect of facing his bad mothers as well as his good mother impels Lear to conceive of Cordelia and himself as forming an impregnable dyad bound together by a complete har-mony of thought and feeling more than by the circumstances of captivity. If he did agree to meet Regan and Goneril, he would have to abandon the fantasy that one good woman like Cordelia can triumph over or negate her evil counterparts, as well as the fantasy that a prison can be a nursery in which Cordelia has no independent being and exists solely for her father as part of his defensive strategy against coming to terms with women who are as human, or as inhuman, as men.

Cordelia's death prevents Lear from trying to live out his fantasy, and perhaps discover once again that a daughter cannot be a mother.[33] When he enters bearing Cordelia in his arms, he is struggling to accept the total and irrevocable loss of the only loving woman in his world, the one person who could possibly fulfill needs that he has, in such anguish, finally come to admit. No wonder that he cannot contemplate such utter, devastating separateness, and in the final scene tries so hard to deny that she is dead. At the end of *King Lear*, only men are left. It remains for Shakespeare to reimagine a world in his last plays in which masculine authority *can* find mothers in its daughters, in Marina, Perdita, and Miranda—the world of pastoral tragicomedy and romance, the genres of wish-fulfillment, rather than the tragic world of *King Lear*.

NOTES

I am grateful to David Leverenz and Louis Adrian Montrose for their sensitive comments on drafts of this essay.

1.   This and all subsequent quotations are taken from the Arden edition of *King Lear*, ed. Kenneth Muir (Cambridge: Harvard University Press, 1952).

2.   See Ilza Veith, *Hysteria: The History of a Disease* (Chicago: University of Chicago Press, 1965).

3.   As Veith (ibid.) shows, during the Middle Ages, hysteria had ceased to be known as a disease and was taken as a visible token of bewitchment. Jordan wrote his treatise to argue for a distinction between the two. Both his work and the pamphlet by Samuel Harsnett denouncing the persecution of witches (from which Shakespeare took much of Poor Tom's language) have the effect of pointing up parallels between hysteria and witchcraft as deviant kinds of behavior associated with women, which are then used to justify denigrating women and subjecting them to strict control. In her essay on the literary and social forms of sexual inversion in early modern Europe whereby women took dominant roles and ruled over men, Natalie Zemon Davis notes that such female unruliness was thought to emanate from a wandering womb and comments, "The lower ruled the higher within the woman, then, and if she were given her way, she would want to rule over those above her outside. Her disorderliness led her into the evil arts of witchcraft, so ecclesiastical authorities claimed . . ." See "Women on Top," in *Society and Culture in Early Modern France* (Stanford, Calif.: Stanford University Press, 1975), p. 125. Hilda Smith notes that a gynecological text published in 1652 calls the entire female sexual structure "The Matrix," subordinating female sexuality to its reproductive function; see her "Gynecology and Ideology in Seventeenth Century England,"

in *Liberating Women's History,* ed. Berenice Carroll (Urbana: Illinois University Press, 1976), pp. 97–114. For a theory of hysteria as a disorder that "makes complex use of contemporaneous cultural and social forms," see Alan Krohn, *Hysteria: The Elusive Neurosis* (New York: International Universities Press, 1978).

4.   Dianne Hunter, "Psychoanalytic Intervention in the History of Consciousness, Beginning with O," *The (M)Other Tongue: Essays in Feminist Psychoanalytic Interpretation,* ed. Shirley Nelson Garner, Claire Kahane, Madelon Sprengnether (Ithaca, N.Y.: Cornell University Press, 1985). Freud suggests that attachment to the mother may be "especially intimately related to the aetiology of hysteria, which is not surprising when we reflect that both the phase and the neurosis are characteristically feminine." "Female Sexuality" (1931), *Standard Edition* 21:221–45.

5.   Gayle Rubin, "The Traffic in Women: Notes on the 'Political Economy' of Sex," in *Toward An Anthropology of Women,* ed. Rayna Reiter (New York: Monthly Review Press, 1975), pp. 184–85.

6.   C. L. Barber, "The Family in Shakespeare's Development," in *Representing Shakespeare: New Psychoanalytic Essays,* ed. Murray Schwartz and Coppélia Kahn (Baltimore: Johns Hopkins University Press, 1980), pp. 199.

7.   See my article, "Excavating 'Those Dim Minoan Regions' Maternal Subtexts in Patriarchal Literature," *Diacritics* (Summer 1982), 32–41, which contains a much condensed version of this essay. The idea of a maternal subtext was first suggested to me by Madelon Gohlke's essay, "'I wooed thee with my sword:' Shakespeare's Tragic Paradigms," in *Representing Shakespeare: New Psychoanalytic Essays* (Baltimore: Johns Hopkins University Press, 1980). She writes of a "structure of relation" in which "it is women who are regarded as powerful and men who strive to avoid an awareness of their vulnerability in relation to women, a vulnerability in which they regard themselves as 'feminine'" (p. 180).

8.   *The True Chronicle Historie of King Leir and His Three Daughters,* in *Narrative and Dramatic Sources of Shakespeare,* ed. Geoffrey Bullough, 7 vols. (New York: Columbia University Press, 1973). 7:337–402.

9.   In his brilliant and wide-ranging essay in this volume, "'Shaping Fantasies:' Figurations of Gender and Power in Elizabethan Culture," Louis Adrian Montrose explicates the patriarchal ideology threaded through *A Midsummer Night's Dream,* whereby the mother's part in procreation is occluded and men alone are held to "make women, and make themselves through the medium of women." He interprets this belief as "an overcompensation for the *natural* fact that men do indeed come from women; an overcompensation for the cultural facts that consanguineal and affinal ties *between* men are established through mothers, wives, and daughters."

10.   Murray Schwartz explored this idea in a series of talks given at the Center for the Humanities, Wesleyan University, February–April 1978.

11.   Lawrence Stone's *The Family, Sex, and Marriage in England, 1500–1800* (New York: Harper & Row, 1978) offers a picture of Elizabethan filial relationships which is both highly suggestive for readings of Shakespeare and much at variance with him; see especially pp. 151–218. For a convenient summary of Stone's account of the Elizabethan patriarchal family, see his essay, "The Rise of the Nuclear

Family in Early Modern England," in *The Family in History*, ed. Charles E. Rosenberg (Philadelphia: University of Pennsylvania Press, 1975), pp. 25–54.

12.   Adrienne Rich, *Of Woman Born: Motherhood as Experience and Institution* (New York: W. W. Norton, 1976; reprint, Bantam, 1977); Dorothy Dinnerstein, *The Mermaid and the Minotaur: Sexual Arrangements and Human Malaise* (New York: Harper & Row, 1976); Nancy Chodorow, *The Reproduction of Mothering: Psychoanalysis and the Sociology of Gender* (Berkeley and Los Angeles: University of California Press, 1979). My article, "Excavating 'Those Dim Minoan Regions,'" mentioned above is in part a review of these books.

13.   Sigmund Freud, "Female Sexuality" (1931), *Standard Edition* 21:228.

14.   Robert Stoller, "Facts and Fancies: An Examination of Freud's Concept of Bisexuality," in *Women and Analysis: Dialogues on Psychoanalytic Views of Femininity*, ed. Jean Strouse (New York: Grossman, 1974), p. 358.

15.   For a reading of Shakespeare in light of this differentiation and the ideology connected with it, see my *Man's Estate: Masculine Identity in Shakespeare* (Berkeley and Los Angeles: University of California Press, 1981).

16.   See reviews by E. P. Thompson, *Radical History Review* 20 (Spring–Summer 1979); 42–50; Alan MacFarlane, *History and Theory* 18 (no. 1, 1979): 103–26; Randolph Traumbach, *Journal of Social History* 13 (no. 1, 1979): 136–43; Richard T. Vann, *Journal of Family History* 4 (Fall 1979): 308–15.

17.   Lawrence Stone, *The Crisis of the Aristocracy, 1558–1641*, abridged ed. (New York: Oxford University Press, 1967), p. 271.

18.   This and the following paragraph appear in *Man's Estate*, pp. 13–14.

19.   Quoted from *Political Works of King James I*, ed. C. H. McIlwain (Cambridge: Harvard University Press, 1918), p. 307; cited in Lawrence Stone, "The Rise of the Nuclear Family," p. 54.

20.   "An Homily of the State of Matrimony," in *The Two Books of Homilies Appointed to be Read in Churches*, ed. John Griffiths (Oxford, 1859), p. 505.

21.   David Leverenz, *The Language of Puritan Feeling: An Exploration in Literature, Psychology, and Social History* (New Brunswick: Rutgers University Press, 1980), p. 86. Leverenz gives a fuller and more psychologically astute interpretation of childrearing than does Stone. Though he is specifically concerned with the Puritan family, he relies on the same sources as Stone—Elizabethan and Jacobean manuals of childrearing and domestic conduct, holding that "almost any point made in Puritan tracts can be found in non-Puritan writings" (p. 91).

22.   Lynda Boose, "The Father and the Bride in Shakespeare," *PMLA* 97 (May 1982): 325–47.

23.   For a subtle and lucid account of pre-oedipal experience, see Margaret S. Mahler, Fred Pine, and Anni Bergman, *The Psychological Birth of the Human Infant: Symbiosis and Individuation* (New York: Basic Books, 1975), pp. 39–120.

24.   Sigmund Freud, "On Narcissism" (1914), *Standard Edition* 14:69–102.

25.   Sigmund Freud, "The Theme of the Three Caskets," *Standard Edition* 12:289–300.

26.   Stone, *Marriage, Sex, and the Family*, pp. 106–109.

27.   John Bowlby, *Attachment and Loss,* 2 vols. (New York: Basic Books, 1969).

28.   *Batman upon Bartholeme* (1582), cited in the Arden edition, p. 118. "The kind life-rend'ring pelican" was a familiar image of Christ in the Middle Ages, wounding herself with her beak to feed her children. Even today, the blood bank of the city of Dublin, administered by an organization called "Mother and Child," is known as "the Pelican." (I am indebted to Thomas Flanagan for this information.)

29.   Stephen J. Greenblatt, "Lear's Anxiety," *Raritan Review* (Summer 1982), 92–114.

30.   Marianne Novy, "Shakespeare and Emotional Distance in the Eliza-bethan Family," *Theatre Journal* 33 (October 1981):316–26.

31.   See. C. L. Barber, "The Family in Shakespeare's Development Tragedy and Sacredness," in *Representing Shakespeare: New Psychoanalytic Essays,* for the idea that "the very central and problematical role of women in Shakespeare—and the Elizabethan drama generally—reflects the fact that Protestantism did away with the cult of the Virgin Mary. It meant the loss of ritual resource for dealing with the in-ternal residues in all of us of the once all-powerful and all-inclusive mother" (p. 196).

32.   Stanley Cavell, "The Avoidance of Love," in *Must We Mean What We Say?* (Cambridge: At the University Press, 1976).

33.   This reading of the play suggests that Shakespeare departed from his sources and let Cordelia die because he wanted to confront as starkly as possible the pain of separation from the mother.

Analysis of Application

Coppélia Kahn's "The Absent Mother in *King Lear*" demonstrates the flexi-bility and synthetic possibilities of psychoanalytic critique. Kahn makes use of Freudian concepts such as "hysteria" and "repression," but she also builds on them with the theories of the feminist psychoanalytic critic Nancy Chodorow; in so doing she constructs a powerful and innovative reading of Shakespeare's tragedy. Her attention to textual detail and to historical data make this essay a particularly useful model for literary and cultural critics-in-training.

In her opening paragraphs, Kahn immediately isolates a set of behaviors and emotions in Lear, ones whose root causes and eventual consequences she will explore. Not unlike a clinical psychoanalyst, Kahn works to amass and interpret data in order to account for Lear's seemingly bizarre and self-destructive actions. She points her readers to Lear's own use of the term "hys-terical" to describe his sorrow, a usage that seems as aberrant as his behavior given its common association with women (*hyster* being Latin for "womb"). But just as the psychoanalyst listens carefully to an analysand's seemingly in-nocuous ("Freudian") slips of the tongue, so, too, does Kahn find avenues for startling insight through Lear's puzzling self-characterization.

Kahn is a skillful critic, not only in her use of, but also in her complication and augmentation of, Freudian concepts. After establishing her methodological base through a brief examination of *Studies in Hysteria*, she turns to Freud's interlocutors, including Gayle Rubin, C. L. Barber, Robert Stoller, and most importantly Nancy Chodorow, in order to construct a gender-sensitive application of and response to Freud. Her essay is noteworthy for its precision in defining its terms and its specific task, as well as for the ways in which it offers both a revisionary reading of a text and revision of a specific theory base on which future readings may be built.

Also noteworthy here is how Kahn handles the possible anachronism of her use of Freudian theory. It is always problematic when critics deploy recent theories of behavior and social organization to analyze earlier time periods and different cultures. But by carefully exploring common familial structures during Shakespeare's day and its crises of parental and, specifically, fatherly authority, Kahn is able to make twentieth-century psychoanalytic theory relevant to a discussion of a tragedy nearly four hundred years old. Without this historical context-setting, Kahn's interpretation would lose much of its credibility.

As Kahn works through her reading of *King Lear*, she pays very careful attention to dialogue, to plot developments, and to other textual details, always grounding her analysis in the concrete and demonstrable. In offering a gutsy and iconoclastic interpretation, Kahn understands that she must provide an abundance of supporting material. This also accounts for her careful and continuous referencing of Freudian theory, so that her reading does not seem to go far afield from established methodologies and the work of other literary critics. In this way, she reinforces her own interpretation and carves out a space for it among more accepted readings of the play.

Thus Kahn is able to argue successfully that the unfolding of the tragedy reveals a process of psychological deterioration and, finally, realization. As her analysis draws to its close, Kahn speculates beyond the play's final scene, to what might have happened if Cordelia and Lear had lived. Her last sentence even suggests that other plays by Shakespeare offer clues to a possible reestablishment of equilibrium in life, which the genre of tragedy allows only through the death of the tragic hero. Throughout, Kahn's essay demonstrates that psychoanalytic critique can be supple and suggestive, offering well-reasoned and well-supported readings without imposing a hasty or harsh diagnosis or dwelling on pathologies.

5

Structuralism and Semiotic Analysis

Overview

While the importance of structuralism—a movement whose heyday has long passed—in a brief overview of current critical methodologies is certainly questionable, it is indisputable that structuralism's offspring—semiotics—still enjoys wide popularity today. While the following discussion will therefore place greatest emphasis on the basic principles of semiotic analysis, it opens with a brief overview of the enduring insights of structuralism. Not only will this provide a foundation for our discussion of semiotics, but it is also necessary as historical background to the discussion of deconstruction (also known as *post*-structuralism) offered in Chapter 6.

Certainly the initial allure of structuralism is still as understandable today as it was powerful at the time. The development of linguistics—the scientific study of language—promised that human expression and behavior might be fully explained by using a standard set of analytical rules to uncover the basic organizing principles of language and culture. The Swiss linguistic Ferdinand de Saussure, examining the ordering principles of what he called "language systems" in the early decades of the twentieth century, posited three component parts that remain central to semiotic analysis today: the sign, the signifier, and the signified. The *signified* is the concept to which a word (for example) refers, such as the concept of a spherical object to which the word "ball" refers or the concept of deep, interpersonal feeling that is designated by the word "love." The *signifier* is then that word, image, or representation that is used to designate the signified, such as the words "ball" or "love" (or the image of a skull and crossbones, for instance, to signify a poisonous substance). The *sign* is Saussure's term for the combination of the signifier and signified: "ball" and "love" as both individual words and the concepts that lie behind them. We depend on signs, and their components parts of signifiers and signifieds, in every aspect of our daily lives. When we order food at a restaurant, give directions to friends, argue for our opinions, or hold a simple conversation, we use words to express concepts in ways that reflect common meanings and accepted definitions; these are signs. In pointing to signs as the basic building blocks of language and meaning systems, Saussure's express purpose was to begin to probe the very rules by which signs, and indeed society itself, are organized. "Semiology" was Saussure's term for his new science of signs, which would be grounded in linguistics but also include more than just the study of language, for it would subsume such fields as sociology and psychology. If one could only isolate the laws that govern signs, one could understand practically everything about human beings, cultural expression, and social activity. This, in a nutshell, was the false promise of structuralism.

Unfortunately, language systems are not reducible to hard-and-fast rules. Structuralism, as the very word implies, depends on a delineation of a clearcut structure, much as one might trace the skeleton within a physical body or the frame holding up a house. Building on Saussure's recognition that signs are intelligible through the way they relate to each other, structuralists such as Claude Levi-Strauss in anthropology and Roman Jakobson in linguistics looked especially for the ways in which meanings are made through oppositions (or binaries); for example, hot/cold, white/black, good/bad. But, of course, meanings are not reducible only to oppositions, though admittedly binaries hold powerful and enduring sway over our consciousness. As the exploration of binaries has given way to investigations of the manifold ways in which both differences and commonalities among signs account for our structures of meaning, structuralism itself has given way to a more flexible, nuanced methodology that is now widely known as "semiotics." Semiotics, though still the study of signs, now emphasizes that signs must be understood through a complex set of sometimes binary, sometimes overlapping associations: linguistic, historical, political, religious, and so forth. Furthermore, semiotics acknowledges that no sign is ever fully understandable or capturable as one might capture a scientific specimen and place it under glass. The title of Jonathan Culler's influential book, *The Pursuit of Signs*, indicates not only the analytical drive toward understanding signs but also the futility of ever achieving full knowledge or possession of them.

The field of semiotics today is an exciting, expansive, and varied one, for signs are not only spoken or written words; they can also be visual representations, symbols, and icons, indeed anything that involves signification. Think, for example, of a box of chocolates on Valentine's Day representing the affection one feels for another person: As the discussion above would indicate, the box of chocolates is indeed a signifier, the affection is that which is signified, and the box-of-chocolates-as-affection is a commonly recognized, but complex, cultural sign. Vis-à-vis the box of chocolates as sign, semiotic analysis could probe, for example, its reflection of an association between love and sweetness, its varied uses in marketing campaigns, and its possible future course in a health-and-diet-conscious society. Indeed, the possibilities for such analysis are endless, and semioticians often focus on very specific "sign systems," exploring small subunits of culture rather than the broad social systems that fascinated early semiologists. Later-twentieth-century theorists such as Roland Barthes and Umberto Eco have examined such specific sign systems as fashion and, of course, literature. Indeed, the popularity of semiotics in literary analysis has led to superb overviews of the field by Terence Hawkes (*Structuralism and Semiotics*) and Robert Scholes (*Semiotics and Interpretation*). Hawkes and Scholes examine both the uniqueness of literary representation and the ways in which it is interconnected with the many other forms of signification. But some of the most productive work in semiotics has been in examining advertising and popular culture. Jack Solomon's *The Signs of Our Time*, an accessible introduction to semiotics (and one from which the present chapter's application is drawn), examines such signs as the religious imagery used in Madonna's early videos and the complex evocation of privilege and luxury in car advertisements. Marshall Blonksy's influential collection of semiotic readings and theories, *On Signs*, explores sign systems evident in everything from film and erotica to televised royal weddings.

All the semioticians mentioned above begin with a specific sign or set of signs and then work to trace its explicit and implicit meanings through an examination of its many relationships to other signs, attempting to explain in as full a manner as possible the power that signs have over us and that we may have over them. Some semioticians work explicitly toward a deconstruction of sign systems (discussed more fully in Chapter 6), while others explore cultural belief systems well beyond the scope of the individual sign (see Chapter 10, on pluralistic cultural analysis), but all provide careful and detailed interpretations of how an individual sign relates to and draws its power from the many signs that surround it.

Key Principles

1 *Language structures our perception of the world around us.*

The most fundamental principle underlying structuralist and semiotic analysis is that there is no objective "reality" that we can know apart from the language that we use to make sense of it. Of course, "love" and "boxes of chocolates" exist as emotional and physical entities, but they acquire meaning primarily through their existence and circulation in language. This assertion reverses traditional assumptions that language exists as a simple descriptive code through which "reality" is transparently communicated. From a structuralist and semiotic perspective, there is nothing transparent about language; it is thick with political beliefs, social values, unreflected-upon judgments, and profound biases. We may naively believe that we control language, but, in fact, language largely controls us. Yet semioticians also believe that by understanding this power of language, we can begin, perhaps, to exercise some reciprocal influence over it.

2 *Language is understandable as a system of signs; furthermore, signs function as a language.*

Another fundamental component of semiotic analysis is the recognition that language and other modes of representation and communication operate as sign systems, that meanings are made through relationships between signs. The overview above traces the basic definitions of the terms "signified," "signifier," and "sign," with the last term indicating the joining of the concept (signified) and the word or other communicative unit that refers to the concept (signifier). Recognizing this three-part nature of signification allows us numerous points of analytical access. Signifiers—words, for example—obviously can be scrutinized in terms of their grammatical arrangement, their different spellings or presentations (boldfaced or italicized, for example), and their variations across cultures or time. Similarly, the many properties of concepts being signified are important for what they tell us about how such properties are represented in language, how values are imposed on otherwise value-free entities, and how culture differentiates and discriminates among similar and dissimilar properties. But certainly the most promising field of research is the analysis of the combination of the two—the sign—and this will be the focus of the remainder of this chapter.

In discussing signs, it is important to remember that signs are not only words, that the term also refers to other bearers of meaning: musical notes, images, fashion, architecture, and such like. Structuralist linguistics sometimes ignored the full range of such important modes of human expression, although anthropologists and other cultural critics working with structuralist methodologies did expand our understanding of what might be considered forms of language. It is obvious that music, for example, can affect our mood; semiotics encourages us to explore how that effect is achieved through a communicative, indeed languagelike, process. Similarly, architecture conveys numerous "meanings"; semioticians would see houses, office buildings, shopping centers, and the like as communicating both explicit and implicit ideas and values. Semiotics allows us to see the many forms of human expression as having internal structures and external relationships with other forms of expression. Oral and written forms of language are just two of the many interconnected languages that make up human consciousness on the individual and collective levels.

3 *A given sign is densely interconnected with other signs.*

Semiotic analysis concerns itself with systems of signs, for no sign possesses meaning in isolation; it does so only through a series of contrasts and comparisons with other signs. Take, for example, the sign "pickup truck," which is analyzable through its many relationships. It is clearly both similar to and different from signs such as "car" or "minivan" in terms of its physical properties and cultural implications. Of course, all three terms indicate a motorized vehicle with a capacity for transporting cargo as well as people, but the type of cargo and the specifics of its design help us understand the complexity of the sign "pickup truck." "Cars" have trunks that carry groceries or other products purchased on shopping trips. "Minivans" carry larger quantities of the same for families, as well as children's sports equipment and perhaps summer camping gear. "Pickup trucks," on the other hand, may also carry any of those, but their cargo space is usually open to the air, perhaps indicating something about the durable nature of what will be hauled. Furthermore, they have a very limited passenger capacity, possibly signifying something about the relatively solitary nature of the driver. They are advertised as being "rugged" and "strong," evoking popular stereotypes of masculinity and power. Thus even though two consumers may have virtually identical transportation needs, they may make very different choices when buying a vehicle, wishing to send distinct messages about their social identities. When beginning semiotic analysis, it is therefore important to ask how a given sign differs from others with which it may share some qualities and how it acquires meaning through both comparison and contrast. What social connotations and implications are attached to a specific sign, and where do they originate? How are certain physical qualities of the signified translated into complex and value-laden social messages in the process of signification? In our pickup truck example, what does a pickup truck "mean" compared to a car or a minivan in terms of the tangible and intangible qualities that it possesses and that its owners wish to possess?

4 *Signs are understandable synchronically.*

Semiotics explores the context of the sign and how meaning is made through that context. One form of such analysis is called "synchronic," meaning that it moves through cultural channels at a given moment in time, without regard to an exploration of history. Synchronic analysis would attempt to explain the overt and covert meanings of a sign with reference only to contemporaneous signs and systems of meaning. In analyzing a sign such as a specific advertisement for a pickup truck—one showing it bouncing across a rugged landscape and climbing steep, slippery mountain slopes—the semiotician might examine the many cultural references that such landscapes draw on. What might the viewer believe that the driver of the pickup truck is doing in that landscape? What presuppositions about leisure time, health, and gender identity underlie such imagery? What power does the ownership of such a pickup truck seem to convey to its owner? Furthermore, what is not shown in the ad? What landscapes, qualities, or lifestyle components seem left behind after purchasing the truck? In exploring such questions, the critic draws on her or his knowledge and research of other signs, showing how the pickup truck advertised is made to seem different from or similar to them. The critic might discover that the advertisement in question evokes images of similar advertisements for beer or cigarettes; in this way, a system of related signs (of masculinity or outlaw identity) emerges as a primary way of making meaning. In tracing such overt and covert meanings, the critic explores how an advertisement operates complexly on viewers, even covertly manipulating them. Semiotic analysis often seeks, in so doing, to empower the audience of signs by making them conscious of such manipulation and thus able to analyze and potentially resist it.

5 *Signs are understandable diachronically.*

But signs also have a history, and the tracing of such chronological aspects of a given sign is known as "diachronic" analysis. Traditionally, much literary and cultural criticism has been of a diachronic nature. But unlike traditional historical criticism, diachronic analysis would not simply place a sign in its historical context (for even more information on new forms of historical research, see Chapter 10); instead it would seek to trace the evolution of the component parts of the sign system—the sign, signifier, and signified—and examine their evolving relationship to other signs. Thus, in our example of a pickup truck, a diachronic analysis of the sign might examine how advertising images of trucks have evolved over time in relationship to changing images of the family, of masculinity, or of leisure time. This is very different from a simple history of pickup trucks, for it focuses intensely on that dense communicative context that allows a sign to convey meaning and explores how those meanings change, often in nearly imperceptible ways, as contexts evolve and signs metamorphose in relationship to some-times subtle changes in related signs.

6 *Literature and literary representation are manifestations of sign systems and provide occasions for their study.*

Literature and literary representation offer many possibilities for semi-otic analysis. Anthropologists and others using structuralist methodologists were fascinated by the ways in which stories, myths, and folktales helped structure culture through such binary oppositions as pure/impure and friend/enemy. And, certainly, literary and other forms of cultural represen-tation may still operate in this binary manner, as critics have discovered in analyzing cold war narratives of Soviet menace and in tracing homophobic portrayals of lesbian and gay threats to social purity (see Chapter 8 for more information about gay/lesbian/queer analysis). But semiotic analysis of liter-ature does not consist only of an exploration of binaries, for the signs sys-tems within and surrounding literature are highly complex. Just as a cultural critic might synchronically or diachronically explore a sign such as a "pickup truck," so, too, could a literary semiotician explore how a sign such as "Moby Dick" in Melville's novel of that name acquires meaning syn-chronically within the pages of the text or how a sign such as "debtors prison" (where indigent Victorian men, women, and children were sent) changed over the course of nineteenth-century literary history as the social context changed. In both cases, the critic would ask many of the questions posed earlier: What is being signified by the signifier? What related signs offer clues to the meaning of the sign? What covert messages are communi-cated through the sign, and how do they draw on an expansive cultural con-text?

But semiotic analysis of literature may have yet another focus, for litera-ture itself is a sign. What do the signs "novel," "poem," "drama," or "essay" mean? How have those signs changed over time, and how have their inter-nal structures and the external means by which they are differentiated from other signs differed across time (diachronically) or differed across contem-poraneous cultures or within a single culture (synchronically)? Northrup Frye's *Anatomy of Criticism*, first published in 1957, is an intriguing and still influential application of specifically structuralist principles to literature's substructures of myths, archetypes, and formal qualities. Yet literature today is not always examined as a distinct system of meaning, which was Frye's express wish. In examining today how a sign such as "poem" differs from a related sign such as "music lyric," the critic might probe how a cul-ture attributes "high" and "low" cultural values to forms of expression, how signs are marketed to certain subsets of society, and perhaps how critics themselves deem certain modes of expression worthy or unworthy of analysis. Thus, again, semiotic analysis takes the practitioner back to some of the basic structuring principles of culture and the human mind.

7 *No sign is ever fully understandable or capturable.*

One quality characterizing contemporary semiotic analysis and differentiating it from some earlier forms of strucuturalist analysis is the recognition that no sign can ever be fully explained. Signs are so complexly interwoven with other signs, expanding outward through culture and time, that an exhaustive and definitive analysis of even the smallest or seemingly most insignificant sign is impossible. The "pickup truck" discussed above can be analyzed with reference to related signs of leisure, gender, class, sexuality, geography, topography, and so forth, and as one explores those related signs, the systems grow ever larger and more complex. As Jonathan Culler makes clear in his influential book, one can only pursue signs and hope to capture part of their meaning.

But semioticians face yet another challenge, for our own language and the systems of reference through which we analyze signs are themselves signs; there is no objective language or purely scientific methodology possible in the analysis of literary and other forms of cultural representation. Unlike some of the early structuralists, who believed that they could create a perfect and comprehensive science of signs, semioticians today recognize that their own terms and analytical products are subject to intense critical scrutiny; they and their writings are also products of existing sign systems and are signs in and of themselves. While some may consider such inherent complexity to be unnerving or paralyzing, it is much more appropriate to see it as exciting and dynamic. Semioticians would suggest that no sign is off limits for analysis; texts both surround and include us. That we, too, create, perpetuate, and potentially alter sign systems can make our work all the more relevant and charged with social and cultural potential.

Bibliography

Barthes, Roland. *Mythologies*, trans. Annette Lavers. New York: Hill & Wang, 1972.

> Of the many works of semiotic analysis that I could list here, *Mythologies* is certainly one of the most influential and enjoyable. Its many brief essays examine a range of cultural texts, from toys to strip shows. While it may be of interest to all, intermediate and advanced readers with some knowledge of the field of semiotics will find it of greatest use.

Blonsky, Marshall, ed. *On Signs*. Baltimore: Johns Hopkins University Press, 1985.

This highly influential collection contains both primary works of semiotic theory and applications devoted to a range of subjects, from literature to architecture. Its level of accessibility varies somewhat, but generally it will be of greatest interest to advanced readers.

Culler, Jonathan. *The Pursuit of Signs: Semiotics, Literature, Deconstruction*. Ithaca, NY: Cornell University Press, 1981.

This superb theoretical study traces the evolution of early forms of structuralism into the contemporary fields of semiotics and deconstruction. Culler's first two chapters, "Beyond Interpretation" and "In Pursuit of Signs," will be of particular interest to both intermediate and advanced readers.

Culler, Jonathan. *Structuralist Poetics: Structuralism, Linguistics, and the Study of Literature*. Ithaca, NY: Cornell University Press, 1975.

This dense introduction to structuralist theory was one of the first that argued for the importance of linguistics-based structuralism in literary analysis. Its sophisticated diction will make it most appropriate for advanced readers.

Frye, Northrup. *Anatomy of Criticism: Four Essays*. Princeton, NJ: Princeton University Press, 1957.

This influential book combines structuralist principles with psychoanalytic theory to create an archetypal or myth-based, criticism, which was very popular in the 1960s. Its dense language and complex responses to previous forms of critical analysis make it most appropriate for advanced readers.

Hawkes, Terence. *Structuralism and Semiotics*. Berkeley: University of California Press, 1977.

This is a solid and highly readable overview of both structuralist and semiotic theory. It is particularly useful for readers interested specifically in literary analysis. Its presupposition of some background knowledge of theory makes it most appropriate for intermediate and advanced readers.

Scholes, Robert. *Semiotics and Interpretation*. New Haven, CT: Yale University Press, 1982.

This introduction to semiotics is devoted almost entirely to its uses in literary analysis. Of particular note are its applications of semiotic theory to stories by James Joyce and Ernest Hemingway. Its presupposition of some familiarity with critical theory makes it most appropriate for intermediate and advanced readers.

Scholes, Robert. *Structuralism in Literature: An Introduction*. New Haven, CT: Yale University Press, 1974.

Much like Scholes's introduction to semiotics above, this introduction to structuralism emphasizes its usefulness in literary analysis. It contains helpful applications of structuralist principles to Romantic poetry and James Joyce's novel *Ulysses*. Its dense language and theoretical sophistication will make it of greatest interest to advanced readers.

Solomon, Jack. *The Signs of Our Time: The Secret Meanings of Everyday Life.* New York: Harper & Row, 1988.

This is a clear and accessible introduction to semiotics, one that pays particular attention to readings of advertising, popular culture, and other nonliterary texts. It provides both a reliable overview of semiotics and an engaging reading experience for all readers, at the beginning through advanced levels.

Application

Reading Prompts

1. Reflect on Solomon's purpose in beginning his essay with a discussion of Alexis de Tocqueville. Mark passages in which he reveals what has changed and what has stayed the same in American culture since Tocqueville wrote *Democracy in America*.

2. Pay careful attention to Solomon's discussion of the reciprocal relationship that exists between advertisers and consumers. As you read, consider the following question: To what extent does the former exercise control over the latter or vice versa?

3. Solomon references Hegel in a discussion of body language as a sign system. Mark or underline passages in which Solomon reveals how certain gestures and expressions operate as signs in advertising.

4. Solomon suggests that McDonald's is one of the most successful manipulators of signs in contemporary American advertising. Mark or underline those passages in which he reveals how and why this is the case.

5. Solomon offers some provocative readings of American advertisements, but after reading it, do you feel that this essay also has an implicit message to readers about their own relationships with ads?

JACK SOLOMON

Masters of Desire:

The Culture of American Advertising

*Amongst democratic nations, men easily attain a
certain equality of condition; but they can never
attain as much as they desire.*

ALEXIS DE TOCQUEVILLE

On May 10, 1831, a young French aristocrat named Alexis de Tocqueville arrived in New York City at the start of what would become one of the most famous visits to America in our history. He had come to observe firsthand the institutions of the freest, most egalitarian society of the age, but what he found was a paradox. For behind America's mythic promise of equal opportunity, Tocqueville discovered a desire for *unequal* social rewards, a ferocious competition for privilege and distinction. As he wrote in his monumental study, *Democracy in America:*

> When all privileges of birth and fortune are abolished, when all professions are accessible to all, and a man's own energies may place him at the top of any of one them, an easy and unbounded career seems open to his ambition . . . But this is an erroneous notion, which is corrected by daily experience. [For when] men are nearly alike, and all follow the same track, it is very difficult for any one individual to walk quick and cleave a way through the same throng which surrounds and presses him.

Yet walking quick and cleaving a way is precisely what Americans dream of. We Americans dream of rising above the crowd, of attaining a social summit beyond the reach of ordinary citizens. And therein lies the paradox.

The American dream, in other words, has two faces: the one communally egalitarian and the other competitively elitist. This contradiction is no accident; it is fundamental to the structure of American society. Even as America's great myth of equality celebrates the virtues of mom, apple pie, and the girl or boy next door, it also lures us to achieve social distinction, to rise above the crowd and bask alone in the glory. This land is your land and this land is my land, Woody Guthrie's populist anthem tells us, but we keep trying to increase the "my" at the expense of the "your." Rather than fostering contentment, the American dream breeds desire, a longing for a greater share of the pie. It is as if our society were a vast high-school football game, with the bulk of the participants noisily rooting in the stands while, deep down, each of them is wishing he or she could be the star quarterback or head cheerleader.

For the semiotician, the contradictory nature of the American myth of equality is nowhere written so clearly as in the signs that American advertisers use to manipulate us into buying their wares. "Manipulate" is the word here, not "persuade"; for advertising campaigns are not sources of product information, they are exercises in behavior modification. Appealing to our subconscious emotions rather than to our conscious intellects, advertisements are designed to exploit the discontentments fostered by the American dream, the constant desire for social success and the material rewards that accompany it. America's consumer economy runs on desire, and advertising stokes the engines by transforming common objects—from peanut butter to political candidates—into signs of all the things that Americans covet most.

But by semiotically reading the signs that advertising agencies manufacture to stimulate consumption, we can plot the precise state of desire in the audiences to which they are addressed. In this chapter, we'll look at a representative sample of ads and what they say about the emotional climate of the country and the fast-changing trends of American life. Because ours is a highly diverse, pluralistic society, various advertisements may say different things depending on their intended audiences, but in every case they say something about America, about the status of our hopes, fears, desires, and beliefs.

Let's begin with two ad campaigns conducted by the same company that bear out Alexis de Tocqueville's observations about the contradictory nature of American society: General Motors' campaigns for its Cadillac and Chevrolet lines. First, consider an early magazine ad for the Cadillac Allanté. Appearing as a full-color, four-page insert in *Time*, the ad seems to say "I'm special—and so is this car" even before we've begun to read it. Rather than being printed on the ordinary, flimsy pages of the magazine, the Allanté spread appears on glossy coated stock. The unwritten message here is that an extraordinary car deserves an extraordinary advertisement, and that both car and ad are aimed at an extraordinary consumer, or at least one who wishes to appear extraordinary compared to his more ordinary fellow citizens.

Ads of this kind work by creating symbolic associations between their product and what is most coveted by the consumers to whom they are addressed. It is significant, then, that this ad insists that the Allanté is virtually an Italian rather than an American car, an automobile, as its copy runs, "Conceived and Commissioned by America's Luxury Car Leader—Cadillac" but "Designed and Handcrafted by Europe's Renowned Design Leader—Pininfarina, SpA, of Turin, Italy." This is not simply a piece of product information, it's a sign of the prestige that European luxury cars enjoy in today's automotive marketplace. Once the luxury car of choice for America's status drivers, Cadillac has fallen far behind its European competitors in the race for the prestige market. So the Allanté essentially represents Cadillac's decision, after years of resisting the trend toward European cars, to introduce its own European import—whose high cost is clearly printed on the last page of the ad. Although $54,700 is a lot of money to pay for a Cadillac, it's about what you'd expect to pay for a top-of-the-line Mercedes-Benz. That's precisely the point the ad is trying to make: the Allanté is no mere car. It's a potent status symbol you can associate with the other major status symbols of the 1980s.

American companies manufacture status symbols because American consumers want them. As Alexis de Tocqueville recognized a century and a half ago, the competitive nature of democratic societies breeds a desire for social distinction, a yearning to rise above the crowd. But given the fact that those who do make it to the top in socially mobile societies have often risen from the lower ranks, they still look like everyone else. In the socially immobile societies of aristocratic Europe, generations of fixed social conditions produced subtle class signals. The accent of one's voice, the shape of one's nose, or even the set of one's chin, immediately communicated social status. Aside from the nasal bray and uptilted head of the Boston Brahmin, Americans do not have any native sets of personal status signals. If it weren't for his Mercedes-Benz and Manhattan townhouse, the parvenu Wall Street millionaire often couldn't be distinguished from the man who tailors his suits. Hence, the demand for status symbols, for the objects that mark one off as a social success, is particularly strong in democratic nations—stronger even than in aristocratic societies, where the aristocrat so often looks and sounds different from everyone else.

Status symbols, then, are signs that identify their possessors' place in a social hierarchy, markers of rank and prestige. We can all think of any number of status symbols—Rolls-Royces, Beverly Hills mansions, even Shar Pei puppies (whose rareness and expense has rocketed them beyond Russian wolfhounds as status pets and has even inspired whole lines of wrinkle-faced stuffed toys)—but how do we know that something *is* a status symbol? The explanation is quite simple: when an object (or puppy!) either costs a lot of money or requires influential connections to possess, anyone who possesses it must also possess the necessary means and influence to acquire it. The object itself really doesn't matter, since it ultimately disappears behind the presumed social potency of its owner. Semiotically, what matters is the signal it sends, its value as a sign of power. One traditional sign of social distinction is owning a country estate and enjoying the peace and privacy that attend it. Advertisements for Mercedes-Benz, Jaguar, and Audi automobiles thus frequently feature drivers motoring quietly along a country road, presumably on their way to or from their country houses.

Advertisers have been quick to exploit the status signals that belong to body language as well. As Hegel observed in the early nineteenth century, it is an ancient aristocratic prerogative to be seen by the lower orders without having to look at them in return. Tilting his chin high in the air and gazing down at the world under hooded eyelids, the aristocrat invites observation while refusing to look back. We can find such a pose exploited in an advertisement for Cadillac Seville in which we see an elegantly dressed woman out for a drive with her husband in their new Cadillac. If we look closely at the woman's body language, we can see her glance inwardly with a satisfied smile on her face but not outward toward the camera that represents our gaze. She is glad to be seen by us in her Seville, but she isn't interested in looking at *us!*

Ads that are aimed at a broader market take the opposite approach. If the American dream encourages the desire to "arrive," to vault above the mass, it also fosters a desire to be popular, to "belong." Populist commercials accordingly transform products into signs of belonging, utilizing such common icons as country music, small-town life, family picnics, and farmyards. All of these icons are incorporated in GM's "Heartbeat of America" campaign for its Chevrolet line. Unlike the Seville commercial, the faces in the Chevy ads look straight at us and smile. Dress is casual; the mood upbeat. Quick camera cuts take us from rustic to suburban to urban scenes, creating an American montage filmed from sea to shining sea. We all "belong" in a Chevy.

Where price alone doesn't determine the market for a product, advertisers can go either way. Both Johnnie Walker and Jack Daniel's are bettergrade whiskies, but where a Johnnie Walker ad appeals to the buyer who wants a mark of aristocratic distinction in his liquor, a Jack Daniel's ad emphasizes the down-home, egalitarian folksiness of its product. Johnnie Walker associates itself with such conventional status symbols as sable coats, Rolls-Royces, and black gold; Jack Daniel's gives us a Good Ol' Boy in overalls. In fact, Jack Daniel's Good Ol' Boy is an icon of backwoods independence, recalling the days of the moonshiner and the Whisky Rebellion of 1794. Evoking emotions quite at odds with those stimulated in

Johnnie Walker ads, the advertisers of Jack Daniel's have chosen to transform their product into a sign of America's populist tradition. The fact that both ads successfully sell whisky is itself a sign of the dual nature of the American dream.

Beer is also pitched on two levels. Consider the difference between the ways Budweiser and Michelob market their light beers. Bud Light and Michelob Light cost and taste about the same, but Budweiser tends to target the working class while Michelob has gone after the upscale market. Bud commercials are set in working-class bars that contrast with the sophisticated nightclubs and yuppie watering holes of the Michelob campaign. "You're one of the guys," Budweiser assures the assembly-line worker and the truck driver, "this Bud's for you." Michelob, on the other hand, makes no such appeal to the democratic instinct of sharing and belonging. You don't share, you take, grabbing what you can in a competitive dash to "have it all."

Populist advertising is particularly effective in the face of foreign competition. When Americans feel threatened from the outside, they tend to circle the wagons and temporarily forget their class differences. In the face of the Japanese automotive "invasion," Chrysler runs populist commercials in which Lee Iacocca joins the simple folk who buy his cars as the jingle "Born in America" blares in the background. Seeking to capitalize on the popularity of Bruce Springsteen's *Born in the USA* album, these ads gloss over Springsteen's ironic lyrics in a vast display of flag-waving. Chevrolet's "Heartbeat of America" campaign similarly attempts to woo American motorists away from Japanese automobiles by appealing to their patriotic sentiments.

The patriotic iconography of these campaigns also reflects the general cultural mood of the early- to mid-1980s. After a period of national anguish in the wake of the Vietnam War and the Iran hostage crisis, America went on a patriotic binge. American athletic triumphs in the Lake Placid and Los Angeles Olympics introduced a sporting tone into the national celebration, often making international affairs appear like one great Olympiad in which America was always going for the gold. In response, advertisers began to do their own flag-waving.

The mood of advertising during this period was definitely upbeat. Even deodorant commercials, which traditionally work on our self-doubts and fears of social rejection, jumped on the bandwagon. In the guilty sixties, we had ads like the "Ice Blue Secret" campaign with its connotations of guilt and shame. In the feel-good Reagan eighties, "Sure" deodorant commercials featured images of triumphant Americans throwing up their arms in victory to reveal—no wet marks! Deodorant commercials once had the moral echo of Nathaniel Hawthorne's guilt-ridden *The Scarlet Letter;* in the early eighties they had all the moral subtlety of *Rocky IV*, reflecting the emotions of a Vietnam-weary nation eager to embrace the imagery of America Triumphant.

The commercials for Worlds of Wonder's Lazer Tag game featured the futuristic finals of some Soviet-American Lazer Tag shootout ("Practice hard, America!") and carried the emotions of patriotism into an even more aggressive arena. Exploiting the hoopla that surrounded the victory over the Soviets in the hockey finals of the 1980 Olympics, the Lazer Tag ads pandered to an American desire for the sort of clear-cut nationalistic triumphs that the nuclear age has rendered almost impossible. Creating a fantasy setting where patriotic dreams are substituted for complicated realities, the Lazer Tag commercials sought to capture the imaginations of children caught up in the patriotic fervor of the early 1980s.

LIVE THE FANTASY

By reading the signs of American advertising, we can conclude that America is a nation of fantasizers, often preferring the sign to the substance and easily enthralled by a veritable Fantasy Island of commercial illusions. Critics of Madison Avenue often complain that advertisers create consumer desire, but semioticians don't think the situation is that simple. Advertisers may give shape to consumer fantasies, but they need raw material to work with, the subconscious dreams and desires of the marketplace. As long as these desires remain unconscious, advertisers will be able to exploit them. But by bringing the fantasies to the surface, you can free yourself from advertising's often hypnotic grasp.

I can think of no company that has more successfully seized upon the subconscious fantasies of the American marketplace—indeed the world marketplace—than McDonald's. By no means the first nor the only hamburger chain in the United States, McDonald's emerged victorious in the "burger wars" by transforming hamburgers into signs of all that was desirable in American life. Other chains like Wendy's, Burger King, and Jack-In-The-Box continue to advertise and sell widely, but no company approaches McDonald's transformation of itself into a symbol of American culture.

McDonald's success can be traced to the precision of its advertising. Instead of broadcasting a single "one-size-fits-all" campaign at a time, McDonald's pitches its burgers simultaneously at different age groups, different classes, even different races (Budweiser beer, incidentally, has succeeded in the same way). For children, there is the Ronald McDonald campaign, which presents a fantasy world that has little to do with hamburgers in any rational sense but a great deal to do with the emotional desires of kids. Ronald McDonald and his friends are signs that recall the Muppets, "Sesame Street," the circus, toys, storybook illustrations, even *Alice in Wonderland*. Such signs do not signify hamburgers. Rather, they are displayed in order to prompt in the child's mind an automatic association of fantasy, fun, and McDonald's.

The same approach is taken in ads aimed at older audiences—teens, adults, and senior citizens. In the teen-oriented ads we may catch a fleeting glimpse of a hamburger or two, but what we are really shown is a teenage fantasy: groups of hip and happy adolescents singing, dancing, and cavorting together. Fearing loneliness more than anything else, adolescents quickly respond to the group appeal of such commercials. "Eat a Big Mac," these ads say, "and you won't be stuck home alone on Saturday night."

To appeal to an older and more sophisticated audience no longer so afraid of not belonging and more concerned with finding a place to go out to at night, McDonald's has designed the elaborate "Mac Tonight" commercials, which have for their backdrop a nightlit urban skyline and at their center a cabaret pianist with a moon-shaped head, a glad manner, and Blues Brothers shades. Such signs prompt an association of McDonald's with nightclubs and urban sophistication, persuading us that McDonald's is a place not only for breakfast or lunch but for dinner too, as if it were a popular off-Broadway nightspot, a place to see and be seen. Even the parody of Kurt Weill's "Mack the Knife" theme song that Mac the Pianist performs is a sign, a subtle signal to the sophisticated hamburger eater able to recognize the origin of the tune in Bertolt Brecht's *Threepenny Opera*.

For yet older customers, McDonald's has designed a commercial around the fact that it employs a large number of retirees and seniors. In one such ad, we see an elderly man leaving his pretty little cottage early in the morning to start work as "the new kid" at McDonald's, and then we watch him during his first day on the job. Of course he is a great success, outdoing everyone else with his energy and efficiency, and he returns home in the evening to a loving wife and happy home. One would almost think that the ad was a kind of moving "help wanted" sign (indeed, McDonald's *was* hiring elderly employees at the time), but it's really just directed at consumers. Older viewers can see themselves wanted and appreciated in the ad—and perhaps be distracted from the rationally uncomfortable fact that many senior citizens take such jobs because of financial need and thus may be unlikely to own the sort of home that one sees in the commercial. But realism isn't the point here. This is fantasyland, a dream world promising instant gratification no matter what the facts of the matter may be.

Practically the only fantasy that McDonald's doesn't exploit is the fantasy of sex. This is understandable, given McDonald's desire to present itself as a family restaurant. But everywhere else, sexual fantasies, which have always had an important place in American advertising, are beginning to dominate the advertising scene. You expect sexual come-ons in ads for perfume or cosmetics or jewelry—after all, that's what they're selling—but for room deodorizers? In a magazine ad for Claire Burke home fragrances, for example, we see a well-dressed couple cavorting about their bedroom in what looks like a cheery preparation for sadomasochistic exercises. Jordache and Calvin Klein pitch blue jeans as props for teenage sexuality. The phallic appeal of automobiles, traditionally an implicit feature in automotive advertising, becomes quite explicit in a Dodge commercial that shifts back and forth from shots of a young man in an automobile to teasing glimpses of a woman—his date—as she dresses in her apartment.

The very language of today's advertisements is charged with sexuality. Products in the more innocent fifties were "new and improved," but everything in the eighties is "hot!"—as in "hot woman," or sexual heat. Cars are "hot." Movies are "hot." An ad for Valvoline pulses to the rhythm of a "heat wave, burning in my car." Sneakers get red hot in a magazine ad for Travel Fox athletic shoes in which we see male and female figures, clad only in Travel Fox shoes, apparently in the act of copulation—an ad that earned one of *Adweek's* annual "badvertising" awards for shoddy advertising.

The sexual explicitness of contemporary advertising is a sign not so much of American sexual fantasies as of the lengths to which advertisers will go to get attention. Sex never fails as an attention-getter, and in a particularly competitive, and expensive, era for American marketing, advertisers like to bet on a sure thing. Ad people refer to the proliferation of TV, radio, newspaper, magazine, and billboard ads as "clutter," and nothing cuts through the clutter like sex.

By showing the flesh, advertisers work on the deepest, most coercive human emotions of all. Much sexual coercion in advertising, however, is a sign of a desperate need to make certain that clients are getting their money's worth. The appearance of advertisements that refer directly to the prefabricated fantasies of Hollywood is a sign of a different sort of desperation: a desperation for ideas. With the rapid turnover of advertising campaigns mandated by the need to cut through the "clutter," advertisers may be hard pressed for new ad concepts, and so they are more and more frequently turning to already-established models. In the early 1980s, for instance, Pepsi-Cola ran a series of ads broadly alluding to Steven Spielberg's *E.T.* In one such ad, we see a young boy who, like the hero of *E.T.*, witnesses an extraterrestrial visit. The boy is led to a soft-drink machine where he pauses to drink a can of Pepsi as the spaceship he's spotted flies off into the universe. The relationship between the ad and the movie, accordingly, is a parasitical one, with the ad taking its life from the creative body of the film.

Pepsi did something similar in 1987 when it arranged with the producers of the movie *Top Gun* to promote the film's video release in Pepsi's television advertisements in exchange for the right to append a Pepsi ad to the video itself. This time, however, the parasitical relationship between ad and film was made explicit. Pepsi sales benefited from the video, and the video's sales benefited from Pepsi. It was a marriage made in corporate heaven.

The fact that Pepsi believed that it could stimulate consumption by appealing to the militaristic fantasies dramatized in *Top Gun* reflects similar fantasies in the "Pepsi generation." Earlier generations saw Pepsi associated with high-school courtship rituals, with couples sipping sodas together at the corner drugstore. When the draft was on, young men fantasized about Peggy Sue, not Air Force Flight School. Military service was all too real a possibility to fantasize about. But in an era when military service is not a reality for most young Americans, Pepsi commercials featuring hotshot flyboys drinking Pepsi while streaking about in their Air Force jets contribute to a youth culture that has forgotten what military service means. It all looks like such fun in the Pepsi ads, but what they conceal is the fact that military jets are weapons, not high-tech recreational vehicles.

For less militaristic dreamers, Madison Avenue has framed ad campaigns around the cultural prestige of high-tech machinery in its own right. This is especially the case with sports cars, whose high-tech appeal is so powerful that some people apparently fantasize about *being* sports cars. At least, this is the conclusion one might draw from a Porsche commercial that asked its audience, "If you were a car, what kind of car would you be?" As a candy-red Porsche speeds along a rain-slick forest road, the ad's voice-over describes all the specifications you'd want to have if you *were* a sports car. "If you were a car," the commercial concludes, "you'd be a Porsche."

In his essay "Car Commercials and 'Miami Vice,'" Todd Gitlin explains the semiotic appeal of such ads as those in the Porsche campaign. Aired at the height of what may be called America's "myth of the entrepreneur," these commercials were aimed at young corporate managers who imaginatively identified with the "lone wolf" image of a Porsche speeding through the woods. Gitlin points out that such images cater to the fantasies of faceless corporate men who dream of entrepreneurial glory, of striking out on their own like John DeLorean and telling the boss to take his job and shove it. But as DeLorean's spectacular failure demonstrates, the life of the entrepreneur can be extremely risky. So rather than having to go it alone and take the risks that accompany entrepreneurial independence, the young executive can substitute fantasy for reality by climbing into his Porsche—or at least that's what Porsche's advertisers wanted him to believe.

But there is more at work in the Porsche ads than the fantasies of corporate America. Ever since Arthur C. Clarke and Stanley Kubrick teamed up to present us with HAL 9000, the demented computer of *2001: A Space Odyssey*, the American imagination has been obsessed with the melding of man and machine. First there was television's "Six Million Dollar Man," and then movieland's *Star Wars*, *Blade Runner*, and *Robocop*, fantasy visions of a future dominated by machines. Androids haunt our imaginations as machines seize the initiative. *Time* magazine's "Man of the Year" for 1982 was a computer. Robot-built automobiles appeal to drivers who spend their days in front of computer screens—perhaps designing robots. When so much power and prestige is being given to high-tech machines, wouldn't you rather be a Porsche?

In short, the Porsche campaign is a sign of a new mythology that is emerging before our eyes, a myth of the machine, which is replacing the myth of the human. The iconic figure of the little tramp caught up in the cogs of industrial production in Charlie Chaplin's *Modern Times* signified a humanistic revulsion to the age of the machine. Human beings, such icons said, were superior to machines. Human values should come first in the moral order of things. But as Edith Milton suggests in her essay "The Track of the Mutant," we are now coming to believe that machines are superior to human beings, that mechanical nature is superior to human nature. Rather than being threatened by machines, we long to merge with them. "The Six Million Dollar Man" is one iconic figure in the new mythology; Harrison Ford's sexual coupling with an android is another. In such an age it should come as little wonder that computer-synthesized Max Headroom should be a commercial spokesman for Coca-Cola, or that Federal Express should design a series of TV ads featuring mechanical-looking human beings revolving around strange and powerful machines.

FEAR AND TREMBLING IN THE MARKETPLACE

While advertisers play on and reflect back at us our fantasies about everything from fighter pilots to robots, they also play on darker imaginings. If dream and desire can be exploited in the quest for sales, so can nightmare and fear.

The nightmare equivalent of America's populist desire to "belong," for example, is the fear of not belonging, of social rejection, of being different. Advertisements for dandruff shampoos, mouthwashes, deodorants, and laundry detergents ("Ring Around the Collar!") accordingly exploit such fears, bullying us into consumption. Although ads of this type are still around in the 1980s, they were particularly common in the fifties and early sixties, reflecting a society still reeling from the witch-hunts of the Mc-Carthy years. When any sort of social eccentricity or difference could result in a public denunciation and the loss of one's job or even liberty, Americans were keen to conform and be like everyone else. No one wanted to be "guilty" of smelling bad or of having a dirty collar.

"Guilt" ads characteristically work by creating narrative situations in which someone is "accused" of some social "transgression," pronounced guilty, and then offered the sponsor's product as a means of returning to "innocence." Such ads, in essence, are parodies of ancient religious rituals of guilt and atonement, whereby sinning humanity is offered salvation through the agency of priest and church. In the world of advertising, a product takes the place of the priest, but the logic of the situation is quite similar.

In commercials for Wisk detergent, for example, we witness the drama of a hapless housewife and her husband as they are mocked by the jeering voices of children shouting "Ring Around the Collar!" "Oh, those dirty rings!" the housewife groans in despair. It's as if she and her husband were being stoned by an angry crowd. But there's hope, there's help, there's Wisk. Cleansing her soul of sin as well as her husband's, the housewife launders his shirts with Wisk, and behold, his collars are clean. Product salvation is only as far as the supermarket.

The recent appearance of advertisements for hospitals treating drug and alcohol addiction have raised the old genre of the guilt ad to new heights (or lows, depending on your perspective). In such ads, we see wives on the verge of leaving their husbands if they don't do something about their drinking, and salesmen about to lose their jobs. The man is guilty; he has sinned; but he upholds the ritual of guilt and atonement by "confessing" to his wife or boss and agreeing to go to the hospital the ad is pitching.

If guilt looks backward in time to past transgressions, fear, like desire, faces forward, trembling before the future. In the late 1980s, a new kind of fear commercial appeared, one whose narrative played on the worries of young corporate managers struggling up the ladder of success. Representing the nightmare equivalent of the elitist desire to "arrive," ads of this sort created images of failure, storylines of corporate defeat. In one ad for Apple computers, for example, a group of junior executives sits around a table with the boss as he asks each executive how long it will take his or her department to complete some publishing jobs. "Two or three days," answers one nervous executive. "A week, on overtime," a tight-lipped woman responds. But one young up-and-comer can have everything ready tomorrow, today, or yesterday, because his department uses a Macintosh desktop publishing system. Guess who'll get the next promotion?

Fear stalks an ad for AT&T computer systems too. A boss and four junior executives are dining in a posh restaurant. Icons of corporate power and prestige flood the screen—from the executives' formal evening wear to the fancy table setting—but there's tension in the air. It seems that the junior managers have chosen a computer system that's incompatible with the firm's sales and marketing departments. A whole new system will have to be purchased, but the tone of the meeting suggests that it will be handled by a new group of managers. These guys are on the way out. They no longer "belong." Indeed, it's probably no accident that the ad takes place in a restaurant, given the joke that went around in the aftermath of the 1987 market crash. "What do you call a yuppie stockbroker?" the joke ran. "Hey, waiter!" Is the ad trying subtly to suggest that junior executives who choose the wrong computer systems are doomed to suffer the same fate?

For other markets, there are other fears. If McDonald's presents senior citizens with bright fantasies of being useful and appreciated beyond retirement, companies like Secure Horizons dramatize senior citizens' fears of being caught short by a major illness. Running its ads in the wake of budgetary cuts in the Medicare system, Secure Horizons designed a series of commercials featuring a pleasant old man named Harry—who looks and sounds rather like Carroll O'Connor—who tells us the story of the scare he got during his wife's recent illness. Fearing that next time Medicare won't cover the bills, he has purchased supplemental health insurance from Secure Horizons and now securely tends his rooftop garden.

Among all the fears advertisers have exploited over the years, I find the fear of not having a posh enough burial site the most arresting. Advertisers usually avoid any mention of death—who wants to associate a product with the grave?—but mortuary advertisers haven't much choice. Generally, they solve their problem by framing cemeteries as timeless parks presided over by priestly morticians, appealing to our desires for dignity and comfort in the face of bereavement. But in one television commercial for Forest Lawn we find a different approach. In this ad we are presented with the ghost of an old man telling us how he might have found a much nicer resting place than the run-down cemetery in which we find him had his wife only known that Forest Lawn was so "affordable." I presume the ad was supposed to be funny, but it's been pulled off the air. There are some fears that just won't bear joking about, some nightmares too dark to dramatize.

THE FUTURE OF AN ILLUSION

There are some signs in the advertising world that Americans are getting fed up with fantasy advertisements and want to hear some straight talk. Weary of extravagant product claims and irrelevant associations, consumers trained by years of advertising to distrust what they hear seem to be developing an immunity to commercials. At least, this is the semiotic message I read in the "new realism" advertisements of the eighties, ads that attempt to convince you that what you're seeing is the real thing, that the ad is giving you the straight dope, not advertising hype.

You can recognize the "new realism" by its camera techniques. The lighting is usually subdued to give the ad the effect of being filmed without studio lighting or special filters. The scene looks gray, as if the blinds were drawn. The camera shots are jerky and off-angle, often zooming in for sudden unflattering close-ups, as if the cameraman was an amateur with a home video recorder. In a "realistic" ad for AT&T, for example, we are treated to a monologue by a plump stockbroker—his plumpness intended as a sign that he's for real and not just another actor—who tells us about the problems he's had with his phone system (not AT&T's) as the camera jerks around, generally filming him from below as if the cameraman couldn't quite fit his equipment into the crammed office and had to film the scene on his knees. "This is no fancy advertisement," the ad tries to convince us, "this is sincere."

An ad for Miller draft beer tries the same approach, re-creating the effect of an amateur videotape of a wedding celebration. Camera shots shift suddenly from group to group. The picture jumps. Bodies are poorly framed. The color is washed out. Like the beer it is pushing, the ad is supposed to strike us as being "as real as it gets."

Such ads reflect a desire for reality in the marketplace, a weariness with Madison Avenue illusions. But there's no illusion like the illusion of reality. Every special technique that advertisers use to create their "reality effects" is, in fact, more unrealistic than the techniques of "illusory" ads. The world, in reality, doesn't jump around when you look at it. It doesn't appear in subdued gray tones. Our eyes don't have zoom lenses, and we don't look at things with our heads cocked to one side. The irony of the "new realism" is that it is more unrealistic, more artificial, than the ordinary run of television advertising.

But don't expect any truly realistic ads in the future, because a realistic advertisement is a contradiction in terms. The logic of advertising is entirely semiotic: it substitutes signs for things, framed visions of consumer desire for the thing itself. The success of modern advertising, its penetration into every corner of American life, reflects a culture that has itself chosen illusion over reality. At a time when political candidates all have professional image-makers attached to their staffs, and the President of the United States is an actor who once sold shirt collars, all the cultural signs are pointing to more illusions in our lives rather than fewer—a fecund breeding ground for the world of the advertiser.

Analysis of Application

"Masters of Desire: The Culture of American Advertising" (excerpted from Jack Solomon's *The Signs of Our Time*) demonstrates the utility of semiotic analysis in exploring sign systems beyond written language and the printed page. Solomon's critique of the semiotics of American advertising is wide-ranging, but it is unified in both diachronic and synchronic ways. First, Solomon hints at a diachronic consistency in American beliefs and behaviors by using the nineteenth-century political theorist Alexis de Tocqueville as a touchstone; Tocqueville observed that despite America's professed belief in equality and democracy, a powerful ideology of competition and striving for individual distinction pervades all of American life. After establishing this enduring conflict in American culture, Solomon narrows his topic to a synchronic analysis of American advertising in the 1980s, exploring why and how advertisers try to meet consumer desires for group conformity and individualism.

Solomon conducts his semiotic analysis by comparing and contrasting advertisements within similar product lines, offering ample support for his interpretations. Just as literary critics use direct quotations and references to images and symbols, Solomon makes succinct reference to the visual, musical, and verbal content, as well as other telling components, of the ads that he analyzes. You will notice that he does not hinder the flow of his discussion with unnecessarily long descriptions; he simply draws quickly and effectively on the most pertinent details. Yet even for readers who do not have firsthand knowledge of the ads in question, their content is quite clear.

Given his overall emphasis on synchronic analysis, Solomon organizes his discussion topically rather than chronologically, although he also retains its unity with frequent references back to his main topic and thesis. As he examines a wide range of advertisements, Solomon explores the conflicts and contradictions of American belief systems regarding class, patriotism, age, and sexuality. As his analysis proceeds, Solomon reveals an American culture heavily invested in fantasy, a culture that both demands and eagerly consumes images of easy answers to complex social and personal questions. In a particularly effective section, Solomon examines how one company, McDonald's, manages to convey distinct and powerful messages simultaneously to very different segments of the American market. It also bears noting that his transition from that section on McDonald's to his next section on sexuality is quite adept in its use of contrast and brief explanation for that contrast.

Semiotic analysis reveals what we do not readily recognize or know about the signs in question; thus Solomon exposes the hidden messages and belief systems underlying advertising's signs. But his implicit purpose is larger than a simple presentation of effective critique; it is also to equip his readers with abilities that will help them decode and even resist the power of advertising. Thus semiotic analysis can be an effective tool in the teaching of critical thinking skills and in critical responses to a wide variety of media. The basic principle of structuralist and semiotic theory—that signs do not acquire their meaning through their grounding in "reality," but rather through their complex relationship to each other and a variety of cultural beliefs—has had a profound effect on contemporary literary and cultural studies. It also allows for effective political critique, as Solomon demonstrates in his last paragraph. Indeed, semiotic analysis makes available for critical scrutiny all of the ways that meanings are made in contemporary culture, suggesting that practically everything—from the clothes we wear to the language that we use—is a potential "text" for critical analysis.

Deconstruction and Post-Structuralist Analysis

Overview

Although this chapter is written to function as a self-contained introduction to the field of deconstruction and post-structuralist analysis, students are urged to read the preceding chapter, "Structuralism and Semiotic Analysis," if time permits. As the term indicates, *post*-structuralism questions but also continues the central project of structuralism: the inquiry into the organizing principles of language and the making of meaning through signification. Many of its fundamental terms are those of its predecessor, including "signifier," "signified," and "sign," with the first term indicating a word, image, or other form of representation that refers to an entity or concept (such as a box of chocolates on Valentine's Day), the second term indicating the concept being referred to (the affection indicated by the box of chocolates), and the third term indicating the combination of the two (a box of chocolates as an indication of affection). But while structuralism is highly confident that the principles by which signs are organized can be fully determined and described, post-structuralism calls into question all such assumptions of comprehension and comprehensiveness, suggesting that conclusions are always fragile and subvertible. Both Derridean deconstruction and the more general field of post-structuralism contend that fixed meanings are only possible when significant destabilizing information and perspectives are energetically suppressed.

For the purposes of this chapter, it is useful to draw something of a distinction between "deconstruction" and "post-structuralism," even though the two terms have been used interchangeably at times. The former, here used in its narrowest sense, refers to a process of linguistic and philosophical analysis that has been largely determined by the theories of the French philosopher Jacques Derrida. The latter refers more generally to the host of inquiries and insights generated recently by theorists and critics who have examined the social construction of "discourse"—language and other forms of representation—and the power deployed and social relationships organized through discourse. While deconstruction is a difficult and sometimes confusing methodology, broader post-structuralist insights underlie some of the most compelling work in literary and cultural analysis today, and they are adaptable for use by a wide variety of students.

Despite their difficulty, the theories of Jacques Derrida certainly deserve consideration here. In works such as *Of Grammatology* and *Writing and Difference*, Derrida offers insights that challenge earlier philosophical notions of truth and objectivity. Derrida takes as a starting point the structuralist notion that meaning is made through relationships among signs rather than through objective representations of reality or truth. But he then uses this principle to question the assumption by structuralists that they, perhaps uniquely, can discover a truth: the enduring structures of signs. He notes that the relationship-based meanings that such theorists propose are actually highly unstable; only by excluding other plausible interpretations can a theorist determine the precise meaning of a given sign. Our example of a box of chocolates on Valentine's Day provides a case in point, for its meaning is never fully knowable or narrowly definable. Of course, its receiver could read the box of chocolates as affection—but could also interpret it suspiciously as an indication of betrayal or, alternately, as a request for forgiveness (for a more sustained discussion of readers' roles in the making of meaning, see Chapter 2). Its meaning is certainly different from that of other affection-related signs (such as a diamond or a greeting card), but its meaning is also "deferred" in that any final understanding of the box of chocolates leads us to comparisons and contrasts with an endlessly expanding, complicated chain of signs. We can be fairly sure that we understand this sign, but we can never be absolutely sure. This, briefly, is one important component of Derrida's complex notion of *différence*—that meaning is made through differences among signs but never made certain and secure through those differences.

In this way Derrida questions and undermines the "logocentrism" that is inherent in the Western philosophical tradition. To understand the term "logocentrism," we should remember the structuralist insight that meaning is often made through a binary relationship between signs, such as love/hate, good/bad, pure/impure. Derrida builds on this point, recognizing that these binaries are almost always hierarchical in value, with the first term being the preferred, privileged one. Yet Derrida also suggests that this ascription of greater weight to the first term only serves as a mask, covering up the threatening, if not predominant, power of the second term. One of the most fundamental of the weighted binaries that Derrida probes, then reverses, and finally shows to be wholly deconstructable is that which privileges "speech" over "writing," which he demonstrates is evident throughout Western philosophy and literature. In speaking to one another, face to face, we can communicate "truth" in clear and transparent ways, or so the cultural fiction goes. Derrida not only shows that in some ways we *really* privilege writing over speech in our culture; he goes on to show that clarity and transparency in signification are never possible, however much we may wish and need to believe that they are. "Logocentrism" is Derrida's term for this deep-rooted but fragile faith that there are, finally, certain and central truths and meanings that signs—and, indeed, the philosophers who speak and write about them—can reference, access, and communicate.

A repudiation of logocentrism underlies most works of post-structuralism, even when their methods and interests differ significantly from Derridean deconstruction of hierarchical binaries. Theorists such as Michel Foucault and Michel de Certeau, while disagreeing with Derrida and each other on certain ideas and processes, are thoroughly committed to exploring the ways in which meaning is always relational and, in so doing, rejecting all claims to enduring and definitive answers. In this way, post-structuralism is related to existentialism (the study of existence without transcendental meaning) and to the earlier work of Friedrich Nietzsche, but it pushes into new territory with its specific focus on how society and texts are structured around notions of truth and objectivity that engender their own opposition even as they offer a facade of unquestionable power.

Indeed, Foucault calls on critics to examine the multiple ways in which power is deployed in society (and in the texts that help constitute and perpetuate social structures) with an eye specifically toward the complexity of possible responses to power deployment. If truth is socially constructed, how are the signs that comprise truth subject to change through critical awareness and individual action? One might take as an example an act such as the calling out of a racial slur by a white man against a man of another race, a reprehensible act that post-structuralists would not defend, but certainly one that they would attempt to understand as fully as possible. While power is clearly deployed oppressively in this situation, there is also a generative aspect to its deployment. The target of the slur may shout back, using the slur as the beginning of a response. He may later participate in a political movement to counter racism or may attempt to deflate the power of the word used by using it himself in other situations. The point for post-structuralists is that any exercise of power, or any other form of signification, is never fully self-contained—it is polyvalent—(see principle 5 below), for its complex meanings are always deferred and complicated through a complex chain of signs and actions. Thus post-structuralist methodologies open up expanded possibilities for social action and critique, as well as exciting new avenues for theoretical speculation and textual analysis.

Key Principles

1 *There is no transcendental signified.*

Deconstruction and post-structuralist theory repudiate the notion that there are enduring truths that can be invoked with certainty in the process of signification, textual creation, and cultural critique. Indeed, some explicit or implicit notion of transcendental truth underlies almost all philosophy and criticism, whether the truth being invoked is a religious belief, an ethical norm, or faith in scientific methodology or objectivity. But by taking the insights of structuralism to some of their logical conclusions, post-structuralism suggests that all truths are fully contextual and the result of relationships among signs, even two truths that one might suppose to underlie post-structuralism itself: that true meanings can be discovered through analysis and that critics can draw conclusions with authority. Post-structuralists would suggest that their own interpretations are never definitive—although they are certainly defensible (because of their ample supporting detail)—and emphasize that their own articulations are certainly fair game for further critique. Earlier forms of literary and cultural analysis failed to invite such critique, and perhaps for good reason, for they arrive at definitive theories and interpretations by presupposing certain values, norms, ideas, and ideals that remain off-limits for discussion and challenge; these are known as a priori assumptions. In effect, such theorists largely predetermine their own conclusions through their dependence on so many a priori assumptions.

As noted above, the term that post-structuralists use to describe this dynamic is "logocentrism," which, as its component parts indicate, suggests the centrality or necessity of the Word (*logos* is Greek for "word"). This concept of the Word, while literally referring to the stability and authority—one might say weighty "presence"—of the spoken pronouncement, also points more generally to the need/desire for a behind-the-scenes, final authority or a metaphysical "presence" that stabilizes meanings and makes them certain and secure. In much philosophy and cultural theory, that "presence"—whether identified with God, science, or even critical authority—is off-limits for analysis. For post-structuralists, however, it is a primary target of analysis. Thus, in beginning their critique, post-structuralists might ask: What are a text's presuppositions and blind spots? What does the text assume to be unassailable "truth"? What foundation—ethical, religious, philosophical, linguistic, or formal—is the text so inflexibly built on that a challenge to it would threaten to bring down the entire structure of reference and meaning? Once discovered, that foundation usually becomes the target of intense post-structuralist inquiry.

2 *Although relationships among signs account for contextual meanings, those relationships are never fixed or fully knowable.*

Post-structuralism, like structuralism, focuses on relationships among signs. But while structuralists posit that a fixed relationship between two or more signs can be discovered and then used as a basis for reliable cultural critique, post-structuralists suggest that such relationships are, in fact, highly contextual; they shift and often betray their own ambiguity, fragility, and inherent biases. As we have seen, structuralists noted that signs often attempt to convey meaning through simplistic opposition: white/black, normal/abnormal, male/female. But post-structuralism not only isolates and describe those oppositions, it also seeks to probe their fragile, hierarchical nature and thereby challenge them. As noted above, in a binary such as speech/writing, greater weight is often attributed to the first term, with the second possessing an instability that only constant reference back to the first term can keep in check. But post-structuralism does not stop after simply locating such biased relationships between signs; it shows just how fragile the definition of the supposedly secure first term is, that only by defining itself (indeed glorifying itself) in opposition to its supposed inferior can it even exist. This is a method of analysis that is pertinent to our example of the calling out of a racial slur by a white man, who attempts thereby to shore up his own sense of power through designating a racial "opposite" as inferior. Post-structuralist critique would reverse that power dynamic, showing that the second term of the cultural binary can actually have great importance as a necessary but always potentially disruptive component of the supposedly superior first term. And post-structuralist critique demonstrates that such binary oppositions are only fragile social constructs, neither real nor fixed, that can be dismantled and discredited as foundational components of our philosophical, social, and cultural systems.

In pointing out the fragility and bias of the binaries underlying even our senses of selfhood and our forms of social organization, post-structuralism seeks implicitly or explicitly to change those valuations. Thus deconstruction and post-structuralism are not divorced from real-world activities and concerns, as some of its detractors suggest, for in pointing out the inherently unfixed and potentially changeable nature of how we make meaning, they open up many possibilities for practical changes in our value judgments and our sociopolitical decisions. In suggesting that truth is never finally discoverable or knowable, they can engender a much more proactive stance toward effecting social change. In undermining our notion of a transcendental signified, they represent a call to action for a more engaged process of making contextual meanings that we can live with and actively defend.

3   *Texts betray traces of their own instability.*

Yet in order to demonstrate the power that such hierarchical binaries and other aspects of logocentrism have in our texts and culture, post-structuralists must amass evidence. While they may be highly critical of texts and their structures of meaning, they must also work with the material provided by those texts. Post-structuralism is rooted in the tradition of close textual reading, and it examines the many ways that texts betray the instability and tenuous nature of their own presuppositions and sign systems. Thus post-structuralist critics might ask: What meaning is textually attributed to a given sign? How is it defined in opposition to other signs? What relationship of value is set up between those signs? Where and how do those signs and the text that surrounds them betray clues to their fragility and ambiguity? How, then, does a reversal of their superficial values, as explored above, lead to different conclusions about the meaning of the sign in question? Indeed, what information must be energetically suppressed in the text in order for its meanings to remain even temporarily secure? What happens, then, when we expose and challenge the text's a priori assumptions or other components of its foundational beliefs and systems of reference that have previously been considered off-limits for discussion? Ample textual evidence must be presented to substantiate all lines of argument and interpretation. In examining how a novel sets up an opposition between images of light and dark, for instance, the critic must make clear textual references to specific passages in which that imagery occurs and point out the value judgments implicit in those images. In locating passages in which darkness functions as the necessary component through which lightness is defined, and without which lightness would lose its own meaning and value, the critic calls into question not just the authority of the text but also the culture's belief systems and value judgments concerning light/dark, white/black, and similar binaries of color and luminance.

A related area of textual interest for post-structuralists is metaphor, the implicit claim that one thing so resembles another thing that their qualities are fully shared, thus rendering further thought or explanation unnecessary. An example is provided by the truism "life is a journey." In accepting such an equation without question, we also accept a host of implicit principles regarding how life should be lived and how time should be organized. Following this metaphor, life, like a journey, must have a goal, or "telos," which is often perceived as a reward or accomplishment (perhaps salvation or immortality). Working backwards from this telos, life is then organized in such a way as to ensure obtaining the reward or reaching the desired destination. In addition to a goal, a sense of linearity is thereby imposed on the conception of life, with "side trips" or "stalled periods" almost unquestionably viewed negatively, simply because of the metaphor initially chosen. In probing the textual uses of such metaphors and their teleological organizing principles, critics would seek to expose and challenge the ways in which truisms have replaced critical thought. In doing so, post-structuralist criticism, which can seem destructive in its thoroughgoing iconoclasm, can actually be quite constructive in its attempt to foster intellectual activity and to replace passive reliance on metaphors and clichés with thoughtful reflection on our lives, texts, and selves.

4 *There is nothing outside of the text.*

Il n'y a pas de hors-texte, a French phrase meaning "there is nothing outside of the text," is a key Derridean concept that is central to deconstruction and post-structuralist theories. It redirects critical attention away from issues such as the intention or the biography of the author and places primary emphasis on the signs present in the text itself. But it would be a mistake to assume, therefore, that post-structuralist critics are interested only in word play or other small textual details. While there is "nothing" outside of the text, "text" is actually an expansive concept for many post-structuralists. Deconstructive critics often focus intensely on print texts such as short stories and novels, but post-structuralist critics more generally examine the larger texts of cultural and social life. Foucault rooted his analysis in the careful examination of medical and legal documents, philosophical treatises, and personal narratives, extrapolating from them to explore the ways in which discourse (the field of signification within a certain subset of society or within society as a whole) helps to create consciousness and to account for broad norms of behavior as well as designations of normality and abnormality. Thus post-structuralism is often intensely political in its implications and, as is the case with Foucault's *Madness and Civilization* and *Discipline and Punish*, can challenge the very nature of our medical establishment and judicial system. But in keeping the concept of "text" central to post-structuralist critique, such theorists return us time and again to those concrete details that must provide the focal points of analysis and the evidence to support conclusions. Thus in examining an intriguing cultural text—say, the deployment of power in a high school classroom—the post-structuralist critic must cite concrete evidence before drawing conclusions. Teacher-training guides might provide a body of work that would allow the critic to explore how the signs teacher/student are defined in binary and hierarchical fashion. But as we have seen, the critic, in exploring how fragile that binary is, would also examine the information that must be suppressed or ignored in order to maintain it. How does the sign "teacher" depend on the existence of the sign "student"? Is there evidence that would demonstrate that students deploy power in their own interests in spite of their lower hierarchical standing? Thus the text in question would include not only the teacher-training manual but also, perhaps, verbal and nonverbal interactions that occurs in classrooms as power is actively negotiated.

5 *The deployment of power is polyvalent, as are all forms of signification.*

Foucault's notion of the "tactical polyvalence of power" demonstrates the enormous potential for such analysis. His basic point, detailed in the first volume of *The History of Sexuality*, is that any exercise of power must be understood as generative as well as oppressive, that power is never unilateral as one traces its consequences and explores its broader contexts. This notion of polyvalence follows the general tendency among post-structuralists to challenge received notions and oversimplifications and to see signs as complexly interactive with other signs. In examining a text such as our teacher/student example above, the post-structuralist critic would first ask: What actions by teachers appear, on the surface at least, to be oppressive in nature? But, then, how do those actions have consequences unforeseen by teachers? How does the self-image or self-definition of students change because of the activity in question? What countering strategies arise that allow students to continue to operate as social beings? In effect, the critic would ask, how are high school students not only passive, but also active, in the many ways that they may work within and against hierarchy-based classroom norms, at times subverting and at other times exploiting them? Foucauldian explorations of power would never excuse oppressive actions or suggest that they are in any way justifiable, but they would seek to explore the tactics used either intentionally or unintentionally, internally or externally, by "the oppressed" so as to understand better how power operates. Indeed, such analysis allows us to see the reempowerment of "victims"—as occurs, for example, in support groups for abuse survivors—as part of a power dynamic that is not explainable simply through the simplistic binary of perpetrator/victim; as always, post-structuralism challenges such binaries.

6 *Cultural and literary criticism is a form of signification.*

And, finally, it is important to see the generation of criticism as itself a form of signification and power deployment. From a post-structuralist perspective, critics too often attempt to "master" texts and readers by positing definitive interpretations. But as with all other exercises of power, literary and cultural critique is both fragile and polyvalent. In examining the work of other critics, post-structuralists examine ways in which the primary text under consideration undermines or thwarts the critic's reading of it. They also scrutinize the text created *by* the critic, looking for suppressed information or facile binaries that, once exposed, threaten to bring down the entire interpretive structure. But in doing so, post-structuralists understand that their own work is subject to the same sort of scrutiny and critical response, that definitive claims and suggestions of unassailable authority will no doubt be greeted with a new round of iconoclastic analysis. To understand and accept this expanded notion of textuality (in which the text being generated is equally subject to critique) is both a challenge and a spur to intense intellectual activity, for it encourages critics to engage in a preemptive self-critique that meets likely responses head-on and energizes the writing with an intellectual dynamism and immediacy that few other methodologies can claim to foster, unless they, too, have been influenced by post-structuralist thinking.

Bibliography

Culler, Jonathan. *On Deconstruction: Theory and Criticism After Structuralism.* Ithaca, NY: Cornell University Press, 1982.

> This is a thorough and well-written overview of deconstruction that builds on Culler's earlier work in *Structuralist Poetics* and *The Pursuit of Signs*. While its presupposition of theoretical knowledge is significant, with patience and diligence, both intermediate and advanced readers will find it of great use.

de Certeau, Michel. *The Practice of Everyday Life*, trans. Steven Rendall. Berkeley: University of California Press, 1984.

> While not as well known as the work of Michel Foucault, the theories of Michel de Certeau are certainly useful for a wide range of textual readings. As a primary philosophical text, this work will pose significant challenges to some readers, but it will be of interest to all advanced students seeking insight into the workings of power in contemporary culture.

Derrida, Jacques. *Acts of Literature*, ed. Derek Attridge. New York: Routledge, 1992.

Derrida, Jacques. *A Derrida Reader: Between the Blinds*, ed. Peggy Kamuf. New York: Columbia University Press, 1991.

While Derrida is always a difficult writer, these books will be of interest to advanced students who wish to acquaint themselves with primary texts in the field of deconstruction. The volume edited by Attridge contains more essays on literature, while Kamuf's provides a more comprehensive general overview of Derrida's writings. It may prove useful even for advanced students to consult a work such as Christopher Norris's *Derrida* or Madan Sarup's *Introductory Guide* (both listed below) as they proceed with a first reading of Derrida's theories.

Foucault, Michel. *The Foucault Reader*, ed. Paul Rabinow. New York: Pantheon Books, 1984.

This is a solid introduction to and sampling of the work of Michel Foucault, one of the leading post-structuralist theorists. It contains selections from all of Foucault's major works, including *Discipline and Punish* and *The History of Sexuality*. Its introduction by Paul Rabinow is useful and accessible, rendering this book of great interest to both intermediate and advanced readers.

Leitch, Vincent B. *Deconstructive Criticism: An Advanced Introduction*. New York: Columbia University Press, 1983.

This is a difficult, but rewarding, introduction to the field of Derridean deconstruction and the theories that comprise post-structuralism. It presupposes considerable knowledge of philosophy and preceding theory, which will make it of interest primarily to advanced readers.

Norris, Christopher. *Deconstruction: Theory and Practice*. New York: Routledge, 1991.

This is an accessible introduction to the basic theories and applications of deconstruction. Its bibliography is superb, and its analysis of deconstruction's relationship to existentialism and earlier philosophical stances is noteworthy. It will serve the needs of both intermediate and advanced readers.

Norris, Christopher. *Deconstruction and the Interests of Theory*. Norman: University of Oklahoma Press, 1989.

Like the other two works by Christopher Norris listed here, this work is accessible and useful. But unlike the others, it contains examples of applied deconstructive criticism, which will make it particularly useful for readers at both the intermediate and advanced levels.

Norris, Christopher. *Derrida*. Cambridge, MA: Harvard University Press, 1987.

    This is an excellent overview of the theories of Jacques Derrida, one of the most influential philosophers of the twentieth century and the "father" of deconstruction. Its general accessibility and clear explanations will make it of interest to both intermediate and advanced readers.

Sarup, Madan. *An Introductory Guide to Post-Structuralism and Postmodernism*. Athens, GA: University of Georgia Press, 1993.

    This is perhaps the most accessible introduction to post-structuralism available today. Its explanations of the theories of Derrida, as well as other recent philosophers such as Michel Foucault and Julia Kristeva, will be of great interest to all readers, from the beginning through the advanced levels.

Wolfreys, Julian. *Deconstruction*Derrida*. New York: St. Martin's Press, 1998.

    This well-written and interesting exploration of Derrida's theories, and their interpretation and use by literary critics today, offers both explanations and applications. Its user-friendly language when discussing complex theoretical concepts makes it appropriate for both intermediate and advanced readers.

Application

Reading Prompts

1. Mark and pay close attention to those passages in which Johnson positions her own reading vis-à-vis those of others. Think about how her essay involves both applied criticism of Melville's *Billy Budd* and meta-discussions of how criticism functions.
2. Johnson suggests that Billy and Claggert operate as signs in the novel. Locate those passages in which she explores how they represent different relationships between signifiers and signifieds.
3. Johnson, revealing some of the linguistic roots of deconstruction, draws an important distinction between what she terms "performative" and "constative" functions of language. Underline or highlight her analysis of how Billy's act of killing Claggert dramatizes the incompatibility of these functions.
4. According to Johnson, historical context operates as a mutable influence on the reading process. Mark those passages in which she reveals "how" this is the case.
5. In Johnson's reading, Captain Vere "functions as a focus for the conversion of polarity into ambiguity and back again." After finishing the essay, consider how that interpretive claim reflects an important feature of deconstruction as a methodology.

Barbara Johnson

Melville's Fist:

The Execution of *Billy Budd*

THE SENSE OF AN ENDING

Truth uncompromisingly told will always have its ragged edges; hence the conclusion of such a narration is apt to be less finished than an architectural finial.

—Melville, *Billy Budd*

The plot of Melville's *Billy Budd* is well known, and, like its title character, appears entirely straightforward and simple. It is a tale of three men in a boat: the innocent, ignorant foretopman, handsome Billy Budd; the devious, urbane master-at-arms, John Claggart; and the respectable, bookish commanding officer, Captain the Honorable Edward Fairfax ("Starry") Vere. Falsely accused by Claggart of plotting mutiny aboard the British man-of-war *Bellipotent*, Billy Budd, his speech impeded by a stutter, strikes his accuser dead in front of the captain, and is condemned, after a summary trial, to hang.

In spite of the apparent straightforwardness of the facts of the case, however, there exists in the critical literature on *Billy Budd* a notable range of disagreement over the ultimate meaning of the tale. For some, the story constitutes Melville's "testament of acceptance," his "everlasting yea," his "acceptance of tragedy," or at least his "recognition of necessity."[1] For others, Melville's "final stage" is, on the contrary, "irony": *Billy Budd* is considered a "testament of resistance," "ironic social criticism," or the last vituperation in Melville's "quarrel with God."[2] More recently, critical attention has devoted itself to the ambiguity in the story, sometimes deploring it, sometimes revelling in it, and sometimes simply listing it.[3] The ambiguity is attributed to various causes: the unfinished state of the manuscript, Melville's change of heart toward Vere, Melville's unreconciled ambivalence toward authority or his guilt about paternity, the incompatibility between the "plot" and the "story."[4] But however great the disagreement over the meaning of this posthumous novel, all critics seem to agree in considering it Melville's "last word." "With the mere fact of the long silence in our minds," writes John Middleton Murry, "we could not help regarding 'Billy Budd' as the last will and spiritual testament of a man of genius."[5]

To regard a story as its author's last will and testament is clearly to grant it a privileged, determining position in the body of that author's work. As its name implies, the "will" is taken to represent the author's final "intentions": in writing his will, the author is presumed to have summed up and evaluated his entire literary output, and directed it—as proof against "dissemination"—toward some determinable destination. The "ending" thus somehow acquires the metalinguistic authority to confer finality and intelligibility upon all that precedes it.

Now, since this sense of Melville's ending is so central to *Billy Budd* criticism, it might be useful to take a look at the nature of the ending of the story itself. Curiously enough, we find that *Billy Budd* ends not once, but no less than four times. As Melville himself describes it, the story continues far beyond its "proper" end: "How it fared with the Handsome Sailor during the year of the Great Mutiny has been faithfully given. But though *properly* the story ends with his life, something in the way of sequel will not be amiss"[6] (emphasis mine here and passim). This "sequel" consists of "three brief chapters": (1) the story of the death of Captain Vere after an encounter with the French ship, the *Athée*; (2) a transcription of the Budd-Claggart affair published in an "authorized" naval publication, in which the characters of the two men are reversed, with Budd represented as the depraved villain and Claggart as the heroic victim; and (3) a description of the posthumous mythification of Billy Budd by his fellow sailors and a transcription of the ballad written by one of them, which presents itself as a monologue spoken by Billy on the eve of his execution. Billy Budd's last words, like Melville's own, are thus spoken posthumously—indeed the final line of the story is uttered from the bottom of the sea.

The question of the sense of Melville's ending is thus raised *in* the story as well as *by* the story. But far from tying up the loose ends of a confusing literary life, Melville's last words are an affirmation of the necessity of "ragged edges":

> The symmetry of form attainable in pure fiction cannot so readily be achieved in a narration essentially having less to do with fable than with fact. Truth uncompromisingly told will always have its ragged edges; hence the conclusion of such a narration is apt to be less finished than an architectural finial. (p. 405)

The story ends by fearlessly fraying its own symmetry, thrice transgressing its own "proper" end; there is something inherently improper about this testamentary disposition of Melville's literary property. Indeed, far from totalizing itself into intentional finality, the story in fact begins to repeat itself—retelling itself first in reverse, and then in verse. The ending not only lacks special authority, it problematizes the very *idea* of authority by placing its own reversal in the pages of an "authorized" naval chronicle. To end is to repeat, and to repeat is to be ungovernably open to revision, displacement, and reversal.[7] The sense of Melville's ending is to empty the ending of any privileged control over sense.

THE PLOT AGAINST THE CHARACTERS

> For Tragedy is an imitation, not of men, but of action and of life, and life consists in action, and its end is a mode of action, not a quality. Now character determines men's qualities, but it is by their actions that they are happy or the reverse.
>
> —Aristotle, *Poetics*

In beginning our study of *Billy Budd* with its ending, we, too, seem to have reversed the "proper" order of things. Most studies of the story tend to begin, after a few general remarks about the nature of good and evil, with a delineation of the three main characters: Billy, Claggart, and Vere. As Charles Weir puts it, "The purely physical action of the story is clear enough, and about its significant details there is never any doubt. . . . It is, therefore, with some consideration of the characters of the three principal actors that any analysis must begin."[8] "Structurally," writes F. B. Freeman, "the three characters *are* the novel"[9] (emphasis in original).

Melville goes to great lengths to describe both the physical and the moral characteristics of his protagonists. Billy Budd, a twenty-one-year-old "novice in the complexities of factitious life," is remarkable for his "significant personal beauty," "reposeful good nature," "straightforward simplicity" and "unconventional rectitude." But Billy's intelligence ("such as it was," says Melville) is as primitive as his virtues are pristine. He is illiterate, he cannot understand ambiguity, and he stutters.

Claggart, on the other hand, is presented as the very image of urbane, intellectualized, articulate evil. Although "of no ill figure upon the whole" (p. 342), something in Claggart's pallid face consistently inspires uneasiness and mistrust. He is a man, writes Melville, "in whom was the mania of an evil nature, not engendered by vicious training or corrupting books or licentious living, but born with him and innate, in short, 'a depravity according to nature'" (p. 354). The mere sight of Billy Budd's rosy beauty and rollicking innocence does not fail to provoke in such a character "an antipathy spontaneous and profound" (p. 351).

The third man in the drama, who has inspired the greatest critical dissent, is presented in less vivid but curiously more contradictory terms. The

Bellipotent's captain is described as both unaffected and pedantic, dreamy and resolute, irascible and undemonstrative, "mindful of the welfare of his men, but never tolerating an infraction of discipline," "intrepid to the verge of temerity, though never injudiciously so" (p. 338). While Billy and Claggart are said to owe their characters to "nature," Captain Vere is shaped mainly by his fondness for books:

> He loved books, never going to sea without a newly replenished library, compact but of the best. . . . With nothing of that literary taste which less heeds the thing conveyed than the vehicle, his bias was toward those books to which every serious mind of superior order occupying any active post of authority in the world naturally inclines: books treating of actual men and events no matter of what era—history, biography, and unconventional writers like Montaigne, who, free from cant and convention, honestly and in the spirit of common sense philosophize upon realities. (p. 340)

Vere, then, is an honest, serious reader, seemingly well suited for the role of judge and witness that in the course of the story he will come to play.

No consideration of the nature of character in *Billy Budd*, however, can fail to take into account the fact that the fate of each of the characters is the direct reverse of what one is led to expect from his "nature." Billy is sweet, innocent, and harmless, yet he kills. Claggart is evil, perverted, and mendacious, yet he dies a victim. Vere is sagacious and responsible, yet he allows a man whom he feels to be blameless to hang. It is this discrepancy between character and action that gives rise to the critical disagreement over the story: readers tend either to save the plot and condemn Billy ("acceptance," "tragedy," or "necessity"), or to save Billy and condemn the plot ("irony," "injustice," or "social criticism").

In an effort to make sense of this troubling incompatibility between character and plot, many readers are tempted to say of Billy and Claggart, as does William York Tindall, that "each is more important for what he is than what he does. . . . Good and bad, they occupy the region of good and evil."[10] This reading effectively preserves the allegorical values suggested by Melville's opening chapters, but it does so only by denying the importance of the plot. It ends where the plot begins: with the identification of the moral natures of the characters. One may therefore ask whether the allegorical interpretation (good vs. evil) depends as such on this sort of preference for being over doing, and if so, what effect the incompatibility between character and action may have on the allegorical functioning of *Billy Budd*.

Interestingly enough, Melville both invites an allegorical reading and subverts the very terms of its consistency when he writes of the murder:

"Innocence and guilt personified in Claggart and Budd in effect changed places" (p. 380). Allowing for the existence of personification but reversing the relation between personifier and personified, positioning an opposition between good and evil only to make each term take on the properties of its opposite, Melville sets up his plot in the form of a chiasmus:

This story, which is often read as a retelling of the story of Christ, is thus literally a cruci-fiction—a fiction structured in the shape of a cross. At the moment of the reversal, an instant before his fist shoots out, Billy's face seems to mark out the point of crossing, bearing "an expression which was as a crucifixion to behold" (p. 376). Innocence and guilt, criminal and victim, change places through the mute expressiveness of Billy's inability to speak.

If *Billy Budd* is indeed an allegory, it is an allegory of the questioning of the traditional conditions of allegorical stability. The requirement of Melville's plot that the good act out the evil designs of the bad while the bad suffer the unwarranted fate of the good indicates that the real opposition with which Melville is preoccupied here is less the static opposition between evil and good than the dynamic opposition between a man's "nature" and his acts, or, in Tindall's terms, the relation between human "being" and human "doing."

Curiously enough, it is precisely this question of being versus doing that is brought up by the only sentence we ever see Claggart directly address to Billy Budd. When Billy accidentally spills his soup across the path of the master-at-arms, Claggart playfully replies, "Handsomely done, my lad! And handsome *is* as handsome *did* it, too!" (p. 350). The proverbial expression "handsome is as handsome does," from which this exclamation springs, posits the possibility of a continuous, predictable, transparent relationship between being and doing. It supposes that the inner goodness of Billy Budd is in harmonious accord with his fair appearance, that, as Melville writes of the stereotypical "Handsome Sailor" in the opening pages of the story, "the moral nature" is not "out of keeping with the physical make" (p. 322). But it is this very continuity between the physical and the moral, between appearance and action, or between being and doing, that Claggart questions in Billy Budd. He warns Captain Vere not to be taken in by Billy's physical beauty: "You have but noted his fair cheek. A mantrap may be under the ruddy-tipped daisies" (p. 372). Claggart indeed soon finds his suspicions confirmed with a vengeance: when he repeats his accusation in front of Billy, the master-at-arms is struck down dead. It would thus seem that to question the continuity between character and action cannot be done with impunity, that fundamental questions of life and death are always surreptitiously involved.

In an effort to examine what is at stake in Claggart's accusation, it might be helpful to view the opposition between Billy and Claggart as an opposition not between innocence and guilt but between two conceptions of language, or between two types of reading. Billy seemingly represents the perfectly *motivated* sign; that is, his inner self (the signified) is considered transparently readable from the beauty of his outer self (the signifier). His "straightforward simplicity" is the very opposite of the "moral obliquities" or "crookedness of heart" that characterize "citified" or rhetorically sophisticated man. "To deal in double meanings and insinuations of any sort," writes Melville, "was quite foreign to his nature" (p. 327). In accordance with his "nature," Billy reads everything at face value, never questioning the meaning of appearances. He is dumbfounded at the Dansker's suggestion, "incomprehensible to a novice," that Claggart's very pleasantness can be interpreted as its opposite, as a sign that he is "down on" Billy Budd. To Billy, "the occasional frank air and pleasant word *went for what they purported to be*, the young sailor never having heard as yet of the 'too fair-spoken man'" (pp. 365–66). As a reader, then, Billy is symbolically as well as factually illiterate. His literal-mindedness is represented by his illiteracy because, in assuming that language can be taken at face value, he excludes the very functioning of *difference* that makes the act of reading both indispensable and undecidable.

Claggart, on the other hand, is the image of difference and duplicity, both in his appearance and in his character. His face is not ugly, but it hints of something defective or abnormal. He has no vices, yet he incarnates evil. He is an intellectual, but uses reason as "an ambidexter implement for effecting the irrational" (p. 354). Billy inspires in him both "profound antipathy" and "soft yearning." In the incompatibility of his attributes, Claggart is thus a personification of ambiguity and ambivalence, of the distance between signifier and signified, of the separation between being and doing: "apprehending the good, but powerless to be it, a nature like Claggart's . . . what recourse is left to it but to recoil upon itself" (p. 356). As a reader, Claggart has learned to "exercise a distrust keen in proportion to the fairness of the appearance" (p. 364). He is properly an ironic reader, who, assuming the sign to be arbitrary and unmotivated, reverses the value signs of appearances and takes a daisy for a mantrap and an unmotivated accidental spilling of soup for an intentional, sly escape of antipathy. Claggart meets his downfall, however, when he attempts to master the arbitrariness of the sign for his own ends by falsely (that is, arbitrarily) accusing Billy of harboring arbitrariness, of hiding a mutineer beneath the appearance of a baby.

Such a formulation of the Budd/Claggart relationship enables one to take a new look not only at the story itself but at the criticism as well. For this opposition between the literal reader (Billy) and the ironic reader (Claggart) is reenacted in the critical readings of *Billy Budd* in the opposition between the "acceptance" school and the "irony" school. Those who see the story as a "testament of acceptance" tend to take Billy's final benediction of Vere at face value; as Lewis Mumford puts it, "As Melville's own end approached, he cried out with Billy Budd: God Bless Captain Vere! In this final affirmation Herman Melville died."[11] In contrast, those who read the tale ironically tend to take Billy's sweet farewell as Melville's bitter curse. Joseph Schiffman writes, "At heart a kind man, Vere, strange to say, makes possible the depraved Claggart's wish—the destruction of Billy. 'God bless Captain Vere!' Is this not piercing irony? As innocent Billy utters these words, does not the reader gag?"[12] But since the acceptance/irony dichotomy is already contained within the story, since it is obviously one of the things the story is *about*, it is not enough to try to decide which of the readings is correct. What the reader of *Billy Budd* must do is to analyze what is at stake in the very opposition between literality and irony. This question, crucial for an understanding of *Billy Budd* not only as a literary but also as a critical phenomenon, will be taken up again in the final pages of the present chapter, but first let us examine further the linguistic implications of the murder itself.

THE FIEND THAT LIES LIKE TRUTH

> Outwardly regarded, our craft is a lie; for all that is outwardly seen of it is the clean-swept deck, and oft-painted planks comprised above the water-line; whereas, the vast mass of our fabric, with all its store-rooms of secrets, forever slides along far under the surface.
>
> —Melville, *White-Jacket*

If Claggart's accusation that Billy is secretly plotting mutiny is essentially an affirmation of the possibility of a discontinuity between being and doing, of an arbitrary, nonmotivated relation between signifier and signified, then Billy's blow must be read as an attempt violently to deny that discontinuity or arbitrariness. The blow, as a denial, functions as a substitute for speech, as Billy explains during his trial: "I did not mean to kill him. Could I have used my tongue I would not have struck him. But he foully lied to my face and in presence of my captain, and I had to say something, and I could only say it with a blow" (p. 383). But in striking a blow in defense of the sign's motivation, Billy actually personifies the very *absence* of motivation: "I did not mean . . ." His blow is involuntary, accidental, properly unmotivated. He is a sign that does not mean to mean. Billy, who cannot understand ambiguity, who takes pleasant words at face value and then obliterates Claggart for suggesting that one could do otherwise, whose sudden blow is a violent denial of any discrepancy between his being and his doing, ends up radically illustrating the very discrepancy he denies.

The story thus takes place between the postulate of continuity between signifier and signified ("handsome is as handsome does") and the postulate of their discontinuity ("a mantrap may be under the ruddy-tipped daisies"). Claggart, whose accusations of incipient mutiny are apparently false and therefore illustrate the very double-facedness that they attribute to Billy, is negated for proclaiming the lie about Billy which Billy's act of negation paradoxically proves to be the truth.

This paradox can also be stated in another way, in terms of the opposition between the performative and the constative functions of language. Constative language is language used as an instrument of cognition—it describes, reports, speaks *about* something other than itself. Performative language is language that itself functions as an act, not as a report of one. Promising, betting, swearing, marrying, and declaring war, for example, are not descriptions of acts but acts in their own right. The proverb "handsome is as handsome does" can thus also be read as a statement of the compatibility between the constative (being) and the performative (doing) dimensions of language. But what Billy's act dramatizes is their radical *incompatibility*— Billy performs the truth of Claggart's report to Vere only by means of his absolute and blind denial of its cognitive validity. If Billy had understood the truth, he would not have performed it. Handsome cannot both be and do its own undoing. The knowledge that being and doing are incompatible cannot know the ultimate performance of its own confirmation.

Melville's chiasmus thus creates a reversal not only of the places of guilt and innocence but also of the postulate of continuity and the postulate of discontinuity between doing and being, performance and cognition. When Billy's fist strikes Claggart's forehead, it is no longer possible for knowing and doing to meet. Melville's story does not report the occurence of a particularly deadly performative utterance, the tale itself performs the radical incompatibility between knowledge and acts.

All this, we recall, is triggered by a stutter, a linguistic defect. No analysis of the story's dramatization of linguistic categories can be complete without careful attention to this glaring infelicity. Billy's "vocal defect" is presented and explained in the story in the following terms:

> There was just one thing amiss in him . . . an occasional liability to a vocal defect. Though in the hour of elemental uproar or peril he was everything that a sailor should be, yet under sudden provocation of strong heart-feeling his voice, otherwise singularly musical, as if expressive of the harmony within, was apt to develop an organic hesitancy, in fact more or less of a stutter or even worse. In this particular Billy was a striking instance that the arch interferer, the envious marplot of Eden, still has more or less to do with every human consignment to this planet of Earth. In every case, one way or another he is sure to slip in his little card, as much as to remind us—I too have a hand here. (pp. 331–32)

It is doubtless this satanic "hand" that shoots out when Billy's speech fails him. Billy is all too literally a "*striking* instance" of the workings of the "envious marplot."

Melville's choice of the word *marplot* to characterize the originator of Billy's stutter deserves special note. It seems logical to understand that the stutter "mars" the plot in that it triggers the reversal of roles between Billy and Claggart. Yet in another sense this reversal does not mar the plot, it constitutes it. Here, as in the story of Eden, what the envious marplot mars is not the plot, but the state of plotlessness that exists "in the beginning." What both the Book of Genesis and *Billy Budd* narrate is thus not the story of a fall, but a fall into story.

In this connection, it is relevant to recall that Claggart falsely accuses Billy of instigating a *plot*, of stirring up mutiny against the naval authorities. What Claggart is in a sense doing by positing this fictitious plot is trying desperately to scare up a plot for the story. And it is Billy's very act of denial of his involvement in any plot that finally brings him *into* the plot. Billy's involuntary blow is an act of mutiny not only against the authority of his naval superiors but also against the authority of his own conscious intentions. Perhaps it is not by chance that the word *plot* can mean both "intrigue" and "story". If all plots somehow tell the story of their own marring, then perhaps it could be said that all plots are plots against authority, that authority creates the scene of its own destruction, that all stories necessarily recount by their very existence the subversion of the father, of the gods, of consciousness, of order, of expectations, or of meaning.

But is Billy truly as "plotless" as he appears? Does his "simplicity" hide no division, no ambiguity? As many critics have remarked, Billy's character seems to result mainly from his exclusion of the negative. When informed that he is being arbitrarily impressed for service on a man-of-war, Billy "makes no demur" (p. 323). When invited to a clandestine meeting by a mysterious stranger, Billy acquiesces through his "incapacity of plumply saying *no*" (p. 359, emphasis in original). But it is interesting to note that although

Billy thus seems to be "just a boy who cain't say no," almost all the words used to describe him are negative in form: innocent, unconventional, illiterate, unsophisticated, unadulterate, etc. And although he denies any discrepancy between what is said and what is meant, he does not prove to be totally incapable of lying. When asked about the shady visit of the afterguardsman, he distorts his account in order to edit out anything that indicates any incompatibility with the absolute maintenance of authority. He neglects to report the questionable proposition even though "it was his duty as a loyal bluejacket" (p. 362) to do so. In thus shrinking from "the dirty work of a telltale" (p. 362), Billy maintains his "plotlessness" not spontaneously but through a complex act of filtering. Far from being simply and naturally pure, he is obsessed with maintaining his own irreproachability in the eyes of authority. After witnessing a flogging, he is so horrified that he resolves "that never through remissness would he make himself liable to such a visitation or do or omit aught that might merit even verbal reproof" (p. 346). Billy does not simply exclude the negative; he represses it. His reaction to questionable behavior of any sort (such as that of Red Whiskers, the afterguardsman, Claggart) is to obliterate it. He retains his "*blank* ignorance" (p. 363) only by a vigorous act of erasing. As Melville says of Billy's reaction to Claggart's petty provocations, "the ineffectual speculations into which he was led were so disturbingly alien to him that *he did his best to smother them*" (p. 362).

> In his *disgustful recoil* from an overture which, though he but ill comprehended, he *instinctively knew* must involve evil of some sort, Billy Budd was like a young horse fresh from the pasture suddenly inhaling a vile whiff from some chemical factory, and by repeated snortings trying to *get it out* of his nostrils and lungs. This frame of mind *barred all desire* of holding further parley with the fellow, even were it but for the purpose of gaining some enlightenment as to his design in approaching him. (p. 361)

Billy maintains his purity only through constant, though unconscious, censorship. "Innocence," writes Melville, "was his blinder" (p. 366).

It is interesting to note that while the majority of readers see Billy as a personification of goodness and Claggart as a personification of evil, those who do not, tend to read from a psychoanalytical point of view. Much has been made of Claggart's latent homosexuality, which Melville clearly suggests. Claggart, like the hypothetical "X—," "is a nut not to be cracked by the tap of a lady's fan" (p. 352). The "unobserved glance" he sometimes casts upon Billy contains "a touch of soft yearning, as if Claggart could even have loved Billy but for fate and ban" (p. 365). The spilling of the soup and Claggart's reaction to it are often read symbolically as a sexual exchange, the import of which, of course, is lost on Billy, who cannot read.

According to this perspective, Claggart's so-called evil is thus really a repressed form of love. But it is perhaps even more interesting to examine the way in which the psychoanalytical view treats Billy's so-called goodness as being in reality a repressed form of hate:

> The persistent feminine imagery . . . indicate[s] that Billy has identified himself with the mother at a pre-Oedipus level and has adopted the attitude of harmlessness and placation toward the father in order to avoid the hard struggle of the Oedipus conflict. . . . That all Billy's rage and hostility against the father are unconscious is symbolized by the fact that whenever aroused it cannot find expression in spoken language. . . . This is a mechanism for keeping himself from admitting his own guilt and his own destructiveness.[13]

> All of Billy's conscious acts are toward passivity. . . . In symbolic language, Billy Budd is seeking his own castration—seeking to yield up his vitality to an authoritative but kindly father, whom he finds in Captain Vere.[14]

> Quite often a patient begins to stutter when he is particularly eager to prove a point. Behind his apparent zeal he has concealed a hostile or sadistic tendency to destroy his opponent by means of words, and the stuttering is both a blocking of and a punishment for this tendency. Still more often stuttering is exacerbated by the presence of prominent or authoritative persons, that is, of paternal figures against whom the unconscious hostility is most intense.[15]

> Although *Billy Budd, Sailor* is placed in historical time . . . the warfare is not between nations for supremacy on the seas but between father and son in the eternal warfare to determine succession.[16]

> When Vere becomes the father, Claggart and Billy are no longer sailors but sons in rivalry for his favor and blessing. Claggart manifestly is charging mutiny but latently is accusing the younger son or brother of plotting the father's overthrow. . . . When Billy strikes Claggart with a furious blow to the forehead, he puts out the "evil eye" of his enemy-rival, but at the same time the blow is displaced, since Billy is prohibited from striking the father. After Claggart is struck and lies on the deck "a dead snake," Vere covers his face in silent recognition of the displaced blow.[17]

> Billy's type of innocence is . . . *pseudoinnocence.* . . . Capitalizing on naiveté, it consists of a childhood that is never outgrown, a kind of fixation on the past. . . . When we face questions too big and too horrendous to contemplate . . . we tend to shrink into this kind of innocence and make a virtue of powerlessness, weakness, and helplessness. . . . It is this innocence that cannot come to terms with the destructiveness in one's self or others; and hence, as with Billy Budd, it actually becomes self-destructive.[18]

The psychoanalytical reading is thus a demystification of the notion of innocence portrayed in *Billy Budd*. In the psychoanalytical view, what underlies the metaphysical lament that in this world "goodness is impotent" is the idea that impotence is good, that harmlessness is innocent, that naiveté is lovable, that "giving no cause of offense to anybody" and resolving never "to do or omit aught that might merit . . . reproof" (p. 346) are the highest ideals in human conduct. While most readers react to Billy as do his fellow crew-members ("they all love him," [p. 325]), the psychoanalysts share Claggart's distrust ("for all his youth and good looks, a deep one," [p. 371]) and even disdain ("to be nothing more than innocent!" [p. 356]).

In this connection it is curious to note that while the psychoanalysts have implicitly chosen to adopt the attitude of Claggart, Melville, in the crucial confrontation scene, comes close to presenting Claggart as a psychoanalyst:

> With the measured step and calm collected air of an asylum physician approaching in the public hall some patient beginning to show indications of a coming paroxysm, Claggart deliberately advanced within short range of Billy, and, mesmerically looking him in the eye, briefly recapitulated the accusation. (p. 375).

It is as though Claggart as analyst, in attempting to bring Billy's unconscious hostility to consciousness, unintentionally unleashes the destructive acting-out of transferential rage. The fatal blow, far from being an unmotivated accident, is the gigantic return of the power of negation that Billy has been repressing all his life. And in his blind destructiveness, Billy lashes out against the "father" as well as against the very process of analysis itself.

The difference between the psychoanalytical and the traditional "metaphysical" readings of *Billy Budd* lies mainly in the status accorded to the fatal blow. If Billy represents pure goodness, then his act is unintentional but symbolically righteous, since it results in the destruction of the "evil" Claggart. If Billy is a case of neurotic repression, then his act is determined by his unconscious desires, and reveals the destructiveness of the attempt to repress one's own destructiveness. In the first case, the murder is accidental; in the second, it is the fulfillment of a wish. Strangely enough, this question of accident versus motivation is brought up again at the end of the story, in the curious lack of spontaneous ejaculation in Billy's corpse. Whether the lack of spasm is as mechanical as its presence would have been, or whether it results from what the purser calls "will power" or "euthanasia," the incident stands as a negative analogue of the murder scene. In the former, it is the absence; in the latter, the presence, of physical violence that offers a challenge to interpretation. The burlesque discussion of the "prodigy of repose" by the purser and the surgeon, interrupting as it does the solemnity of Billy's "ascension," can have no other purpose than to dramatize the central importance for the story of the question of arbitrary accident versus determinable motivation. If the psychoanalytical and the metaphysical readings, however incompatible, are both equally supported by textual evidence, then perhaps Melville, rather than asking us to choose between them, is presenting us with a context in which to examine what is at stake in the very oppositions between psychoanalysis and metaphysics, chance and determination, the willed and the accidental, the unconscious and the moral. . . .

THREE READINGS OF READING

It is no doubt significant that the character around whom the greatest critical dissent has revolved is neither the good one nor the evil one but the one who is explicitly presented as a *reader*, Captain Vere. On some level, readers of *Billy Budd* have always testified to the fact that reading, as much as killing, is at the heart of Melville's story. But how is the act of reading being manifested? And what, precisely, are its relations with the deadliness of the spaces it attempts to comprehend?

As we have noted, critical readings of *Billy Budd* have generally divided themselves into two opposing groups, the "testament of acceptance" school on the one hand and the "testament of resistance" or "irony" school on the other. The first is characterized by its tendency to take at face value the narrator's professed admiration of Vere's sagacity and the final benediction of Vere uttered by Billy. The second group is characterized by its tendency to distance the reader's point of view from that of any of the characters, including the narrator, so that the injustice of Billy's execution becomes perceptible through a process of reversal of certain explicit pronouncements within the tale. This opposition between "acceptance" and "irony" quite strikingly mirrors, as we mentioned earlier, the opposition within the story between Billy's naiveté and Claggart's paranoia. We will therefore begin our analysis of Melville's study of the nature of reading with an examination of the way in which the act of reading is manifested in the confrontation between these two characters.

It seems evident that Billy's reading method consists of taking everything at face value, while Claggart's consists of seeing a mantrap under every daisy. Yet in practice, neither of these methods is rigorously upheld. The naive reader is not naive enough to forget to edit out information too troubling to report. The instability of the space between sign and referent, normally denied by the naive reader, is called upon as an instrument whenever that same instability threatens to disturb the content of meaning itself. Billy takes every sign as transparently readable as long as what he reads is consistent with transparent peace, order, and authority. When this is not so, his reading clouds accordingly. And Claggart, for whom every sign can be read as its opposite, neglects to doubt the transparency of any sign that tends to confirm his own doubts: "the master-at-arms *never suspected the veracity*" (p. 357) of Squeak's reports. The naive believer thus refuses to believe any evidence that subverts the transparency of his beliefs, while the ironic doubter forgets to suspect the reliability of anything confirming his own suspicions.

Naiveté and irony thus stand as symmetrical opposites blinded by their very incapacity to see anything but symmetry. Claggart, in his antipathy, "can really form no conception of an *unreciprocated* malice" (p. 358). And Billy, conscious of his own blamelessness, can see nothing but pleasantness in Claggart's pleasant words: "Had the foretopman been conscious of having done or said anything to provoke the ill-will of the official, it would have been different with him, and his sight might have been purged if not sharpened. As it was, innocence was his blinder" (p. 366). Each character sees the other only through the mirror of his own reflection. Claggart, looking at Billy, mistakes his own twisted face for the face of an enemy, while Billy, recognizing in Claggart the negativity he smothers in himself, strikes out.

The naive and the ironic readers are thus equally destructive, both of themselves and of each other. It is significant that both Billy and Claggart should die. Both readings do violence to the plays of ambiguity and belief by forcing upon the text the applicability of a universal and absolute law. The one, obsessively intent on preserving peace and eliminating equivocation, murders the text; the other, seeing nothing but universal war, becomes the spot on which aberrant premonitions of negativity become truth.

But what of the third reader in the drama, Captain Vere? What can be said of a reading whose task is precisely to read the *relation* between naiveté and paranoia, acceptance and irony, murder and error?

For many readers, the function of Captain Vere has been to provide "complexity" and "reality" in an otherwise "oversimplified" allegorical confrontation:

> Billy and Claggart, who represent almost pure good and pure evil, are too simple and too extreme to satisfy the demands of realism; for character demands admixture. Their all but allegorical blackness and whiteness, however, are functional in the service of Vere's problem, and Vere, goodness knows, is real enough.[19]

> *Billy Budd* seems different from much of the later work, less "mysterious," even didactic. . . . Its issues seem somewhat simplified, and, though the opposition of Christly Billy and Satanic Claggart is surely diagrammatic, it appears almost melodramatic in its reduction of values. Only Captain Vere seems to give the story complexity, his deliberations acting like a balance wheel in a watch, preventing a rapid, obvious resolution of the action. . . . It is Vere's decision, and the debatable rationale for it, which introduces the complexity of intimation, the ambiguity.[20]

As the locus of complexity, Captain Vere then becomes the "balance wheel" not only in the clash between good and evil but also in the clash between "accepting" and "ironic" interpretations of the story. Critical opinion has pronounced the captain "vicious" and "virtuous," "self-mythifying" and "self-sacrificing," "capable" and "cowardly," "responsible" and "criminal," "moral" and "perverted," "intellectual" and "stupid," "moderate" and "authoritarian."[21] But how does the same character provoke such diametrically opposed responses? Why is it the judge that is so passionately judged?

In order to analyze what is at stake in Melville's portrait of Vere, let us first examine the ways in which Vere's reading differs from those of Billy Budd and John Claggart:

1. While the naive/ironic dichotomy was based on a symmetry between *individuals,* Captain Vere's reading takes place within a social *structure:* the rigidly hierarchical structure of a British warship. While the naive reader (Billy) destroys the other in order to defend the self, and while the ironic reader (Claggart) destroys the self by projecting aggression onto the other, the third reader (Vere) subordinates both self and other, and ultimately sacrifices both self and other, for the preservation of a political order.

2. The apparent purpose of both Billy's and Claggart's readings was to determine character; to preserve innocence or to prove guilt. Vere, on the other hand, subordinates character to action, being to doing. "A martial court," he tells his officers, "must needs in the present case confine its attention to the *blow's consequence*, which consequence justly is to be deemed not otherwise than as the *striker's deed*" (p. 384).

3. In the opposition between the metaphysical and psychoanalytical readings of Billy's deed, the deciding question was whether the blow should be considered accidental or (unconsciously) motivated. But in Vere's courtroom reading, both these alternatives are irrelevant: "Budd's intent or nonintent is nothing to the purpose" (p. 389). What matters is not the cause but the consequences of the blow.

4. The naive or literal reader takes language at face value and treats signs as *motivated*; the ironic reader assumes that the relation between sign and meaning can be *arbitrary* and that appearances are made to be reversed. For Vere, the functions and meanings of signs are neither transparent nor reversible but fixed by socially determined *convention*. Vere's very character is determined not by a relation between his outward appearance and his inner being but by the "buttons" that signify his position in society. While both Billy and Claggart are said to owe their character to "nature," Vere sees his actions and being as meaningful only within the context of a contractual allegiance:

Do these buttons that we wear attest that our allegiance is to Nature? No, to the King. Though the ocean, which is inviolate Nature primeval, though this be the element where we move and have our being as sailors, yet as the King's officers lies our duty in a sphere correspondingly natural? So little is that true, that in receiving our commissions we in the most important regards ceased to be natural free agents. When war is declared are we the commissioned fighters previously consulted? We fight at command. If our judgments approve the war, that is but coincidence. (p. 387)

Judgment is thus for Vere a function neither of individual conscience nor of absolute justice but of "the rigor of martial law" (p. 387) operating *through* him.

5. While Billy and Claggart read spontaneously and directly, Vere's reading often makes use of precedent (historical facts, childhood memories), allusions (to the Bible, to various ancient and modern authors), and analogies (Billy is like Adam, Claggart is like Ananias). Just as both Billy and Claggart have no known past, they read without memory; just as their lives end with their reading, they read without foresight. Vere, on the other hand, interrogates both past and future for interpretative guidance.

6. While Budd and Claggart thus oppose each other directly, without regard for circumstance or consequence, Vere reads solely in function of the attending historical situation; the Nore and Spithead mutinies have created an atmosphere "critical to naval authority" (p. 380), and, since an engagement with the enemy fleet is possible at any moment, the *Bellipotent* cannot afford internal unrest.

The fundamental factor that underlies the opposition between the metaphysical Budd/Claggart conflict on the one hand and the reading of Captain Vere on the other can be summed up in a single word: history. While the naive and the ironic readers attempt to impose upon language the functioning of an absolute, timeless, universal law (the sign as either motivated or arbitrary), the question of *martial* law arises within the story precisely to reveal the law as a historical phenomenon, to underscore the element of contextual mutability in the conditions of any act of reading. Arbitrariness and motivation, irony and literality, are parameters between which language constantly fluctuates, but only historical context determines which proportion of each is perceptible to each reader. Melville indeed shows history to be a story not only of events but also of fluctuations in the very functioning of irony and belief:

The event *converted into irony for a time* those spirited strains of Dibdin. . . . (p. 333)

Everything is *for a term venerated* in navies. (p. 408)

The opposing critical judgments of Vere's decision to hang Billy are divided, in the final analysis, according to the place they attribute to history in the process of justification. For the ironists, Vere is misusing history for his own self-preservation or for the preservation of a world safe for aristocracy. For those who accept Vere's verdict as tragic but necessary, it is Melville who has stacked the historical cards in Vere's favor. In both cases, the conception of history as an interpretive instrument remains the same: it is its *use* that is being judged. And the very direction of *Billy Budd* criticism itself, historically moving from acceptance to irony, is no doubt itself interpretable in the same historical terms.

Evidence can be found in the text for both pro-Vere and anti-Vere judgments:

> Full of disquietude and misgiving, the surgeon left the cabin. Was Captain Vere suddenly affected in his mind? (p. 378)

> Whether Captain Vere, as the surgeon professionally and privately surmised, was really the sudden victim of any degree of aberration, every one must determine for himself by such light as this narrative may afford. (p. 379–80)

> That the unhappy event which has been narrated could not have happened at a worse juncture was but too true. For it was close on the heel of the suppressed insurrections, an aftertime very critical to naval authority, demanding from every English sea commander two qualities not readily interfusable—prudence and rigor. (p. 380)

> Small wonder then that the *Bellipotent*'s captain . . . felt that circumspection not less than promptitude was necessary. . . . Here he may or may not have erred. (p. 380)

The effect of these explicit oscillations of judgment within the text is to underline the importance of the act of judging while rendering its outcome undecidable. Judgment, however difficult, is clearly the central preoccupation of Melville's text, whether it be the judgment pronounced *by* Vere or *upon* him.

There is still another reason for the uncertainty over Vere's final status, however: the unfinished state of the manuscript at Melville's death. According to editors Hayford and Sealts,[22] it is the "late pencil revisions" that cast the greatest doubt upon Vere; Melville was evidently still fine-tuning the text's attitude toward its third reader when he died. The ultimate irony in the tale is thus that our final judgment of the very reader who takes history into consideration is made problematic by the intervention of history; by the historical accident of the author's death. History here affects interpretation not only within the content of the narration but also within the very production of the narrative. And what remains suspended by this historical accident is nothing less than the exact signifying value of history. Clearly, the meaning of "history" as a feature distinguishing Vere's reading from those of Claggart and Budd can in no way be taken for granted.

JUDGMENT AS POLITICAL PERFORMANCE

> When a poet takes his seat on the tripod of the Muse, he cannot control his thoughts. . . . When he represents men with contrasting characters he is often obliged to contradict himself, and he doesn't know which of the opposing speeches contains the truth. But for the legislator, this is impossible: he must not let his laws say two different things on the same subject.
>
> —Plato, *The Laws*

In the final analysis, the question is not, What did Melville really think of Captain Vere? but rather, What is at stake in his way of presenting him? What can we learn from him about the act of judging? Melville seems to be presenting us less with an object for judgment than with an example of judgment. And the very vehemence with which the critics tend to praise or condemn the justice of Vere's decision indicates that it is judging, not murdering, that Melville is asking us to judge.

And yet Vere's judgment *is* an act of murder. Captain Vere is a reader who kills, not, like Billy, instead of speaking, but rather, precisely by means of speaking. While Billy kills through verbal impotence, Vere kills through the very potency and sophistication of rhetoric. Judging, in Vere's case, is nothing less than the wielding of the power of life and death through language. In thus occupying the point at which murder and language meet, Captain Vere positions himself astride the "deadly space between." While Billy's performative force occupies the vanishing point of utterance and cognition, and while the validity of Claggart's cognitive perception is realized only through the annihilation of the perceiver, Captain Vere's reading mobilizes both power and knowledge, performance and cognition, error and murder. Judgment is cognition functioning as an act. This combination of performance and cognition defines Vere's reading not merely as historical but as political. If politics is defined as the attempt to reconcile action with understanding, then Melville's story offers an exemplary context in which to analyze the interpretive and performative structures that make politics so problematic.

Melville's story amply demonstrates that the alliance between knowledge and action is by no means an easy one. Vere indeed has often been seen as the character in the tale who experiences the greatest suffering; his understanding of Billy's character and his military duty are totally at odds. On the one hand, cognitive exactitude requires that "history" be taken into consideration. Yet what constitutes "knowledge of history"? How are "circumstances" to be defined? What sort of causality does "precedent" imply? And what is to be done with overlapping but incompatible "contexts"? Before deciding upon innocence and guilt, Vere must define and limit the frame of reference within which his decision is to be possible. He does so by choosing the "legal" context over the "essential" context:

> In a *legal view* the apparent victim of the tragedy was he who had sought to victimize a man blameless; and the indisputable deed of the latter, *navally regarded*, constituted the most heinous of military crimes. Yet more. The *essential right and wrong* involved in the matter, the clearer that might be, so much the worse for the responsibility of a loyal sea commander, inasmuch as he was not authorized to determine the matter on that primitive basis. (p. 380)

Yet it is precisely this determination of the proper frame of reference that dictates the outcome of the decision; once Vere has defined his context, he has also in fact reached his verdict. The very choice of the *conditions* of judgment itself constitutes a judgment. But what are the conditions of choosing the conditions of judgment?

The alternative, it seems, is between the "naval" and the "primitive," between "Nature" and "the King," between the martial court and what Vere calls the "Last Assizes" (p. 388). But the question arises of exactly what the concept "Nature" entails in such an opposition. In what way, and with what changes, would it have been possible for Vere's allegiance to be to "Nature"? How can a legal judgment exemplify "primitive" justice?

In spite of his allegiance to martial law and conventional authority, Vere clearly finds the "absolute" criteria equally applicable to Billy's deed, for he responds to each new development with the following exclamations:

> "It is the divine judgment on Ananias!" (p. 278)

> "Struck dead by an angel of God! Yet the angel must hang!" (p. 378)

> "Before a court less arbitrary and more merciful than a martial one, that plea would largely extenuate. At the Last Assizes it shall acquit." (p. 388)

> "Ay, there is a mystery; but, to use a scriptural phrase, it is a 'mystery of iniquity,' a matter for psychologic theologicans to discuss." (p. 385)

This last expression, which refers to the source of Claggart's antipathy, has already been mentioned by Melville's narrator and dismissed as being "tinctured with the biblical element":

> If that lexicon which is based on Holy Writ were any longer popular, one might with less difficulty define and denominate certain phenomenal men. As it is, one must turn to some authority not liable to the charge of being tinctured with the biblical element. (p. 353)

Vere turns to the Bible to designate Claggart's "nature"; Melville turns to a Platonic tautology. But in both cases, the question arises, What does it mean to seal an explanation with a quotation? And what, in Vere's case, does it mean to refer a legal mystery to a religious text?

If Vere names the "absolute"—as opposed to the martial—by means of quotations and allusions, does this not suggest that the two alternative frames of reference within which judgment is possible are not nature and the king, but rather two types of textual authority: the Bible and the Mutiny Act? This is not to say that Vere is "innocently" choosing one text over another, but that the nature of "nature" in a legal context cannot be taken for granted. Even Thomas Paine, who is referred to by Melville in his function as proponent of "natural" human rights, cannot avoid grounding his concept of nature in biblical myth. In the very act of rejecting the authority of antiquity, he writes:

> The fact is, that portions of antiquity, by proving every thing, establish nothing. It is authority against authority all the way, till we come to the divine origin of the rights of man, at the Creation. Here our inquiries find a resting-place, and our reason finds a home.[23]

The final frame of reference is neither the heart nor the gun, neither nature nor the king, but the authority of a sacred text. Authority seems to be nothing other than the vanishing-point of textuality. And nature is authority whose textual origins have been forgotten. Even behind the martial order of the world of the man-of-war, there lies a religious referent: the *Bellipotent*'s last battle is with a French ship called the *Athée*.

Judgment, then, would seem to ground itself in a suspension of the opposition between textuality and referentiality, just as politics can be seen as that which makes it impossible to draw the line between "language" and "life." Vere, indeed, is presented as a reader who does not recognize the "frontier" between "remote allusions" and current events:

> In illustrating of any point touching the stirring personages and events of the time he would be as apt to cite some historic character or incident of antiquity as he would be to cite from the moderns. He seemed unmindful of the circumstances that to his bluff company such remote allusions, however pertinent they might really be, were altogether alien to men whose reading was mainly confined to the journals. But considerateness in such matters if not easy to natures constituted like Captain Vere's. Their honesty prescribes to them directness, sometimes far-reaching like that of a migratory fowl that in its flight never heeds when it crosses a frontier. (p. 341)

Yet it is by inviting Billy Budd and John Claggart to "cross" the "frontier" between their proper territory and their superior's cabin, between the private and the political realms, that Vere unwittingly sets up the conditions for the narrative chiasmus he must judge.

As was noted earlier, Captain Vere's function, according to many critics, is to insert "ambiguity" into the story's "oversimplified" allegorical opposition. Yet, at the same time, it is Captain Vere who inspires the most vehement critical oppositions. In other words, he seems to mobilize simultaneously the seemingly contradictory forces of ambiguity and polarity.

In his median position between the Budd/Claggart opposition and the acceptance/irony opposition, Captain Vere functions as a focus for the conversion of polarity into ambiguity and back again. Interestingly, he plays exactly the same role in the progress of the plot. It is Vere who brings together the "innocent" Billy and the "guilty" Claggart in order to test the validity of Claggart's accusations, but he does so in such a way as to effect not a clarification but a reversal of places between guilt and innocence. Vere's fatherly words to Billy trigger the ambiguous deed upon which Vere must pronounce a verdict of "condemn *or* let go." Just as Melville's readers, faced with the ambiguity they themselves recognize as being provided by Vere, are quick to pronounce the captain vicious *or* virtuous, evil *or* just; so, too, Vere, who clearly perceives the "mystery" in the "moral dilemma" confronting him, must nevertheless reduce the situation to a binary opposition.

It would seem, then, that the function of judgment is to convert an ambiguous situation into a decidable one. But it does so by converting a difference *within* (Billy as divided between conscious submissiveness and unconscious hostility, Vere as divided between understanding father and military authority) into a difference *between* (between Claggart and Billy, between Nature and the King, between authority and criminality). A difference *between* opposing forces presupposes that the entities in conflict be knowable. A difference *within* one of the entities in question is precisely what problematizes the very *idea* of an entity in the first place, rendering the "legal point of view" inapplicable. In studying the plays of both ambiguity and binarity, Melville's story situates *its* critical difference neither within nor between, but in the *relation between the two* as the fundamental question of all human politics. The political context in *Billy Budd* is such that on all levels the differences *within* (mutiny on the warship, the French revolution as a threat to "lasting institutions," Billy's unconscious hostility) are subordinated to differences *between* (the *Bellipotent* vs. the *Athée*, England vs. France, murderer vs. victim). This is why Melville's choice of historical setting is so significant; the war between France and England at the time of the French Revolution is as striking an example of the simultaneous functioning of differences within and between as is the confrontation between Billy and Claggart in relation to their own internal divisions. War, indeed, is the absolute transformation of all differences into binary differences.

It would seem, then, that the maintenance of political authority requires that the law function as a set of rules for the regular, predictable misreading of the "difference within" as a "difference between." Yet if, as our epigraph from Plato suggests, law is thus defined in terms of its repression of ambiguity, then it is itself an overwhelming example of an entity based on a "difference within." Like Billy, the law, in attempting to eliminate its own "deadly space," can only inscribe itself in a space of deadliness.

In seeking to regulate the violent effects of difference, the political work of cognition is thus an attempt to situate that which must be eliminated. Yet in the absence of the possibility of knowing the locus and origin of violence, cognition itself becomes an act of violence. In terms of pure understanding, the drawing of a line between opposing entities does violence to the irreducible ambiguities that subvert the very possibility of determining the limits of what an "entity" is:

> Who in the rainbow can draw the line where the violet tint ends and the orange tint begins? Distinctly we see the difference of the colors, but where exactly does the first blendingly enter into the other? So with sanity and insanity. In pronounced cases there is no question about them. But in some supposed cases, in various degrees supposedly less pronounced, to draw the exact line of demarcation few will undertake, though for a fee becoming considerate some professional experts will. There is nothing nameable but that some men will, or undertake to, do it for pay. (p. 379)

As an act, drawing a line is inexact and violent; and it also problematizes the very possibility of situating the "difference between" the judge and what is judged, between the interests of the "expert" and the truth of his expertise. What every act of judgment manifests is not the value of the object but the position of the judge within a structure of exchange. There is, in other words, no position from which to judge that would be outside the lines of force involved in the object judged.

But if judging is always a *partial* reading (in both senses of the word), is there a place for reading beyond politics? Are we, as Melville's readers, outside the arena in which power and fees are exchanged? If law is the forcible transformation of ambiguity into decidability, is it possible to read ambiguity *as such*, without that reading functioning as a political act?

Melville has something to say even about this. For there is a fourth reader in *Billy Budd*, one who "never interferes in aught and never gives advice" (p. 363): the old Dansker. A man of "few words, many wrinkles" and "the complexion of an antique parchment" (p. 347), the Dansker is the very picture of one who understands and emits ambiguous utterances. When asked by Billy for an explanation of his petty troubles, the Dansker says only, "Jemmy Legs [Claggart] is down on you" (p. 349). This interpretation, entirely accurate as a reading of Claggart's ambiguous behavior, is handed down to Billy without further explanation:

> Something less unpleasantly oracular he tried to extract; but the old sea Chiron, thinking perhaps that for the nonce he had sufficiently instructed his young Achilles, pursed his lips, gathered all his wrinkles together, and would commit himself to nothing further. (p. 349)

As a reader who understands ambiguity yet refuses to "commit himself," the Dansker thus dramatizes a reading that attempts to be as cognitively accurate and as performatively neutral as possible. Yet however neutral he tries to remain, the Dansker's reading does not take place outside the political realm; it is his very refusal to participate in it, whether by further instruction or by direct intervention, that leads to Billy's exclamation in the soup episode ("There now, who says Jemmy Legs is down on me?"). The transference of knowledge is no more innocent than the transference of power, for it is through the impossibility of finding a spot from which knowledge could be all-encompassing that the plays of political power proceed.

Just as the attempt to know without doing can itself function as a deed, the fact that judgment is always explicitly an act adds a further insoluble problem to its cognitive predicament. Since, as Vere points out, no judgment can take place in the "*Last* Assizes," no judge can ever pronounce a Last Judgment. In order to reach a verdict, Vere must determine the consequences not only of the fatal blow but also of his own verdict. Judgment is an act not only because it kills, but because it is in turn open to judgment:

> "Can we not convict and yet mitigate the penalty?" asked the sailing master. . . .
> "Gentlemen, were that clearly lawful for us under the circumstances, consider the consequences of such clemency. . . . To the people the foretopman's deed, however it be worded in the announcement, will be plain homicide committed in a flagrant act of mutiny. What penalty for that should follow, they know. But it does not follow. *Why?* They will ruminate. You know what sailors are. Will they not revert to the recent outbreak at the Nore?" (p. 389)

The danger is not only one of repeating the Nore mutiny, however. It is also one of forcing Billy, for all his innocence, to repeat his crime. Billy is a politically charged object from the moment he strikes his superior. He is no longer, and can never again be, plotless. If he were set free, he himself would be unable to explain why. As a focus for the questions and intrigues of the crew, he would be even less capable of defending himself than before, and would surely strike again. The political reading, as cognition, attempts to understand the past; as performance, it attempts to eliminate from the future any necessity for its own recurrence.

What this means is that every judge is in the impossible position of having to include the effects of his own act of judging within the cognitive context of his decision. The question of the nature of the type of historical causality that would govern such effects can neither be decided nor ignored. Because of his official position, Vere cannot choose to read in such a way that his reading would not be an act of political authority. But Melville shows in *Billy Budd* that authority consists precisely in the impossibility of containing the effects of its own application.

As a political allegory, Melville's *Billy Budd* is thus much more than a study of good and evil, justice and injustice. It is a dramatization of the twisted relations between knowing and doing, speaking and killing, reading and judging, which make political understanding and action so problematic. In the subtle creation of Claggart's "evil" out of a series of spaces in knowledge, Melville shows that gaps in cognition, far from being mere absences, take on the performative power of true acts. The *force* of what is not known is all the more effective for not being perceived as such. The crew, which does not understand that it does not know, is no less performative a reader than the captain, who clearly perceives and represses the presence of "mystery." The legal order, which attempts to submit "brute force" to "forms, measured forms," can only eliminate violence by transforming violence into the final authority. And cognition, which perhaps begins as a power play against the play of power, can only increase, through its own elaboration, the range of what it tries to dominate. The "deadly space" or "difference" that runs through *Billy Budd* is not located between knowledge and action, performance and cognition. It is that which, within cognition, functions as an act; it is that which, within action, prevents us from ever knowing whether what we hit coincides with what we understand. And this is what makes the meaning of Melville's last work so *striking*.

NOTES

1.   E. L. Grant Watson, "Melville's Testament of Acceptance," *New England Quarterly* 6 (June 1933): 319–27; the expression appears in both John Freeman, *Herman Melville* (New York: Macmillan Co., 1926), p. 136 and in Raymond M. Weaver, *The Shorter Novels of Herman Melville* (New York: Liveright, 1928), p. li; William E. Sedgwick, *Herman Melville: The Tragedy of Mind* (Cambridge: Harvard University Press, 1944), pp. 231–49; F. Barron Freeman, *Melville's "Billy Budd"* (Cambridge: Harvard University Press, 1948), pp. 115–24.

2.   Joseph Schiffman, "Melville's Final Stage: Irony," *American Literature* 22, no. 2 (May 1950): 128–36; Philip Withim, "*Billy Budd:* Testament of Resistance,"

Modern Language Quarterly 20 (June 1959): 115–27; Karl E. Zink, "Herman Melville and the Forms—Irony and Social Criticism in *Billy Budd*," *Accent* 12, no. 3 (Summer 1952): 131–39; Lawrance Thompson, *Melville's Quarrel with God* (Princeton: Princeton University Press, 1952).

3.   Kenneth Ledbetter, "The Ambiguity of *Billy Budd*," *Texas Studies in Literature and Language* 4, no. 1 (Spring 1962): 130–34; S. E. Hyman, quoted in R. H. Fogle, "*Billy Budd*—Acceptance or Irony," *Tulane Studies in English* 8 (1958): 107; Edward M. Cifelli, "*Billy Budd*: Boggy Ground to Build On," *Studies in Short Fiction* 13, no. 4 (Fall 1976): 463–69.

4.   Lee T. Lemon, "*Billy Budd*: the Plot Against the Story," in *Studies in Short Fiction* 2, no. 1 (Fall 1964): 32–43.

5.   John Middleton Murry, "Herman Melville's Silence," *Times Literary Supplement*, 10 July 1924, p. 433.

6.   Herman Melville, *Billy Budd*, in *Billy Budd, Sailor, and Other Stories*, ed. Harold Beaver. (New York: Penguin Books, 1967), p. 405; emphasis mine. Unless otherwise indicated, all references to *Billy Budd* are to this edition, which reprints the Hayford and Sealts reading text.

7.   It is interesting that reversibility seems to constitute not only *Billy Budd*'s ending but also its origin: the *Somers* mutiny case, which commentators have seen as a major source for the story, had been brought back to Melville's attention at the time he was writing *Billy Budd* by two opposing articles that reopened and retold the *Somers* case, forty-six years after the fact, in antithetical terms.

8.   Charles Weir, Jr., "Malice Reconciled," *Critics on Melville*, ed. Thomas Rountree. (Coral Gables, Fla.: University of Miami Press, 1972), p. 121.

9.   Freeman, *Melville's "Billy Budd,"* p. 73.

10.   William York Tindall, quoted in William T. Stafford, ed., *"Billy Budd" and the Critics* (Belmont, Calif.: Wadsworth, 1969), p. 188.

11.   Lewis Mumford, quoted in Stafford, *"Billy Budd" and the Critics*, p. 135.

12.   Schiffman, "Melville's Final Stage," p. 133.

13.   Richard Chase, *Herman Melville: A Critical Study*, excerpted in Stafford, *"Billy Budd" and the Critics*, p. 174.

14.   Ibid., p. 173.

15.   Otto Fenichel, *The Psychoanalytic Theory of Neuroses*, quoted in ibid, p. 176.

16.   Edwin Haviland Miller, *Melville* (New York: Persea Books, 1975), p. 358.

17.   Ibid., p. 362.

18.   Rollo May, *Power and Innocence* (New York: W. W. Norton, 1972), pp. 49–50.

19.   Tindall, *"Billy Budd" and the Critics*, p. 187.

20.   John Seelye, *Melville: the Ironic Diagram* (Evanston, Ill.: Northwestern University Press, 1970), p. 162.

21.   Kingsley Widmer, *The Ways of Nihilism:* A Study of Herman Melville's Short Novels (Los Angeles: Ritchie, Ward, Press, for California State Colleges, 1970), p. 21; Hannah Arendt, *On Revolution* (New York: Viking Press, 1963), pp. 77–83; Widmer, *Nihilism*, p. 33; Milton Stern, *The Fine Hammered Steel of Herman*

Melville (Urbana: University of Illinois Press, 1957), pp. 206–50; Weir, "Malice Reconciled," p. 121; Withim, *"Billy Budd,"* p. 126; Weir, "Malice Reconciled," p. 121; Thompson, *Melville's Quarrel*, p. 386; Weir, "Malice Reconciled," p. 124; Leonard Casper, "The Case against Captain Vere," *Perspective* 5, no. 3 (Summer 1952): p. 151; Weir, "Malice Reconciled," p. 121; Thompson, *Melville's Quarrel*, p. 386; James E. Miller, *"Billy Budd:* The Catastrophe of Innocence," *MLN* 73 (March, 1958): p. 174; Widmer, *Nihilism*, p. 29.

    22.   See especially pp. 34–35, Editors' Introduction, *Billy Budd, Sailor* (Chicago: University of Chicago Press, 1962).

    23.   Thomas Paine, *The Rights of Man* (Garden City: Anchor Press, 1973), p. 303.

Analysis of Application

From its epigraph forward, Barbara Johnson's "Melville's Fist: The Execution of *Billy Budd*" uses the text of Melville's novel to deconstruct not only some of the sign systems operating within it but also some of the ones found in critical responses to the novel. In effect, Johnson's project is to explore the ambiguity that lies just underneath the surface of many seemingly simple, straightforward acts of signification. A telling of "truth," she implies, is often a revelation of complexity and "ragged edges," even when the "teller" is a critical authority or textual interpreter.

    Yet beyond this central insight, what makes Johnson's essay noteworthy is that as she explores such ambiguity, she also offers compelling—even if deconstructable—readings of the sign systems within the novel. In setting up the various textual oppositions between Billy and Claggert—innocence and guilt, literality and irony—Johnson builds a powerful argument as she makes succinct reference to scenes and characterizations in a series of quotations from the novel. Johnson firmly establishes the values and surface qualities of the novel's binaries before she begins to explore their fragility, reversibility, and mutable, constructed nature.

    Woven throughout her analysis of the novel are her responses to other critics of Melville's work. In citing those critics, she both helps establish her own position as a knowledgeable scholar and widens the impact of her critique, for she challenges not only the novel's binaries but also those found in previous readings of it. Indeed, her analysis coheres partly through the touchstone represented by the concept "reading," an activity performed both inside and outside of the text. In juxtaposing psychoanalytical and metaphysical readings of the novel she simultaneously traces the ambiguities and multiplicities found in *Billy Budd*, which seems fully capable of supporting a startling variety of critical responses.

    Johnson explores the a priori assumptions of the text's characters and their respondents. In the section "Three Readings of Reading," she juxtaposes the reading strategies of Billy, Claggert, and Vere and isolates a foundational difference to account for their dramatically divergent visions, which she sums up in a single word: "history." And in isolating differing relationships to concepts such as "universality" and "contextuality" in the novel, Johnson is again able to draw parallels between the binaries inside and outside the confines of Melville's text, for the differing presuppositions regarding history account for the differing critical responses to *Billy Budd*. Indeed, the degree of critical belief in and dependence on notions such as "timelessness" and contextual "determination" and/or "mutability" remains one of the hottest of topics in literary and cultural theory today.

Thus, in her last section of analysis, Johnson shifts our focus from Melville's intent to what is at stake in an act of judging intent or meaning. And rather than argue for the truth of a particular interpretation, Johnson demonstrates how the act of interpretation inevitably demands the suppression of ambiguity, for the text itself always threatens to destabilize a given reading. Thus as her analysis draws to its end, she even complicates her reading of reading by suggesting that the novel confronts us with the impossibility of rendering fully authoritative judgment; every judge must "include the effects of his own act of judging within the cognitive context of his decision. . . . Melville shows in *Billy Budd* that authority consists precisely in the impossibility of containing the effects of its own application." Johnson's analysis moves between the microtextual and the meta-theoretical in ways that make it an exemplary work of post-structuralist critique. Resisting definitive answers, it seeks to complicate rather than dictate and to provoke rather than preempt future criticism.

7

Feminist Analysis

Overview

The field of feminist literary and cultural analysis has produced some of the most vibrant intellectual work of recent years. While all feminist methodologies focus intensely on gender (the social roles performed by the sexes) and explore the complex ways in which women have been denied social power and the right to various forms of self-expression, the many perspectives that fall under the heading "feminism" vary widely. Feminist analysis draws on (and also has influenced) every other field covered in this book; its many applications include work on the intersections of gender and class, sexuality, race/ethnicity, psychology, literary form, post-structuralist theory, and so forth. While the following overview is necessarily broad, it covers the most important insights common to all these areas of interest and also traces some of the major disagreements within the field of feminism. As a politically charged and provocative theoretical domain, feminism is far from homogeneous and harmonious, yet its very contestatory nature captures the dynamism and excitement of recent developments in theory as a cultural and critical phenomenon.

Key to all feminist analysis is a recognition of the different degrees of social power that are granted to and exercised by women and men. Feminism can trace its philosophical and political roots back many centuries, but there has been an explosion of interest in women's rights and possible avenues for social empowerment in recent years. Patriarchy, the social structure empowering men throughout much of history, has come under intense critical scrutiny. While individuals from the various subfields of feminism may disagree strongly on the root causes and numerous effects of patriarchal domination of women, certainly they share a commitment to enriching women's lives and senses of their own history and sociopolitical potential. Feminist literary and cultural analysis works toward this end, focusing on representations of gender in literary and other cultural texts and the social implications of those representations. Like Marxist and materialist analysis (discussed in Chapter 3), and even at times sharing its theories, feminist analysis sees texts as thoroughly social. In working with and through texts, feminists believe that critics can help bring about significant social change.

The exact type of social change that feminist critics wish to effect varies dramatically. While all would see traditional forms of male power as oppressive and would ground their analysis in specific textual manifestations of that power and women's responses to it, feminist methodologies and premises are quite diverse. One way of approaching this diversity is to consider the vexing question of just how different and/or how similar women and men are. Some feminists (from Mary Wollstonecraft in the eighteenth century to Gloria Steinem today) emphasize certain fundamental similarities between men and women that exist beyond any artificial social roles. For many such feminists, the key to a more egalitarian world is effecting change through the socioeconomic system at hand, liberalizing oppressive laws, and ensuring equal access to existing power structures, such as political and educational institutions and the business world. For the most part, the goal of these critics and theorists is to reveal, analyze, and redress situations in which women's equality with men is denied.

Working from a dramatically different set of premises are other feminists who believe that women's interests and abilities are fundamentally or essentially different from those of men. Sometimes termed "essentialists," these critics and theorists often point out specific biological differences between men and women, suggesting that women's emotional and nurturing capacities are distinct from men's testosterone-driven engagement with the world around them. Their goal is to achieve the proper social valuation of women's unique qualities and perspectives as well as to change existing social systems to reflect women's ways of knowing and being.

These very different perspectives have had a profound impact on the many movements and submovements within feminism and the related field of gay/lesbian/queer studies (see Chapter 8). Some works of feminist analysis fit clearly within one of the two categories, while others draw on both perspectives. To cover the many different manifestations and subfields of feminist theory would take far more space than we have here (students are urged to consult the overviews of current feminist methodologies listed in this chapter's bibliography), but certain influential recent movements do warrant brief discussion. Some of the most important feminist work of the past few years is that which addresses the inherent racial and ethnic blind spots in much feminist theory and criticism, suggesting that the gender oppression experienced by women of color differs significantly from that of white women. Critics such as bell hooks suggest that social constructs of race and gender should not be analyzed in isolation from each other. hooks offers a multidimensional methodology in which gender is only one important component of a critical inquiry into oppression that includes attention to white women's oppression of African American women and the unique gender dynamics of the African American community (see also Chapter 9). Similarly interested in arriving at a multifaceted methodology are materialist feminists (some of whom self-identify as socialist or Marxist feminists). Materialist feminists wish to explore not only how men have traditionally exercised power over women but also how that power is manifested in and reinforced by capitalism and the exploitation of the working class (see Chapter 3); they insist that oppressive constructs of both gender and class demand concerted revisionary attention. And finally, drawing on some of the most exciting recent work in philosophy and psychology, there are the post-structuralist feminists. Some post-structuralists posit that the only possible escape from the complex power that the binary man/woman (see Chapter 6) holds over us is by tapping into a prelinguistic, essential "femininity" that disrupts language and the power manifested therein. Julia Kristeva, Helene Cixous, and Luce Irigaray are among the leading theorists of this specifically French feminist movement, which has proved enormously influential in recent years (see Chapter 6 for more information on post-structuralism). Other recent critics have been influenced even more profoundly by Foucauldian and social-constructionist thought (see also Chapter 6); these include Judith Butler, whose work on gender "performance" has been very widely cited in literary and cultural studies, and Elizabeth Grosz, who has worked toward a theory of corporeal feminism that shares with Butler an emphasis on how bodies display and perform genders and sexualities in culturally entrenched but still challengeable ways.

Thus there are many different perspectives on gender-based oppression and possible avenues for countering it. The following principles attempt to bridge some of those enormous gaps but also to help students move toward a well-defined and narrowly focused feminist methodology. Principles 1–3 underlie all feminist analysis, while principles 4–8 are unique to individual methodological subcategories within feminism. Depending on the text at hand and the core beliefs of the student, principles 1–3 can be combined with any one (or more) of the remaining principles as a solid basis on which to begin analysis and construct an interpretation of a literary or other cultural text.

Key Principles

1 *Language, institutions, and social power structures have reflected patriarchal interests throughout much of history; this has had a profound impact on women's ability to express themselves and the quality of their daily lives.*

Key to all feminist methodologies is the belief that patriarchal oppression of women throughout history has been profound and multifaceted. That multidimensional quality has meant that feminist respondents to patriarchy have both drawn and significantly expanded on insights in psychology, political science, history, sociology, and literary and cultural studies. Indeed, these fields have traditionally neglected the study of women and oppression, thereby helping perpetuate patriarchy through their very premises and designations of legitimate subject matter. Early feminist work often consisted of pointing out those blind spots, raising women's consciousness of their own oppression, and tracing exactly how and why women have been subordinated to men throughout history and in many fields of study. The roots and manifestations of patriarchy are dauntingly complex, as Gerda Lerner has explored in her groundbreaking book *The Creation of Patriarchy*. Numerous possibilities offer themselves as foundational components of patriarchy, including women's reproductive capacity (which led to an insistence on their "naturally" domestic role), their relatively smaller physical size (which allowed men to dominate them physically), and the mandates of narrow religious belief systems (which also worked to naturalize male power and render it unquestionable). No doubt all of these have aided at times in the reinforcement of patriarchy's power, which helps explain why male privilege has been so thoroughly entrenched in our core beliefs, social institutions, and perceptions of selfhood.

But feminist critics and theorists are interested not only in exploring how men have exercised such power so widely but also in how women's experiences of selfhood have been affected by the power exercised over them. What capacities in women have been deemed "unnatural" and therefore punished if demonstrated? What manifestations of discontent and self-doubt have resulted from a constant experience of oppression? Feminists speak of women being relegated to the status of objects, pointing out that they have traditionally been valued for their beauty and usefulness to men. What behaviors and constricted senses of self does that dehumanization lead to? How have women, at times, even internalized oppression and used patriarchal criteria in valuing and evaluating themselves and other women? If we take as an example in the following principles a narrative of one woman's struggle for economic and psychological self-determination—

which is the central plot line of Charlotte Brontë's *Jane Eyre*—we see how the varying emphases and questions discussed above will direct our attention to the larger social forces that impede our heroine's economic advancement as well as to her own inner struggles to define and assert herself in ways that break prescribed social roles. The potential scope of inquiry allowed by, and even at times demanded by, feminist analysis is indeed very wide.

2 *Yet at the same time, women have resisted and subverted patriarchal oppression in a variety of ways.*

But certainly feminism is not a field that seeks simply to point out victimization. Feminists of every persuasion recognize that women have also resisted and subverted patriarchal oppression at times. Early feminist work sought to recover oppositional voices of women from the past, showing how previous attempts at challenging patriarchy were expressed and how such expressions fared. And even within the relatively narrow scope of action allowed to women under patriarchy, complex forms of resistance are evident. Within the family structure and the home, women have always exercised forms of power, as they have negotiated to meet their own economic, psychological, and intellectual needs as well as those of others. Though sometimes defined solely as mothers, wives, governesses, and/or teachers, women have found ways of influencing social structures in complex and often covert ways. It is indeed a testament to their resilience that some women have worked within an oppressive system to carve out productive lives, finding even in domesticity and ancillary roles ways of expressing themselves and exercising power. In a powerful scene from Brontë's *Jane Eyre*, the heroine leaves behind her unfulfilling position as a teacher at a girls' school to seek a slightly broader scope of action as a governess, even as she fully admits that it is only a "new" form of servitude. Yet even in that incremental move outward, the critic can find a complex negotiation with an oppressive social structure and evidence of one woman's determination to meet her own economic, psychological, and eventually emotional needs in ways that challenge certain norms.

In examining women's history, sociology, and psychology, feminist critics would explore precisely what self-definitions and avenues for expression were available to women at a given time. How did women respond to those restrictions? Were there any explicit voices of rebellion? Among those women who lived by the rules, so to speak, how did some find fulfillment in what may seem today to be very narrow existences? How did they exercise power at home, in the marketplace, and within their social circles or restricted fields of employment? Where and how did they find companionship and support within groups of other women? In *Jane Eyre* or almost any other narrative exploring forms of economic and psychological self-determination, our heroine will no doubt find microcommunities of support and solace that demonstrate where and how resistance to social norms could find expression and nurturance, even in rigidly patriarchal eras. In conducting research on cultural phenomena involving women, you may soon discover that because women's voices and interests have often been deemed unworthy of recording and archiving, it is sometimes difficult to find substantial data from the past to use in analyzing the complexity of women's existences. Yet texts do exist that help us understand and respond to manifestations of oppression that existed many years or even centuries ago—and that may persist in modified forms to this day.

3   *This combination of patriarchal oppression and women's resistance to it is apparent in many literary and other cultural texts.*

Indeed, literary texts provide invaluable and intriguing sources of data. They contain abundant information about the daily components of past lives and the microcosmic effects of some of the broadest social dynamics, although, of course, they can hardly be considered objective sources of such information. Since many texts were written when the social oppression of women was considered natural, they often reflect patriarchy in substantially unmodified ways. Throughout history, texts written by men have tended to reflect, overtly or covertly, their own positions of power and often highly patriarchal attitudes toward women. Thus feminist criticism of writers such as John Milton, Charles Dickens, and Ernest Hemingway have often focused on how they portrayed women characters and what biases those characterizations demonstrate. And, of course, even texts written by women are not free of patriarchy. Thus feminist criticism of women authors has extensively probed certain writers' complex responses to the social situations surrounding them. Some, such as Brontë in *Jane Eyre* and Zora Neale Hurston in *Their Eyes Were Watching God*, spoke out in remarkably forceful ways about social restrictions on women's lives. Others, such as Jane Austen and Flannery O'Connor, expressed their ideas in ways that were less clearly antagonistic toward patriarchal power structures but that still reflected complex understandings of women's desires for fulfillment and self-expression.

The feminist critic will draw carefully on textual details as the process of argumentation and interpretation proceeds. What characterizations and narrator comments help reveal the gender belief systems present in a text? In *Jane Eyre* this might lead us to examine the attitudes of characters such as

Brocklehurst, the hypocritical and oppressive minister in the novel's early chapters, as well as the initial characterization of Rochester, Jane's employer and love interest. Also, do characters disagree on women's roles, either explicitly in their dialogue or implicitly in the way they live their lives? In Brontë's novel, numerous female characters—Miss Temple, Helen Burns, Jane Eyre—could be compared to see how they define themselves and reflect, reject, or revise standard notions of women's roles and rights. Which of these women characters thrive and which fail to thrive, and why? How do they successfully exercise power in the realms to which they are assigned? Do some step out of the roles assigned to them? If so, what is their fate and what message or theme is communicated through that fate? Do rebellious or nonconformist men appear in the text, and how do their fates differ from those of nonconformist women? All works of feminist criticism will draw carefully on textual detail—quotations, plot developments, and themes—but many also look beyond the text, to the time period of its setting or creation, to understand in as full a manner as possible how a given text variously supports, alters, and/or rejects prevailing gender belief systems.

4 *For some feminists, the most important way to resist patriarchy is to challenge laws and other institutional barriers to women's equality.*

Some forms of feminism are interested primarily in emphasizing the fundamental similarities between women and men as well as in opening access to the prevailing economic and political system so as to ensure equal opportunity and a level playing field for all. From the late eighteenth century to the present day, many feminist theorists have suggested that oppression is most productively countered by opening up institutions such as the educational system and the political process to as large a number of people as possible. This is a perspective that a critic might also bring to the analysis of a text. In analyzing a work of literature or other cultural text, the feminist critic might focus on the differential treatment of women and men. What advantages or opportunities are allowed to men? In *Jane Eyre*, for example, why does John Reed (Jane's cousin) have career and personal options that she never has? What specific social and legal barriers keep women from achieving the level of personal success and economic security available to men? Even with very recent texts, you might ask why female characters still need to struggle to enter arenas such as business, the literary profession, politics, and other highly valued fields. What accommodations do women have to make in order to enter such fields, or how do they construct alternate avenues for empowerment if they are wholly denied access to them? Certainly such questions could easily advance research into Jane Eyre's struggle for economic self-determination, as the critic explores which specific barriers to advancement she encounters and suggests possibilities for challenging them. Feminist analysis never accepts the status quo as perfect or undeserving of modification, but as we see here, some forms of feminism do not seek a radical revision in the common social emphasis on personal achievement and individual responsibility. In analyzing literary and other cultural texts, some feminist analysis works to further the overall empowerment of women by exploring their fundamental equality with men.

5 *For more essentialist feminists, resistance often means focusing on the differences between men and women as well as ensuring the social valuation and expression of the latter's unique abilities.*

While "essentialist" is a term used pejoratively by some social constructionists, here it indicates those feminist perspectives that focus on fundamental and enduring differences between the sexes and that offer thoroughgoing critiques of male-centered norms. Responding to the oppression of their day, some early feminists even called for separatism, suggesting that only by forming single-sex communities could women distance themselves from and eventually slough off the corrupting influence of men. Today, some essentialists focus on women's reproductive capacity and the nurturance that they demonstrate as mothers; such theorists, activists, and critics adhere at times to women-centered spiritual belief systems. Yet whatever their distinct beliefs, all such feminists would thoroughly question values traditionally associated with men, such as the emphasis on cutthroat competition and the aggressive drive for domination. Instead, most would assert the profound worth of characteristics traditionally associated with women: nurturance, cooperation, and emotion. In analyzing a text, such critics would look at the distinct qualities of men's and women's perspectives on the world, their familial and community ties, and their inherent values. If, as some of the feminists mentioned above advocate, women become integrated into the prevailing political and economic system, what positive qualities would they lose? How do women, when they are apart from the company of men, demonstrate important values that seem practically unknown to most men? How do many of the values and roles associated with men, both historically and in the pages of a text, lead to profound social injustices? Where in the text can one isolate glimmers of hope that alternate systems are possible, ones built not on hierarchy and competition but instead on mutual caring and concern? Even in a text such as *Jane Eyre*, which clearly does not call for separatism, the heroine calls out to a "mother" presence in the universe as she seeks the strength to flee a potentially abusive relationship, and she then finds a supportive community with two sisters—Diana and Mary—who help her resist the demands of their brother, St. John. In such scenes and interactions, even a narrative such as *Jane Eyre* that basically leaves unchallenged the economic and sexual status quo may reveal an implicit valuation of women's unique qualities and forms of interaction. In probing such essentialist implications, the critic can construct a powerful critique of certain male-centered norms that impede positive social change.

6 *For feminists interested in issues of race and ethnicity, both sexism and racism demand analysis in literary and other cultural texts.*

African American feminists and other feminists of color point out that feminist theory has often ignored the many ways in which race and ethnicity compound the dynamic of oppression for many women. Indeed, feminism has often erased differences among women in order to clarify and assert more forcefully a specific gender-related agenda. But in doing so they also erase the many ways in which women can act oppressively toward each other and ignore the complexities of African American, Latina, Asian American, and Native American lives. In exploring those lives, feminists interested in issues of race and ethnicity draw on the theories of class and cultural identity explored in Chapters 3 and 9, then expand those insights with a specific focus on women's lives and interests. What are the racial politics and cultural norms of the communities—ethnic minority and/or majority—portrayed in a text? What are their expectations of gender behavior and familial responsibility? Indeed, how do religious beliefs and specific cultural traditions and histories affect men's and women's self-perception and their perception of proper gender roles? How do minority women's and minority men's interactions with white or economically privileged groups converge and diverge, and how do their shared experiences of oppression lead to forms of solidarity or manifestations of tension within their own community? How does the text demonstrate that women are not a homogeneous group and that women of color have their own unique stories to tell and triumphs to experience? All these are questions that could generate a nuanced examination of how a heroine from an ethnic minority community might battle forces very different from those of a heroine such as Jane Eyre—ones of racism and sexism, within and outside her own ethnic group—as she moves toward self-expression and self-determination. Indeed, *Jane Eyre* itself could be critiqued for the ways in which it implicitly supports certain social values that affect women from social and economic backgrounds different from those of its author and heroine.

7 *For materialist feminists, resistance to patriarchy must include thorough questioning of the class system as well as the gender system.*

Feminism has been greatly enriched by the recognition that dramatic class differences exist among women and that an analysis of women's experiences of oppression cannot be neatly divorced from an analysis of capitalism and class oppression (as discussed more fully in Chapter 3). Many Marxist and materialist feminists point out that women have always worked, both inside and outside the home, and that any critique of their lives must include attention to their status as laborers. Furthermore, class-based oppression and the pernicious ideologies of competitive capitalism exacerbate the oppression of women in both working-class and upper-class communities. While there is considerable disagreement among feminists interested in issues of class about whether class or gender should receive primary critical emphasis in a given reading, all would agree that these systems of oppression are thoroughly interrelated. Critics such as Teresa Ebert, Donna Haraway, and Gayatri Spivak (whose work also draws on post-structuralist and post-colonial theory) ask questions such as: What class tensions exist in the text under scrutiny? How do economic worries and the effects of specific material deprivations (such as access to housing, education, and employment) exacerbate gender-related tensions? What forms of labor do the women of the text perform, and how is that labor valued or ignored? How might a modification or thorough overhaul of the economic system portrayed in the text change the lives of its women characters and help alleviate their experience of gender-related oppression? All of these could help generate a careful probing of the many factors contributing to the economic oppression of a heroine such as Jane Eyre, of groups of women in a text, or even of women exploited by other women of a different class. It might also allow the critic to explore solutions to such manifestations of oppression that are more than simply personal or self-motivated, that are instead structural and system-altering in their implications, if not explicit agenda.

8 *For post-structuralist feminists, man/woman is a hierarchical binary that may be challenged through intense critical scrutiny. This may include an exploration of prelinguistic experiences of essential femininity or attention to gender as "performance."*

Post-structuralist theories (see Chapter 6) have had a profound impact on feminism, and vice versa. Seeing the binary of man/woman as one clearly favoring the former term, post-structuralist feminists have looked at the many ways in which male-centered (phallocentric) norms pervade language, culture, and fields such as psychology and anthropology. In seeking to disrupt these norms, some post-structuralist feminists have sought access to more essential women's experiences of their body and nature, ones that may even biologically or genetically precede the determining influence of language and its inherent biases. French feminists such as Helene Cixous and Luce Irigaray challenge the norms of male discourse and writing, suggesting that women's writing and experience of the world may be diffuse and multidimensional rather than linear and directive. While French and Anglo American post-structuralist feminism is a complex field that cannot be summed up briefly here, critics influenced by it would first examine a text with a specific interest in its language and basic organizing principles, particularly the ways in which these relate to the binary man/woman. Such critics might then find text-related ways of challenging this binary, searching for the ways in which the text reveals its own biases and blind spots, as well as isolating and then challenging those presuppositions that underlie the whole meaning-making structure of the text. In particular, the critic might examine how women's experiences of self and language have the potential to disrupt men's experience of primacy and secure selfhood. For example, in Jane Eyre's drive toward self-determination, how do her words and actions undermine male-centered definitions and hierarchies? How do her dreams or evocation of a natural "maternal" presence represent a challenge to phallocentrism? As always, the proof must be in the details of the text, as nuances of language, disruptive actions, and fine differences of consciousness prove the inherently fictitious nature of men's assertion of primacy and unassailable power.

More recent theorists of "performativity" and corporeal feminism have also drawn on post-structuralist insights, but with a much greater emphasis on the constructed nature of reality and how those constructions help determine relationships with our own bodies and those of others. Judith Butler, in *Gender Trouble* and *Bodies That Matter*, has emphasized that gender roles are performed in both highly visible and elusive ways: in the clothes we wear, the gestures we make, the often-stylized interactions that we have with each other. All these "performances" must be repeated in order to remain "real" to us; that repetition, though, is subvertible if the social scripts determining our performances are critically challenged. Similarly, Elizabeth Grosz, in *Volatile Bodies*, examines the ways in which gender roles are inscribed on the body by sciences and philosophies that take male bodies as their frame of reference. She suggests that by examining women's corporeal experiences—including childbirth and menstruation—male-centered norms can be challenged without resorting to an essentialism that erases the ways in which our bodies are given meaning through social customs and our language system. Through such body-scrutinizing theories, the literary and cultural critic would examine textual references to and values placed on the bodies of characters or other figures, the ways in which individuals enact social scripts through their bodies, subverting or reinforcing social norms thereby, and the critical insights that can be generated by examining the tensions created by nonconforming bodies or performances, or even ones that simply threaten to become so. Students wishing to use these latest theories of post-structuralist feminism will wish to consult Chapter 6 for more information on the ways whereby the visible "signs" of gender reflect and work to control our worldviews. As Jane Eyre or any other heroine struggles for self-determination and self-expression, crises of gender definition may be displayed in "body language," in changes in clothing and adornment, and in physical reflections (such as illness, weight change, exercise or inertia) of the larger social battles that she wages. In delving into these recent insights into gender and sexuality, students will be intellectually challenged and their writing energized by a brisk engagement with the subtle yet powerful ways in which gender roles pervade our lives and shape our very sense of self.

Bibliography

Butler, Judith. *Bodies That Matter: On the Discursive Limits of "Sex."* New York: Routledge, 1993.

> This difficult but rewarding book builds on Butler's insights in *Gender Trouble*, listed below, and offers readings of gender "performances" in fictional, theoretical, and film texts. Its theoretical sophistication will make it of greatest interest to advanced readers.

Butler, Judith. *Gender Trouble: Feminism and the Subversion of Identity.* New York: Routledge, 1990.

> This is one of the most influential recent works of feminist theory, providing a superb overview of post-structuralist feminism and Butler's exciting notion of gender as "performance." Its conceptual difficulty and presupposition of theoretical knowledge, however, will make it of greatest use to advanced readers.

Grosz, Elizabeth. *Volatile Bodies: Toward a Corporeal Feminism.* Bloomington: Indiana University Press, 1994.

> This superb overview of recent feminist theories and the debates over essentialism and constructionism offers a new emphasis on the ways in which gender roles affect and reflect our physical bodies. Its theoretical density will make it of greatest interest to advanced readers.

hooks, bell. *Ain't I a Woman: Black Women and Feminism*. Boston: South End Press, 1981.

This groundbreaking work established bell hooks as one of the preeminent theorists of race and gender. Clearly written and forcefully expressed, it will be of interest to students at all levels.

Humm, Margaret, ed. *Modern Feminisms: Political Literary Cultural*. New York: Columbia University Press, 1992.

This is a useful and comprehensive collection of primary texts that demonstrate the range of current feminist methodologies. It contains examples of all of the movements discussed in this chapter. As with all collections, its level of accessibility varies widely, but students at all levels will find its introductory essays useful, with intermediate and advanced students finding its primary texts of particular interest.

Jardine, Alice, and Paul Smith, eds. *Men in Feminism*. New York: Methuen, 1987.

While it often presupposes advanced knowledge of theory, this collection covers its topic area comprehensively and memorably. Its dialogues and essays show the range of opinions concerning men's possible roles in feminist movements. Students at the advanced level will find it particularly useful.

Lerner, Gerda. *The Creation of Patriarchy*. New York: Oxford University Press, 1986.

This accessible and comprehensive work traces the early roots and manifestations of patriarchal oppression of women. While it does not contain applied literary readings, it will provide useful historical information for intermediate and advanced readers.

Moi, Toril. *Sexual/Textual Politics*. New York: Methuen, 1985.

This brief book is an idiosyncratic but intriguing response to recent feminist theories in America, Great Britain, and France, with a particularly useful overview of post-structuralist methodologies. Its presupposition of theoretical knowledge will make it of greatest interest to advanced readers.

Munt, Sally, ed. *New Lesbian Criticism: Literary and Cultural Readings*. New York: Columbia University Press, 1992.

This collection contains very useful examples of applied lesbian feminist criticism. Its introduction and its overview of the field by Bonnie Zimmerman will make it of great interest to readers at the intermediate and advanced levels.

Newton, Judith, and Deborah Rosenfelt, eds. *Feminist Criticism and Social Change: Sex, Class, and Race in Literature and Culture*. New York: Methuen, 1985.

This collection contains primary texts and applied readings in all of the fields mentioned in its subtitle, but it is particularly useful for its introduction, which discusses the necessity of developing a materialist feminism. While its level of

accessibility varies somewhat, this collection will be appropriate for most students at the intermediate and advanced levels.

Showalter, Elaine, ed. *The New Feminist Criticism: Essays on Women, Literature, Theory.* New York: Pantheon, 1985.

This collection contains examples of all the areas of feminist inquiry covered in
this chapter, with accessible overviews and clear applications. While its level of
accessibility varies, it will be of interest to most readers at the intermediate and
advanced levels.

Tong, Rosemarie. *Feminist Thought: A Comprehensive Introduction.* Boulder,
CO: Westview Press, 1989.

While this introductory guide is not as complete as its title suggests (it contains
no coverage of theories of race and ethnicity, for example), it nevertheless provides a very clear overview of many important forms of feminist analysis. Its
clarity and accessibility will make it useful for all readers.

Warhol, Robyn, and Diane Price Herndl, eds. *Feminisms: An Anthology of
Literary Theory and Criticism,* 2nd ed. New Brunswick: Rutgers University Press, 1997.

This is the most substantial and comprehensive collection of primary texts in
feminist literary and cultural analysis available today. It contains examples of all
of the movements and submovements in feminist theory covered in this chapter. While its level of accessibility varies, it will be of interest to students at
both the intermediate and advanced levels.

Weedon, Chris. *Feminist Practice and Poststructuralist Theory,* 2nd ed. Blackwell: New York, 1997.

This is a clearly written overview of post-structuralism and its possible uses in
feminist cultural critique. Although it contains no examples of literary readings,
its accessibility and clarity will make it of interest to both intermediate and advanced readers.

Application

Reading Prompts

1. In her introductory paragraphs, Vermillion traces the implications of somatophobia—fear of and disdain for the body—for a number of groups,
focusing finally on black women who have been raped and have written
about their experiences. Highlight or underline those passages in which
she reveals the particularly arduous task such women face as they construct a "new image" of themselves and their "selves."
2. Mark and pay careful attention to those passages in which Vermillion
suggests how Harriet Jacobs at once uses and responds to the stereo-

types present in a previous century of literary portrayals of raped and seduced heroines.

3. Vermillion suggests that rape and racism function together as muting forces in Angelou's *I Know Why the Caged Bird Sings*. Highlight and pay careful attention to the evidence that she uses to support this claim.

4. Highlight and reflect on the weight of evidence that Vermillion offers to support her assertion that Angelou successfully "reembodies," reclaims, and reasserts her "self."

5. Vermillion focuses on the genre of autobiography. At the end of her essay, what possibilities for feminist empowerment does she imply are offered by that genre?

MARY VERMILLION

Reembodying the Self:

Representations of Rape in *Incidents in the Life of a Slave Girl* and *I Know Why the Caged Bird Sings*

A study of a woman's written record of her own rape can illustrate the dual consciousness that Susan Stanford Friedman identifies as a primary characteristic of female life-writing. According to Friedman, a woman's alienation from her culturally defined self motivates the creation of an alternate self in her autobiography.[1] Because patriarchal cultural definitions of a woman center on her body and sexual status, the rape victim not only becomes painfully aware of her culturally defined self, but she also confronts a hideous paradox as she tries to construct an alternate self. In trying to perceive herself as whole and untouched, the rape victim runs the risk of fragmenting her identity, of excluding her body from what she considers as the rest of her self. Such negation of her body is a natural continuation of the actual rape: the victim tells herself that *she* was not there during the rape—it was not *she* whom he raped. Unanswerable questions then loom. If she was not there, then who was? Who is this "she," this "self" who exists bodiless?[2]

The rape victim's uncertainties about her own subjectivity stem in part from a long tradition in Western patriarchal thought—what Elizabeth Spelman terms "somatophobia," fear of and disdain for the body. Spelman demonstrates that patriarchal thinkers from Plato onward have channeled most of this disdain toward the female body.[3] I will briefly examine the partnership of misogyny and somatophobia in Shakespeare's *The Rape of Lucrece* because his poem influenced the two autobiographers whom I examine in the second and third parts of this essay. Maya Angelou specifically refers to the poem, and it shaped the novels of seduction that Harriet Jacobs critiques in her autobiography.[4] Shakespeare describes the raped Lucrece as privileging her innocent mind over her violated body: "Though my gross blood be stain'd with this abuse, / Immaculate and spotless is my mind."[5] Stephanie Jed describes how somatophobia springs from such a Platonic duality between body and mind: "Implicit in every construct of a chaste or integral mind is the splitting off of the body as the region of all potential contamination."[6] The dire but logical consequences of this splitting off emerge when Lucrece views her violated body through patriarchy's eyes. Perceiving her body as her husband's damaged property, she gives the following rationale for killing herself:

> My honor I'll bequeath unto the knife
> That wounds my body so dishonored.
> 'Tis honor to deprive dishonor'd life,
> The one will live, the other being dead.
> So of shame's ashes shall my fame be bred,
> For in my death I murther shameful scorn:
> My shame so dead, mine honor is newborn.[7]

Informing Lucrece's deadly resolution are somatophobia and two other key aspects of patriarchal ideology: the identification of the female with her body and the equation of female "honor" and chastity. The destruction of Lucrece's body perpetuates these patriarchal conceptions of womanhood.[8]

The woman who records her own rape must—if she does not wish to do with her pen what Lucrece does with her sword—close the distance between her body and whatever her society posits as a woman's integral self (i.e., sexual reputation, mind, soul, desire, or will). She must reclaim her body. While this written reclamation is difficult for any woman, it presents a special problem for the black woman because of the meanings that hegemonic white cultures have assigned to her body. According to Spelman, somatophobia supports both sexist and racist thinking because these hegemonic cultures have posited women as more bodylike than men and blacks as more bodylike than whites. Within these two hierarchical relationships, the black woman is implicitly perceived as the most bodylike, and this perception fosters her oppression in somatophobic societies.[9] Numerous scholars have demonstrated that both the institutions of slavery and antebellum writing constructed the black woman as the sum total of her bodily labor and suffering. Antebellum writers—including abolitionists and black males—depicted the black woman as breeder, wet nurse, field laborer, and, most significant, sexually exploited victim. So pervasive were these images of the black woman's body that the National Association of Colored Women's Clubs, founded in 1896, targeted for its most vehement attacks negative stereotypes of black women's sexuality.[10] Angela Davis and bell hooks illustrate how these nineteenth-century stereotypes inform twentieth-century racist images of the black woman as promiscuous and bestial.[11] Because of this long history of negative stereotypes, the black woman who records her own rape faces the arduous task of reaffirming her sexual autonomy without perpetuating the racist myths that associate her with illicit sexuality. She must recover and celebrate her body without reinforcing racist perceptions of her as mere body.

This task is, of course, also a crucial project for contemporary black feminists. Reviewing Spike Lee's film, *She's Gotta Have It* (1986)—in which a black woman, Nola Darling, is raped—hooks writes:

> She [Darling] has had sex throughout the film; what she has not had is a sense of self that would enable her to be fully autonomous and sexually assertive, independent and liberated. . . . A new image, the one we have yet to see in film, is the desiring black woman who prevails, who triumphs, not desexualized, not alone, who is 'together' in every sense of the word.[12]

How two black women who have suffered rape (or its threat) begin to construct this "new image" will be my focus as I examine Harriet Jacob's and Maya Angelou's autobiographies.

Jacobs, in *Incidents in the Life of a Slave Girl* (1861), adopts the pseudonym Linda Brent and describes how, as a young enslaved girl, she coped with the threat of rape from her master, Dr. Flint.[13] In order to escape this threat, as well as slavery itself, Brent deliberately chooses to have sexual relations with another white man, Mr. Sands. Many critics have argued that Jacob's narration of these events echoes and subverts various components of nineteenth-century sentimental discourse—particularly the seduction plot and the basic tenets of "true womanhood" (piety, purity, submissiveness, and domesticity).[14] In my examination of these subversions, I will focus on how Jacobs critiques somatophobia and degrading images of the black female body. Brent's decision to have sexual relations with Sands marks a turning point in Jacob's reembodying strategies. Before this point, she obscures her own corporeality in order to counter negative stereotypes about black women, and after this point, she begins constructing new positive images of the black female body.

For over one hundred years preceding Jacob's writing of her autobiography, sentimental novelists portrayed both raped and seduced heroines as believing, like Shakespeare's Lucrece, that their sexual activities sever their integral selves from their bodies. In Susanna Rowson's *Charlotte Temple* (1791), for instance, when the eponymous heroine leaves her paternal home with her seducer, she mourns, "It seemed like the separation of soul and body."[15] Sentimental heroines who undergo such a separation (i.e., lose their "sexual purity")—be it by their own choice or not—face a bout of madness or muteness usually followed by a slow, painful death.[16] Inscribing the "fallen" woman's body as damaged male property, the sentimental novel identifies the female with her body and promotes somatophobia. Furthermore, in dishing out the same "punishment" to both raped and seduced

heroines, the sentimental novel as a literary mode obscures seduction's crucial difference from rape: seduction requires a contest of wills, while rape
requires the mastery of one will over another. In disguising this difference,
the sentimental novel erases female volition. Jacobs, I believe, must have
recognized that such an erasure reinforced the slaveholder's negation of the
enslaved woman's will.[17] In order to reclaim her own volition, she appropri-
ates the sentimental novel's obfuscation of rape and seduction. By portraying in the language of seduction her former master's legally sanctioned
threat to rape her, Jacobs refutes his idea that she was his property, "subject
to his will in all things."[18]

Jacobs further accentuates her own volition by depicting the unequal
contest between Brent's and Flint's bodies as an equal contest of words.
Observing that Jacob's autobiography contains more reconstructed dialogue than any male-authored slave narrative, William Andrews maintains
that Brent's and Flint's dialogues pivot on arguments of the slave woman's
rights to define herself.[19] I want to argue that Jacobs also uses dialogue to
challenge the hegemonic culture's perception of her as mere body. Flint
tries to control Brent by whispering foul words into her ear, and Jacobs
writes that he *"peopled* my young mind with unclean images, such as only a
vile monster could think of" (27, emphasis added). With the choice of the
word "peopled," Jacobs merely hints that Flint would like to "people" his
plantation through Brent's body. She portrays the sexual threat that Flint
poses as a predominantly psychological/spiritual one and thus lessens her
reader's tendency to associate her body with illicit sexuality. Jacobs continues to mystify her former master's physical power and legal right to rape
her by confining it to verbal expressions. She primarily depicts his economic mastery over Brent not as his ability to overpower her physically but
as his power to perpetuate her slavery in his last will and testament. Jacobs
further confines Flint's power to words as she portrays him sending Brent
letters, making speeches, and, ironically, promising to make her a lady, a
category from which black women were excluded by the white planter culture.[20] Even after Brent runs away, it is Flint's words, and not his body, that
threaten her. In her first hiding place the sight of Flint gives her a "gleam
of satisfaction" (100), but the sound of his voice "chills her blood" (103).
Brent's differing reactions to Flint highlight Jacob's primary strategy in
recording his threat to her body. As Flint's body nears Brent's, as he enters
the house she hides in, Jacobs describes him as a mere voice. In recording
Flint's attempts to disembody her, she disembodies him.

In thus obscuring the corporeality of Flint's threat of rape, Jacobs mini-
mizes her own body and thereby strikes a blow against the racist stereotype
of the black woman as sexually exploited victim. The pen with which she

strikes, however, is double-edged, and like Lucrece's dagger, annihilates her own body. In the early part of her autobiography, Jacobs, like Lucrece, privileges an interior self over her body and nearly erases its presence in her text.

Brent's decision to have sexual relations with Sands, however, begins Jacob's rewriting of her body into her life story. Most feminist readers of Jacob's narrative interpret her discussion of this incident as her most powerful rejection of sentimental discourse and "true womanhood."[21] I want to emphasize that Jacob's reversals of the seduction plot's conventions also enable her to reject the body/mind duality that promotes somatophobia. When Flint asks if she loves the father of her unborn child, she retorts, "I am thankful that I do not despise him" (59). Unlike the stock seduced maiden, Brent has no uncontrollable passion for Sands. Reasoning that he will buy and free her and the children they have, Brent exerts her own will to escape Flint's. "It seems," she states, "less degrading to give one's self, than to submit to compulsion. There is something akin to freedom in having a lover who has no control over you except that which he gains by kindness and attachment" (56). Mary Helen Washington calls this declaration "the clearest statement of . . . the need for control over one's female body."[22] Jacobs, I believe, seizes this control by insisting upon a connection between her sexuality and autonomy: "I knew what I did, and I did it with deliberate calculation" (55). By thus emphasizing that Brent willed her sexual activity, Jacobs critiques the somatophobic sentimental convention that severs an unchaste woman's body from her integral self, and she inscribes Brent's union with Sands as a union of her own body and will.

After Brent escapes Flint's plantation, his pursuit of her is so rigorous that she is forced to hide for seven years in a crawl space in her grandmother's attic. Of these years in hiding Andrews writes that "her disembodied presence in patriarchal society lets her become for the first time Dr. Flint's manipulator instead of his tool."[23] While I acknowledge this power shift, I want to further explore Andrew's use of the word "disembodiment." Confined to a coffinlike space and temporarily losing the use of her limbs, Brent is indeed disembodied in her situation. Yet it is, I maintain, in describing this very disembodiment that Jacobs embodies herself in her text. Her descriptions of Brent's physical sufferings in the attic reinforce the bond between her body and her will. Jacobs engages a pattern of first cataloging Brent's physical ills and then comparing them favorably to her state as a slave:

> I was eager to look on their [her children's] faces; but there was no hole, no crack through which I could peep. This continued darkness was oppressive. It

seemed horrible to sit or lie in a cramped position day after day, without one gleam of light. Yet I would have chosen this, rather than my lot as a slave. (114)

Here Brent's physical suffering accentuates not only her ability to choose but also the reason behind her choice—her children's freedom.

Jacobs also emphasizes this connection between Brent's will, body, and children by juxtaposing her agony in hiding with the pain of the slave mother whose children have been sold (122). This recurrent figure who has lost both her will and the fruit of her body represents the completely disembodied black woman. She is Jacob's antitype and has no wish to continue her life. "Why *don't* God kill me?" asks one (16). "I've got nothing to live for now," says another (70). In Chapter 13, "The Church and Slavery," Jacobs uses the disembodied slave mother to demonstrate how the somatophobic privileging of an interior self over the body disembodies the black race. In this scene not only does the childless woman voice her suffering and loss, but Jacobs also minutely records her physical torment. The woman stands and beats her breast, then sits down, "quivering in every limb." The white constable who presides over the Methodist class meeting disregards her longing for her sold children, her physical suffering, and the many enslaved people who weep in sympathy with her. He stifles a laugh and says, "Sister, pray to the Lord that every dispensation of his divine will may be sanctified to the good of your poor needy soul" (70). This "spiritual" advice disembodies the woman and her friends, leaving them only their singing voices: "Ole Satan's church is here below. / Up to God's free church I hope to go" (71). While these words disparage the white constable, they also confirm his privileging of soul over body. Critiquing the slaveholder's religion within her rewriting of the seduction plot, Jacobs juxtaposes the "Christian" slaveholder's devaluation of the black body with the sentimental novel's devaluation of the female body and thereby unveils the somatophobia in both discourses.[24]

She further contests both of these disembodying discourses with her descriptions of Brent's activities in her attic hideaway. It is in this part of the text that Brent—tearful, hysterical, and sleepless—most resembles the sentimental heroine. Brent's crawling exercises, her drilling of peepholes, her sewing, reading, and letter writing oddly mimic domestic industriousness. During the second winter, in which cold stiffens her tongue, Brent's muteness and delirium echo that of a "fallen" and dying sentimental heroine. Jacobs thus parallels Brent's attic with the private space that usually confines the sentimental heroine: the kitchen, the parlor, the upstairs chamber, the deathbed, and the grave. Jane Tompkins calls such female space "the closet of the heart" and observes that sentimental fiction "shares with the evangelical reform movement a theory of power that stipulates that all true action is not material, but spiritual."[25] Jacobs challenges this stipulation by emphasizing the drastic material change that Brent works from within her "closet of the heart." As Valerie Smith observes, Brent "uses to her advantage all the power of the voyeur."[26] She prevents her own capture by embroiling Flint in an elaborate plot to deflect his attention, and she meets with Sands to secure his promise to free her children. In her hiding place she not only has a mystical vision of her children, but she actually succeeds in gaining their freedom from slavery.

This uniting of spiritual and material action reenacts Jacob's earlier textual union of Brent's body and will, and it situates her maternity as a powerful symbol of her autonomy.[27] In her autobiography, Jacobs transforms her body from a site of sexual oppression to a source of freedom—freedom from slavery for herself and her children and freedom from somatophobic racist ideologies that demean the black female body. With one of Brent's early experiences in the North, however, Jacobs suggests that her maternity is not the only cause for celebrating her body. Brent sees portraits of her friend Fanny's children and remarks, "I had never seen any paintings of colored people before, and they seemed to me beautiful" (162). With this statement, Jacobs subtly indicates that her readers must likewise see the black race anew. Jacob's autobiography, like Fanny's portraits, insists that the value and worth of the black female body exists outside of its functions in a patriarchal slaveholding society.

Important differences obviously exist between Jacob's antebellum autobiography and Maya Angelou's twentieth-century record of her rape at age eight in *I Know Why the Caged Bird Sings* (1969). One important difference is the way in which somatophobia manifests itself in their texts. Because Angelou does not have to contend with the nineteenth-century patriarchal ideology of "true womanhood," she is freer to portray her rape, her body, and her sexuality. Yet Jacobs describes herself as beautiful and sexually desirable, while Angelou, as a child and young adult, sees herself as ugly. Jacobs posits somatophobia outside herself and critiques it as part of slaveholding culture, while Angelou portrays her younger self internalizing and finally challenging the somatophobia inherent in twentieth-century racist conceptions of the black female body. Despite these differences, Angelou's text contains reembodying strategies similar to those of Jacobs. Both women contest somatophobia by questioning religious ideologies, rewriting white literary traditions, and celebrating their bodies and motherhood as symbols of their political struggles. In order to challenge racist stereotypes that associate black women with illicit sexuality, both writers obscure their corporeality in the early part of their texts by transforming the suffering connected with rape into a metaphor for the suffering of their race. In Jacob's text rape is a metaphor for the severed body and will of the slave, and Angelou similarly uses her rapist's violation of her body and will to explore the oppression of her black community.

Angelou first connects her rape with the suffering of the poor. "The act of rape on an eight-year-old body," she writes, "is a matter of the needle giving because the camel can't."[28] In this description, Angelou subtly links her rapist with the wealthy man whom Jesus warned would have a difficult time getting into heaven, and she reinforces this link by alluding to Jesus's words in her ironic description of a black revival congregation's sentiments: "The Lord loved the poor and hated those cast high in the world. Hadn't He Himself said it would be easier for a camel to go through the eye of a needle than for a rich man to enter heaven?" (108). As she continues to imagine the congregation's thoughts, Angelou makes the connection between her rape and the plight of the poor in class society more racially explicit, and, like Jacobs, she also demonstrates that privileging a future world over the present perpetuates black oppression:

> They [the congregation] basked in the righteousness of the poor and the exclusiveness of the downtrodden. Let the whitefolks have their money and power and segregation and sarcasm and big houses and schools and lawns like carpets, and books, and mostly—mostly—let them have their whiteness. (110)

With the image of the camel and the needle, Angelou transforms her rape into a symbol of the racism and somatophobia that afflict Maya and her race throughout much of *Caged Bird*.

Rape in Angelou's text, however, primarily represents the black girl's difficulties in controlling, understanding, and respecting both her body and her words in a somatophobic society that sees "sweet little white girls" as "everybody's dream of what was right with the world" (1). Angelou connects white definitions of beauty with rape by linking Maya's rape with her first sight of her mother, Vivian Baxter. Angelou's description of Vivian echoes that of the ghostlike whites who baffle young Maya. Vivian has "even white teeth and her fresh-butter color looked see-through clean" (49). Maya and her brother, Bailey, later determine that Vivian resembles a white movie star. Angelou writes that her mother's beauty "literally assailed" Maya and twice observes that she was "struck dumb" (49–50). This assault by her mother's beauty anticipates the physical assault by Mr. Freeman, her mother's boyfriend, and Maya's muteness upon meeting her mother foreshadows her silence after the rape. With this parallel Angelou indicates that both rape and the dominant white culture's definitions of beauty disempower the black woman's body and self-expression.

Angelou further demonstrates the intimate connection between the violation of Maya's body and the devaluation of her words by depicting her self-imposed silence after Freeman's rape trial. Freeman's pleading looks in the courtroom, along with Maya's own shame, compel her to lie, and after she learns that her uncles have murdered Freeman, she believes that her courtroom lie is responsible for his death. Angelou describes the emotions that silence Maya: "I could feel the evilness flowing through my body and waiting, pent up, to rush off my tongue if I tried to open my mouth. I clamped by teeth shut, I'd hold it in. If it escaped, wouldn't it flood the world and all the innocent people?" (72). Angelou's use of flood imagery in this crucial passage enables her to link Maya's inability to control her body and her words. Throughout the text Maya's failure to keep her bodily functions "pent up" signals the domination of her body by others. The autobiography's opening scene merges her inability to control her appearance, words, and bodily functions. Wanting to look like a "sweet little white girl," Maya is embarrassed about her own appearance and cannot remember the words of the Easter poem she recites. With her escape from the church, Angelou implicitly associates Maya's inability to rule her bladder with her inability to speak:

> I stumbled and started to say something, or maybe to scream, but a green persimmon, or it could have been a lemon, caught me between the legs and squeezed. I tasted the sour on my tongue and felt it in the back of my mouth. Then before I reached the door, the sting was burning down my legs and into my Sunday socks. I tried to hold, to squeeze it back, to keep it from speeding. (3)[29]

Maya's squeezing back in this passage anticipates her stopping the flood of her words after the rape, and Angelou also connects this opening scene of urination with one of Freeman's means of silencing Maya. After ejaculating on a mattress, he tells her that she has wet the bed, and with this lie, he denies her knowledge about her own body and confounds her ability to make a coherent story out of his actions.

This inability to create a story about her body pervades the remainder of *Caged Bird* as Maya struggles to cope with her emerging womanhood. Angelou, however, is not content to let the mute, sexually abused, wishing-to-be-white Maya represent the black female body in her text. Instead, she begins to reembody Maya by critiquing her admiration for white literary discourse. An early point at which Angelou foregrounds this critique is in Maya's meeting with Mrs. Bertha Flowers. Presenting this older black woman as the direct opposite of young Maya, Angelou stresses that Flowers magnificently rules both her words and her body. Indeed Flowers's bodily control seems almost supernatural: "She had the grace of control to appear warm in the coldest weather, and on the Arkansas summer days it seemed she had a private breeze which swirled around, cooling her" (77). She makes Maya proud to be black, and Maya claims that Flowers is more beautiful and "just as refined as whitefolks in movies and books" (79). Although Maya begins to respect and admire the black female body, white heroines still provide her standard for beauty, and Angelou pokes fun at the literary discourse that whitens Maya's view of Bertha Flowers and womanhood:

> She [Flowers] appealed to me because she was like people I had never met personally. Like women in English novels who walked the moors (whatever they were) with their loyal dogs racing at a respectful distance. Like the women who sat in front of roaring fireplaces, drinking tea incessantly from silver trays full of scones and crumpets. Women who walked over the 'heath' and read morocco-bound books. (79)

This humorous passage demonstrates that Maya's self-perception remains dangerously regulated by white culture. Angelou treats such regulation less comically when Flowers breaks Maya's self-imposed silence by asking her to read aloud. The first words Maya speaks after her long spell of muteness are those of Charles Dickens.

Angelou dramatizes the danger that a borrowed voice poses to Maya in her description of Maya's relationship with Viola Cullinan. Maya makes fun of this white woman, whose kitchen she briefly works in, until she discovers that Cullinan's husband has two daughters by a black woman. Then Maya—in a gesture of sisterhood and empathy that is never returned by Cullinan—pities her employer and decides to write a "tragic ballad" "on being white, fat, old and without children" (91). Such a ballad would, of course, completely exclude Maya's own experience: black, thin, young, and (near the end of her autobiography) with child. Through Maya's speculation that Cullinan walks around with no organs and drinks alcohol to keep herself "embalmed," Angelou implies that Maya's potential poetic identification with Cullinan nearly negates her own body. Cullinan's empty insides echo Maya's own perception of herself after the rape as a "gutless doll" she had earlier ripped to pieces (72).

Angelou's most complex and subtle examination of Maya's attachment to white literary discourse occurs when she lists as one of her accomplishments the memorization of Shakespeare's *The Rape of Lucrece*. Christine Froula maintains that Maya's feat of memory suggests the potential erasure of black female reality by white male literary discourse.[30] More specifically, I believe, Angelou's reference to *Lucrece* subtly indicates that Maya's

propensity for the verbal and the literary leads her to ignore her own corporeality. After their rapes both Maya and Lucrece turn to representations
of suffering women. Maya reads about Lucrece, and Lucrece, finding a
painting of the fall of Troy, views Hecuba's mourning the destruction of
her city and husband, King Priam. Unlike Lucrece, Maya seeks strength
not from pictorial representations of female bodies but from print, and this
preference for the verbal over the pictorial suggests her tendency to privilege literature over her own physical reality. Lucrece decides to speak for
the mute sufferers in the painting, and Shakespeare writes, "She lends them
words, and she their looks doth borrow."[31] Maya's situation is an inversion
of Lucrece's lending of words and borrowing of looks. The once mute
Maya can borrow Lucrece's words, but she must somehow lend these words
her own "looks" if she does not wish Shakespeare's equation of Lucrece's
virtue and whiteness to degrade her own blackness.[32] In remembering *The
Rape of Lucrece* Maya must also remember or reconstruct her own body.

One of the ways that she accomplishes this is by celebrating the bodies
of other black women. In the only story Maya creates within *Caged Bird*,
she augments her grandmother's physical and verbal powers. After a white
dentist refuses to treat Maya because she is black, Maya imagines her
grandmother ten feet tall, arms doubling in length. As this fantasy grandmother orders the dentist out of town and commands him to quit practicing dentistry, her words, too, metamorphose: "Her tongue had thinned and
the words rolled off well enunciated. Well enunciated and sharp like little
claps of thunder" (161). With Maya's brief fantasy, Angelou demonstrates
how her own autobiography functions. Maya's story, which empowers her
grandmother's body and speech, attacks the dentist's derogatory behavior;
Angelou's autobiography, which celebrates Maya's body and words, critiques the rape and racial oppression she suffers.

Maya finds, however, that her body and words exist uneasily together.
While in the early part of the narrative Maya depends heavily on
literature,[33] in the text's final San Francisco section, all words, particularly
those packaged as literature, fail to account for her adolescent body's
changes. Reading Radclyffe Hall's *The Well of Loneliness* (1928) leads Maya
to mistakenly interpret these changes as signals that she is becoming a lesbian. When Maya confronts her mother with this fear, Angelou further
demonstrates the inability of the verbal to explain the physical. Vivian's requiring Maya to read aloud the dictionary definition of the word "vulva"
echoes strangely Flowers's asking Maya to read aloud from Dickens. Unlike
Dickens's prose, however, Noah Webster's and Vivian's words lose their
soothing power as soon as Maya is confronted with a stronger physical reality—her own admiration for her girlfriend's fully developed breasts. This

scene in which Maya shifts her attention from words to bodies paves the way for Angelou's concluding celebration of the black female body.

Seeking physical rather than verbal knowledge of her sexuality, Maya determines to have sex with one of "the most eligible young men in the neighborhood" (239). Their encounter, which "is unredeemed by shared tenderness" (240), leaves sixteen-year-old Maya pregnant and alone. The young man quits talking to her in her fourth month, and Maya's brother, who is overseas, advises her not to tell her parents until she graduates from high school. Yet it would be wrong to see Maya's motherhood as "a tragic way to end the book and begin life as an adult."[34] While Angelou portrays the pain and confusion resulting from Maya's pregnancy, she places a far greater emphasis on her newfound autonomy. Even Maya's naive style of seduction accentuates her feminist stance. She asks the young man, "Would you like to have a sexual intercourse with me?" (239). In posing this straightforward question, Maya claims control of her body and her identity for the first time in the text. Just as Jacobs describes Brent's union with Sands as a union of her body and will, Angelou celebrates Maya's encounter with the young man. She accentuates Maya's reclamation of her body and volition by ironically alluding to the violation she suffered as an eight-year-old. "Thanks to Mr. Freeman nine years before," asserts Angelou, "I had had no pain of entry to endure" (240).

By detailing how the pregnant Maya copes with her isolation, Angelou pays further tribute to Maya's increased autonomy and acceptance of her own body. Beginning to reject the literary myths that led her to deny her own agency, Maya accepts complete responsibility for her pregnancy: "For eons, it seemed, I had accepted my plight as the hapless, put-upon victim of fate and the Furies, but this time I had to face the fact that I had brought my new catastrophe upon myself" (241). This acceptance of responsibility also leads Maya to a greater acceptance of her own body's powers: "I had a baby. He was beautiful and mine. Totally mine. No one had bought him for me. No one had helped me endure the sickly gray months. I had had help in the child's conception, but no one could deny that I had had an immaculate pregnancy" (245). Angelou's use of the word "immaculate" not only challenges racist stereotypes that associate black women with illicit sexuality, but it also suggests the Maya has shed her earlier conceptions of her body as "dirty like mud" (2) and "shit-colored" (17). Because the eight-year-old Maya perceives her own mother as looking like the "Virgin Mary" (57), the word "immaculate" also indicates that the teenage Maya begins to see in herself the power and beauty she sees in Vivian.

Maya's lack of confidence in her body briefly returns, however, in the autobiography's final paragraphs. Vivian's suggestion that Maya sleep with

her child accentuates her worry that she is too clumsy to handle a baby.
Vivian banishes this fear by waking Maya and showing her the baby sleeping under a tent that Maya unconsciously formed with her body and a blan-
ket. "See," Vivian whispers, "you don't have to think about doing the right
thing. If you're for the right thing then you do it without thinking" (246).
Presenting the mother/child bond as a symbol of Maya's newfound autonomy, this closing scene reverses her earlier privileging of the verbal over
the physical and celebrates the harmonious interaction of her body and will.

Rape can destroy a woman's autonomy and self-image, yet Jacobs and Angelou transform this potentially destructive event into an opportunity to celebrate their resistance to somatophobia and negative stereotypes about the
black female body. An early scene in *Caged Bird* serves as a synecdoche for
the reembodiment both Angelou and Jacobs accomplish in recording their
experiences of rape. Three "powhitetrash" girls ape the posture and singing
of Maya's grandmother, yet she emerges victorious and beautiful from this
degradation and calms the enraged Maya. Afterward Maya rakes away the
girls' footprints in the lawn and creates a new pattern: "a large heart with lots
of hearts growing smaller inside, and piercing from the outside rim to the
smallest heart was an arrow" (27). These connected hearts, which represent
the bond between Maya and her grandmother, encapsulate Angelou's and
Jacob's celebration of black motherhood as a sign of personal autonomy. In
the grandmother's triumph over the white girls who mock and caricature her
body, and in young Maya's erasure of their footprints, I see Angelou's and
Jacob's refutation of negative stereotypes about their bodies. Maya's newly
raked pattern resembles their autobiographies—their writings (or rightings)
of the black female body outside of dominant cultural definitions.

NOTES

1.   Susan Stanford Friedman, "Women's Autobiographical Selves: Theory
and Practice," in *The Private Self: Theory and Practice of Women's Autobiographical
Writings*, ed. Shari Benstock (Chapel Hill: Univ. of North Carolina Press, 1988), 37.

2.   Susan Griffin argues that even the fear of rape causes women to negate
their bodies: "The fear of rape permeates our lives. . . . the best defense against this
is not to be, to deny being in the body." See *Rape: The Power of Consciousness* (New
York: Harper, 1979), qtd. in Jacquelyn Dowd Hall, "'The Mind That Burns in
Each Body': Women, Rape, and Racial Violence," in *Powers of Desire: The Politics of
Sexuality:* ed. Ann Snitow, Christine Stansell, and Sharon Thompson (New York:
Monthly Review Press, 1983), 333.

3.   Elizabeth V. Spelman, *Inessential Woman: Problems of Exclusion in Feminist
Thought* (Boston: Beacon Press, 1988), 30, 126–31. While I assume that disdain for

the female body is inherent in patriarchal ideology, I do not perceive this ideology as monolithic, and I discuss somatophobia's differing manifestations in Shakespeare's, Harriet Jacobs's, and Maya Angelou's times.

4.   Ian Donaldson provides a detailed analysis of the role of the Lucretia myth in Samuel Richardson's *Clarissa* (1747–48), a novel that greatly influenced American novels of seduction before and during Jacobs's time. See *The Rapes of Lucretia: A Myth and Its Transformations* (Oxford: Clarendon, 1982), 57–82.

5.   William Shakespeare, *The Poems*, ed. F. T. Prince (London: Methuen, 1974), 1655–56.

6.   Stephanie H. Jed, *Chaste Thinking: The Rape of Lucretia and the Birth of Humanism* (Bloomington: Indiana Univ. Press, 1989), 13.

7.   Shakespeare, 1184–90. Shakespeare's sources similarly privilege an integral self over the body.

8.   There are many good feminist readings of *Lucrece*. My reading is most influenced by Coppélia Kahn, "The Rape in Shakespeare's *Lucrece*," *Shakespeare Studies* 9 (1976): 45–72.

9.   Spelman, 126–32.

10.   Darlene Clark Hine, "Rape and the Inner Lives of Black Women in the Middle West: Preliminary Thoughts on the Culture of Dissemblance," *Signs* 14 (1989): 917–20. In examining dissemblance, Hine also states that antebellum black women had to "collectively create alternative self-images and shield from scrutiny these private empowering definitions of self" in order to function in white patriarchal America (916). I will show how Jacobs and Angelou make their empowering self-definitions public in their autobiographies.

11.   Because of the vast scholarship on negative stereotypes about the black woman's body, I will cite only those works that most strongly informed this essay. bell hooks, *Ain't I a Woman: Black Women and Feminism* (Boston: South End Press, 1981), 15–86: Angela Y. Davis, *Women, Race and Class* (New York: Random House, 1981); Hazel V. Carby, *Reconstructing Womanhood: The Emergence of the Afro-American Woman Novelist* (New York: Oxford Univ. Press, 1987), 20–61; Barbara Christian, *Black Feminist Criticism: Perspectives on Black Women Writers* (New York: Pergamon Press, 1985), 1–30; Christian, *Black Women Novelists: The Development of a Tradition, 1892–1976* (Westport: Greenwood Press, 1980); Sondra O'Neale, "Inhibiting Midwives, Usurping Creators: The Struggling Emergence of Black Women in American Fiction," in *Feminist Studies/Critical Studies*, ed. Teresa de Lauretis (Bloomington: Indiana Univ. Press, 1986), 139–56; Sander L. Gilman, "Black Bodies, White Bodies: Toward an Iconography of Female Sexuality in Late Nineteenth-Century Art, Medicine, and Literature," in *"Race" Writing, and Difference*, ed. Henry Louis Gates, Jr. (Chicago: Chicago Univ. Press, 1985), 223–61; Barbara Omolade, "Hearts of Darkness," in *Powers of Desire: The Politics of Sexuality*, ed. Ann Snitow, Christine Stansell, and Sharon Thompson (New York: Monthly Review Press, 1983), 350–70; Frances Foster, "'In Respect to Females. . . .': Differences in the Portrayals of Women by Male and Female Narrators," *Black American Literature Forum* 15(1981): 66–70; Hall; and Hine.

12.   bell hooks, *Talking Back: Thinking Feminist, Thinking Black* (Boston: South End Press, 1989), 140. hooks's challenge is indeed a difficult one. As Barbara Christian observes, "The garb of uninhibited passion wears better on a male, who after all, does not have to carry the burden of the race's morality or lack of it" (*Novelists*, 40).

13.   All the names in Jacobs's text are pseudonyms. Dr. Flint is a fictitious name for Jacobs's former master, James Norcom. In this paper I will refer to the author of the autobiography as Jacobs, and to the actor within it as Brent. In order to avoid confusion, I will call the other people Jacobs writes about by their pseudonyms.

14.   For the basic tenets of "true womanhood" see Barbara Welter, *Dimity Convictions: The American Woman in the Nineteenth Century* (Columbus: Ohio Univ. Press, 1976), 21. For discussions of Jacobs's subversion of sentimental discourse see Carby, 20–61; Jean Fagan Yellin, "Texts and Contexts of Harriet Jacobs' *Incidents in the Life of a Slave Girl: Written by Herself* " in *The Slave's Narrative*, ed. Charles T. Davis and Henry Louis Gates, Jr. (New York: Oxford Univ. Press, 1985), 262–82; Yellin, introduction, *Incidents in the Life of a Slave Girl*, by Harriet Jacobs, ed. Yellin (Cambridge: Harvard Univ. Press, 1987), xiii–xxxiv; Valerie Smith, *Self-Discovery and Authority in Afro-American Narrative* (Cambridge: Harvard Univ. Press, 1987), 35–43; Joanne M. Braxton, "Harriet Jacobs' *Incidents in the Life of a Slave Girl:* The Re-Definition of the Slave Narrative Genre," *Massachusetts Review* 27 (1986): 379–87; Claudia Tate, "Allegories of Black Female Desire; or, Rereading Nineteenth-Century Sentimental Narratives of Black Female Authority," *Changing Our Own Words: Essays on Criticism, Theory, and Writing by Black Women* (New Brunswick: Rutgers Univ. Press, 1989), 108–11; and Mary Helen Washington, *Invented Lives: Narratives of Black Women 1860–1960* (Garden City: Doubleday, 1987), 3–15.

15.   Susanna Rowson, *Charlotte Temple*, ed. Clara M. and Rudolf Kirk (New Haven: College and Univ. Press, 1964), 117. For an excellent discussion of how eighteenth-century English novels represented a split between the rape victim's body and mind see Frances Ferguson, "Rape and the Rise of the Novel," *Representations* 20 (1987): 88–110.

16.   Welter, 23.

17.   As Susan Staves observes, the idea of seduction is incomprehensible "if women have no rights over their own bodies but are simply the property of men to use as they will, as female slaves were the property of slaveowners." See "British Seduced Maidens," *Eighteenth-Century Studies* 14 (1981): 116.

18.   Harriet Jacobs, *Incidents in the Life of a Slave Girl*, ed. Jean Fagan Yellin (Cambridge: Harvard Univ. Press, 1987), 27. Future references to this text will be inserted parenthetically.

19.   William L. Andrews, "Dialogue in Antebellum Afro-American Autobiography," in *Studies in Autobiography*, ed. James Olney (New York: Oxford Univ. Press, 1988), 94. Braxton observes that Brent "uses 'sass' the way Frederick Douglass uses his fists and his feet, as a means of expressing her resistance" (386).

20.   Carby's second chapter in *Reconstructing Womanhood*, "Slave and Mistress: Ideologies of Womanhood under Slavery" (20–39), is an excellent study of how nineteenth-century conception of "lady" and "womanhood" depended upon the exclusion of black women.

21.   Carby, 57–59; Yellin, introduction, xxx–xxxi; Tate, 108–09; Washington, xxiii, 6–7.

22.   Washington, xxiii.

23.   Andrews, *To Tell a Free Story: The First Century of Afro-American Autobiography 1760–1865* (Urbana: Univ. of Chicago Press, 1986), 259.

24.   For a discussion of how privileging a discrete spiritual realm increased patriarchal authority's control over the bodies of enslaved people and white women in antebellum America, see Karen Sanchez-Eppler, "Bodily Bonds: The Intersecting Rhetorics of Feminism and Abolition," *Representations* 24 (1988): 49–50.

25.   Jane Tompkins, *Sensational Designs: The Cultural Work of American Fiction* (New York: Oxford Univ. Press, 1985), 150–51.

26.   Valerie Smith, 32.

27.   For discussions of Jacobs's depiction of her motherhood as a source of her personal autonomy; see Carby, 40–61; Tate, 107–10; and Braxton, *passim*.

28.   Maya Angelou, *I Know Why the Caged Bird Sings* (New York: Bantam, 1969), 65. Future references to this text will be inserted parenthetically. I will refer to the author of *Caged Bird* as Angelou, and to the actor within it as Maya. In my reading of the early part of Angelou's autobiography, I am indebted to Sidonie Smith's discussion of Maya's quest after her "self-accepted black womanhood," to Liliane K. Arensberg's analysis of Maya's dependence on books, and to Francoise Lionnet's exploration of how Angelou makes her body the source and model of her creativity. See Smith, "The Song of the Caged Bird: Maya Angelou's Quest for Self-Acceptance," *Southern Humanities Review* 7 (1973): 365–75; Arensberg, "Death as Metaphor of Self in *I Know Why the Caged Bird Sings*," *CLA* 20 (1970): 275–76; Lionnet, *Autobiographical Voices: Race, Gender, Self-Portraiture* (Ithaca: Cornell Univ. Press, 1989), 130–68. I differ from these readers in that I discuss the somatophobia and racism in white literary discourse as significant obstacles that Maya must overcome before she can begin to recover from her rape and take pride in her body.

29.   For another examination of this opening scene and for a consideration of Angelou's other images of flowing liquids and rhythms, see Lionnet, 134–35, 146. Unlike Lionnet, I emphasize Maya's attempts to control her body and words.

30.   Christine Froula, "The Daughter's Seduction: Sexual Violence and Literary History," *Signs* 11 (1986): 673.

31.   Shakespeare, 1498. He devotes over two hundred lines to Lucrece's viewing of this painting (1367–1569) and contrasts the muteness of the painted Hecuba with Lucrece's venting of grief and outrage at her rape:

On this sad shadow [Hecuba] Lucrece spends her eyes,
And shapes her sorrow to the beldame's woes,
Who nothing wants to answer her but cries,

And bitter words to ban her cruel foes;
The painter was no god to lend her those,
And therefore Lucrece swears he did her wrong,
To give her so much grief, and not a tongue. (1457–64)

32.   The following lines typify the many times Shakespeare makes this equation throughout his poem: "This heraldry in Lucrece' face was seen, / Argued by beauty's red and virtue's white" (64–65).

33.   Arensberg, 275–76, and Lionnet, *passim*. Neither critic discusses Maya's dependence on literature in the San Francisco section of *Caged Bird*.

34.   Stephanie A. Demetrakopoulos, "The Metaphysics of Matrilinearism in Women's Autobiography: Studies of Mead's *Blackberry Winter*, Hellman's *Pentimento*, Angelou's *I Know Why The Caged Bird Sings*, and Kingston's *The Woman Warrior*," in *Women's Autobiography: Essays in Criticism*, ed. Estelle C. Jelinek (Bloomington: Indiana Univ. Press, 1980), 189.

Analysis of Application

Mary Vermillion's "Reembodying the Self" offers an intriguing feminist analysis of two texts, Harriet Jacobs's *Incidents in the Life of a Slave Girl* and Maya Angelou's *I Know Why the Caged Bird Sings;* these are works that she interprets with reference to a history of specifically male literary representations of raped and seduced women. Her literary and cultural critical task is a difficult one: to trace how women who write about their own experiences of rape succeed in reasserting authority over their own bodies and reclaiming a self that includes sexuality and a positive sense of physicality. Throughout she emphasizes not only the power of patriarchal notions of women's bodies and sexuality but also the power of individual women to resist dominant definitions and impositions.

Vermillion's essay succeeds structurally because it isolates its specific purpose in an introductory section that examines somatophobia in its differential impact on men, women, and, finally, black women specifically. Vermillion then focuses on her precise textual interest: autobiographical accounts of rape written by black women. She investigates a complex cultural milieu, from Plato through Shakespeare and then eighteenth-century novelists, as she explores the arduous task faced by black women who work to assert their autonomous, sexual selves after enduring an act that denies autonomy and denigrates, even threatens to destroy, those selves. In separate sections, she carefully examines the nuances of self-representation and self-empowerment that are present in two texts that, although written a century apart, still share certain characteristics because they respond to a similar, long-standing cultural heritage, even as they diverge in other characteristics because of their different historical contexts.

In both sections of analysis, Vermillion focuses on "reembodying" strategies, specific acts taken by women who have been raped as they work to reassert their autonomy and sexual selves. For Jacobs, this involves using her body sexually to achieve certain goals and finally asserting her maternity as a "symbol of her of autonomy." Angelou also chooses sexual self-expression and then comes to celebrate her childbearing and maternal roles as ones of power and recovered selfhood. In both sections, Vermillion draws carefully on quotations from the autobiographical texts, from the works of other literary and cultural critics, and from a long history of somatophobic and patriarchal representations of women, as she constructs a finely nuanced interpretation of two women's successful struggles with personal trauma and social oppression.

Of course, no one work of feminist analysis can adequately represent all the possible methodologies and interests that fall under the heading "feminism." Vermillion, however, touches on several issues raised in this chapter's overview and list of principles. She isolates a history of oppressive conceptions of women's bodies and sexualities; she then reveals her own interest in discovering effective resistance to such conceptions; she complicates and enriches her argument with an examination of race- as well as gender-based oppression; and, finally, she reflects some of the latest interests in corporeality—the ways that our physical bodies are sites for intense social and cultural struggles over definitions and desires. It is also worth noting that Vermillion focuses on a genre—autobiography—that allows her to establish links between literary representation and life outside the text. Thus there is a social immediacy and real-world applicability to the analysis that she offers. She thereby reflects a long history in feminist criticism of making the work that critics do socially relevant. Yet Vermillion also sticks close to the texts at hand, using textual detail throughout and ending her essay with an example of a powerful synecdoche. While another critic's opinions, interests, and application of feminist theory might differ significantly from Vermillion's, her essay is exemplary in its structure, use of evidence, and delineation of a precise outlook and purpose.

Gay/Lesbian/
Queer Analysis

Overview

As with the field of feminist textual and cultural analysis (discussed in the preceding chapter), that of gay/lesbian/queer analysis actually encompasses many different methodologies, drawing potentially on theories of post-structuralism, gender, race, class, and psychology. Indeed, its areas of interest are also numerous; they are as diverse as the many possibilities of human desire and the self-definitions that desire can generate or influence. Even so, there are some significant analytical commonalities that can be discussed profitably within the space of a brief chapter. Primary among these is that all practitioners of gay/lesbian/queer analysis focus on sexuality as a particularly important component of human identity, social organization, and textual representation; this differentiates it clearly from most other fields. But more specifically, critics working in this field explore precisely why and how desire between members of the same sex has been socially valued and textually represented far differently than has desire between men and women.

While textual evidence of same-sex desire dates back to the ancient Greeks, sustained analysis of it has been generated most openly and energetically since the advent of the nationally prominent gay rights movement in the late 1960s and early 1970s (which followed more localized and often covert movements of previous decades). From the start, the power of words and representations was central to this movement. "Gay" became a term of political commitment, one signaling an explicit rejection of the medical label "homosexual" (which since its coinage in the late nineteenth century had often carried with it an implied diagnosis of illness). Even so, the frequent use of "gay" as an umbrella term covering both men and women posed new problems concerning whose interests were reflected by it, for it obscured the unique problems faced by same-sex-desiring women who were doubly oppressed because of their gender and sexuality; this has led, of course, to a common and more precise differentiation between "lesbians" and "gay" men. The complex ways in which these two groups' interests both converge and diverge highlight the challenges generated by any identity label, which always obscures some differences in order to dramatize others. Recent years have seen new debates over such political issues of identity. Two decades after the birth of the gay rights movement, the brash reclaiming of the term "queer" (propelled by the need to build coalitions in response to the AIDS crisis) again linked the interests of sexually nonconforming men and women, including transgendered individuals. As might be expected, its erasure of distinctions among such groups continues to be a topic of heated discussion.

As is the case with any field growing out of political engagement, debates among gay/lesbian/queer critics, theorists, and activists are actually a sign of health and intellectual vigor. And no topic has generated more useful and substantive discussion than that of the historical contingency and cultural specificity of same-sex-desire. Some theorists posit a core identity for same-sex-desiring individuals that has endured through the ages; this stance is often termed "essentialism" because of its suggestion of a transhistorical "essence." Other theorists suggest that desire is largely dependent on historical circumstances and prevailing social definitions; this stance is known as "constructionism" because of its insistence on the socially constructed, highly contingent nature of any form of sexual desire and expression. It is impossible to resolve the disagreement between the two camps here, but it is important to note that they do not have to be perceived as irreconcilably polarized. While it is highly improbable that homosexuality has remained unchanged over the ages (given that everything else has changed significantly, including gender roles and definitions of social class), recent scientific research suggesting some connection between genetics or physiology and sexual identity might indicate that same-sex desire has persisted as a significant trait for some people throughout the ages. But certainly we must recognize that the ways in which such a trait either did or did not lead to a privately or publicly identifying stance (known today as a "coming-out" statement) have varied widely. Indeed, one of the most important avenues for research into textual representations of gay/lesbian/queer identity is the examination of exactly how a given age defines sexual and other forms of social identity, what language an individual or group uses to self-identify, what sort of response that identity elicits from others, and what impact historically specific forms of self-identification have on textual representation.

As with Marxist, materialist, and feminist analysis, gay/lesbian/queer analysis therefore demands not only a careful examination of the text but also research into context. The critic must understand the norms and terminology of a given time period (it would be anachronistic, for example, to transplant current notions of urban lesbian identity into considerations of Renaissance texts). Similarly, the critic cannot make facile assumptions across cultures (in many parts of the world, for example, men hold hands while walking down the street; but they are not thereby indicating sexual involvement, however accurately one might interpret similar activity by men in New York as a forthright indication of their sexuality). Thus it is imperative that literary and cultural critics collect not only textual but also extratextual—historical and cultural—evidence before drawing conclusions about the meaning of any supposed sign of sexual identity or activity. Nothing about sexuality or sexual identity can be posited as obvious or self-evident.

Indeed, the entire notion of sexual identity as obviously real is currently under considerable scrutiny. In recent years, queer theory has come to question the very bases on which we claim and manifest a specifically sexual identity. Drawing on post-structuralism (discussed in Chapter 6), as well as work in social theory, queer theory has sought to question all assumptions of "normality," including lesbian and gay demands to be treated as "normal." For example, even as many gay and lesbian activists have focused on the legalization of same-sex marriages, some queer theorists have been far more interested in critiquing marriage as a limited and outdated model. Similarly, bisexual theorists and activists have questioned the legitimacy of polarized sexual identities, suggesting that more fluid sexual possibilities exist than are recognized by the heterosexual/homosexual paradigm. What does it mean that many individuals manifest both heterosexual and homosexual behaviors at some time in their lives and that those behaviors change over time? Transgender and transsexual theorists have even worked to disrupt the notion that only two sexes exist and have challenged the belief that the sex to which one is assigned at birth constitutes one's natural identity, especially given new technologies that allow dramatic changes in what had been considered fixed biological fact. All the above stances have opened up new possibilities for the analysis of literary and other cultural texts; representations of sexual activity and identity and the processes by which sexuality is given social value can serve as the basis for compelling investigations of how we define ourselves and others and to what degree we treat human diversity with respect or disapproval.

Key Principles

1 *Even though sexuality is often considered a highly private matter, it is thoroughly connected to our social existence.*

Gay/lesbian/queer analysis foregrounds sexuality as an important aspect of social existence. This is not to say that critics working in the field are sex-obsessed, but rather that they treat sexuality as a legitimate topic for analysis, which means that a given essay, article, or book may be wholly devoted to it (just as one might be devoted to an investigation of race or class). Indeed, sexuality has significance far beyond the physical acts that partly comprise it; prevailing attitudes about sexual, emotional, and erotic activity can tell us much about systems of social classification, about a society's economic and political priorities, and about the degree to which human diversity and personal freedom are respected at a given time and place. In probing, for example, whether a sexually involved couple (unmarried heterosexual or homosexual) are allowed to cohabit, for example, the critic can explore the social valence of religion, the impact of economic conditions on the norms of adult cohabitation, and the ways in which a given culture may need a social scapegoat and perhaps find one in sexual nonconformists. And because sexuality has been so often linked explicitly with reproduction, it is a subject area particularly well situated to offer insight into the processes by which culture itself reproduces, how it ensures its own survival and that of its values.

2 *Negative social attitudes about expressions of sexual desire between members of the same sex have had a profound impact on many individuals' public and private lives.*

While the debate about how many people are gay, lesbian, or bisexual today (or at some time in the past) is unresolvable, expressions of same-sex desire are evident in texts from the classical Greek era to the present day. It is also clear that expressions of sexual desire between members of the same sex have been treated far differently than expressions of sexual desire between men and women. While classical Greek society viewed as legitimate—and even idealized—some manifestations of same-sex desire (between adult men and youths in Plato's *Symposium*, for instance), such activity has been severely proscribed in most of the Western world since that time. Two terms have been coined to describe this general dynamic of oppression: "homophobia" (which suggests an irrational fear of same-sex-desiring people) and "heterosexism" (which suggests a social and institutional prejudice against same-sex-desiring people and the active forms of discrimination that follow from it). The force of homophobia and hetero-sexism is indisputable, shown most dramatically in statistical data on the high rate of violent assaults on gays and lesbians, in oppressive laws concerning sexual contact between consenting adults of the same sex, and in common literary and artistic portrayals of evil or pathetic sexual "deviants." In simply examining the options available to same-sex couples compared to male/female couples during the same time period—their ability to marry or simply live together without social stigma, to walk hand-in-hand down the street, to visit each other in the hospital during times of grave illness, or to share health insurance—the critic can chart the concrete manifestations and precise contours of homophobia and heterosexism at a given time and place.

3 *Yet social attitudes about sexuality have changed dramatically over time.*

But even though same-sex desire has often been condemned and certainly has been subject to active forms of discrimination, social attitudes about sexuality and the terms through which notions of proper and improper forms of sexual expression have been expressed have changed significantly over time. More than two thousand years ago, Plato theorized that all individuals sought out their perfect complement and that this complement could be of the opposite or the same sex, but his relatively nondiscriminatory model had little social influence after the ancient Greek era. With the rise of Christianity and its restriction of sexual propriety to the framework of marriage and reproduction, same-sex desire and other forms of desire that fell outside the prescribed parameters (such as adulterous desire) came under powerful new social regulations, although these, too, were by no means uniform. Some scholars have suggested that "sodomites" (a quasi-biblical term for individuals who have had sexual contact with another person of the same sex) were often treated no more harshly than adulterers or other sexual nonconformists (though certainly that treatment could still be quite harsh). Others have shown that in certain communities such individuals were singled out for punishment as clear threats to an entire social framework of mandated reproduction (which expanding nations and economies depended on to ensure their future prominence). And with the medical and psychiatric designation of the "homosexual" as a diagnosable "case" in the late nineteenth century, the terms changed again, with a new emphasis placed on the causes, and even possible cures, for what was perceived as an affliction. And finally, with the rise of civil rights movements and with expanded notions of sexual freedom during the last half of the twentieth century, social definitions of sexuality again shifted, with varying uses of terms such as "gay," "lesbian," and "queer" demanding careful attention to context and precise time period. Thus at various times in history, even a simple act such as two adult women or men setting up housekeeping together might be socially interpreted and responded to in very different ways. An investigation into why that variation exists will take the critic into analysis of differing economic, religious, and gender norms as they have existed across times and cultures.

Indeed, it is very important to remember that sexual acts, narrowly defined, are not all that the forces of homophobia and heterosexism regulate and proscribe. A wide range of attachments, friendships, bondings, and other interpersonal connections may be analyzed by examining a given culture's treatment of same-sex-desiring couples. Leslie Fiedler and Eve Sedgwick are only two of the many critics who have examined the homoerotic and homosocial subcurrents in American and British society and literature. Works by writers such as Hermann Melville and Charles Dickens may demonstrate intense emotional bondings between male characters; such relationships may have little to do with actual genital sexual contact, but how they are demonstrated and regulated may tell us much about how some forms of bonding are allowed while others harshly treated in a given culture, as well as about how "pure" forms of friendship and emotional attachment help cement social bonds, even though that cement always threatens to crumble when attachment becomes even slightly too intense or slips incrementally toward proscribed physical interactions. Thus gay/lesbian/queer analysis has many implications for the lives of heterosexual individuals, who may find their own close friendships with members of the same sex viewed suspiciously during times of virulent homophobia.

4 *Social attitudes about sexuality have differed significantly for men and women.*

But attitudes toward men's and women's sexuality have differed significantly not only over time but even within the same time period. Given the profound force of patriarchy (the wielding of most forms of political and social power by men during much of Western history), men's same-sex desires have been treated very differently from women's. In some circumstances, desire between men has been perceived as a profoundly dangerous threat to the very foundation of society, since that foundation was defined specifically as male and was thought to be ensured by men's doing exactly as the "common good" dictated (in other words, engaging in reproductive sex within marriage). On the other hand, certain powerful men have managed at times to use their power to act as they wished, flaunting sexual norms without fear of reprisal because of their social standing and ability to "buy" tolerance. Social attitudes about expressions of same-sex desire between women have varied as well. At times, the very existence of women's sexuality has been denied; in some instances, this could mean even less freedom than that allowed men because any manifestation of sexuality (except in the form of a passive response to reproductive demands) was seen as unnatural and therefore as requiring a harsh social response. On the other hand, sexual expressions between women have sometimes been completely ignored as being meaningless or even impossible, thus allowing sexual diversity to exist under cover, so to speak, without severe penalty. "Boston marriages"—instances of unmarried women cohabiting, at times for all their adult lives—were often tolerated during the nineteenth century, partly because women were not seen as capable of sexual existence apart from men. These wide variations and uneven implications of social power structures demonstrate just how complex and idiosyncratic relationships between individuals and their cultural contexts can be, which makes the work of the literary and cultural critic both exciting and difficult.

5 *Social attitudes about sexuality have differed significantly across cultures, regions, classes, and ethnic groups.*

The preceding principles demand precision in any discussion of sexuality, and that need for precision extends as well to discussion of cultural, class-related, and ethnic issues. Social rules, religious belief systems, customs, and laws vary widely among world cultures. Notions of American lesbian or gay experience cannot be transplanted to North Africa or Polynesia, for example, where forms of same-sex eroticism that are very different from American experiences may be allowed within certain narrow confines. Even within the same nation, attitudes can vary widely by region; lesbian and gay experiences in the rural South of the United States are quite different from those in San Francisco. Similarly, attitudes can vary widely among ethnic groups, whose traditions, religious influences, and degree of access to support networks can play important roles in an individual's experience and expression of same-sex desire. Finally, social class also has an impact on the relative freedom with which one can pursue a nonconformist lifestyle; as mentioned above, with wealth can sometimes come the ability to flaunt social rules. On the other hand, difficult economic conditions may mean that unmarried adults of the same sex must live together in order to survive, which may also mean that a "closeted" same-sex couple can create a covert existence for themselves. While daunting, these many variables do not mean that interpretation is hopelessly complex and therefore impossible; instead they help provide the very subject matter of interpretation. Sexuality may (or may not) be a limited component of a given individual's daily life, but it is so thoroughly connected with multiple aspects of that individual's social existence that it almost always provides a very productive field for literary and cultural analysis.

6 *All notions of "normality"—sexual, gender-related, and otherwise—are appropriate subjects for critique and historical investigation.*

Given the many variables mentioned above, it is clear that notions of "normality" demand careful scrutiny, and queer theory, in particular, takes the injunction to question everything very seriously. It probes how definitions of the "normal" have come into being and how they work to regulate lives. As mentioned in the overview, the common paradigm of monogamous coupling is one that some critics and activists have found highly confining and reflective of unquestioned social customs. Some queer critics have suggested that lesbians and gays who simply mirror heterosexual conventions, such as marriage, are in fact assimilationist, in that they accept without critical scrutiny certain dominant roles and conventions, seeking to assimilate themselves into society rather than critique and, if necessary, change it in fundamental ways. Other theorists have suggested that the very categories "homosexuality" and "heterosexuality" are time-bound and restrictive, and that more fluid, "bisexual" human potentials are especially productive avenues for investigation. Still others have critiqued our restrictive notions of biological sex to explore how those individuals who do not fit into narrow categories such as "man" and "woman" (through biology, behavior, and/or forms of personal self-identification) further complicate and can help illuminate the dynamics of sexual desire and the roles that social definitions play in sexuality. While those theorists self-identifying as lesbian or gay often take a fixed sexual identity as one of the few givens in a discussion, many queer critics accept little as fixed or self-evident (for more information on the post-structuralist background of queer analysis, see Chapter 6).

7 *Social attitudes about sexuality resonate through literary and other cultural texts.*

As we have seen through investigations of methodologies such as feminism and materialism, literary and other cultural texts reflect the belief systems circulating in the society from which they emerge. Thus social attitudes about sexuality will be reflected in texts, just as attitudes about gender and class are reflected there. But authors are not simple mouthpieces for political and other social institutions; they shape and modify the belief systems surrounding them in individualistic fashions. The many aspects of human diversity that help account for this individualism of aesthetic expression may include, of course, an author's own sexuality. This is not to suggest, however, that it is always necessary to pinpoint the sexuality or sexual practices of a given author; indeed, sexual identity is often impossible to establish, given that many people conceal or deny the full range of their sexual desires. And even if it is possible to establish through clear biographical evidence that an author is gay or lesbian, it is erroneous to assume immediately that this identity will be manifested clearly or treated with tolerance in a given text; homosexuals certainly can act in a heterosexist manner because of their social training and perceptions of audience expectations (the term sometimes used to describe this dynamic is "internalized homophobia"). Thus it is always necessary to judge themes, characterizations, and other textual concerns with great care, because the belief systems surrounding a text may intrude in ways that cannot be reduced to authorial biography or intent.

And these belief systems affect not only the creation of texts but also their reception and social uses. Those authors who do incorporate into their works themes that are clearly relevant to gay or lesbian identities have sometimes been ignored by critics and literary anthologists. At other times, anthologies may include only those works that do not portray lesbian or gay sexualities, even if others exist by the same author that do contain gay- or lesbian-relevant themes and characterizations. On the other hand, the gay and lesbian market for books, movies, and other texts has been recognized recently as being very lucrative, so new strategies to meet the needs of such an audience have further complicated how texts circulate through our culture. These complex extratextual connections between sexuality and textuality provide many opportunities for cultural analysis.

8 *Social attitudes about sexuality may be discernible in the themes of literary and other cultural texts.*

Many works of analysis that deploy gay/lesbian/queer methodologies focus primarily on a text's thematic reflections of social attitudes about sexuality. Some texts contain explicit references to gay/lesbian/queer demands for justice or recognition, but for those that do not, relevant analysis could begin as a response to some of the following basic questions. Does the text promote a notion of proper sexual and affectional attachment as existing only within the confines of the traditional marriage between a man and a woman? How are gender or sexually nonconforming characters related to the themes of the work—are they villains, heroes, incidental to the plot, or completely absent from it? Where does a given text draw the lines on expressions of affection between members of the same sex, and how does this relate to its portrayal of health and happiness? Are some manifestations of sexual nonconformity treated with tolerance (such as affairs between men and women) and others condemned (such as the possibility of same-sex desire)? In addressing such questions, it is only necessary to continue probing why and how a text defines sexual "normality" to begin to generate gay/lesbian/queer analysis.

9 *Social attitudes about sexuality may be discernible in the characterizations present in literary and other cultural texts.*

As suggested in the preceding discussion, a focus on individual characterizations may be particularly revealing. If you perceive gender and sexually nonconforming characters in the text, can you explain precisely how they diverge from the norms of their historical and cultural context? Do you find any clues in the text to account for why they are nonconforming? Are they portrayed as born that way or created through environmental factors? Are such characters punished for their behavior or portrayed as requiring punishment for the good of society? If such characters are portrayed positively, how do they manage to thrive in the face of forces that mandate conformity? Must they make compromises in order to survive? What internal qualities do they possess or acquire that account for their ability to endure? Do they struggle with questions about their own sexuality or sexual identity? If so, what factors account for how they resolve their struggle? In answering such questions, you will move inevitably between text and context, considering perhaps how characterizations relate to specific theories about sexual and gender nonconformity circulating in the culture and time period from which the text emerged.

10 *Explorations of the interrelationship of sexuality and textuality may draw on different theories, such as those concerning class, race, psychology, and form, and as well as those of post-structuralism and the New Historicism.*

Gay/lesbian/queer analysis is a rubric containing many different methodological emphases. Materialist queer analysis examines how class-based oppression is intertwined with and has exacerbated the oppression of lesbians and gay men. Theorists of race and ethnicity have pointed out that gay and lesbian analysis often ignores the experiences of people of color, and they have urged critics to explore those experiences as well as the racism entrenched in some sectors of the gay and lesbian community. Other critics examine Freudian and post-Freudian theories of sexual identity development, looking at how individual texts can be explored with reference to those theories. Indeed, new developments and insights in other methodologies help generate new insights in the field of gay/lesbian/queer analysis. But gay/lesbian/queer analysis also offers its own unique insights and certainly has pushed the boundaries of contemporary literary and cultural analysis. It is a field that addresses in strikingly overt and direct fashion precisely how individuals and groups have come to love and/or hate each other and how their relationships are reflected in the literature and art that they create.

Bibliography

Abelove, Henry, et al., eds. *The Lesbian and Gay Studies Reader.* New York: Routledge, 1993.

> This is the most comprehensive collection to date of essays in the field of gay and lesbian literary and cultural studies. While it will be useful to many readers for its extensive bibliography, its conceptual difficulty and presumption of theoretical knowledge will make it of greatest interest to advanced readers.

Bristow, Joseph. *Sexuality.* New York: Routledge, 1997.

> This helpful overview of theories of sexuality covers all the major concepts and debates propelling gay/lesbian/queer studies. Its level of accessibility and clarity will make it of interest to intermediate and advanced readers.

Cruikshank, Margaret. *The Gay and Lesbian Liberation Movement.* New York: Routledge, 1992.

> This very accessible overview of the history of the struggle for gay and lesbian rights will provide necessary background information and some clear explanations of theoretical debates for beginning and intermediate readers.

Fiedler, Leslie. *Love and Death in the American Novel.* New York: Stein & Day, 1966.

> While not a work of gay criticism and often exhibiting a pathologizing attitude toward homosexuality, this early critical consideration of homoeroticism in nineteenth-century American literature was revolutionary for the way it foregrounded male/male erotic attachment as a key and ongoing component of American identity. It psychoanalytic readings may be of interest to both intermediate and advanced readers.

Foucault, Michel. *The History of Sexuality: An Introduction*, vol. 1. New York: Vintage, 1978.

> Foucault's theories of sexuality and power have played a key role in the development of gay and lesbian studies and are particularly important in recent work in queer theory. The vocabulary and conceptual sophistication of this text will make it of greatest interest to intermediate and advanced readers.

Hall, Donald E., and Maria Pramaggiore, eds. *RePresenting Bisexualities: Subjects and Cultures of Fluid Desire*. New York: New York University Press, 1996.

This collection of essays complicates the discussion of gay and lesbian representations and queer theory with a specific focus on fluid sexuality and bisexual characterizations. Its level of difficulty and presupposition of theoretical knowledge will make it of greatest interest to advanced readers.

Jagose, Annamarie. *Queer Theory: An Introduction*. New York: New York University Press, 1996.

This brief and relatively accessible introduction covers the basics of gay and lesbian analysis and the distinctive theoretical roots of queer theory. Its clarity will make it of interest to all readers.

Morton, Donald, ed. *The Material Queer: A LesBiGay Cultural Studies Reader*. Boulder, CO: Westview Press, 1996.

This collection of excerpts and essays focuses specifically on the intersection of Marxist theory and theories of sexuality. While its introduction and editorial commentary are strident at times, it usefully supplements other works that ignore issues of social class. Its vocabulary and conceptual sophistication will make it of greatest interest to advanced readers.

Sedgwick, Eve. *Between Men: English Literature and Male Homosocial Desire*. New York: Columbia University Press, 1985.

This groundbreaking work of gay-positive analysis locates currents of homoerotic desire and homophobic reaction in works from four centuries of British literature. It revolutionized the terminology of gay studies and contributed importantly to its more widespread acceptance within the academy. Its clarity of expression and explanations of theories will make it appropriate for both intermediate and advanced readers.

Sedgwick, Eve. *Epistemology of the Closet*. Berkeley: University of California Press, 1990.

This important work of theory and applied analysis offers insights into the importance of sexual categories in society and in textual representation. Its complexity and presupposition of theoretical knowledge will make it of greatest interest to advanced readers.

Stryker, Susan, ed. The Transgender Issue [Special issue]. *GLQ: A Journal of Lesbian and Gay Studies* 4, no. 2 (1998).

This groundbreaking special issue of a prominent gay and lesbian studies journal contains sophisticated inquiries into the relationship between new theories of sexuality and the burgeoning field of transgender/transsexual studies. Its contributors include activists and academics, and both intermediate and advanced readers will find essays of interest in it.

Warner, Michael, ed. *Fear of a Queer Planet: Queer Politics and Social Theory.* Minneapolis: University of Minnesota Press, 1993.

> This is the most important collection to date of works in queer theory. Its essays and introduction cover most of the compelling issues and insights in the field. While it offers few examples of applied literary analysis and its essays often require an extensive background knowledge of theory, it is an important collection for advanced readers.

Application

Reading Prompts

1. Early in his essay, Porter traces a wide range of previous perspectives in criticism of Marlowe's and Shakespeare's sexualities. Highlight or underline passages revealing Porter's own purpose in examining the sexualities apparent in these authors' works and lives.

2. Porter focuses finally on the figure of Mercutio from *Romeo and Juliet;* mark those passages in which he justifies and qualifies his use of this character.

3. Porter offers an interpretation of Mercutio's "phallicism," a term he uses to indicate Mercutio's association with penis imagery and symbolism. Pay careful attention to his analysis of why Shakespeare incorporates that phallicism into his play.

4. Textual erasures of and critical responses to the phrase "open-arse" help Porter critique a climate of canonized heterosexuality. Locate and evaluate his evidence in support of his interpretive claims concerning that phrase.

5. After reading this essay, consider the following question: How is Porter's analysis sensitive to historical contexts and complexities while still contributing to recent discussions about gay studies and gay rights?

Joseph A. Porter

Marlowe, Shakespeare, and the Canonization of Heterosexuality

Relations between Marlowe and Shakespeare, particularly as manifested in the character of Mercutio in *Romeo and Juliet*, serve as an index of the Western canonization of heterosexuality at the expense of homosexuality through the past four centuries. That exceedingly complex history, only recently starting to be told, continues to unfold in the present, with the ongoing denial, containment, and suppression of homosexuality countered by powerful recent movements toward undoing the orthodox hierarchy that privileges heterosexuality. Our evolving views of relations between the two playwrights, and our processing of the figure of Mercutio, continue to show where we stand in the battle of the sexualities, whether for maintenance of orthodoxy, or for its affirmative-action inversion in a privileging of homosexuality, or (as here) for peaceful coexistence and the elimination of hierarchy as a stage toward our freeing ourselves from the very categories of homosexuality and heterosexuality.[1]

Bearing in mind that "sexuality," like "homosexuality" and "heterosexuality," dates only from the early nineteenth century, and that these terms are variously problematic, as Eve Kosofsky Sedgwick, Jonathan Goldberg, Alan Bray, and others are currently helping us see, Marlowe's sexual stance might be described as intermittently misogynistic, aggressively sensual, and flagrantly homoerotic. I list the three characteristics in increasing degree of provocativeness or subversiveness. The misogyny shows in moments like Tamburlaine's off-the-cuff totalizing remark that "women must be flattered," and also in a stinginess notable even for the time with female dramatic roles. Marlowe's urgent sensuality, more often present than his misogyny and nearly always incipient, shows in many ways, including the apparent readiness of his imagination to eroticize, and perhaps above all in the sheer corporeality of his imagined world. In that world the human body of either gender is the most insistently corporeal of objects: it realizes with peculiar provocativeness the renascent and newly problematic (because newly secular) appreciation of the body that had come up from the Italy of Botticelli and Michelangelo to an England comparatively starved for pictures and statues of nudes.

The most provocative and subversive component of Marlowe's sexuality, however, is the preference flaunted in the vivid homoeroticism of *Hero and Leander*, in the love of Edward and Gaveston in *Edward II*, and at other points in his work such as the opening scene of *Dido, Queen of Carthage* with Jupiter dandling Ganymede on his knee. Marlowe may also have expressed his sexual preference in the claim "That all they that love not tobacco and boys were fools," attributed to him by Richard Baines in his list of charges against Marlowe sent to the queen three days after Marlowe's death. In "Sodomy and Society: The Case of Christopher Marlowe," Jonathan Goldberg treats some of the difficulties this last piece of evidence presents, which include the possibility that it was fabricated as part of a government action.[2] Since, as has seemed at least possible to many recent commentators, Marlowe's very death may have been a government-ordered assassination, we need put no great faith in the disinterested accuracy of Baines's report, which was clearly intended to discredit at least. Even as a fabrication, however, it bears some weight since its plausibility may be assumed. As with the anticlerical and sacrilegious remarks Baines also attributes to Marlowe, so with the remark about tobacco and boys: there is reason to suspect that Marlowe had behaved in ways that made it seem he could well have made the remark, whether or not he actually did make it. Baines's report, then, if not evidence of Marlowe's homoerotic stance, exemplifies the treatment of such "evidence": that is, Baines's or his superiors' confidence that pederasty (like any other homosexual practice) would discredit Marlowe manifests a stance apparent in the commentary on Marlowe (and writers such as Richard Barnfield) from the Renaissance to the present. With due acknowledgment that this stance toward "homosexuality" varies with time in weight and tenability, it appears in criticism past and present, antipathetic and ostensibly tolerant.[3]

A second way of processing Marlowe's sexuality is by ignoring it. This has been the most common response, both of detractors and proponents, from shortly after Marlowe's death to the present. Some detractors have ignored Marlowe's sexuality as part of a general downplaying of him, or because the subject in their opinions is per se inappropriate for discussion, or even because they prefer not to denigrate homosexuality. Most of the ignoring of Marlowe's sexuality, however, has been at the hands of his champions and proponents. In some cases they have doubtless shared the detractors' reluctance, for reasons of propriety, to discuss the matter at all; some must have been inclined to save Marlowe from the "taint" he had paraded in self-advertisement and self-destructiveness. Editors in particular have followed this line, usually providing in notes and commentary a kind of bowdlerized-into-wonderland Marlowe; nor does any edition to date yet take significant cognizance of Marlowe's sexuality. While the recent climate of criticism has made it less easy to paper over Marlowe's sexuality, we still have a widespread inability or refusal to grant its pervasive importance in his life and work, and in his reception. When that importance is granted, even now, it may be with the most surprising indirectness. Michael Goldman, one of Marlowe's most influential recent commentators, says almost nothing directly about Marlowe's minority sexuality, while indirectly acknowledging it—flaunting it, even—with the "ravished" acting style he recommends for Marlowe's drama.[4]

A third possible treatment of Marlowe's sexuality is to acknowledge it and its importance in an unprejudicial response to his work. To an extent we can see this treatment in the wave of homoerotic and largely Ovidian poetry that sweeps through the 1590s, which includes Shakespeare's *Venus and Adonis,* and which seems importantly initiated by the example of Marlowe's *Hero and Leander.* In Marlowe criticism and editorial procedures, however, some of which is otherwise of a very high order, this sort of response (which I take as a desideratum) appears as a scant glimmer. During the two-session seminar on "Marlowe and Shakespeare" at the 1985 meeting of the Shakespeare Association of America, virtually no attention was given to questions of sexuality and sexual preference.

As for Shakespeare's sexuality, while there seems to be more to go on, both in the life and in the works, the evidence is also more ambiguous and contradictory than with Marlowe. Apparent evidence from the life includes all the tantalizing facts we have about his marriage, fatherhood, and long absence from his family, as well as the complete absence of suggestions of any sort of sexual impropriety. Evidence from the work, too voluminous and complex for more than a glance here, includes: the celebration of heterosexuality in many of the plays, above all *Antony and Cleopatra;* the various sorts of protofeminism and celebration of the female in most of the same plays: the eruptions of what has been called sexual loathing or fear of the female, especially in *Hamlet, Lear,* and the dark lady sonnets; the loving sonnets to the young man; the narrative poems, one with rape as its titular subject and the other portraying something approaching a goddess's rape of a mortal male; and a multitude of *sexually* complex moments and situations in the plays and poems. Compared to Marlowe's, Shakespeare's sexual stance seems to me less misogynistic and sexist and far more protofeminist, less aggressively sensual, and generally if perhaps not exclusively heterosexual. Furthermore, still painting with broad strokes, I would say not only that Shakespeare is more retiring than Marlowe on the subject of sexuality (as on most subjects), but also that the subject itself is less prominent in Shakespeare.

My take on the evidence, of course, constitutes a part of the cultural processing of Shakespeare's sexuality. Given Shakespeare's early prominence and later canonization, stakes in the processing of his sexuality have been much higher than with Marlowe. Therefore, while in general Shakespeare's sexuality has not seemed so much at issue as Marlowe's, and in particular has not seemed so subversive, still where the subject has arisen there has been a hotter contest for its determination, more strident claims and charges, and heavier ammunition. Here I have in mind not merely the shadowland of claims that Shakespeare actually was Marlowe, or that he was female, but also, for instance, the broad daylight Victorian manufacture of that sentimentalized Shakespeare of heroines fitted out with girlhoods. In our century the *Sonnets* have of course been prime battleground. Most recently Joseph Pequigney argues that Sonnets 1–126 detail physical intimacies in an amorous friendship that is "sexual in both orientation and practice," these sonnets comprising "the grand masterpiece of homoerotic poetry"; and Eve Kosofsky Sedgwick begins her *Between Men* with "Swan in Love: The Example of Shakespeare's Sonnets," a subtle and powerful treatment of relations among gender, power, and "homosocial" desire in the sonnets.[5]

When Shakespeare in *As You Like It* has the silly shepherdess Phebe quote Marlowe—"Dead shepherd, now I find thy saw of might,/'Who ever loved that loved not at first sight?'"—the directness and the assured lightness of touch seem earned, since in itself the moment scarcely hints at how much of Shakespeare's energy during most of the preceding decade has been absorbed in a struggle with his mighty rival, before and after Marlowe's death in 1593. Whether or not Marlowe is, as some maintain, the "rival poet" of the sonnets, he was certainly a commercial rival even after his death, and he was also (insofar as the two can be separated) an artistic rival. While clarification of much about their tangled artistic relations must await more precise dating of their works in the years near Marlowe's death, enough is clear for us to be able to characterize the general dynamic as notably including Shakespeare's response to the challenge posed by Marlowe. Shakespeare's response to Marlowe is characteristically complex and delayed, in part considered and in part barely if at all conscious, and at once a containment of subversiveness and a creation of subtle new subversiveness.

Phebe's quotation serves as something of a valedictory from Shakespeare to Marlowe. Following it, Shakespeare's concern with Marlowe subsides markedly, and appears only in such sporadic traces as those in the Player's speech in *Hamlet*, which at "one or perhaps two points" seems to echo the *Dido* of Marlowe and Nashe.[6] Before Phebe's valedictory, however, Shakespeare's massive engagement with Marlowe shows, as is generally recognized, in the correspondence between three pairs of complete works by the two authors—the Ovidian poems *Hero and Leander* and *Venus and Adonis*, the history plays *Edward II* and *Richard II*, and the two plays *The Jew of Malta* and *The Merchant of Venice*, the one a kind of tragedy and the other a kind of comedy—as well as in numerous local features of Shakespeare, some of them of great interest. Marjorie Garber, for instance, has argued persuasively that in Hal's killing of Hotspur in *1 Henry IV* Shakespeare represents his dramatic victory over Marlowe.[7]

As I maintain in *Shakespeare's Mercutio*, using the character of Mercutio in *Romeo and Juliet* as a partial simulacrum of Marlowe, dead some two years, Shakespeare carries out a major and hitherto largely unremarked phase of his negotiations with the memory of the rival.[8] With Mercutio, those negotiations concern, among other things, sexual matters. Indeed, leaving aside questions of the sonnets, I would say that in the plays Mercutio plays the major and indeed virtually the sole part in Shakespeare's processing of the challenge presented by Marlowe's sexuality.

Before elaborating, it may be well to insert a few caveats. My claim is not that Shakespeare's Mercutio must be taken in any simple, obvious, or reductive way as really or merely "a homosexual" with the hots for Romeo, although I know he has been read and played that way. Nor am I claiming that *Romeo and Juliet* is a *drame à clef* wherein Mercutio is "really" Marlowe, nor even that Mercutio's Marlovianness is simple, uniform, or determinate. Nor finally do I claim that Shakespeare was fully conscious in using Mercutio for a negotiation with Marlowe's homoeroticism. That negotiation seems to have been partly conscious, given such a detail as the echo of *Tamburlaine* in Benvolio's announcement of Mercutio's death, but here as with much else in Shakespeare important operations seem to take place beneath the level of full consciousness.[9]

Shakespeare, choosing what was already a fairly canonical story of heterosexual love for his play, seems to have relied entirely on the version in Arthur Brooke's *The Tragical History of Romeus and Juliet* (1562).[10] Brooke's Mercutio is a rudimentary figure who appears at the Capulet ball as a potential rival of Romeo's for Juliet. The sketched figure, that is, exhibits some of the conventional heterosexual interest of a young gallant, and there is no suggestion that he and Romeo even know each other. His main *raison d'être* in the poem is to occasion the first words between Juliet and Romeo, for after he and Romeo each have grasped one of Juliet's hands she turns to Romeo to complain of Mercutio's "icy hand." Thereafter Brooke's poem contains no mention of Mercutio.

Shakespeare's elaboration of Brooke's trace Mercutio begins in a sense, with the erasure of the potential Mercutio-Juliet bond. The erasure if very thorough. At the Capulet ball, Shakespeare gives Mercutio neither lines nor stage directions, nor any acknowledgment of his presence, not even where it might seem most natural, as when the Nurse informs Juliet of the identities of guests as they depart at the end of the scene. Shakespeare's Mercutio and Juliet never touch hands or speak to each other, nor does either ever speak of the other. Furthermore, while the play contains several occasions where one might naturally be spoken of to the other, neither ever hears mention of the other.

By a certain conservation of imaginative weight, the erased Mercutio-Juliet bond reappears in Shakespeare as the bond uniting Mercutio and Romeo. Their friendship is, of course, a part of the camaraderie that also bonds each of these two with Benvolio, in a version of the liminal fraternities studied by Victor Turner and others. Within that fraternity, however, the Mercutio-Romeo bond is much the most prominent and consequential. Soon after Mercutio's last exit, the play twice comes close to naming the bond, when Romeo calls Mercutio his "very friend" and when Montague says his son was "Mercutio's friend." "Friendship" will do as a name for the bond so long as we recognize that, on Mercutio's part at least, the affectional state might as easily be named love, and that, while what we would call homosexual desire plays no conspicuous role in Mercutio's friendship for Romeo, still the erotic and indeed the phallic figure more prominently here than in any other significant friendship in Shakespeare.[11]

Given all this, along with Shakespeare's great expansion of the role of a character whose Marlovian resonances extend even to his name, it would seem that Shakespeare's response to Marlowe's sexuality must be legible in Mercutio. The general nature of that response is summarized, *mutatis mutandis*, in Nicholas Brooke's remark about Marlowe's political heterodoxy:

> Marlowe seems to have been for Shakespeare . . . the inescapable creator of something initially alien which he could only assimilate with difficulty.[12]

While we might not wish to credit Marlowe as "creator" of homoeroticism (any more, perhaps, than as creator of his political heterodoxy), Shakespeare does seem to deserve credit for accepting the challenge of Marlowe's sexuality, at least in Mercutio.

The opening of *Romeo and Juliet* , with Sampson and Gregory talking of thrusting maids to the wall, drawing a tool, and having a naked weapon out, is the most relentlessly phallic opening in all of Shakespeare's play, and in only a few passages from anywhere in his work is the phallus more

prominent. The opening ranks the phallus alongside the feud as a major
theme, and sets up equations between phallus and weapon, and between
male heterosexuality and the violent subjugation of women. At the same
time, since the two servants are comic, Shakespeare uses them to call into
question the institution of patriarchal sexism, an institution some of whose
costs Shakespeare recognizes in much of the play. The parodic heterosexual
phallocentrism of the opening lines, that is, sounds a characteristic Shakespearean note, the note we call antisexist or protofeminist.

The point is worth making because commentators have sometimes
blurred together with the play's opening its three additional notably phallic
passages, all in Mercutio's speech, and all with the phallocentrism still more
prominent and concentrated than in the opening: Mercutio's talk of sinking
in love, pricks and pricking, and beating love down; his long bawdy inter-
change with Benvolio about raising a spirit; and his talk with Romeo and
Benvolio, and then the Nurse, of love's bauble, of his own "tale," and of the
prick of noon. Given that in each passage it is Mercutio who introduces the
phallicism and primarily sustains it, and given the proportional prominence
of such talk in Mercutio's total of lines, he is easily Shakespeare's most
phallic character. And several points should be made immediately about his
insistent references to the phallus.

While Mercutio's phallicism is as aggressive as the Capulet servants',
his is in a thoroughly different key to start with, by virtue of his social class
and friendships. Furthermore, while Sampson boasts to Gregory of the tool
with which he thrusts maids to the wall, in Mercutio we find neither boast-
ing nor envisioned male aggression toward women. Indeed he begins his
first phallic passage with "And, to sink in it, should you burden love—/ Too
great oppression for a tender thing"—a mock counsel to Romeo against
love on the grounds that heterosexual intercourse per se is overly aggressive
against women. The roughness in the remainder of his counsel, "If love be
rough with you, be rough with love; / Prick love for pricking and you beat
love down," is directed not against women but against love, which has
changed gender from female to male in Romeo's intervening speech. Nor
do we find misogyny or particular aggressiveness toward women in Mercutio's other concentrations of phallic speech. Nor, it may be worth noting, is
Mercutio's disapproval of Romeo's infatuation and heterosexuality at all
sternly prescriptive. Rather it is genial and tolerant, and the increasingly
sensual catalog of Rosaline's parts that introduces the second concentration
of phallicism is appreciative throughout. In an important respect Mercutio's phallic talk reverses Sampson's. While Sampson talks boastfully
and exclusively about his own phallus, and induces the compliant though
not entirely credulous Gregory to talk about it too, only a portion of

Mercutio's bawdy, and that not boastful, is about his own "tale." The other phalli that come up more or less explicitly in his speech are love's, noon's, a stranger's, and Romeo's. Mercutio, that is, very readily grants the phallus to others, notably including his friend Romeo.

Mercutio's references to his friend's phallus suggest the sexual dynamics of the friendship. The quibbling figurativeness of "If love be rough with you, be rough with love; / Prick love for pricking and you beat love down" makes the sentence exceptionally resistant to close paraphrase. Still, the exhortation is not only phallic but also opposed to heterosexual love, or antivenereal, so that (being rough with the sentence) we might paraphrase it as "Use your phallus against love." A lightened and, as it were, genially resigned antivenerealism appears as well in the context of "in his mistress' name / I conjure only but to raise up him" with its sensually appreciative but irreverent talk of Rosaline. But Mercutio's phallicism is the stronger and more apparent agenda. Mercutio here exhibits a generous and interested attitude toward Romeo's phallus, as if he has a personal investment, as we say, in his friend's erection. The nature of that investment might seem, on the basis of the line and a half quoted above, to involve the idea of Mercutio's taking Rosaline's place not only as conjurer but also as container of Romeo's phallus, and it is true that Rosaline has receded from active participation with the stranger, her circle around his spirit, to a mere deputizing name at Mercutio's raising of Romeo. But that fleeting, apparently subliminal trace of sexual desire on Mercutio's part for Romeo, which seems to reappear in Mercutio's image of biting Romeo by the ear,[13] is preceded by the genially explicit talk of Rosaline as sexually active and attractive, and is followed shortly by the third reference to Romeo's phallus, in Mercutio's mock wish that Romeo were a poperin pear, another image that (like "raise up him") reduces the friend to his genitals, while naming the phallus precisely for its use in heterosexual intercourse.

These references of Mercutio's to Romeo's phallus add up to a highly mercurial stance that combines an opposition to love, an amiable erotic permissiveness, and a phallocentrism that admits traces of homoeroticism. The stance amounts to an invitation, and it is one Romeo is unable to accept. His repartee with Mercutio never seems quite wholehearted; when Mercutio shifts into the bawdy Romeo hangs back and Romeo's love for Juliet is notably uncarnal and unphallic. Just as the play authorizes Romeo's greater allegiance to love than to family honor in the feud, so it also authorizes his greater allegiance to Juliet than to Mercutio. The generally neglected point, however, is that by radically expanding Brooke's minor Mercutio, Shakespeare gives Romeo's heterosexual love an opposition other than and different in quality from the opposition of the feud. That is, in *Romeo and Juliet*, while acknowledging the (here disastrous) power of heterosexual love, Shakespeare uses Mercutio and his appeal to entertain Marlovian homosexuality as fully as he can.

To elaborate this last point: through Mercutio, while Marlowe's sexual orientation is not paraded, neither is it cancelled, denied, or ignored. Rather, in this play at least, Shakespeare in the arena of the erotic demonstrates the sort of mastery that Stephen Greenblatt and others have taught us to see in him, as he admits and incorporates the subversive element, to some extent containing it, and to some extent rendering it still more subversive. Here, in other words, Shakespeare mounts his strongest case against the enshrinement of heterosexuality at the expense of homosexuality. The strength of the case is in part a function of the force of the general challenge of Marlowe's example as felt by Shakespeare, and in part a function of the strength of Shakespeare's general response.

With Mercutio, then, Shakespeare seems to carry out a profound and nonjudgmental acknowledgment of Marlowe's minority sexuality, and does so by way of what in 1595 is still for him an exceptional, even unprecedented, degree of imaginative identification. The identification shows in the warmth and generosity of Mercutio's fraternal bonding to Romeo, and in his phallic bawdiness, neither feature especially noteworthy in Shakespearean characters before Mercutio or, for that matter, after him either. The imaginative empathy may account for particulars of Mercutio's behavior as well, the most remarkable possibly being the wish he expresses to his absent friend, "O Romeo, that she were, O that she were / An open-arse and thou a poperin pear!" This seems to be the only direct and explicit reference to sodomy in the canon.[14] Of course the sodomy imagined in these lines is heterosexual, but its uniqueness in Shakespeare suggests that it derives from Mercutio's Marlovianness—as if Shakespeare has Mercutio wish for his friend heterosexual intercourse as it might easily have been imagined, in passing, by Marlowe. So understood, the moment marks an exceptional imaginative reach.

Mercutio, however, is about as far as Shakespeare goes with the conversion of Marlovian homosexuality into phallocentric male friendship charged with erotic overtones and undertones. Shakespeare lets the homosexual Marlowe into the realm of the canonical heterosexual, not only to give him some free rein but also to kill him off. While the heterosexual lovers die too, their deaths are later and their love is finally accorded the sanction of their society. In what may be the next play, *The Merchant of Venice*, Antonio's melancholy manifests some lingering dissatisfaction with the accommodation achieved through Mercutio and his death, but while Antonio lives to the end of his play much of the life has now gone out of the Marlowe simulacrum. In *The Merchant of Venice* friendship is supplanted by undying heterosexual love; then Shakespeare is off and running through a series of plays conspicuously deficient in celebrations of male-male bonding, and generally without celebratory or even acquiescent moments of the homoerotic.

Still, with Mercutio Shakespeare has entertained the Marlovian stance. He has shown himself open to an alternate sexuality. The negotiation with Marlowe and his sexuality in the creation of Mercutio may well have been instrumental in giving Shakespeare an exceptional freedom from the prescriptivism that must demonize homosexuality. As is well known, he seems not unsympathetic to the more or less explicit homosexuality of Achilles and Patroclus in *Troilus and Cressida*, and restricts derision of it to the "deformed and scurrilous" Thersites.

The imaginative capaciousness and generosity with which Shakespeare comes to terms with Marlovian homoeroticism in Mercutio has not usually been matched or even approached in our culture's nearly four-hundred-year processing of Mercutio. In numerous and changing ways that history has been one of suppression, reduction, bowdlerizing, sentimentalizing, and denial of his fraternal phallocentric bawdy and of the nature and vigor of his bonding with Romeo, as well as of much else about him. The manifold attack on Mercutio, which may for convenience be termed a drive for his containment, is visible in adaptations, in promptbooks, in editorial practice, in records of performance (including film and video), and in critical commentary on the texts and performances of the play. The drive for containment of Mercutio varies in scope and intricacy from Francis Gentleman's considered view that *Romeo and Juliet* would have been better if Shakespeare had left Mercutio out of it altogether, to the ingenious cutting in the 1906 production that reduces Mercutio's catalog of Rosaline's parts to her "bright eyes, / And the demesnes that there adjacent lie."[15]

At the same time, Mercutio through the four centuries has continued to exert the subversive appeal that, according to Dryden, made Shakespeare have to kill him off midway through the play, so that the drive for containment has always been opposed by forces working for the restoration and acceptance of an authentic Mercutio. The volatile and continuing contest that has been and continues to be waged over Mercutio may be seen as a small but not insignificant part of the dialectic of sexualities. Indeed, given Shakespeare's prominence, especially in the past two centuries, I maintain that the processing of Mercutio can serve as a useful series of bulletins from the front in the struggle over the privileging of heterosexuality. Before concluding, then, I wish briefly to consider three of those bulletins. While the academy's conservatorship of Shakespeare brings all of what I have said above into the general purview of the subject of Shakespeare and the academy, with these three matters I will try to lay open some more specifics.

In this century, and especially in the permissive climate of twenty years ago, Mercutio seems finally to begin to come into his own, after the centuries-long night of seldom remitting censorship. Franco Zeffirelli's 1968 *Romeo and Juliet* , with John McEnery playing Mercutio, was a landmark. Zeffirelli had directed a stage version of the play earlier, and some of what he had worked out there reappears in the film.[16] Still, the film manifests some fundamental rethinking of the play, rethinking especially evident in, and possibly originating with, the part of Mercutio. One of the important innovations was the choice of an actor appreciably older than those playing Romeo, Juliet, and Benvolio. The age discrepancy works with some subtlety to enlist audience interest in—and perhaps sympathy for, and perhaps anxiety about—"an aging manic-depressive, idling his time away in the company of men half his own age."[17] The Marlovian-Shakespearean phallicism is abundantly present, as in the moment when Mercutio in the waist-deep watering trough raises the shank of his sword out of the water at the phallic angle. The strength and potential eroticism of his bond with Romeo also manifests itself, as in the two moments when they touch foreheads. Nor does the Zeffirelli-McEnery Mercutio exhibit any trace of the un-Marlovian heterosexual flirtatiousness the character shows in Shakespeare's source and often in adaptations and stagings of Shakespeare's play, though nowhere in Shakespeare's dialogue.

While the great popularity of the film clearly derived from Zeffirelli's playing to the sixties cult of innocent youth with his principals—and the film does celebrate and partly canonize youthful heterosexual desire—at the same time the influence of McEnery's Mercutio may prove to have been more consequential. Five years later, for instance, in the Terry Hands 1973 Stratford stage production of the play, Mercutio becomes, according to Evans, "an aggressive homosexual."[18]

Evans's reactions to both film and stage productions in his introduction to the 1984 New Cambridge *Romeo and Juliet* represent one sort of academic response to the late twentieth-century acknowledgment or exaggeration, in performance, of Shakespeare's engagement with Marlovian homoeroticism. Of the Hands production Evans writes,

> Such character perversion, all too common today in Shakespeare productions generally, is nothing more than a meretricious attempt, at whatever drastic cost to the integrity of the play, to make Shakespeare "our contemporary"; only if the friendship of Romeo, Benvolio and Mercutio can be given an exciting nuance of homosexuality does the play become relevant for a modern audience— so runs the directors' justification.

As for the Zeffirelli film, Evans disapproves of it as "narrowly conceived and reductionist" because of its "emphasis on youth" which seems to him to diminish "the larger aspects of their [Romeo's and Juliet's] love, its developing maturity and final dignity." Evans does not mention the Zeffirelli-McEnery Mercutio's strong traces of the protohomoerotic or indeed anything about the role.[19] His very neglect of it seems a function of his concern that the play be understood as enshrining a dignified heterosexual love.

Elsewhere in the academy reception has been more favorable to recent performances of Mercutio that counter the canonization of heterosexuality. Jack J. Jorgens appreciates the prominence Zeffirelli gives Mercutio, noting, for instance, that with Mercutio's death the entire film is "drained of its busy look and festive colors"; Jorgens acknowledges the depth of this Mercutio's attachment to Romeo:

> There is deep friendship, even love, between Romeo and Mercutio. Mercutio's mercurial showmanship seems aimed at Romeo, and his anger, when Romeo is off sighing for love or making a milksop of himself before Tybalt, is tinged with jealousy. How could a friend abandon his male comradery for "a smock"?

And E. A. M. Colman writes of the film that "*Romeo and Juliet* demands a good deal of critical reorientation if . . . Zeffirelli's . . . presentation of Mercutio is justified by the text." Despite a certain circularity here—not merely "the text" but also a particular given critical orientation is necessarily implicated in determining whether the presentation is "justified" or not— Colman clearly acknowledges the disruptive importance of the Zeffirelli-McEnery Mercutio.[20]

Feminist and psychoanalytic critical treatments of Mercutio comprise a second index of the part Mercutio is currently playing in the contest for and against the canonization of heterosexuality in the academy. While the MLA Delegate Assembly's passage of a resolution opposing discrimination on the basis of sexual orientation clearly results from interrogation inside the academy of the received assumptions grounding such discrimination, all too often in academic discourse these assumptions continue to be promulgated as fact. Mercutio serves as an exceptionally good gauge of this discourse, by virtue of his homosocial-homoerotic resonances and opposition to heterosexual love in what has become far more canonical a story of heterosexual love than it was when it came to Shakespeare's hand.

The strengths and weaknesses of both feminist and psychoanalytic treatments of Shakespeare have been widely discussed. Most recently Richard Levin has exposed widespread error and falsehood in feminist thematic readings of the tragedies; he suggests that the deficiencies derive not only from the thematism but also from a fallacious feminist-psychoanalytic conception of masculinity.[21] Levin does not address the preconceptions about sexual orientation in the critics he surveys, but his admirable concluding call for the abandonment of psychoanalytic stances that must make one gender or the other inherently pathological may be immediately extrapolated to psychoanalytic stances that privilege heterosexuality by making adult homosexuality a pathology.

Levin's concerns resemble mine enough to lead him to notice some suppression of Mercutio in the criticism he surveys, as when he notes the misrepresentation by Coppélia Kahn of Romeo's motive in attaching Tybalt—not, as Kahn claims, to uphold the Montague honor, but rather "to avenge Mercutio."[22] If we shift focus from gender to sexual orientation, however, it is easy to see that, for feminist-psychoanalytic criticism espousing the doctrine that adult male homosexuality is either an irrelevance or a pathology, Mercutio has a good deal besides mere maleness working against him. And a conspicuous resurgence of the ongoing movement to contain Mercutio appears precisely in this body of criticism.

In "Coming of Age in Verona," for example, Kahn maintains that Mercutio "represents" the "attempted sublimation" of "virile energy . . . into fancy and wit," and that he "suggests" that feuding functions psychologically as a definition of manhood.[23] If these slippery and jargon-bound claims seem provisionally tenable, the same is not true of Kahn's "Love is only manly, he [Mercutio] hints, if it is aggressive and violent and consists of subjugating women, rather than being subjugated by them." In fact, Mercutio nowhere hints at approval of "subjugating women." Nor does he hint that a particular sort of heterosexual love is "manly." Indeed, as Kahn herself observes, Mercutio "mocks . . . all [heterosexual] love."[24] Kahn's otherwise helpful essay traduces Mercutio in such ways because he threatens the psychological dogma that prescribes the supplanting of homosexual by heterosexual bonding in the life of the "healthy" individual, and also because he stands outside the feminist reflex division of men into two sorts: those who wish to dominate women and those who love women in a way characterized by mutuality, a division that depends on the prescriptive assumption that only heterosexual men bear discussion. Mercutio serves, that is, as a particularly sensitive emblem of the extent to which current feminist and psychoanalytic modes of criticism constitute a new stronghold in the academic privileging of heterosexuality.

The bibliographical and critical history of a particular half-line of Mercutio's provides still another yardstick for measuring his changing phallic subversiveness and the varying acceptance and containment it elicits. At the beginning of act 2, Romeo enters alone and after two lines withdraws, hiding himself from the next two entrants, his friends Mercutio and Benvolio, whom he overhears summoning him wittily and in vain, until they give up the search and exit. The apostrophe "O Romeo, that she [Romeo's love] were, O that she were / An open-arse and thou a poperin pear!" in Mercutio's last speech in the scene contains, as I have said, what seems to be Shakespeare's only explicit reference to sodomy, but the "open-arse" does not appear in printed texts of the play before 1954.

The intricate and not yet fully understood story of the disappearance and recovery of what is now generally, though not quite universally, taken to be the phrase as Shakespeare wrote it may be summarized as follows. Shakespeare seems to have written something like "open-arse" or "openers," which the compositor of the Bad First Quarto (1597) understood in its reported form and replaced with the euphemism "open *Et cetera*," and which the compositor of the Good Second Quarto (1599), probably working from Shakespeare's foul papers, misread and set as "open, or." The Q2 reading reappears in Q3 (1609) and in the First Folio (1623), but since it makes no sense it is generally superseded thenceforth by the Q1 reading, until a flurry of independent restorations in the mid-1950s. In 1953, Kökeritz suggests the reading "open-arse"; the following year, Hosley prints the line as "An open-arse or thou a poperin pear"; and in 1955 Wilson and Duthie give the line the form, and thus the coherence, it has in virtually all subsequent editions.

There is no way to know how often in the three and a half centuries between Q1 and the mid-1950s the "open-arse" may have been divined, but we do know that it was suggested in print at least once, in Farmer and Henley's *Slang and its Analogues* (1902), not an especially obscure work. So the reluctance of editors through half a century to adopt the reading may betoken not simply procedural conservatism but also a continuing drive to protect Mercutio, and through him Shakespeare, from what was perceived as scandalous, a drive that to the present day maintains the superseded line in one edition in general use, the Pelican.

Sqeamishness about the "open-arse" continues even after its general adoption in editions of the play. In editors' notes on the passage a nearly uniform silence prevails about the envisioned sodomy, broken only by what seems a muffled pun in the note by Wilson and Duthie about "'or' as the seat of the [textual] corruption."[25] Eric Partridge, writing during the last decade of the exclusive reign of "et cetera" in editions, glosses it confidently "Pudend," although in his notes on this phrase and on "medlar" he seems not only to foresee the imminent "arse" but also to attempt to bowdlerize it in advance.[26]

In 1974, well after "open-arse" has carried the day, Colman writes with
a comparatively generous appreciation of Mercutio; nevertheless, he too
goes to some lengths to detoxify the phrase:

> It is unlikely that Mercutios of Shakespeare's own day spoke the term "open-
> arse" here, as both the Bad and Good quartos . . . suppress it, and some such
> action as Benvolio's clapping his hand over Mercutio's mouth seems called for.

This ingenious bit of hypothetical stage business seems called for largely by
Colman's disapproval of the implied image of sodomy, about which he remarks rather primly: "Clearly, all that Romeo needs to do about so broad a
sally is to keep out of the way and flatly disregard it."[27] Furthermore, Colman is at best misleading about how the two Quartos "suppress" the of-
fending phrase, since the Q2 "open, or" seems a compositor's misreading
or misunderstanding rather than the sort of censorship that explains the Q1
et cetera.

Colman's expedients with Mercutio's image of sodomy may suggest
what I believe to be the case: that the struggle over the canonization of heterosexuality is proceeding in his own thought, and perhaps beneath the
level of full consciousness. In his summary discussion of homosexuality and
sodomy, he restates conventional reassurances about the innocence of Elizabethan friendship, although here and in his chapter on the sonnets he does
admit the possibility of homosexual eroticism. And a double standard is apparent in his discussion of the act implied by Mercutio's image: when heterosexual, the act is "anal intercourse," when homosexual, "sodomy."[28]
Colman finds few references to either in Shakespeare; however, while he
passes over the first scarcity without comment, of the second he remarks
that when "the plays glance at sodomy it is with reticence and distaste. . . .
Shakespeare seems to have shared in the conventional disapproval of
sodomy."[29] True enough of Shakespeare, perhaps, and perhaps also truer of
Colman than he acknowledges.

Hence the general screening out of homosexual bawdy for which
Joseph Pequigney takes Colman, Partridge, and many other commentators
on Shakespeare, to task. Pequigney is openly against the prescriptive privileging of heterosexuality, and at times he is not averse even to a certain
privileging of homosexuality. Thus some of the screening Pequigney finds
in Colman may seem as fabricated as a few of the more strained homosexual glosses Pequigney gives the sonnets. Still, partisanship of even the most
outspoken sort is an intricate matter here, as witness Pequigney's passing
treatment of Mercutio. This scholar, who finds many more homosexual
meanings in the sonnets than do all previous commentators together,

screens every trace of the sexual out of his understanding of the friendship between Mercutio and Romeo.

Because of his lineage and pedigree, and because of the manifold uses Shakespeare puts him to, Mercutio plays an idiosyncratic and comparatively prominent part in the ongoing struggle for and against the canonization of heterosexuality. Since the struggle goes on throughout our culture, Mercutio's part is only a small component of it, and would be vanishingly small but for Shakespeare's continuing prominence. Nevertheless, Mercutio's part in the struggle is complex, changing, and far from entirely predictable, and the same seems likely to be true to some extent of other Shakespearean characters—indeed of any other component of Shakespeare's or anyone else's art, and even possibly of any object of attention.

With Mercutio, while the struggle goes on outside the academy, most notable in productions of *Romeo and Juliet* and in nonacademic responses to them, the academy's custodianship of Shakespeare means that the struggle proceeds within the walls at least as vigorously as without, and of course the walls are permeable to the influence of defeats and victories. We in the academy, in any case, seem best situated to read bulletins from all fronts. The task of reading them demands patience, tenacity, imagination, and all other hermeneutic skills we can muster, but it can be done, and doing it will help us avoid providing unintentional support for one contested doctrinal position or another.

NOTES

1.   By "canonization" I mean what the term means generally in ecclesiastical and current literary-critical discourse; by "processing" I mean psychological and cultural reception, interpretation, response, and other sorts of treatments, whether they be conscious or not.

2.   Jonathan Goldberg, "Sodomy and Society: The Case of Christopher Marlowe," *Southwest Review* 69 (1984): 371–78.

3.   See Alan Bray, *Homosexuality in Renaissance England* (London, 1982); Wilbur Sanders, *The Dramatist and the Received Idea* (Cambridge, 1968); and Judith Weil, *Christopher Marlowe* (Cambridge, 1977).

4.   Michael Goldman, "Marlowe and the Histrionics of Ravishment," in *Two Renaissance Mythmakers: Christopher Marlowe and Ben Jonson*, ed. Alvin Kernan (Baltimore, 1977).

5.   Joseph Pequigney, *Such Is My Love* (Chicago, 1985), 1; Eve Kosofsky Sedgwick, *Between Men: English Literature and Male Homosocial Desire* (New York, 1985).

6.   William Shakespeare, *Hamlet*, ed. Harold Jenkins (London, 1982), 479.

7.   Marjorie Garber, "Marlovian Vision/Shakespearean Revision," *Research Opportunities in Renaissance Drama* 22 (1979): 7. I would argue that the moment also

figures the same irrationally assumed responsibility for Marlowe's death that first appears as a flicker of attribution of responsibility for Mercutio's death to Romeo, in Mercutio's dying words: "I was hurt under your arm."

8.   Joseph Porter, *Shakespeare's Mercutio: His History and Drama* (Chapel Hill, 1988).

9.   Benvolio's "brave Mercutio is dead, / That gallant spirit hath aspir'd the clouds" echoes the "And both our soules aspire celestiall thrones" in Tamburlaine's vow of undying friendship to Theridamas.

10.   Arthur Brooke, *The Tragical History of Romeus and Juliet*, ed. J. J. Munro (New York, 1908).

11.   Ronald A. Sharp, *Friendship and Literature* (Durham, 1986), treats with exceptional acuteness the subject of the erotic as a component of friendship.

12.   Nicholas Brooke, "Marlowe as Provocative Agent in Shakespeare's Early Plays." *Shakespeare Survey* 14 (1961): 44.

13.   Here and throughout I'm citing William Shakespeare, *Romeo and Juliet*, ed. Brian Gibbons (London, 1980); see Gibbons's note on 2.4.77.

14.   See Eric Partridge, *Shakespeare's Bawdy* (London, 1948); E. A. M. Colman, *The Dramatic Use of Bawdy in Shakespeare* (London, 1974); Frankie Rubenstein, *A Dictionary of Shakespeare's Sexual Puns and Their Significance* (London, 1984); along with Pequigney, these and other critics find various indirect, inexplicit, and metaphorical references to sodomy in Shakespeare.

15.   See my *Shakespeare's Mercutio*; Francis Gentleman, *The Dramatic Censor* (London, 1770); and Folger Shakespeare Library Promptbook, *Rom.* 29.

16.   See Jill L. Levenson, *Shakespeare in Performance: "Romeo and Juliet"* (Manchester, 1987).

17.   Colman, *Dramatic Use of Bawdy*, 70.

18.   William Shakespeare, *Romeo and Juliet*, ed. G. Blakemore Evans (Cambridge, 1984), 45.

19.   Probably these traces were lost on him, or on his conscious mind, as were the names of the leading actors, Leonard Whiting and Olivia Hussey, whom he has confused with John Stride and Judi Dench, performers in stage productions. See Evans's edition, 45–48.

20.   Jack J. Jorgens, *Shakespeare on Film* (Bloomington, Ind., 1977), 89, 84; Colman, *Dramatic Use of Bawdy*, 171.

21.   Richard Levin, "Feminist Thematics and Shakespearean Tragedy," *PMLA* 103 (1988): 125–38.

22.   Ibid., 128; and see Coppélia Kahn, *Man's Estate: Masculine Identity in Shakespeare* (Berkeley, 1981). In more detail in *Shakespeare's Mercutio*, I discuss the effort to contain/suppress Mercutio and thereby to continue the canonization of heterosexuality.

23.   Coppélia Kahn, "Coming of Age in Verona," in *The Woman's Part: Feminist Criticism of Shakespeare*, ed. Carolyn Ruth Swift Lenz, Gayle Greene, and Carol Thomas Neely (Urbana, 1980), 176.

24.   Ibid., 176–77.

25.   William Shakespeare, *Romeo and Juliet*, ed. John Dover Wilson and George Ian Duthie (Cambridge, 1955), 152–53.

26.   In *Shakespeare's Bawdy*, Partridge's note on et cetera cross-references "medlar," where we find the oddly defensive claim that in "Shakespeare, 'medlar' means *either* pudend or podex or the pudend-podex area."

27.   Colman, *Dramatic Use of Bawdy*, 69.

28.   Ibid., 100, 7.

29.   Ibid., 7.

Analysis of Application

Joseph A. Porter's "Marlowe, Shakespeare, and the Canonization of Heterosexuality" is a useful example of gay-positive, revisionary analysis of both literature and the norms of literary criticism. Porter takes two well-known Elizabethan playwrights, both of whom have been the subject of previous speculation concerning same-sex desire in their lives and plays, and works toward a delineation of the precise ways in which the widespread social privileging of heterosexuality has erased gay-positive readings of their works. Porter is careful to locate his analysis within both historical and critical contexts, avoiding charges of anachronism by using terms such as "homoerotic" rather than "homosexual" to discuss the subtexts of the works he considers. Even so, he is clearly interested in pointing out manifestations of same-sex desire in those works and challenging forthrightly the canonization of heterosexuality in recent critical discourse.

Although Porter's analysis could range widely over the many possibly homoerotic scenes and figures in plays and poems by Shakespeare and Marlowe, he instead focuses primarily on one character: Mercutio from *Romeo and Juliet*. Porter makes a strong case that Shakespeare on several occasions found ways of responding, through dramatic portrayals, to the diverse challenges posed by his contemporary and rival Marlowe, and he provides compelling evidence that Mercutio can be read as a figure through whom Shakespeare grapples with Marlowe's identity and sexuality two years after the latter's death. In examining Mercutio's thinly veiled "phallic" references and erotic "invitations" to Romeo, Porter demonstrates how a gay-positive reading can open up new avenues for speculation about tensions within a work of literature, between authors, and among critical respondents to cultural texts. Porter thereby makes a credible case for how Shakespeare may be considered "open to an alternate sexuality," even if his critics are not.

But Porter's essay is useful not only because it illuminates a primary text such as *Romeo and Juliet* but also because it demonstrates gay criticism's clear debt to, but also divergence from, feminist critique. Porter makes his own pro-feminist sympathies explicit from the beginning of the essay, but he also offers pointed criticism of some feminist critics who ignore possible nuances of characterization regarding sexually nonconforming men and thereby help to perpetuate a "privileging of heterosexuality." Indeed, an analysis of the work of Coppélia Kahn (whose essay on *King Lear* appears in Chapter 4) provides an important occasion for Porter to issue a challenge to his scholarly colleagues to de-privilege heterosexuality in their own readings.

Porter's essay is also noteworthy for its careful attention to detail—in particular, the erasures of and varied responses to a single phrase from *Romeo and Juliet:* "open-arse." In charting how that explicit reference to sodomy (anal sex) was taken out of the play for centuries by editors and how controversial the phrase still is among critics, Porter is able to drive home his central point: that homoeroticism has been, and in many ways still is, devalued among Shakespeare's learned devotees. And in a final challenge to his fellow scholars of the Elizabethan era, Porter is just as critical of those who privilege homosexuality in texts and whom he believes are as guilty of oversimplification and biased reading practices as their homoeroticism-erasing peers. While no one work of gay-positive literary criticism can adequately represent the full range of possible subjects and methodologies that fall under the broad heading of gay/lesbian/queer analysis, Porter's essay is exemplary in its tackling of both microtextual and larger meta-theoretical issues regarding same-sex desire and in his challenge to all critics to allow complexity and a respect for sexual diversity to resonate through their readings of texts.

CHAPTER 9

Race, Ethnicity, and Post-Colonial Analysis

Overview

An analysis of race, ethnicity, and/or post-coloniality can enrich any critical reading, or it can provide an exciting central focus in analyzing a literary or other cultural text. As with Marxist and materialist analysis (see Chapter 3) and feminist analysis (see Chapter 7), an investigation of race, ethnicity, and/or post-coloniality explores the complex relationship between a text and its social context, tracing the many ways in which the belief systems of a time and place are reflected in and potentially altered by literary and other forms of representation. Central to all such critique is the recognition that racism (the differential treatment of people based on racial identity) and ethnocentrism (the viewing of one's own ethnic group's perspectives as universally legitimate and appropriate for all) have been thoroughly entrenched in language, literature, art, and social institutions. Even so, such oppression has not gone unchallenged; oppositional voices and revisionary viewpoints existed in the past and have grown in strength in recent years. Indeed, many students using this methodology will find their analysis energized with a sense of clear political relevance as they investigate textual reflections of some of the most powerful belief systems underlying our senses of self and other, both today and in the past.

First it is necessary to establish working definitions of the three terms mentioned in this chapter's title. "Race" has been used loosely at times to indicate practically any group of people who self-identify separately from others, but for our purposes the term refers specifically to the ways that physiological characteristics (such as skin tone) are combined with distinctions in social history (such as region of original habitation) to distinguish

265

and identify groups of people. "Ethnicity," although often equated with "race," in this discussion refers more directly to nonphysiological aspects of cultural identity, such as religious affiliation and/or shared customs or language. Nation of origin also may be an important aspect of ethnicity, as is the case with the many American descendants of European ancestry who are ethnically, but not necessarily racially, diverse (e.g., Italian Americans or Polish Americans). "Post-coloniality" is quite distinct from the other terms, because it focuses more directly on national and regional legacies of imperialism and colonialism (the domination and occupation of certain nations and regions of the world by others). These three terms thus indicate different possible emphases in literary and cultural analysis, but they share a commitment to challenging oppression based on cultural identity, seeking to enrich our understanding of the diverse experiences and rich heritages of all groups and peoples.

As laudable and even unquestionable as that may seem to us today, such was not always the case. For centuries, science, popular culture, and even religion lent powerful support to racist beliefs. Groups that were branded sub- or even nonhuman simply because of linguistic and/or physiological differences were enslaved and subjected to other forms of physical and psychological oppression. Literary and other cultural texts have reflected that oppression, often from the standpoint of the oppressor, whose art and literature have commonly helped justify broad social belief systems and the more specific acts that follow from biased definitions and designations. To be sure, the most pernicious qualities and consequences of racism have also been subject to limited forms of written critique for several centuries (by the Quakers in the United States, for instance), but only in recent years has a concerted critical inquiry into racism's literary and cultural manifestations gained widespread attention and support.

In the wake of the civil rights movements of the 1950s and 1960s in the United States, the field of literary and cultural studies began to confront some of its own blind spots and implicit biases. Not only were widely revered literary works reexamined for their reflections of dominant values and oppressive belief systems, but also the traditional notion of a narrowly circumscribed canon of masterpieces was reevaluated for the biases that underlay its exclusionary principles. Thus writers such as William Shakespeare and James Fenimore Cooper came under new scrutiny for the ways in which their portrayals of nonwhite characters helped reinforce oppressive notions of race and ethnicity. Furthermore, previously ignored writers from racial and ethnic minority groups, such as Jean Toomer and Zora Neale Hurston, began to receive the critical attention they had long deserved. Thus an attention to issues of race and ethnicity has changed literary and cultural studies in dramatic ways, expanding both the list of texts deemed worthy of analysis and its avenues of inquiry into those texts. Similarly, even more recent attention to post-coloniality has brought to the foreground a host of writers, such as Chinua Achebe from Nigeria and Jamaica Kincaid from Antigua, whose works grapple with the complex consequences of Anglo American and European domination of other nations. Furthermore, it has allowed insight into the ways in which canonical writers such as Jane Austen and Joseph Conrad have helped shape cultural belief systems regarding "civilization" and "foreignness." The broad field of race, ethnicity, and post-colonial analysis includes some of the most exciting critical work being done today, by theorists such as Henry Louis Gates, Edward Said, Gayatri Spivak, and bell hooks. It explores how images and issues of cultural identity can reveal some of the fundamental structures through which society makes meaning as well as how those structures must change if culturally sanctioned oppression is ever to end.

The following pages will examine key principles underlying the analysis of race, ethnicity, and post-coloniality in literary and other cultural texts. Such analysis is often combined with the insights of other methodologies covered in this book; thus one finds feminist post-colonial analysis, materialist emphases in the analysis of ethnicity, and gay/lesbian/queer analysis enriched with a focus on racial identity. But rather than attempt to summarize the perspectives of the many groups that draw on and participate in the expansive field of studies in race, ethnicity, and post-coloniality today, this chapter will emphasize the broader ways in which texts reflect, reinforce, and/or work to revise social belief systems; furthermore, it will emphasize the role that literary and cultural critics can play in exposing oppression and effecting social change. As always, students are urged to consult works from the annotated bibliography to expand their understanding of the diverse voices that have contributed to this exciting field.

Key Principles

1 *Categories of race and ethnicity have been used in ways that have empowered and oppressed.*

Much as feminist analysis focuses on the ways in which gender categories have been used throughout history to oppress women, an analysis of race, ethnicity, and/or post-coloniality begins with the recognition that the social meanings ascribed to categories of race and ethnicity have led to profound injustices. Racism and ethnocentrism have been forces plaguing almost every society and region of the world, as differences in appearance, language, and customs have been used to designate groups of *us* and *them* (or "self" and "other"), with the unique characteristics of *them* perceived as a threat to the security and interests of *us*. Anger, suspicion, and hatred have developed from the ignorance that geographic and linguistic separation breeds. But as common as xenophobia—the fear of the foreigner and/or outsider—has been throughout all of human history, the manifestations and horrific consequences of racism have grown exponentially in the past 500 years, with the increased intermingling of peoples and the rapidly growing sophistication of technologies of war and oppression. Economic and technological advantages have allowed certain groups—namely, those of European origin—to dominate and exploit others with historically unparalleled force. And that component of force is key here, for one very useful way of distinguishing racism from other social currents, such as fear of those who are different or anger at oppressors, is to see it as race-based value judgments with clear social power behind them. Thus a term such as "reverse racism," when used to indicate the anger of the oppressed, is not particularly useful for nuanced critique, because it obscures the origins and long history of, as well as the primary responsibility for, an entrenched dynamic of oppression. That foundation of racial and social injustice demands continuing attention and critique, even as its many consequences and pernicious legacies are apparent in the bloody wars, terrorist attacks, and urban crime statistics that make headlines every day.

2 *This differentiation of peoples is reflected in and reinforced by language and metaphor.*

Since one of the most commonly recognized indicators of racial identity is skin color, it is especially telling that Western culture has attributed profoundly unequal meanings to different colors and even subtle shadings. Whiteness and lightness have long been equated with goodness and purity, as well as intellectual and spiritual superiority. Darkness is traditionally associated with evil and debasement. Thus one of the most fundamental ways in which Western culture has made meaning—through opposing whiteness to blackness and assigning clear values to them—has led to racist judgments and actions, masking their social construction with an appearance of "naturalness." Indeed, literary and cultural analysis may begin with a tracing of the ways in which such an opposition reveals itself within a text, continuing on to examine the consequences for characters and groups of a reliance on the binaries white/black and light/dark in ascribing social value (see Chapters 5 and 6 for more information on binary structures and possibilities for their disruption).

But such underlying binaries are not the only linguistic component and manifestation of race and racism, for language has also been used in very self-conscious exercises of power. Hateful and derogatory terms are often created by the powerful to "put people in their place" and demonstrate precisely who has the ability to name others and assign them a social role and value. Some textual analysis focuses on such linguistic reflections of power, as well as the many responses to that power shown by the oppressed (including the appropriating of an oppressive term for use within the oppressed group itself, in an attempt to deflate its power). As Henry Louis Gates has explored in *The Signifying Monkey*, oppressed groups have often shaped language to serve their own needs, making words "signify" in powerfully different ways. Indeed, the battle for social power and recognition is often reflected in a battle over language, for in asserting a right to name itself and express itself, a group asserts its ownership of itself, demonstrating that whatever forms of oppression—slavery, imprisonment, and expropriation—may have existed in the past, the group is, in fact, neither owned by nor inherently subordinate to any other.

Thus, if we take as a brief example Hollywood film portrayals of African Americans, we find a number of possible avenues of inquiry propelled by the perspectives and insights mentioned above. For instance, one cultural critic might examine a film such as D. W. Griffith's *The Birth of a Nation*, analyzing the racist implications of some of its plot line by tracing its use of the imagery of lightness and darkness to ascribe moral and social value. Another critic might examine language in a given film or set of films, analyzing, for example, the use of Black English (or caricatures thereof) to ask whether it designates comic inferiority to a dominant group (as in the exaggerated speech and mannerisms of characters such as Prissy in *Gone with the Wind*) or the creation of a subcultural space in response to forces of racism or ethnic oppression (as in dramas of black urban existence such as *Boyz in the Hood* and *Do the Right Thing*). Indeed, investigation of the use of a single word—the infamous "n" word, for example—to determine whether it indicates and denigrates "otherness" from *outside* of a community or communicates values and meanings *within* a community is a clear example of the complex powers of and analytical possibilities provided by processes of signification and resignification, as Gates and others have explored.

3 *This differentiation of peoples, as well as forces of economic greed and expansionism, are also reflected in a centuries-long history of imperialism and colonization.*

Enslavement, occupation, exploitation, and even extermination have been some of the most horrific manifestations of race-based value judgments.

During the seventeenth, eighteenth, and nineteenth centuries European nations scrambled for control over other regions of the world, displacing and oppressing the peoples inhabiting those regions. At stake, of course, were vast natural resources and also national pride, with the latter centering on which nation could lay claim to the largest and richest empire. But greed and egotism were not the only forces driving imperialism, for a well-articulated belief in a profound, even quasi-sacred, duty to bring "civilization" to "untamed" continents and "savage" peoples was also used to justify exploitation and colonization. Rich cultural traditions and complex indigenous civilizations were destroyed as European religions, languages, and values were introduced and often brutally imposed. Only in the middle to latter decades of the twentieth century did some of the most overt forms of imperialism begin to wane as local populations revolted against colonizing forces and as more covert forms of imperial control replaced outright military occupation.

The field of post-colonial studies examines the legacy of this brutal deployment of power and the lingering effects of European domination of the indigenous peoples of Africa, Asia, and North, Central, and South America. It seeks to explore the political and cultural aftermath of colonization and to examine the profound changes wrought on colonized peoples. The questions it may seek to address are diverse. What forms of protest literature and art arose under colonialism? How were colonizers and the colonized represented in such mediums? How were the self-perceptions and senses of self-worth of indigenous peoples changed by the imposition of foreign languages, values, and social definitions? What attempts to recover traditions and other preexisting aspects of culture have followed the retreat of imperial armies? How have those attempts fared as European traditions and cultural norms have continued to be disseminated through music, film, and other cultural forms? How do lingering economic disparities, international trade policies, and corrupt political institutions continue as subtle effects of imperialism? How do literary and other cultural texts address these issues and offer implicit or explicit solutions to complex social and cultural problems?

To make some of this more concrete, we might think for a moment of the possibilities for post-colonial analysis of Native Americans in film. In addressing the questions above, the critic might first establish the existence of certain beliefs among both American colonizers and twentieth-century filmmakers by carefully examining historical documents from the era of westward expansion and then corresponding images of savage Indians in much of film history. Such analysis might then turn to an important instance of Native American self-representation in film, such as Chris Eyre's

1998 film *Smoke Signals*, to explore the complex negotiations that Native Americans must undertake today with their own cultural history and traditions, as well as with their complex identities as twentieth-century Americans who are exposed to the very same pop cultural stereotyping discussed above. In exploring this intriguing melange of old and new, of oppression and resistance, of disempowerment and reempowerment, the critic may discover that human beings often demonstrate stunning personal resilience, even though their lives have been culturally and economically impoverished by the racist and ethnocentric actions of others.

4 *This differentiation of peoples and its political consequences are reflected not only in literary and other forms of representation but also in our very notion of literature.*

Indeed, literary and other cultural texts—films, historical documents, music, and advertisements—provide important sources of data for the analysis of racism, ethnocentrism, and other forms of oppression. As discussed in preceding chapters on materialist and feminist analysis, literary representations not only reflect but often help construct and maintain the worldviews of their audience. They provide insight into belief systems of the past and may exert a continuing influence long after their initial appearance. But recognizing this is neither to posit a simple cause-and-effect relationship between what one reads and how one acts nor to suggest that representations in novels, plays, and poems can ever provide objective sources of data. Rather, the literary and cultural critic must be attuned to the implicit biases that underlie a text's characterizations and themes and, at the same time, be aware of the many ways in which readers may respond to a given text, perhaps accepting, rejecting, or complexly negotiating with its belief systems (see Chapter 2 for more information on possible reader responses to a text). Those belief systems may be apparent in subtle and overt ways throughout the text, in its form, metaphors, symbols, and themes. Thus the critic may explore a text's characterizations, its portrayal of villainy or heroism, in order to pinpoint the roles and social values attributed to the groups it portrays.

But, of course, literary and cultural analysis is never free of its own biases. Our very notion of what falls within a category such as "masterpiece," "film classic," and even "literature" itself reflects numerous cultural values. While formalist and New Critics may reference notions of enduring aesthetic value to support judgments about what is or is not literary (see Chapter 1), those notions reflect the cultural histories of empowered social groups. Thus critics interested in race, ethnicity, and post-coloniality do not necessarily restrict their analysis to those texts traditionally designated as masterpieces, for numerous other cultural forms also allow insight into how groups have lived, defined themselves, and defined others. Rich cultural traditions exist in folktales, regional music and drama, storytelling, and other genres that may have been demeaned as "popular" rather than "literary" in past critical evaluations. Certainly sustained analysis of the portrayal of African Americans in film would demand attention to the many popular but now largely forgotten films written for and shown in the African American community in the 1940s and 1950s. Exploring why a work or set of works was neglected by previous critics and historians is often the starting point for intriguing analysis. Indeed, film history, literary history, and cultural history are themselves texts available for analysis to the critic interested in race, ethnicity, and post-coloniality, since their ways of making meaning are as complex and culturally revealing as literary texts.

But even as critics interested in race, ethnicity, and post-coloniality work to establish new forms of cultural and literary history that include the voices of those who have often been ignored or silenced, it is important that they remember that those voices are not always unequivocally opposed to or completely different from those representing the racist or ethnocentric belief systems of the dominant culture. Indeed, one important form of analysis in this field is examination of the ways in which dominant belief systems pervade and influence even those voices raised in opposition to them. Thus critics at times examine the "internalized oppression"of groups subjected to social prejudice, some of whose members may even use highly oppressive concepts and categories to judge themselves and others in their group (as Spike Lee explores in his film *Jungle Fever*). The range of textual responses from among the oppressed includes voices of collusion as well as those calling for radical change. Attention to race, ethnicity, and post-coloniality demands a recognition of human differences and nuances of belief and behavior within all groups, for gross oversimplification and facile generalizations are some of the root causes of persistent forms of racism and ethnocentrism.

5 *Thus an understanding of textual reflections of racism and ethnocentrism demands an attention to the cultural history and belief systems of the social group(s) being portrayed and discussed.*

Important for all analysis in the study of race, ethnicity, and post-coloniality is a careful attention to the history and culture of the social groups under consideration. In exploring the self-representation of African Americans in film or white filmmakers' representations of Native Americans, critics must acquaint themselves with aspects of African American or Native American history and culture in order to discuss knowledgeably the ways in which social beliefs and biases are reflected in or challenged by texts. In claiming authority without knowledge or research, the critic runs a high risk of simply replicating the biases that continue to circulate throughout our culture. To attempt to critique the heavily skewed representations of savage Indians in 1950s Westerns without a solid knowledge base is to risk missing some of the most important clues to the ethnocentrism of such films, from their misrepresentations of the dynamics of aggressor and aggressed upon to their offensive homogenization of Native American cultures and forms of social organization. Rather than being peripheral to the critic's analysis, these data provide some of its core material.

6   *The analysis of racism and ethnocentrism in texts from the past may have relevance to the ways we live our lives today.*

Thus literary and cultural critics should understand as fully as possible the social context from which a given text emerged and ponder how it reveals beliefs and struggles that persist to this day (see Chapter 10 for information on the New Historicism). A literary critic, for example, might wish to research the social forces at work in the African American community during the time in which James Baldwin's *Go Tell It on the Mountain* is set in order to analyze the text's references to the African American church and representations of the industrial North and rural South. Equally important for the same or another critic might be an examination of Baldwin's continuing relevance to unsolved social problems today. Similarly, a post-colonial critic might explore the characterizations in E. M. Forster's *A Passage to India* in light of colonial anxieties especially prevalent during the early decades of the twentieth century in order to comprehend more fully the metaphors and tensions of the text; beyond this, however, the critic might also discover that the novel allows an exploration of continuing tensions on the Indian subcontinent today. Indeed, this process of sorting out historical relationships, exploring how belief systems have sometimes changed and sometimes endured, characterizes some of the latest developments in literary and cultural analysis, energizing examination of texts from the seemingly distant past. Often the belief systems portrayed in those texts are not at all distant. In placing 1930s and 1940s Nazi film representations of "demonic Jews" side by side with similar portrayals in white supremacist propaganda today, a critic might demonstrate in chilling fashion how hatred and bigotry can endure among groups and subcultures even when social contexts change and many people's consciousness of oppression has been raised dramatically.

7 *Textual analysis of race, ethnicity, and post-coloniality can serve as a starting point for positive forms of social change in the future.*

As frequently as studies in race, ethnicity, and post-coloniality look to the past for texts and for historical evidence, a firm belief the underlies all such work is that through the analysis of oppression literary and cultural critics can help shape the future. Thus, much like work informed by materialist, feminist, and gay/lesbian/queer theories (see Chapters 3, 7, and 8), the textual analysis of race, ethnicity, and post-coloniality has an immediacy and impact that is undeniable. Cultural critics such as bell hooks have looked to representations in literature, television, and film to seek ways of changing the world by raising people's awareness of hidden textual meanings and the cultural, as well as social, dynamics of oppression. Indeed, it is hardly surprising that hooks and others have often combined an attention to race and ethnicity with an exploration of gender, class, and sexuality to provide multifaceted insights into literary and cultural representation (as is discussed more fully Chapter 10). In researching and analyzing how cultural forces have separated and differentially valued groups of people, literary and cultural critics tackle some of the most profound social problems facing the world today. In probing the responses of groups in the past and examining emerging voices of revision, critics in all of the fields of contemporary analysis mentioned above position themselves as political agents working to redress injustice and to further understanding, in the hope of helping create a more equitable future for all peoples.

Bibliography

Allen, Paula Gunn. *Studies in American Indian Literature: Critical Essays and Course Designs.* New York: Modern Language Association, 1983.

> While this book is designed especially for instructors, its superb overviews of issues in American Indian studies and its discussion of current trends in literary theory will make it of interest to many readers at both the intermediate and advanced levels.

Anzaldua, Gloria. *Borderlands/La Frontera: The New Mestiza.* San Francisco: Aunt Lute Books, 1987.

> In this book and in the collection *This Bridge Called My Back* (co-edited with Cherrie Moraga), Anzaldua helped establish the field of Chicana and mestiza studies. Anzaldua offers a rich personal and theoretical narrative that will be accessible to readers at all levels.

Ashcroft, Bill, Gareth Griffiths, and Helen Tiffin, eds. *The Post-Colonial Studies Reader*. New York: Routledge, 1995.

This dense but important and wide-ranging overview of the field of post-colonial studies includes essays by Gayatri Spivak, Homi Bhabha, Chinua Achebe, and other important scholars. Its presupposition of theoretical knowledge will make it of greatest interest to advanced readers.

Gates, Henry Louis, ed. *Black Literature and Literary Theory*. New York: Routledge, 1990.

This collection of essays by important scholars in the field of African American literary studies includes a superb introduction by Henry Louis Gates that overviews the field. While many of the essays presume advanced theoretical knowledge, Gates's introduction will make it of interest to intermediate as well as advanced readers.

Gates, Henry Louis. *The Signifying Monkey: A Theory of Afro-American Literary Criticism*. New York: Oxford University Press, 1988.

This is one of the most influential theoretical works published in recent years, one in which Gates develops a theory of "signification" that draws and also expands on post-structuralist theory, as well as previous articulations in the field of African American literary studies. Its theoretical sophistication and vocabulary will make it of greatest interest to advanced readers.

hooks, bell. *Black Looks: Race and Representation*. Boston: South End Press, 1992.

This is one of many books by bell hooks that explores images of race in contemporary culture, but it is noteworthy for its critique of the pop star Madonna as well as its reflections on black masculinity and the common ground possible among African Americans and Native Americans. hooks is an accessible writer whose work will be of interest to students at all levels.

Kim, Elaine H. *Asian American Literature: An Introduction to the Writings and Their Social Context*. Philadelphia: Temple University Press, 1982.

While this overview of the field of Asian American literary studies is several years old, its clarity and insight into American literary history make it of continuing significance. While it presumes some knowledge of literary and social criticism, it will be of interest to readers at both the intermediate and advanced levels.

Loomba, Ania. *Colonialism/Postcolonialism*. New York: Routledge, 1998.

This is a clear and comprehensive introduction to the field of post-colonial theory. In addition to covering major concepts and theorists, it includes brief applications of theory to texts from the nineteenth and twentieth centuries. Its accessible language will make it of interest to both intermediate and advanced readers.

Said, Edward W. *Culture and Imperialism.* New York: Vintage, 1993.

> In this book and in his earlier work *Orientalism*, Edward Said helped establish the field of post-colonial studies. His work is particularly significant for its accessible and nuanced treatment of both canonical and lesser-known literary figures. Said's writings will be of interest to all readers.

Stanley, Sandra Kumamoto, ed. *Other Sisterhoods: Literary Theory and U.S. Women of Color.* Urbana: University of Illinois Press, 1998.

> This collection of original essays covers many of the emerging issues and theories in the diverse fields of interest discussed throughout this book. But beyond the importance of its essays, the bibliographies attached to them also make this collection of great interest to intermediate and advanced readers.

Application

Reading Prompts

1. Before Joyce A. Joyce focuses specifically on the racial implications of Richard Wright's use of figurative language and metaphor in *Native Son*, she offers key definitions of terms, addresses previous criticism, and examines Wright's use of sentence structure to reveal important tensions in the novel. Consider how this lead-in helps strengthen her main argument and anchor her authority as an interpreter of the text.

2. Highlight or underline places in her essay where Joyce draws explicit parallels between Bigger and King Lear. Why would she do so?

3. Joyce suggests that "whiteness" and "blackness" function in the novel as interrelated terms. Mark or highlight passages in which Joyce demonstrates that their apparent opposition represents society's views only, masking a more fundamental commonality underlying all human existence.

4. Joyce suggests that Bigger is "blind" through much of the novel. Mark those passages in which she explains in precisely which ways this is so.

5. After you finish reading this essay, consider the following question: How does the novel's final sun image reveal Bigger's new insights as he approaches death, what are those insights, and how do they relate to the novel's tragic form?

JOYCE A. JOYCE

The Figurative Web of Native Son

The crux of tragedy is ambiguity in the characterization of the hero and irony embodied in the events that affect the hero's life. Richard Wright's *Native Son* epitomizes this duality in the personality of Bigger Thomas. With Bigger's consciousness at the center of the novel, Wright creates the mood of exploration and anxiety[1] through his portrayal of Bigger as paradoxically indifferent and violent, fearful and prideful, sullen and passionate. As shown in Chapter 3, the narrator, identified with Bigger's consciousness, ensures that we perceive simultaneously Bigger's vulnerability and his violent temperament. Thus the narrator's guidance along with the ambiguity in Bigger's character explains why it is possible not only to feel sympathy for but also to like Bigger Thomas, who is both murderer and hero. Yet, the sublimity of the novel lies in the connection between Wright's characterization of Bigger and his unique use of sentence structure and figurative language. For *Native Son* is a linguistically complex network of sentences and images that reflect the opposing or contradictory aspects of Bigger's psyche and thus synthesize the interrelationship between Wright's subject matter and his expression of it.

Much of the criticism on *Native Son* has focused too exclusively on the image of the snow and the metaphor of blindness. It has overlooked the tightly knit web which Wright creates through his figurative use of the colors black, white, and yellow and the interrelationship between the images of the snow, the sun, the wall (the "white looming mountain"), the metaphor of blindness, and Wright's sentence patterns.[2] Similarly, naturalistic and existential views of Bigger as either a victimized or isolated figure limit the dimensions of Bigger's character and give no attention to how Wright's use of language punctuates the irony and ambiguity of Bigger's personality. Irony in Bigger's characterization, in the sequence of events that affect his life, and in the language is the foundation upon which Wright builds his tragic theme. The fact that Bigger is at once separate from others (that is, individual) and at the same time connected to them (that is, universal) parallels the ambiguous, interlocked symbols of the snow, the sun, and the wall, and the colors white, yellow, and black. For as is the case with the elements of Bigger's personality, these symbols have contrapuntal meanings that parallel and, at the same time, contrast with each other.

When Wright says that the rhythms of Bigger's life vacillate between "indifference and violence; periods of abstract brooding and periods of intense desire; moments of silence and moments of anger," he himself links the ambiguity of Bigger's personality to the language he uses to depict that personality. The periodic, balanced, and compound sentences in the novel unite with the symbols to supplement Wright's theme.[3] Just as the colors black, white, and yellow, blindness, snow, the sun, and the wall all achieve symbolic depth as representations of Bigger's ambiguous character, the rhythm of many sentences highlights the discrepancy between Bigger's perception of himself and the view of him held by others. Hence the figurative language and the rhetorical function of the sentences coalesce as integral embodiments of Wright's single purpose—to depict the nature of truth through his characterization of Bigger Thomas. For the ironic nature of Bigger's psyche, of the events that affect his life, and of the language that describes him exemplify the dialectic of the tragic form described by Sewall: "It [the tragic form] is a way . . . of making an important—and 'tragic'—statement about the nature of truth. In tragedy, truth is not revealed as one harmonious whole; it is many-faceted, ambiguous, a sum of irreconcilables—and that is one source of its terror".[4]

The periodic sentences which summarize past events, introduce Bigger's state of mind, and justify his actions both alleviate the intensity of the terror evoked by Bigger's harsh actions and emphasize the changes in his state of mind at different intervals. In Book 3, when Bigger is first confined, Wright uses a series of participial phrases to describe the hope and rebelliousness which motivated Bigger in Books 1 and 2.

> Having been thrown by an accidental murder into a position where he had sensed a possible order and meaning in his relations with the people about him; having accepted the moral guilt and responsibility for that murder because it made him feel free for the first time in his life; having felt in his heart some obscure need to be at home with people and having demanded ransom money to enable him to do it—having done all this and failed, he chose not to struggle any more.[5]

These earlier feelings are juxtaposed to the new and more dominant feelings of resignation and helplessness stated succinctly in the final independent clause. A manipulative tool of the third-person limited narrator, this periodic sentence does far more than assure the reader's perception of the sudden changes in nuances that have taken place in Bigger's consciousness. It illuminates that complex ability of the human psyche to hold conflicting feelings simultaneously as it analyzes them and discards those that fail to be beneficial.

Not only do the periodic sentences reveal the contrasts within Bigger's own consciousness; they also exemplify the irreconcilable differences between Bigger's attitude and that of his family toward his rebelliousness. Interpreting Bigger's response to the shame and humiliation on the faces of his family as they visit him in jail, the narrator explains: "While looking at his brother and sister and feeling his mother's arms about him; while knowing that Jack and G. H. and Gus were standing awkwardly in the doorway staring at him in curious disbelief—while being conscious of all this, Bigger felt a wild outlandish conviction surge in him: *They ought to be glad!*" (252). This series of elliptical clauses stresses the emotional chasm that separates Bigger from all others in his Black environment. Moreover, these clauses illustrate a perfect balance between form and meaning. For just as the elliptical clauses depend on the independent clause to complete their meaning, it is in this scene that Bigger, upon hearing of the assaults upon his family, begins to perceive the relationship between his actions and the well-being of his family. Thus the periodic sentence suggests the simultaneity of irreconcilable opposites: Bigger's alienation from others as well as his connection to something outside himself.

The balanced and compound sentences prove to be even more illuminative of this paradox. In the scene in which Bigger succumbs to Buckley's coercion and signs a confession, Wright uses a balanced sentence which juxtaposes Bigger's physical helplessness to his emotional strength:

> He lay on the cold floor sobbing; but really he was standing up strongly with contrite heart, holding his life in his hands, staring at it with a wondering question. He lay on the cold floor sobbing; but really he was pushing forward with his puny strength against a world too big and too strong for him. He lay on the cold floor sobbing; but really he was groping forward with fierce zeal into a welter of circumstances which he felt contained a water of mercy for the thirst of his heart and brain.(264)

Here, contrasting ideas occur within the same grammatical structure. The repeated independent clause which emphasizes Bigger's intense despair contrasts with the varying independent clauses which describe the hope Bigger feels despite the severity of his circumstances. No other group of sentences more aptly illustrates the paradoxical nature of Bigger's personality. Whereas the Bigger of Books 1 and 2 is simultaneously fearful and prideful, indifferent and violent, the Bigger of Book 3 is at once physically impotent and emotionally resolute.

As is the case with Bigger's personality, irreconcilable opposites also underlie the harsh realities of racially and socially segregated communities in *Native Son*. Achieving a superb balance between form and content, Wright uses the compound sentence to stress the power whites have over Blacks as well as the aberrations engendered in both by stereotypes based on class and sex. The compound sentence accompanies the metaphorical function of the colors black and white in their representation of the social, economic, and political forces that govern Bigger's life. These elements of language manifest the cosmological order that divides society into groups— Black and white, rich and poor, male and female.

The series of compound sentences which describes Bigger's immediate thoughts concerning his murder of Mary accentuates the overwhelming severity of the codes controlling the interaction between the Black and white worlds in the novel: "He stood with her body in his arms in the silent room and cold facts battered him like waves sweeping in from the sea; she was dead; she was white; she was a woman; he had killed her; he was black; he might be caught; he did not want to be caught; if he were they would kill him" (77). Whereas the balanced and periodic sentences discussed above focus on the paradoxical elements within Bigger's psyche, the compound sentence highlights the incongruity between Bigger's world view and that of the white world. The simile comparing the "cold facts" of Bigger's thoughts to "waves sweeping in from the sea" suggests, as does Wright's use of setting, that the forces of the white world are as powerful and as invincible as those of the natural environment.

But the apparent invincibility of the white world in *Native Son* is underlaid with frailties. Bigger escapes immediate detection as Mary's murderer only because the Daltons and the rest of the whites who question him fail to see the full scope of his humanity. A series of stark compound sentences describing Bigger's response to Mrs. Dalton's questioning shows how her stereotyped notions of race, class, and sex render her psychologically ineffective in communicating with Bigger and in seeing through his mask of humility: "She must know this house like a book, he thought. He trembled with excitement. She was white and he was black; she was rich and he was poor; she was old and he was young; she was the boss and he was the worker. He was safe; yes" (109). Perfect examples of the irony that is the essential element holding all parts of the novel together, this series of compound sentences and the use of polysyndeton explicitly place racial, class, and age categories in equal grammatical structures while their implicit message is a condemnation of the injustices that arise from these categories.

Wright's ingenious use of periodic, balanced, and compound sentences is only part of the intricate language system through which Bigger's tragic fate evolves. Complementing Bigger's ambiguous characterization and the ironic events that shape his destiny are the interconnections among the rhythmic sentence patterns; the colors black, white, and yellow; the images of the wall, the sun, and the snow; and the metaphor of blindness. In their figurative function, the wall and the color black unite with the balanced sentence in their portrayal of Bigger's helplessness and physical impotence. Suggestive of the entrapment described in the balanced sentence, black represents the fear and humiliation Bigger feels in the face of the white world. Upon Bigger's initial visit to the Dalton home, the fear and shame he feels in the presence of whites are so intense that he remains on the verge of hysteria during the entire interview with Mr. Dalton. Thus when Bigger first meets Mr. Dalton, the word *black* accentuates the psychological chasm that separates the two men: "Grabbing the arms of the chair, he pulled himself upright and found a tall, lean, white-haired man holding a piece of paper in his hand. The man was gazing at him with an amused smile that made him conscious of every square inch of skin on his *black* body" (39, emphasis mine). Mr. Dalton's "amused smile" reflects the superiority, power, and emotional distance characteristic of a representative from the godlike world that controls Bigger's life. It is no accident that this white-haired man holds a (white) piece of paper. These symbols are markers for the subjugation that causes Bigger to recoil in acute awareness of his blackness. Consequently, Wright's use of *black* interacts with setting. For just as Mr. Dalton is identified with the power and stability cultivated by his environment, Bigger's encounter with that environment produces feelings of inferiority and entrapment.

Although the word *black* appears throughout the novel, two other passages make especially vivid its metaphorical dimensions. The first occurs in the scene in which Bigger murders Bessie. Despite the fact that Bessie coerces Bigger into confiding in her, once she learns of the magnitude of his crime she desperately wants to retreat. Bigger must then keep her with him until he realizes that her extreme fear will only accelerate his capture. Soon after he decides that he has to kill her, they step into a deserted building to rest. Wright uses *black* three times in this single passage to underscore Bessie's despair and impotence:

> He [Bigger] put his shoulder to it [the door] and gave a stout shove; it yielded grudgingly. It was *black* inside and the feeble glow of the flashlight did not help much. . . . He circled the spot of the flashlight; the floor was carpeted with *black* dirt and he saw two bricks lying in corners. He looked at Bessie; her hands covered her face and he could see the damp of tears on her *black* fingers. (196, emphasis mine)

Black in this passage connects with Wright's use of setting to reflect Bigger's growing feelings of entrapment and fear. It also suggests that Bessie's cowering and feelings of remorse stem from her humiliation at her blackness as well as her fear of the white world.

The other scene in which *black* is used with especially strong significance occurs during Rev. Hammond's visit with Bigger in jail in Book 3. Rev. Hammond epitomizes the Black community's acceptance of the guilt and shame that arise from their blackness. Bigger intuitively associates the newspapers' descriptions of him as brutish, ignorant, and inferior with Rev. Hammond's passivity and penitence:

> He [Bigger] stared at the man's jet-*black* suit and remembered who he was. . . . And at once he was on guard against the man. . . . He feared that the preacher would make him feel remorseful. He wanted to tell him to go; but so closely associated in his mind was the man with his mother and what she stood for that he could not speak. In his feelings he could not tell the difference between what this man evoked in him and what he read in the papers. . . . (240, emphasis mine)

Here *black* is the touchstone for Bigger's response to Rev. Hammond, his Job-like rejection of this counselor's religious palaver. The use of the word *black* appears to be inadvertent in the one-line paragraph after Rev. Hammond's prayer for Bigger: "Bigger's black face rested in his hands and he did not move" (243). Actually, *black* functions here as the symbolic finale of the suffering, shame, and penitence expressed in the prayer. When Bigger eventually pulls the preacher's cross from around his neck, he demonstrates his final rejection of the humiliation linked to his blackness.

A traditional metaphor for impotence and resistance[6] the image of the wall accompanies *black* and Wright's use of setting to reflect his character's state of mind by representing limiting situations or obstructions that challenge Bigger. Wright's rhythmic use of the image of the wall satisfies T. R. Henn's description of what he refers to as dominant images in his discussion of those characteristic of the tragic structure. A dominant image is "one or more images that, by specific statement or inference, provide a framework or theme for the play; and in terms of which part or all of the dramatic statement is made. These will be of varying degrees of subtlety. . . ."[7] Of more than twenty-nine instances in which Wright depicts Bigger or Bessie physically backed against a wall, the two most powerful scenes, filled with persistent references to wall, both take place in the basement of the Dalton home.

In both scenes the basement and the furnace containing Mary's burning body unite as the focus of the ultimate tests that confront Wright's

hero. In addition to the fact that the basement becomes the gathering place
for the newspaper reporters and Britten, Mr. Dalton's private detective, the
droning furnace also serves as a constant reminder of Bigger's vulnerability.
Dominating these scenes, the walls of the basement surrounding Bigger
emphasize the extent of his entrapment and the severity of his physical impotence. After he has burned Mary's body and chosen to remain in the Dalton home, his first major challenge is to withstand Britten's hostility and to
delude him as he has the Daltons. As Britten questions him, Bigger ponders
on the furnace: "The fire sang in Bigger's ears and he saw the red shadows
dance on the walls" (133). The more Britten confronts Bigger, the more
Bigger thinks of the furnace and meets Britten's challenges with his mask of
pusillanimity. When Britten finally thinks he has successfully identified
Bigger as a Communist, the wall exemplifies the threatening power of the
white world and Bigger's concomitant physical helplessness: "Britten followed Bigger till Bigger's head struck the wall. Bigger looked squarely into
his eyes. Britten, with a movement so fast that Bigger did not see it,
grabbed him in the collar and rammed his head hard against the wall"
(137). Literally backing Bigger up against the wall, Britten, like a god, epitomizes the insensitivity and overwhelming authority of the white world.

Wright concentrates references to the wall in those sections where the
power of the white world is most intense in its threat to Bigger. In the climactic scenes that begin with Peggy's discovery of the kidnap note and end
with her telling Bigger to clean the furnace, the narrator points out seven
times that Bigger stands or leans against a wall. As soon as Bigger plants the
kidnap note at the Daltons' front door, he shrewdly joins the reporters and
Britten in the basement. The reporters' excitement over the kidnap note
spurs a new series of flashing cameras which increases the inevitability of
Bigger's fate. Moreover, it is in this scene that Wright's rhythmic use of the
furnace coalesces with the image of the wall. Bigger's constant thoughts of
the furnace, his failure to clean it before the ashes back up, and the failure
of the furnace to warm the house all function as associative elements of the
image of the wall, finally resolving into a physical and metaphoric trap.

Thus the reporter's taking the shovel and Bigger's fleeing for his life as
all the reporters stand amazed at what they believe to be Mary's bones are
the natural results of the physical setting represented by the wall. R. E.
Baldwin sums up nicely how the recurring image of the wall reflects Bigger's powerlessness and impotence. Describing the progression of the
novel, Baldwin says:

> The general outlines of development can be sketched by tracing the rich im-
> agery of rooms, walls, curtains, and other forms of isolation, enclosure, and

definition of social groupings. The basis element of this imagery is the single room; both as a feature of physical setting and as a metaphoric formulation in Bigger's mind, the single room merges with thematic issues to provide a manageable summary of Wright's basic view.[8]

An essential element of Wright's "basic views" is the emotional impotence characteristic of the parties on either side of the wall that segregates a community by race. Adapting the traditional polemic of *black* and *white*, Wright uses the color white to represent the obstructions which deny Bigger's humanity and black (and its associated image of the wall) to signal Bigger's entrapment and physical impotence. Striking image patterns therefore collaborate with Bigger's characterization to express the tragic theme. For just as Bigger's personality embodies irreconcilable opposites, the colors black and white and their associated images manifest the paradoxical experiences that reinforce the tragic plot. While the context of certain passages throughout the novel quantifies and qualifies the meaning of a particular image, the individual meanings are heightened by their interrelationship and interdependence.

While the color black clearly exemplifies Bigger's physical relationship to the white world, white further strengthens Wright's portrayal of Bigger's dilemma by underscoring the moral disorder of the powerful white world. The color white also appears rhythmically throughout the novel, heightening Wright's depiction of the shallowness and insensitivity of the world which controls Bigger's life. Bigger's home environment and his extreme self-consciousness about his blackness, and the Daltons' wealthy community and their self-assurance, reflect two mutually exclusive worlds with diametrically opposed world views. A look at the description of the Daltons' neighborhood reveals how the color white symbolizes the emotional distance and economic power of the white world:

> But while walking through this quiet and spacious *white* neighborhood, he did not feel the pull and mystery of the thing as strongly as he had in the movie. The houses he passed were huge; lights glowed softly in windows. The streets were empty, save for an occasional car the zoomed past on swift rubber tires. This was a cold and distant world; a world of *white* secrets carefully guarded. He could feel a pride, a certainty, and a confidence in these streets and houses. . . . All he had felt in the movie was gone; only fear and emptiness filled him now. (37–38, emphasis mine)

Of all the references to whiteness, this one describing Bigger's entrance into the white world emerges as the most important because it stresses how environmental differences account for psychological ones. The reality of the Daltons' white world rekindles Bigger's sense of helplessness, for their environment is an integral element of their overwhelming power.

The interrelationship between Wright's use of *white* to represent the white world's authority and hostility and the image of the wall to suggest Bigger's impotence when confronted by the white world shows how the image clusters in *Native Son* collaborate or interlock with each other as expressions of the tragic theme. Interestingly enough, in the scene in which Bigger is forced to visit his family under the watchful eyes of Jan, Max, the Daltons, and Buckley, it is these whites who the narrator consistently says are standing along the wall. Exercising their control of Bigger's destiny and his family's, these representatives of the white world insensitively deny them the privacy that would spare them their shame. The wall highlights the aloofness and the abuse of authority that typify the actions of the white characters in the novel. Unavoidably aware of the staring white faces, Bigger struggles to redress the lie he has just told his mother: "Yes; he had to wipe out that lie [Bigger has told his mother that he will be out of jail in no time], not only so that they might know the truth, but to redeem himself in the eyes of those *white* faces behind his back along the *white wall*. . . . he would not lie, not in the presence of that *white mountain looming* behind him" (253, emphasis mine). The "white looming mountain," with its suggestions of both muteness and massiveness, symbolizes at once the psychological limitations as well as the political and economic power of those whites who watch Bigger and his family.

In the same way that *black*, the metaphor of the wall, and the "white looming mountain" are connected, *white* and the metaphor of blindness merge as associative figurative patterns evoking shallowness and a lack of perception. The description of Mrs. Dalton and of her actual physical blindness demonstrates the link between Wright's use of *white* and blindness. The narrator uses the same terms to describe Mrs. Dalton throughout the novel as he does when Bigger first meets her: ". . . he saw coming slowly toward him a tall, thin, white woman, walking silently, her hands lifted delicately in the air and touching the walls to either side of her. . . . Her face and hair were completely white; she seemed to him like a ghost" (40). In the murder scene, when Mrs. Dalton enters the bedroom as Bigger leans over Mary, the narrator says, "A white blur was standing by the door, silent, ghostlike" (73). The consistent descriptions of Mrs. Dalton as a "white blur" and a "ghostlike figure" suggest the insubstantiality of her philanthropic ideology. Like her daughter, she does not understand that the social, political, and economic elements of the different environments which nurture her and Bigger instill in them totally different psychological responses to the world around them and forbid their having a meaningful relationship.

The language she and her husband use in discussing Bigger as they consider his future reflects their emotional distance and their mechanical treatment of him. Responding to her husband's hesitancy to encourage Bigger to go back to school, Mrs. Dalton says, "I think it's important emotionally that he feels free to trust his environment. . . . Using the analysis contained in the case record the relief sent us, I think we should evoke an immediate feeling of confidence . . ." (40). Mrs. Dalton's "strange words" evidence that she does not feel for Bigger as a fellow human being, a point made earlier in Chapter 2. Although her conception of herself as superior is so ingrained into her psyche that she is not aware of it, her natural manner of speaking reveals it at every turn. And when Max questions Mr. Dalton during Bigger's trial, the hypocrisy and blindness that characterize the Daltons' attitude toward Bigger is explicitly revealed. For Max has Mr. Dalton confess that he does not think it proper to employ Blacks in his real estate offices, and that he does not think it proper to lease apartments to Blacks in white neighborhoods. Blindly, then, the Daltons believe that they improve the quality of life for Blacks by hiring them in menial positions and by donating thousands of dollars to keep young Black men entertained at recreation centers. Hence what superficially looks like naivete is the Daltons' insensitivity to Bigger's plight. Their viewing him as a fellow human being would demand that they relinquish their roles as superior, godlike beings and give Bigger equal status among them and their kind. This stance of superiority, lodged deeply and immovably in the white unconscious, lies at the root of the Daltons' blindness as well as Britten's and Buckley's hostility toward Bigger.

Consequently, in the tradition of the great tragedians before him, Wright uses the metaphor of blindness to reveal a lack of insight in his characters. As is the case with Oedipus and King Lear, Bigger too suffers from the blindness rooted in his own lack of self-knowledge, and this reinforces the tragic drama. The irony inherent in the relationship among Tiresias, the blind seer, and Oedipus, who physically blinds himself when he gains insight, and Gloucester, whose eyes are stamped out because he did not see his son's treachery, is the prototype of Bigger's gain of insight from his inadvertent act of murder and from the brutality necessitated by his trying to conceal it. Just a blindness and suffering ultimately liberate these characters of classical tragedy, so is Bigger brought to enlightenment by the horrors which materialize from the darkness of his self-ignorance.

The passage in which Bigger scrutinizes his new vision of this relationship to the white world captures the essence of this metaphoric, many-faceted blindness:

No, he did not have to hide behind a wall or a curtain now; he had a safer way of being safe, an easier way. What he had done last night had proved that. Jan was blind. Mary had been blind. Mr. Dalton was blind. And Mrs. Dalton was blind; yes, blind in more ways than one. . . . She had thought that Mary was drunk, because she was used to Mary's coming home drunk. And Mrs. Dalton had not known that he was in the room with her; it would have been the last thing she would have thought of. He was black and would not have figured in her thoughts on such an occasion. Bigger felt that a lot of people were like Mrs. Dalton, blind. . . . (91)

What Bigger perceives is how "manipulating appearances is really a way of inducing blindness."[9] Because he understands the way in which "values determine how one sees,"[10] he is able, for some time, to deceive the white world by exploiting its stereotypical notions of his blackness.

Madness, interwoven with blindness, is another attribute that Bigger shares with classical tragic heroes. A monumental study already alluded to above, Robert B. Heilman's *This Great Stage: Image and Structure in King Lear*, makes a distinction between that play's pattern of sight and madness which can also be applied to the function of the trancelike, phantasmagoric state that often overwhelms Bigger:

> . . . the sight pattern tends to take man at the level of the *recognition and identification of phenomena*, that of immediate practical decision. . . . The madness pattern, however, is concerned with the ways in which men *interpret phenomena*, the meanings which they find in experience, the general truths which they consciously formulate or in terms of which they characteristically act, the kind of wisdom, or sophistication, which they achieve. What men see and what men believe, of course, are intimately related. . . . [11]

On the level of identification of phenomena, Bigger (before his murder of Mary) and the other characters in *Native Son*—like Lear and Gloucester— all "miss the point of what is going on around them."[12] Moreover, until Bigger is shocked out of his blindness, his mind is incapable of interpreting his experiences in a manner that would enable him to learn from them and exert better control over his life. Therefore, when confronted by the white world, he panics and slips into a trance.

This trance or phantasmagoric hysteria is equivalent to Lear's madness. Although descriptions of Bigger's dreamlike state permeate Books 1 and 2, the murder scene most acutely illustrates the intensity of Bigger's trance, which reflects his inability to grasp the complexity of his experiences. The "madness" begins when he is forced to carry Mary's body up the stairs to her room: "He felt strange, possessed, or as if he were acting upon a stage in front of a crowd of people" (72). Bigger's trancelike state, induced by the extreme fear that causes him to lose control, demonstrates his inability to sustain contact with reality, as evidenced by the splitting of his consciousness into two distinct selves. Later in the same scene when Mrs. Dalton enters Mary's room, "a hysterical terror seized him, as though he were falling from a great height in a dream" (73). Because Bigger lacks self-knowledge and an insight into the pattern of his encounter with the white world, he blindly succumbs to his own vulnerability.

The obvious, reasonable solutions to his dilemma never occur to him because he fears the white world so intensely. Hence, instead of summoning Mary's parents or leaving her in the basement in her drunken condition, he carries her up the stairs to her room, accelerating, like Oedipus, his own tragic fate. As discussed in Chapter 3, after being completely seized with terror and killing Mary by pressing the pillow too tightly over her face, he finally realizes that, for some time, he had lost total contact with the world around him: "Gradually, the intensity of his sensations subsided and he was aware of the room. He felt that he had been in the grip of a weird spell and was now free. The fingertips of his right hand were pressed deeply into the soft fibers of the rug and his whole body vibrated from the wild pounding of his heart" (75). The "weird spell" resulting from Bigger's fear is the direct cause of Mary's death.

Characteristic of the paradoxes indigenous to tragedy, Bigger's trance-like condition ironically propels him into rebelliousness which manifests the chaos of his world. The blindness and the trance merge as expressions of the total breakdown of natural order that Wright describes in *Native Son*. The novel presents a world divided into groups, with one group having complete dominance over the other. Wright's point is that this imposition of hierarchy where none should exist is a "breach of nature" that has at its source nothing less than the problem of evil itself.[13] Consequently, all parts of *Native Son*—its title, Bigger's characterization, his being thrust deeper into his fate, his fear, and the elements of language—collaborate as integral elements of a cosmological order in which nothing is as it should be. In this world where irony is the controlling principle and distortion of natural order a given fact, an act of murder gives Bigger sight and fear emboldens him. Clearly, the young outraged college student, thrown into Bigger's cell because he has gone completely mad over problems of racial injustice, functions as foil to Bigger, suggesting another extreme reaction to the breakdown of natural order that besets their world.

Snow is another dominant image in *Native Son*, joining the color white and the metaphor of blindness to form an image group that evokes the hostility, insensitivity, and lack of perception of the white world and emphasizing the unnatural power the white world holds over the Black. The white color of snow is caused by the complete reflection of sunlight from the frozen water crystals; this reflection is often intense and blinding to the eyes. Hence in this single image Wright makes final the connection among the negative attributes of the others. Just as whiteness and blindness connote animosity and shallowness, the ambivalent snow—a traditional image of danger and destruction—symbolizes the malevolence of the white world and by implication identifies Bigger's animal-like will to survive.

Although the snow is more than a symbol of white hostility because of its function as the external counterpart of Bigger's rebellion, traditional criticism on the novel has seen the snow only as a "persistent symbol of white hostility."[14] But because the snow surrounds, impedes, and betrays Bigger as he flees for his life and because he must fight against it to survive, this image evokes his defiance at the same time that it represents the animosity of the white world. A superb craftsman, Wright is consistent in his habit of concentrating images in those scenes where the hero faces the greatest challenges. Snow dominates Book 2, which begins with Bigger's deception of the white world and ends with his inevitable capture. The last forty-two pages of Book 2, which encompass events from the discovery of Mary's bones to Bigger's capture, contain no fewer than sixty-one references to snow. Although it snows during all of Book 2, the figurative function of snow increases in impact as Bigger flees for his life. Nine references to snow pervade the single paragraph that describes Bigger's escape after the reporter takes the shovel from him. Tiptoeing up the stairs of the basement to his room and lifting the window,

> . . . he felt a cold rush of air laden with snow. . . . He groped to the window and climbed into it, feeling again the chilling blast of snowy wind. . . . he looked into the snow and tried to see the ground below. . . . His eyes were shut and his hands were clenched as his body turned, sailing through the snow. . . . he lay buried in a cold pile of snow, dazed. Snow was in his mouth, eyes, ears: snow was seeping down his back. . . . He had not been able to control the muscles of his hot body against the chilled assault of the wet snow over all his skin. . . . he struggled against the snow, pushing it away from him. (187)

Because the white world is now able to identify Bigger as Mary's murderer, the threatening power it has over him will become even more hostile. This malevolence—beastlike in its force—is suggested by the rhythmic repetition of the word *snow*.

As Bigger flees through the streets of Chicago, he fights his way through the driving snow, which has fallen quite heavily, encumbering traffic and thus increasing in its force. The danger and hostility symbolized by the snow merge with whiteness—its associative metaphor—in the scene which warns that the vigilantes have almost surrounded the hero. As Bigger looks through the newspaper, searching the maps for the location of the mob, the narrator explains: "There was another map of the South Side. This time the shaded area [showing where the mob was] had deepened from both the north and south, leaving a small square of white in the middle of the oblong Black Belt. He stood looking at that tiny square of white as though gazing down into the barrel of a gun" (216). The "small square of white" in the map echoes the white piece of paper Mr. Dalton held earlier in his hand. Instead of cowering and giving in to his fear as he had in his initial visit to Mr. Dalton's home, Bigger chooses to fight to the end.

His physical journey ends, soon afterwards, on the roof of a tenement building near "a white looming bulk." Fighting instinctively, Bigger uses the barrel of his gun to knock unconscious the first of the men who discover him on the roof. The snow warns, however, that the mob will overpower Bigger's courage. As he slides about over the roof, "he felt snow in his face and eyes" (222). And finally, when the mob spots him and fires its first shot, he comes to the huge, white, snow-covered obstruction, a point in which all the important figurative elements of the novel up to now—the colors black and white, the wall, and snow—suddenly unite. The multiplicity of this image evidences what Heilman sees as characteristic of life itself. In discussing the image patterns in *King Lear*, he writes, "Nearly every pattern has its dichotomy, and the dichotomies tend to coincide and even coalesce into a general definition of reality."[15] Analogously, the humiliation and fear Bigger feels because of his black skin, the social, economic, political, and psychological limitations imposed by the wall of segregation, the hostility and power of the white world, and the limitations of sight and comprehension all coalesce in the "white looming bulk," a huge water tank draped in snow.

Before he reaches the looming bulk, Bigger wonders what it is and whether he will somehow be able to use it to his advantage: "He wove among the chimneys, his feet slipping and sliding over the snow, keeping in mind that white looming bulk which he had glimpsed ahead of him. Was it something that would help him? Could he get upon it, or behind it, and hold them off?" (224). Ironically, the water tank becomes the weapon that makes Bigger's capture final. Once he crawls to the top and hangs on to the tank, the vigilantes—unsuccessful at all other attempts—spray icy water upon him with a hose attached to the tank. His body stiff and frozen, Bigger finally loses his grip, landing on the roof with his face in the snow. His being "dragged across the snow of the roof" and stretched out on the ground later in the snow as if he were about to be crucified suggest the outcome of the abusive power one group holds over another in a world that has chosen oppression and chaos over harmony and natural order.

The complex, often paradoxical nature of the figurative language Wright uses to depict the unnatural cosmological order in *Native Son* perfectly parallels the contradictory, irreconcilable elements of Bigger's personality. At the same time that the colors black and white, the wall, blindness, Bigger's trancelike state, and the snow have their individual symbolic meanings, they also merge into a unified whole as a collective expression of the phenomena that affect Bigger's consciousness. A part of Bigger's consciousness always remains undisclosed to those around him, but he must also be defined—like the rest of us—in terms of his relationship to the world around him. Because Bigger is existentially isolated from his family and friends and at the same time is subject to the influence of the environment, he emerges as a complex human personality whose pride and fear catapult him into a realm of experiences where he willfully challenges the forces that attempt to subdue him.

Reflecting those juxtapositions of opposites that comprise the complexity characteristic of the human psyche, the snow works together with its diametrically opposed image—the sun—to show Bigger as both murderer and hero respectively. In the same way that the snow represents the animosity of the white world and simultaneously identifies Bigger as a menace, the sun shares a relationship with its corresponding color yellow, which evokes both heroism and danger. This final image group completes the tightly interwoven relationship of the figurative constituents in *Native Son*. The sun—the seat of life and energy[16]—highlights Bigger as hero while its associated color yellow connects with the color white to prefigure danger.

Although yellow—the attribute of Apollo, the sun-god—traditionally indicates magnanimity, intuition, and intellect,[17] it is also coupled with white by its position on an upward-tending color scale in which black and white represent two extremes.[18] Yellow light abounds in those scenes where Bigger is quite vulnerable to forces that pursue him, and becomes increasingly forceful as it develops an affinity with the white snow in the final, climactic scene of Book 2. As Bigger darts about on the roof of the tenement buildings, he desperately struggles to avoid the continuous, intense flashes of yellow light from the searchlights the vigilantes use in their pursuit. In the passage in which the first flash of yellow light occurs, the narrator—in his role as interpreting guide—explains that the yellow lights are the inescapable manifestations of Bigger's equally inescapable fate:

> His eyes jerked upward as a huge, sharp beam of yellow light shot into the sky. Another came, crossing it like a knife. Then another. Soon the sky was full of them. They circled slowly, hemming him in; bars of light forming a prison, a wall between him and the rest of the world; bars weaving a shifting wall of light

into which he dared not go. He was in the midst of it now; this was what he had been running from ever since that night Mrs. Dalton had come into the room and charged him with such fear that his hands had gripped the pillow with fingers of steel and had cut off the air from Mary's lungs. (218)

The yellow bars of light are prefigured early in Book 1 by the red-hot iron that Bigger feels in his throat when he thinks of whites and of his mother's premonition. Suggesting the magnitude of the forces that over-power Bigger, yellow now merges with the image of the wall to become an element of setting. For both these images, along with the threatening snow, symbolize the effect of the moral, social, economic, and political laws aimed at stifling Bigger's life.

The sun contrasts with the snow, illuminating Bigger as the hero deter-mined to maintain his pride and to subvert those forces that deny his hu-manity. The use of the sun to counteract negative responses to a rebellious protagonist beautifully evidences Wright's skill at sustaining a balance be-tween the subjectivity rooted in the author's identification with his charac-ters and the objectivity reflected in the artist's superb mastery of his craft. Forming an affinity with the interpretive, third-person limited narrator, the sun—symbolic of reflection and willpower[19]—appears primarily in the scenes where Bigger questions his relationship to the white world and where his role in his own fate becomes increasingly clear first to the reader and finally to Bigger himself.

The sun pervades Books 1 and 3, presaging Bigger's destiny in the be-ginning and heralding his transcendence at the end. In the early scenes, the sun illuminates the elements in Bigger's environment and in his personality that later undergird that act of will responsible for his defiance of the estab-lished order of the white world. A scene from Book 1 serves as a good ex-ample of this function of the sun. Intensely frustrated because they are hemmed in, forbidden to participate in the mainstream of life, Bigger and Gus hang along the street and listlessly share their fantasies. As they watch an airplane move across the sky, Bigger discloses his wish to fly a plane. When Gus responds with "God'll let you fly when He give you your wings up in heaven" (15), he is expressing their despair at the extent of the control the white world has over them. The sun image that immediately follows evokes the intensity of Bigger's dissatisfaction with that world's power and foreshadows his imminent rebellion:

They laughed again, reclining against the wall, smoking, the lids of their eyes drooped softly against the sun. Cars whizzed past on rubber tires. Bigger's face was metallically black in the strong sunlight. There was in his eyes a pensive, brooding amazement, as of a man who had been long confronted and tantalized by a riddle whose answer seemed always just on the verge of escaping him, but prodding him irresistibly on to seek its solution. (15)

The lack of insight and comprehension that characterizes Bigger in Book 1 is also responsible for the constant rifts between him and his gang. Because his overwhelming pride keeps him from acknowledging even to himself his intense fear of whites, he contrives a fight with Gus in a futile attempt to hide his real feelings. Once the fight is over and Bigger has completely severed his relations with his friends, the sun highlights his alienation:

> He shut the knife and slipped it in his pocket and swung the door [of Doc's poolroom] to the street. He blinked his eyes from the bright sunshine; his nerves were so taut that he had difficulty in breathing. . . .
>   He had an overwhelming desire to be alone; he walked to the middle of the next block and turned into an alley. . . . When he reached the end of the alley, he turned into a street, walking slowly in the sunshine, his hands jammed deep into his pockets, his head down, depressed. (35)

In Book 3 as Bigger lies in his jail cell awaiting his death, the narrator explains that Bigger has stopped responding to any stimuli from the world around him: "Most of the time he sat with bowed head, staring at the floor; or he lay full length upon his stomach, his face buried in the crook of an elbow, just as he lay now upon a cot with the pale yellow sunshine of a February sky falling obliquely upon him through the cold steel bars of the Eleventh Street Police Station" (233). The paleness of the sunshine suggests that, having accepted responsibility for his actions, Bigger feels that he has failed and wants to die. Yet, at the inquest, when Bigger sees that the white world intends to mock him, "to use his death as a bloody symbol of fear to wave before the eyes of the black world" (235), his pride forces him to fight again.

This time the battle takes place exclusively in an emotional arena. Completely entrapped physically by the white world, Bigger must again exercise his newly acquired inner strength and vision. His awakened determination is symbolized by the yellow sunshine that splashes across the sidewalks and buildings outside, where a huge crowd stares at him as he is led from the police station. Instead of taking Bigger directly to the designated Cook County Jail, the police first drive him to the Daltons' home and attempt to have him parody himself by acting out the steps of his crime. Again, the sun shines as the motorcade begins to move through the streets, and when it reaches Drexel Boulevard, the narrator points out that the Daltons' big brick house is completely "drenched in sunshine." Throughout the novel, the sun is directly associated with Bigger, but in this scene Wright uses it ironically.

While the Dalton home is of course in mourning, it is drenched in sunlight to symbolize that Mary's death is Bigger's source of life.

In the final scenes of the novel, the sun becomes the reflector of Bigger's spiritual state. To convince the judge to give Bigger a life term in prison rather than sentence him to death, Max feels that his only recourse is to explain to the judge how Bigger sees the world and his relationship to it. Early in Book 3, then, Max engages Bigger in a long discussion that ignites a new kind of fire in Bigger. For the first time, Bigger begins to lift the veil of hate that had earlier blinded him. Inspired by Max's questions, Bigger experiences new feelings and perceives the connection between his previous feelings and actions. Emphasizing the intensity and depth of Bigger's recognition of a wholeness that binds all people together, Wright has Bigger create his own sun image as a metaphor for his feelings:

> Another impulse rose in him, born of desperate need, and his mind clothed it in an image of a strong blinding sun sending hot rays down and he was standing in the midst of a vast crowd of men, white men and black men and all men, and the sun's rays melted away the many differences, the colors, the clothes, and drew what was common and good upward toward the sun. . . . (307)

This important passage marks the pinnacle of Bigger's revelation.

Bigger now recognizes his affinity with the rest of humanity. Before and especially after his murder of Mary, he felt unconnected to the human world. He was an observer of life, alienated emotionally from his family and friends and denied the social and economic fruits of the American dream he craved intensely. On the eve of his death, he understands that despite the evil effects of racism, we all hold our own value, our own worth within ourselves, and it is this inherent value and our common desires that give each of us a vital place in the scheme of things. The fact that Wright has Bigger imagine his own sun (rather than use the natural sunshine, as he does in all other scenes) punctuates Bigger's final acceptance of his own humanity. For he now understands that although he challenged the white world and attempted to shape his own destiny, he had at the same time internalized the negative image of himself created by that white world.

Bigger's creation of his own sun image attests to his tragic purification and explains the nonvindictiveness that characterizes his acceptance of the judge's refusal of his appeal. He is not surprised to learn that the governor refuses to commute his death sentence to life imprisonment. After receiving the telegram from Max, "he lay down again on the cot, on his back, and stared at the tiny bright-yellow electric bulb glowing in the ceiling above his head. It contained the fire of death" (351). According to T. R. Henn, "Fire is of transcendent value to man. . . . it is given by the gods only as lightning or as the sun. . . ."[20] The yellow bulb contains the fire of Bigger's spiritual strength. The light that emanates from the yellow bulb symbolizes the paradox that enfolds *Native Son*. Associated with the sun, which represents spiritual strength and the creative force, yellow here continues to prefigure the threat the white world poses to Bigger. However, having found consolation through the vision entailed in his own sun image, Bigger has attained a spiritual peace that makes him ready to face his death.

NOTES

1.   Richard B. Sewall, *The Vision of Tragedy* (New Haven, CT: Yale University Press, 1980), 25.

2.   For individual discussions of the metaphors of blindness and the snow, see Dennis E. Baron, "The Syntax of Perception in Richard Wright's *Native Son,*" *Language and Style* 9 (1976): 17–28; Kenneth Kinnamon, *The Emergence of Richard Wright* (Urbana, IL: University of Illinois Press, 1972); Milton and Patricia Rickels, *Richard Wright* (Austin, TX: Steck-Vaughn, 1970); Edward Margolies, *The Art of Richard Wright* (Carbondale, IL: Southern Illinois University Press, 1969).

3.   For a prior reading of the sentence patterns and the colors black, white, and yellow, see Joyce A. Joyce, "Style and Meaning in Richard Wright's *Native Son,*" *BALF* 16 (1982): 112–115.

4.   Richard B. Sewall, 13.

5.   Richard Wright, *Native Son* (New York: Harper & Brothers, 1940), 234. Future references to this text will be inserted parenthetically.

6.   J. E. Cirlot, *A Dictionary of Symbols*, trans. Jack Sage (New York: Philosophical Library, 1962), 343.

7.   T. R. Henn, *The Harvest of Tragedy* (London: Methuen, 1956), 135.

8.   R. E. Baldwin, "Creative Vision of *Native Son,*" *Massachusetts Review* 14 (1973): 387.

9.   Robert B. Heilman, *Magic in the Web: Action and Language in* Othello (Lexington, KY: University of Kentucky Press, 1956), 58.

10.   Robert B. Heilman, *This Great Stage: Image and Structure in* King Lear (Baton Rouge, LA: Louisiana State University Press, 1956), 25.

11.   Heilman, *This Great Stage*, 180.

12.   Heilman, *This Great Stage*, 180.

13.   Heilman, *This Great Stage*, 174.

14.   Kinnamon, 136.

15.   Heilman, *This Great Stage*, 178.

16.   Sir James Frazer, *The Golden Bough: A Study in Magic and Religion* (New York: Macmillan, 1947), 79.

17.   Cirlot, 52.

18.   Cirlot, 51.

19.   Cirlot, 303.

20.   Henn, 60.

Analysis of Application

Joyce A. Joyce's "The Figurative Web of *Native Son*," demonstrates clearly how close reading practices (often linked to very traditional forms of analysis) can work to strengthen an argument with a clear sociopolitical message. Rooted firmly in formalist analysis (discussed in Chapter 1), Joyce's commentary builds on a history of previous considerations of tragedy as a genre and Wright's novel as an aesthetic creation. Yet she also establishes her own particular interest and argument: the ambiguity and interrelationship of imagery in Wright's novel, and how that imagery relates to the work's insights on race relations and to its hero's tortured but changing sense of self.

In her opening analysis of Wright's use of compound sentences, Joyce demonstrates how the novel sets up oppositions between white/black, rich/poor, and other identity categories. But Joyce is not interested in simply tracing those patterns of imagery; her larger goal is to demonstrate that the surface oppositions mask a reality of thorough interconnection and confusion. Whiteness may be associated with power, but it is also shown to be fragile. Blackness may be linked to despair, but it is also a starting point for growth and self-awareness. In taking us back to the text time and again, Joyce teases out the complexity of images that have been read previously (and simplistically) through many of the same binaries that the novel itself works to critique.

Yet Joyce has still another purpose, for she is also interested in establishing Wright's place among the great tragedians, including Sophocles and Shakespeare. Thus she points out all the components of classical tragedy in the novel: paradox, blindness, madness, and eventual insight. That she links these so carefully and convincingly with both the novel's pattern of imagery and its specifically social message demonstrates how the analysis of race and ethnicity can draw effectively on detail in the text yet retain its extratextual relevance. Joyce carefully explores the complexity of Bigger's characterization as she sets up the insights that mark the end of the journey of Wright's tragic hero. Her reading of Bigger's "creation of his own sun image," his movement past hatred, and his recognition of his own internalization of a racist society's negative image of him is convincingly argued. But even as Bigger acquires new knowledge as he approaches death, Joyce reinforces the real and continuing social problems that surround him, concluding with a reading of the yellow bulb that hangs above his head as symbolizing both creative strength and lingering threat. Throughout, her critique is directed not only at the racist society of the novel's setting but also, implicitly, at a history of literary criticism that has yet to value properly Wright's own artistic abilities.

Thus Joyce's essay exemplifies many of the principles explored earlier in this chapter. It explores the dynamics of oppression and the ways in which that oppression is achieved and reinforced through language and metaphor. It shows the blindness of literary history itself, in the ways that it has valued certain tragedians and ignored others. It traces the effects of its hero's internalized oppression and path toward personal and social healing. And it does all these through a focused reading of the text. While no one critical piece can represent all the possibilities for the study of race, ethnicity, and post-coloniality, Joyce's essay can help students focus their own analysis on textual complexities and ground it in concrete detail.

The New Historicism and Pluralistic Cultural Analysis

Overview

For the most part, previous chapters have covered individual methodologies as if they are always used alone and in isolation from one another. But many recent works of literary and cultural analysis draw on and reflect at least two, if not more, of those methodologies; indeed, some of the most supple readings of literature and culture today see texts as inextricably and simultaneously connected to a variety of political, social, and ideological systems. "The New Historicism" and "cultural studies" have become catch phrases for much of this work, though certainly some people conducting new forms of historical and cultural analysis do not accept them as accurately describing their own readings, which may still have a largely feminist, materialist, or other focus (see earlier chapters for more information on the historical bases for those methodologies). These are highly contested categories, ones demanding some precision in their use here. The New Historicism, for our purposes, is a synthetic methodology, drawing on several of the forms of analysis covered earlier in this book, but always with a firm base in historical research on past eras and pre-twentieth-century literary texts. Cultural studies is a similarly pluralistic field, engaged in the interplay between text and context, but it usually focuses on twentieth-century or present-day works and often emphasizes nonliterary genres. Although these forms of analysis could be said to lack the concentration of insight that a more narrowly focused reading might provide, their breadth offers a distinct advantage: an ability to understand a text's reflection of multiple, coexisting systems of meaning, thereby emphasizing textual and historical complexity to a greater degree.

The New Historicism is perhaps best understood in contrast to more traditional forms of historical analysis. As many of us know from experience with school textbooks, history is often presented as the story of great men and their activities, a pageant of political leaders, generals, religious figures, influential thinkers, and other (usually male) actors who might be said to perform upon the grand stage of national and international affairs. But given the insights explored in Chapters 2–9 of this book—especially those derived from recent critical attention to the gender, racial, sexual, and class biases inherent in many forms of representation and cultural valuation—it was inevitable that what constitutes history would itself come under intense critical scrutiny and revision. In the 1970s and 1980s, popular history, such as that practiced by Studs Terkl and Howard Zinn, along with feminist historical inquiry, such as that conducted by Bonnie Anderson and Judith Zinsser, demonstrated that those individuals usually ignored by history textbooks were affected in very diverse ways by such events as wars, revolutions, and governmental policy changes. Indeed, the notion of a perfectly linear historical timeline, indicating a steady developmental sequence, obscured the numerous ways in which many people's lives did not change for the better in a neatly progressive fashion because sexism, heterosexism, racism, and other oppressive forces remained substantially unchallenged for many years; in some cases, these forces even intensified as time went on. As we saw in our discussion of post-colonial analysis (Chapter 9), many lives in Africa, the Americas, and Asia were actually made materially worse by the supposed advance of civilization. For any given moment in time, there are numerous possible stories and histories that would offer very different insights into the ways people's lives reflected their time, place, race, gender, sexuality, and economic situation.

Of course, certain forms of historical analysis have long played key roles in literary studies. A critic might relate the theme or plot of a given work to a major event in history, such as the U.S. Civil War or the French Revolution. Another long-practiced form of history-based literary analysis has been to relate the concerns of a text to the biography of the author, finding in literature a reflection of the life story and experiences of its creator (see Chapter 4 for a brief discussion relevant to this topic). The New Historicism would not deny that such perspectives allow certain insights into literature but would insist on their very limited scope, for they are far from definitive.

The birth of the New Historicism as a specifically literary critical phenomenon is often linked to the publication in 1980 of Stephen Greenblatt's

Renaissance Self-Fashioning, a work that drew new attention to the ways in which literature reflects not only the intentions of its creators as self-conscious respondents to their time periods but also the ways in which a variety of systems of power and responses to power are reflected in a given text. Building on some of the insights of Michel Foucault (who is discussed in Chapter 6), Greenblatt shows how seemingly insignificant occurrences—a conversation at a dinner party, an attempt by a father to subdue the will of his infant son—can serve as starting points for a discussion of how individuals were socialized during their day, how some resisted that socialization to a greater or lesser degree than others, and what interests were served by the norms of a particular time and place. Of course, Greenblatt, as a literary critic rather than a historian, turns in each of his chapters to literature itself as a source of data and insight, even if he often starts with an anecdote related in a letter, journal, or historical document. Indeed, the New Historicism makes a strong case for the important role played by literary texts in the creation and replication of systems of power, even as they affected the nonreading public. The literate segment of the population has usually held considerable institutionalized power over others in society; its concerns, fears, hopes, and strategies for retaining forms of social control are inevitably represented in the works that it has written, bought, and otherwise circulated. To be sure, there were many individuals who never read or responded to even the best-known literary works, but even those individuals lived their lives in a context of economic, political, gender, and other systems of power that are evident in the pages of contemporary texts.

But no one practicing or influenced by the New Historicism would assign to high cultural forms—such as poetry, drama, novels, or essays—a unique importance for understanding a time period. This is the reason that critics today often turn to other, more popular sources of information to advance their insights and enrich their analysis: journalism and news reportage, letters and diaries, popular songs and theatrics, fashion, film, advertising, and television. All these allow access into the many ways in which people have expressed their beliefs, hopes, and fears, and all are equally valid sources of data for understanding the diversity of human perception and experience. This is also one of the primary insights of what is often called "cultural studies," which emphasizes that the study of culture today and in the past should involve the full range of ways in which people individually and collectively express and have expressed themselves. While the New Historicism is a field that fixes its critical eye firmly on the past and often turns to literature, cultural studies may focus solely on popular media and other cultural forms, making no mention of literature, and it may be concerned solely with the present day. But linking the two fields is an awareness that narrow methodological allegiances produce narrow readings of texts and culture, and that a supple methodological base often produces a supple and complex reading. This eclecticism also suggests that no methodology, application, or perspective is ever truly definitive. While a given New Historicist or cultural studies reading will certainly draw conclusions about its subject, it would never insist on its own conclusiveness, for there is always a new perspective on every issue, a new way of understanding the consequences of even what seems the most clear-cut of actions, and another avenue for investigating historical and cultural complexity.

Key Principles

1 *History is not linearly progressive and is not reducible to the activities of prominent individuals.*

As you begin to generate history-based literary and cultural analysis, you will, of course, conduct historical research. But as you approach that research, you should remember that history is itself a story that is constructed out of an immense amount of possible data and interpretations of data (as feminists have suggested, his-story is often just that, a story told by men). The history that we encounter in textbooks inevitably reflects the belief systems of the books' writers, and just as inevitably, some of the class, ethnic, gender, and other beliefs of the society producing those writers, though certainly these forces may be critically engaged by the writers themselves. Yet too often they are not, and certainly the common attempt to reduce history to a simple timeline of wars, revolutions, major political crises, and changes in governmental policy is to ignore the many ways in which people's lives have been differently affected (and sometimes unaffected) by such grand actions. After all, Columbus only "discovered" America from the perspective of the Europeans; the many indigenous peoples already living in the territory that he claimed for Spain were well aware of the existence of the land beneath their feet. His arrival hardly signaled "forward progress" for them; instead, it marked the beginning a slow process of cultural decimation. Similarly, histories and tales of colonial glory in Africa or Asia often ignore the perspectives of those local peoples being subjected to colonial rule, as well as the diseases, forms of enslavement, and other cruelties that they faced. You should always keep this recognition of dramatic differences in perspective in mind as you conduct your research.

2 *The mundane activities and conditions of daily life can tell us much about the belief systems of a time period.*

The bulk of people's lives, their degree of happiness, and their goals and desires are hardly reducible to or understandable through the activities of their political or military leaders. If you think about how you spend your own day and what impinges on your time and determines your own sense of well-being, you can easily see that issues such as child care, recreation, employment conditions, and access to health care and education are some of the most important factors in life today, but ones that may or may not make history books in the future. As you conduct historical research, consider where you might find evidence of such relatively mundane, but still highly important, aspects of daily life. Indeed, see what you can learn about a society, its values and valuations, through an understanding of common daily activities and material struggles. Productive sources for historical research might include popular news reports, diaries, letters, autobiographies, speeches, sermons, travel journals, scientific and medical reports, and census accounts or other sources of data on populations. In beginning to analyze, let us say, an adventure narrative—a story of an individual or a family on the "frontier" of civilization—you can well imagine the many different perspectives and types of information that might be useful to you. By exploring the mundane activities of the adults and children at the time and place of your narrative's setting, you will begin to acquire insight into the text's own perspective and interests; you will discover the choices that it makes about what to represent and what to omit. And by expanding your research to explore the daily lives of others on that same "frontier" of civilization—the indigenous peoples, the servants, the laborers, and the transients, all of whom are often considered marginal or forgettable—you will also begin to uncover who, precisely, the text values most highly, as you move toward seeing the text as occupying a certain cultural position and presenting a certain limited perspective. Use your imagination and do not be afraid to pursue unorthodox avenues for uncovering new histories and different vantage points on the time period or culture in which a literary work or other text was produced.

3 *Literary and other cultural texts are connected in complex ways to the time period in which they were created. Systems of social power are both reflected in and reinforced by such texts.*

Indeed, it is never very useful to speak of literature as "timeless," because doing so erases the ways in which the complexity of a given time period is reflected in the concerns expressed in a text and in the reception of it. It also ignores the fact that texts actually help produce the belief systems of their time period. Critics today often speak of a reciprocity between texts and contexts, of how they influence each other. As you actively explore that complex relationship, you may wish to begin by looking for the ways in which the text could only have been written at the time it was, at what is unique and most clearly time-bound in its plot, theme, or construction. Yet also bear in mind that in reading and otherwise interacting with texts, an audience comes to know something about itself and its past, that texts help us process and understand both our own contexts and those of other eras. Fundamental to semiotic, structuralist, and post-structuralist theories (see Chapters 5 and 6) is the recognition that our beliefs and lifestyles are formed through acculturation processes, that language and principles of social ordering transmit values to us. This transmission occurs in our educational process, in our interactions with parents and friends, and in our exposure to literary and other cultural texts. Certainly what some people believe today about "frontier" life in North America and the "progress" of civilization in Africa, Asia, and Central and South America, they know primarily from fictional sources and limited textbook accounts that reflect a certain set of beliefs and viewpoints. This is not to set up a simple cause-and-effect relationship between what people read and what they believe or how they act, but it does allow us to explore and understand more fully where peoples' beliefs and actions *may* come from and, certainly, how they are reinforced.

Thus beyond a simple recognition that a text interacts with its historical context, New Historicist research demands that you examine more specifically the systems of power that were operating at the time and that are reflected and reinforced in the text. These systems of power are, of course, numerous and diverse. As you will remember from discussions in previous chapters, the same individual is a member of many different social subsets, ones of class, gender, sexuality, and race, as well as age, religion, region, political party, and so forth. In each of these categories the individual simultaneously is defined by society and responds to that process of definition. Texts may reflect and participate in any or all of those processes of definition and responses to definition. To return to our example above, almost any adventure narrative will reveal belief systems concerning nation, gender, ethnicity, class, and often religion. Of course, your own choice of which systems of power and processes to investigate will reflect the parameters of your assignment, your own interests, and the text in question.

4 *Many different types of cultural texts can reflect and advance social interests.*

It is important to remember that it is not literature alone that captures and participates in the belief systems of a given time and place. Cultural studies today often looks at very different forms of expression from those emphasized by earlier types of specifically literary analysis. "Text" today can mean many things—music, fashion, film, and so forth—that are as useful a starting point for historical and cultural understanding as a printed work of fiction or poetry. Certainly if you think about recent retellings of classic adventure tales—such as film versions of *The Last of the Mohicans* or *Heart of Darkness* (adapted in *Apocalypse Now*)—you can begin to see that contemporary cultural studies opens many doors for investigating how new contexts and social interests—such as environmentalism, civil rights movements, and the Vietnam War—lead to very different emphases and perspectives in storytelling. Moreover, cultural studies allows critics to expand their discussion to address visual imagery, costuming, and body language as well as the precise words used in a text. Indeed, in examining texts from film, advertising, and other media, you may wish to consult Chapter 5 for information on semiotics and the sign systems that reflect and construct a society's beliefs and interest. Of course, it is always important to keep in mind that this reflection of context may or may not be attributable to the conscious intention of the text's creator; none of us are wholly self-conscious of our own beliefs and biases. In fact, this emphasis on the hidden quality of textual meaning is precisely why literary and cultural analysis is such an exciting and complex endeavor.

5   *A synthetic methodology or pluralistic approach still requires both precision and unity.*

After choosing your text and the belief systems or social processes that you wish to examine, you must still construct a unified argument and use your methodology or methodologies consistently and appropriately. If you decide to examine an adventure narrative's reflection of class and gender biases in its representation of indigenous peoples, you should not only conduct historical research to support your reading but also consult Chapters 3 and 7 of this book for more information on how to analyze classism and sexism in a text. But always bear in mind that examining such disparate forces may lead you far afield from your thesis statement. Your analysis must have an overall sense of unity and focus, one that may derive from your attention to a specific moment in time, a specific character, or perhaps a larger force accounting for the various beliefs and processes that you analyze. Be sure to acquaint yourself fully with the text, with its context, and with your methodologies to ensure that you maximize your insights and avoid the lack of clarity and sense of disorganization that can result from choosing too many topics or points of entrance into a text. Always keep your readers' needs firmly in mind; those needs include a clear sense of purpose to an essay and a credible methodology, free from contradictions and unexplained choices.

6 *Many of the above rules apply equally to interpreters of literary texts and to the interpretations that they generate.*

As we have explored in other chapters, the writings of literary and cultural critics also reflect choices and transmit values. Indeed, New Historicist and pluralistic cultural analysis demand a significant degree of self-awareness and social consciousness on the part of its practitioners. Even as contemporary critics reveal and analyze the biases and idiosyncrasies of texts, authors, characters, and audiences, it is necessary for them also to recognize their own perceptual limitations and what systems of power and belief they may be reflecting and reinforcing through their work. This is not to say that it is necessary to include in one's analysis an apology for one's own blind spots or a laundry list of the various aspects of one's own identity; that would not only be tedious but would also imply that one knows all about oneself and one's limitations, an impossibility for any of us. Even so, the way we present ourselves, our "ethos," clearly will lead our readers to see us as sensitive and thoughtful, or crass and un-self-reflective. Any act of analysis requires an assumption of authority over a text or topic, yet authority does not have to mean a presumption of complete mastery. New Historicists and cultural critics know that their analysis examines the lives of complex and fallible human beings; critics of literature and culture must always remember that they, too, are complex and fallible human beings.

7 *Therefore no reading of a literary or other cultural text is definitive.*

Readings of texts provide insight into the complexity of human thought and experience. It would be arrogant or naive to believe that such complexity can ever be covered fully in a given essay or other analytical project. New Historicist and pluralist cultural analysis would therefore never suggest that it is conclusive or that it provides the "last word" on a text's meaning, even though it will and must draw conclusions. The many methods of analysis covered in the book that you have in hand reflect some of the most pressing social concerns and interests today; these will inevitably, and no doubt dramatically, change in the future. Literary and cultural analysis is a field that can never be exhausted, for new readings of even the best-known texts will always be possible as new avenues for insight, new forms of data, and new ways of approaching historical complexity become available to us.

Bibliography

Anderson, Bonnie S., and Judith P. Zinsser. *A History of Their Own.* 2 vols. New York: Harper & Row, 1988.

> This is a useful example of feminist historiography, one that points out the blind spots in traditional accounts of European history. Though its subject matter is limited to Europe, it may provide a starting point for historical research for beginning to advanced readers.

Booth, Wayne C. *Critical Understanding: The Powers and Limits of Pluralism.* Chicago: University of Chicago Press, 1979.

> This influential book by a major critic and theorist argues against dogmatism in critical analysis, suggesting instead that various theories and methodologies may allow different but still valid insights into texts. Its vocabulary and presupposition of theoretical knowledge will make it of greatest interest to advanced readers.

Brannigan, John. *New Historicism and Cultural Materialism.* New York: St. Martin's Press, 1998.

> This overview of the principles of the New Historicism and that field's relationship to Marxist and materialist theory contains useful applications to texts, including Conrad's *Heart of Darkness* and Gilman's "The Yellow Wall-Paper." Its user-friendly language will make it appropriate for both intermediate and advanced readers.

Cox, Jeffrey N., and Larry J. Reynolds, eds. *New Historical Literary Study: Essays on Reproducing Texts, Representing History.* Princeton, NJ: Princeton University Press, 1993.

> This collection of essays covers many of the theoretical debates in historiography and historicist literary analysis. Its vocabulary and methodology make it most appropriate for advanced readers.

During, Simon, ed. *The Cultural Studies Reader.* New York: Routledge, 1993.

> This massive collection of primary theoretical texts and applications in the field of cultural studies examine issues as diverse as cultural studies' relationship to history, spaciality, advertising, music, and television. Because of their theoretical density, most of its essays will be of interest primarily to advanced readers.

Foucault, Michel. *Discipline and Punish: The Birth of the Prison.* New York: Vintage, 1977.

> This is one of Foucault's most influential works (see also his *History of Sexuality, vol. 1,* discussed in Chapter 8 and its bibliography); it contains his intriguing theories of surveillance and social control. Its vocabulary and presupposition of theoretical knowledge will make it most appropriate for advanced readers.

Greenblatt, Stephen. *Renaissance Self-Fashioning: From More to Shakespeare.* Chicago: University of Chicago Press, 1980.

> This is a highly influential work of New Historicist analysis, with individual chapters on Shakespeare, Wyatt, Spenser, Marlowe, and other important Renaissance writers and their complex relationships to their time period. Its diction and methodology make it most appropriate for advanced readers.

Hamilton, Paul. *Historicism.* New York: Routledge, 1996.

> A volume in the advanced introductory series *The New Critical Idiom*, this work thoroughly covers the philosophical and theoretical background to the current debate on historical evidence and understanding. It is a useful work for advanced readers.

Scott, Joan W. *Gender and the Politics of History.* New York: Columbia University Press, 1988.

> This influential work of feminist history and theory reexamines the ways in which history is made and the interests reflected therein. Scott is a lucid writer and though her theoretical base is often quite sophisticated, this work may be of interest to both intermediate and advanced readers.

Storey, John, ed. *What Is Cultural Studies?* New York: St. Martin's Press, 1996.

> This useful reader contains essays addressing the question posed by its title, probing also the relationship between cultural studies and Marxism, feminism, and other important methodological emphases. Its essays vary in vocabulary and theoretical density, but most will be appropriate for advanced readers.

Veeser, H. Aram, ed. *The New Historicism.* New York: Routledge, 1989.

> This collection of essays explores many of the debates within the broad field that has become known as the New Historicism, including objections to the field's "watered-down" quality expressed by scholars working in materialist and feminist analysis. Its introduction and wide range of materials will make it of interest to intermediate and advanced readers.

Veeser, H. Aram, ed. *The New Historicism Reader.* New York: Routledge, 1994.

> This collection of essays (a follow-up to the one listed above) contains works of applied criticism in the field of the New Historicism, showing a wide range of possible styles and subject matters. It may be useful for both intermediate and advanced readers.

Application

Reading Prompts

1. Locate and highlight the distinct identity-based issues and emphases that are addressed in the essay's discussion of *Great Expectations*.

2. Locate and evaluate the nonfictional sources the essay draws on to contextualize the novel. How does the novel reflect a particular time and place?

3. Pay careful attention to the reciprocal relationship that is suggested between the novel and the Contagious Diseases Acts; highlight passages in which that relationship is explained.

4. Locate and highlight those passages that explain the extent to which Dickens's intentions are pertinent or not to the essay and its conclusions.

5. Near the end of the essay, a question is posed—"was the glass, is the glass, half empty or half full?" How does that question relate to the essay's perspective on changes in discourse?

Donald E. Hall

Great Expectations
and Harsh Realities

In an 1863 article for *Fraser's*, George Whyte-Melville manages to capture the confusion and intensity of the ongoing social dialogue concerning women's rights and domain. He opens 'Strong-minded Women' by relating an argument he claims to have overheard between 'two very youthful disputants':

> 'It was Eve,' said the little boy with an honest assumption of male superiority, 'that made Adam do wrong, and she was a woman.' 'But it was the devil that tempted Eve,' retorted his sister; developing thus early that feminine subtlety of argument which sets all reasoning at defiance; 'and *he was a man!*' [1]

Indeed, this passage tells us much about the general Victorian muddle concerning the origins and fixity of gender roles. Discourses of religion and 'reason,' hardly in easy agreement themselves, seem complicated even further by certain innate abilities in women, ones that disrupt facile categories and preconceived notions. To be sure, something like a veneer of discursive control remains in the hands of the male essayist. His assertion that women's thought processes run counter to reason reflects a long history of male arrogation of clear-headedness and wisdom, an arrogation that circularly enabled and substantially constituted the theory and practice of 'patriarchy,' and one underlying his use of the adjective 'honest' to characterize the boy's 'assumption of superiority,' Nevertheless, the semantics here are quite slippery; after all, his is only an *assumption* of superiority and Whyte-Melville tacitly admits that there is no adequate counter response possible to the 'subtlety' of the girl's argument. Evil seems to have begun with the machinations of an arrogant man; the anti-patriarchal sister traces causes and effects accurately, even though the author clearly does not relish admitting so.

And even as this important concession, that there is a base of truth behind some feminist assertions, is never wholly lost in the remainder of Whyte-Melville's essay, when he looks beyond individuals engaging in an isolated argument and expands his scope to examine a large social contest between groups of men and women, Whyte-Melville, himself, seems to leave all 'reason' behind. He speaks of the public perception of anti-patriarchal women as 'the enemy' and includes himself among those who view 'strong-minded women' in such a way: 'If they [women] could but unite their forces, earth's whole dynasty would be changed and woman would become the mistress of the creation'.[2] But breathing a sigh of relief, he predicts that such will never be the case: 'By an immutable law of nature, it seems decreed that unity, the first element of strength, should exist under no circumstances in any sisterhood whatever'.[3] Certainly Whyte-Melville's misrepresentation of feminist goals as 'totalitarian' is worth noting, for whether it indicates a fundamental misapprehension or an intentional sensationalism, it certainly operates discursively to inflame rather than calm male fears; of course it also allows him to offer himself (generously) as someone able to relieve those fears with his assurances of irreparable factionalism among women. But more importantly, this summary dismissal itself seems remarkable, even bizarre. Of course Victorian women were far from univocal in their support for even moderate feminist demands; to expect that they would be otherwise is to deny human differences among individual women. But his claim that all unity among even small groups of women was impossible is mystifying, for such groups *were* making substantial inroads into a patriarchal social power structure; organized women were effectively challenging the exclusionary policies and practices summed up in Whyte-Melville's claim that 'there can be no doubt, man is the nobler nature, woman the weaker vessel'.[4]

What is the discursive consequences of admitting the truth of one's 'enemies'' grievances but summarily dismissing their ability or right to redress those wrongs? Of setting up a simplistic 'if . . . then . . .' scenario, where the first clause may well be achievable by those individuals, but the second clause wholly misrepresents or mistakes the consequences of that achievement? One finds such disparities, contradictions, half-hearted admissions, and misrepresentations throughout the works I have examined in *Fixing Patriarchy;* to probe not only the reasons behind, but also the effects of such perplexing literary articulations has been my purpose here. Indeed, the latter will receive most pointed attention in the pages that follow, which focus specifically on the compelling relationship between representation and social 'reality,' one traced finally through a historically contextualized close reading of Dickens's *Great Expectations* from 1861. The 1860s provide remarkable evidence of a discursive matrix (or matrix of discourses thoroughly interconnected) that simultaneously reflected and enabled seemingly disparate actions within the sociopolitical and literary context of that period. In 1870, a substantially expanded Married Women's Property Rights Act was passed; in the last years of the 1860s, hopes ran high for the passage of a women's suffrage bill (which I discuss more fully in my conclusion). During the same decade, however, the brutal Contagious Diseases Acts were passed, and in 1870, the suffrage movement lost its closest parliamentary vote of the century, followed by what several commentators have termed a near half century of suffrage-related 'doldrums'.[5] But linking such acts of accommodation and retrenchment were certain common metaphors, representations, and configurations, an enabling and polyvalent discourse that not only connected fictionalized male attacks on empowered women to anti-feminist legislative action, but also allowed broad movements toward a gradual accommodation of feminists and certain feminist demands. Indeed, this matrix contains both reactionary ideological stands and the seeds of resistance.

Certainly it is not difficult to call Whyte-Melville's bluff, for collective action by women was relatively common by the 1860s. As Mary Poovey has noted, societies to further women's employment opportunities had existed since the mid-1850s, and the *English Woman's Journal*, established in 1858, became a new 'vehicle for linking . . . sympathizers throughout the country'.[6] A national feminist community was slowly developing, while smaller 'communities of women' had already attracted numerous and often very vocal members. The essayist Dora Greenwell, usually a conservative voice in debates on gender roles, comments in the *North British Review* in 1862 on the remarkable changes she sees occurring around her:

> Does not woman show, even in her accomplishments, a continually increasing appreciation of the solid and fundamental? She *knows* more of what she *does*. Her attainments are no longer like the flowers in a child's garden, stuck in without a root to hold by, but living blossoms, unfolding from principles—those everlasting 'seeds of things'.[7]

The vehicle for such 'blossoming' is 'association': 'There is something, too, that awakens our sympathy in the movement which is now making in favor of the higher class of female workers by the Society for Promoting the Employment of Women, in opening out for them less thronged and footworn tracks than those of tuition and needlework'.[8] Greenwell even goes so far as to call for a greater number of similar organizations: 'Should no scheme of associated female labour be organized? Sisterhoods, we know, have often been constructed on pernicious principles, but they are capable of being so organized as to become a blessing alike to themselves and to the world'.[9] Although she applauds the '*conservative* element which belongs to community,' she states that 'social progress' can only be effected through 'association' and 'working in concert'.[10] Finally, Greenwell asserts that while

'Woman has already done much for herself *by herself*' she hopes that soon men too will offer their 'generous co-operation'.[11]

As I have indicated, such 'generous co-operation' was not generally forthcoming; Whyte-Melville's response eighteen months later character-izes the defensiveness inherent in common male reactions to community-building among women. . . . W.E. Aytoun, in a *Blackwood*'s essay that appeared just six months after Greenwell's piece, speaks derisively of the 'cackling which we hear about the abstract rights of woman'.[12] He, like Whyte-Melville, goes on to decry all feminist activity as attempts at 'gy-necocracy' and identifies the most dangerous proponents of such female political hegemony as members of vague 'associations' in which the 'fe-male members have taken the lead'.[13] Organized women, he indicates, threaten a formerly stable and benevolent male power structure in what he characterizes as a zero-sum and violent 'contest for the possession of the breeches'.[14]

Why did associations between women elicit such hysterical reactions from some men? Nina Auerbach suggests some useful answers to this ques-tion in stating that 'a community of women is a rebuke to the conventional ideal of a solitary woman living for and through men, attaining citizenship in the community of adulthood through masculine approval alone';[15] 'em-blems of female self-sufficiency,' such communities challenge patriarchal insistence on natural, fixed 'spheres,' with men alone possessing the ability to determine stable and productive 'communal' policy. And Auerbach's commentary is equally pertinent to the present study when she links male anxiety over young women acting and living together to a fear of 'contagion which gives their conjunction the status of a profound taboo. Such a com-munity can only arouse the "dormant" horror of female sexuality: depths of sleeping perversion blossoming in its inhabitants, and so, perhaps, do em-barrassing memories of the bordello in the man who contemplates it'.[16] In-deed, an awakening, 'blossoming,' subjectivity, nurtured in an 'Other' community, could only have 'perverse' qualities ascribed to it. Thus women together were commonly seen by men as wickedly self-indulgent, capri-cious, and even depraved. As unpredictably and exuberantly desiring be-ings, their desires could hardly be trusted to coincide with the wishes or interests of patriarchs, were feared, in fact, as potentially sociopathic, even psychopathic. Thus Aytoun describes hordes of women warriors ripping the trousers off men and afterwards celebrating their 'conquest' among themselves, women whom he later imagines as ghoulish doctors, driven mad by their transgressions, striding 'bare-armed' into men's chambers to threaten surgically their health and destroy their mental well-being. These gross misrepresentations are somewhat amusing from a twentieth-century perspective but had considerable social consequences in their day. Uncontrolled and antagonistic, virulent and sexually threatening, women independent of men and working together were commonly represented as communities pervaded by mental and physical disease, ones that were violent threats to the bodily safety and psychological well-being of the true (new) unfortunates of Victorian society: upstanding, overburdened, grossly underappreciated patriarchs.

After all, *their* bodies constituted the (most important parts of the) body of the nation; *their* health was the nation's health. And exacerbating such hubristic uneasiness was the fact that the female sex itself was commonly associated with *disease* during and after the nineteenth century. As Barbara Ehrenreich and Deirdre English have demonstrated, 'the theories which guided the doctor's practice . . . held that woman's *normal* state was to be sick. This was not advanced as an empirical observation, but as physiological fact'.[17] A binary construction of gender inevitably led to an association between women and disease or ill-health, since the signifier 'man' was fundamentally equated with all that was solid, healthful, and good. Viewing women through patriarchal lenses, doctors 'established that women are sick, that this sickness is innate, and stems from the very possession of the uterus and ovaries'.[18] Given such an equation, it is easy to see how feminist rebellion and organization also came to be associated with especially pernicious forms of disease and contagion. Whyte-Melville speaks of the 'fast young lady,' a term denoting both the transgressive, feminist-minded woman and possibly the sexually unconventional one as well; in her example, he finds that the potential disease of women in general has moved from dormancy to active virulence:

> It is her power of imitation that leads her to wear men's shirts, hats, collars, breast-pins, boots, &c., and a morbid craving for remark—the diseased growth of that love of approbation which is so beautiful a quality in her sex, that causes her to drive, smoke, and talk public-school slang, doing all these things in the most offensive and unladylike manner the while.[19]

'Diseased growth,' 'morbid cravings'—Julia Kristeva argues in *Powers of Horror* that the diseased and abject demarcate the 'foul lining'[20] of patriarchal order; thus when 'male, phallic power is vigorously threatened by the no less virulent power of the other sex,' then '[t]hat other sex, the feminine, becomes synonymous with a radical evil that is to be suppressed'.[21] This 'feminine'/feminist evil is associated with contagion, decay, and all other signifiers denoting the breakdown and transgression of boundaries; historically it is a social 'evil' that has elicited diverse but often violent male strategies of disease containment.

. . . [S]uch a perception of a contagion passing between women informed Dickens's characterization of the Miss Wade/Tattycoram community in *Little Dorrit;* anti-male activity passed as a form of mental and ocular
disease from Miss Wade to her protégée and elicited concerted and anxi-
ety-driven efforts by Arthur Clennam and Mr Meagles to cure Tattycoram
and reestablish healthy male authority over her body (eyes) and desires. But
fictional representations were not alone in being influenced by the connections that Auerbach, English, Ehrenreich, and Kristeva note. Lives were
brutally affected. A particularly deplorable consequence of the deep-seated
and complex male fear of groups of women spreading sickness was the passage in 1864 of the Contagious Diseases Acts; in the name of public health,
the CDAs allowed for the incarceration and forced physical examination of
all women who were suspected of being prostitutes and therefore possible
transmitters of venereal disease. But besides being considered 'unnatural'
and morally, as well as physically, diseased because of their sexual activity,
prostitutes were also considered as a group to be antagonistic toward men.
As E.M. Sigsworth and T.J. Wyke have documented, prostitutes were
viewed as active agents of vice, a 'vicious and profligate sisterhood',[22] whose
machinations destroyed men's lives; venereal diseases were spread by the
guilty to the innocent'.[23] Thus Susan Kent notes that 'Victorians regarded
the prostitute as the seducer of young men, the corrupter of morals, and
the carrier and personification of disease, who entered her profession out of
vanity, pleasure-seeking, and greed'.[24] In parliamentary and journalistic debates on the topic, it was commonly asserted that selfish and aggressive
women were acting in concert to attack the health and security of innocent
patriarchs and their families:

> The typical Pater-familias living in a grand house near the park, sees his sons
> allured into debauchery, dares not walk with his daughters through the streets
> after nightfall, and is disturbed from his night-slumbers by the drunken
> screams and foul oaths of prostitutes reeling home with daylight.[25]

In the words of one contemporary commentator, such prostitutes constituted a 'multitudinous amazonian army [that] the devil keeps in constant
field service'.[26]

Although historian William O'Neill, writing over a century later, expresses a profound astonishment and disbelief that such laws could have
ever been passed given that they 'violated . . . Christian moral standards,
feminine integrity, and the most fundamental principles of English justice',[27] it is imperative to recognize that these Acts appeared from a context
of explicit challenges to male authority and male attempts to contain the
'contagion' that feminism itself represented. Judith Walkowitz, in her

superb overview of Victorian attitudes toward prostitution, has argued that prostitutes themselves were often women who 'were more inclined to self-assertion' than their contemporaries.[28] And as Olive Banks notes, there was a clear 'connection between support for the Acts and anti-feminism'.[29] In fact, Kent argues that feminists themselves were often perceived as prostitutes and were vociferously denounced as 'public women,'[30] ones who had the audacity to flaunt their 'desiring' state openly. But with the exception of two incidents in which feminists were physically attacked in 1872, they generally were not treated with as much overt violence as prostitutes. However, the reverse dynamic made the treatment of prostitutes particularly brutal. As Walkowitz, Banks, and Kent each imply, the enactment of laws punishing certain groups of women for challenging male health was at least partially an act of displacement by some men; the aggression felt toward women who were actively challenging male social power was vented on a convenient target. Ironically, of course, the brutality of the CDAs did more to galvanize women, who organized throughout Britain to campaign for their repeal, than any other action by parliament in the nineteenth century. Until their suspension in 1883, the Acts formed a locus of concern for feminists that led them to fight effectively against patriarchal objectification of women, including the traffic in young female prostitutes and the propagation of pornography.

Women opposed to patriarchy acted; certain men, determined to protect their interests, responded. But inevitably those responses themselves generated new avenues for challenges to male authority. In Foucault's words:

> Discourses are not once and for all subservient to power or raised up against it . . . discourse can be both an instrument and an effect of power, but also a hindrance, a stumbling-block, a point of resistance and a starting point for an opposing strategy. Discourse transmits and produces power; it reinforces it, but also undermines and exposes it, renders it fragile and makes it possible to thwart it.[31]

Thus discourse(s) can change significantly over and in time, producing both varying mechanisms for solidifying and justifying power, as well as new and diverse sites of resistance to power. It is for this reason that I examine three temporally separated novels by Charles Dickens in the body of a study that ranges widely over single or roughly contemporary works by other authors. Placing *Great Expectations* beside *Martin Chuzzlewit* and *Little Dorrit* uncovers not only the evolution of one male writer's defenses regarding effective feminist challenges to patriarchy, but also certain discursive and perceptual changes that clearly impacted on men's resistance to and even ability to resist the political agenda of the Victorian feminists. As the essays quoted above demonstrate, there were both admissions of effectiveness and harsh reaction, contradictions and telling representations that indicate a society in flux.

Before moving on to *Great Expectations* a bit of recapitulation is warranted. In *Martin Chuzzlewit*, the most explicit threats to male power and equanimity were on American soil, where Mrs Brick and her friends vocally challenged patriarchal authority. Nevertheless, certain members of British society, notably the more aggressive women of the Chuzzlewit family, themselves embodied a form of female separatism and 'self-interestedness' that reflected some of the demands of American feminists, even as the danger to men represented by the egotism of Sairey Gamp and Betsy Prig highlighted newly pronounced male fears of women working together for their own benefit. And in *Martin Chuzzlewit* Dickens makes little attempt to understand the motivations behind such collaboration; the novel makes no positive connection between Merry Chuzzlewit's abuse at the hands of Jonas and other women's attempts to remain independent and protect their own interests.

But the novel had other social implications as well, for it suggests clearly that 'if women become nurses, they may kill men.' As Mary Poovey has demonstrated, women did become nurses in increasing numbers at mid-century and certainly did not kill men. In fact, the relative efficiency with which Florence Nightingale manipulated cultural constructions of femininity to legitimize nursing as a 'woman's' profession demonstrates how such 'extreme' warnings can fail, can in fact work polyvalently. While Poovey argues that the characterization of Sairey Gamp in 1844 'galvanized the prejudices and anxieties of a large sector of the English public,'[32] within the next decade and a half, Nightingale became immensely popular as a cultural icon who was effective at rewriting cultural discourse concerning nursing. Extreme stereotypes and harsh fictional characterizations of female nurses may have hindered efforts by women trying to enter the new profession, but once female nurses proved themselves 'able,' the simplistic construct was supplanted. A polyvalent discourse on threatening, empowered women had a self-subverting quality; exaggerated warnings and fears were substantially disproven as new evidence of fluidity continued to undermine oppressive constructions of fixity. Indeed, a rigidly binary structuring of gender roles became ever less credible as its fundamental relationship to the 'reality' of diverse human abilities became increasingly and glaringly problematic.

. . . Victorian attitudes were changing steadily, and by the time we reach *Little Dorrit* thirteen years after *Martin Chuzzlewit*, Dickens portrays

two explicitly identified 'patriarchs' as selfish, greedy, and wholly remiss in
their duties toward their dependants. In response to such male corruption
and incapacity, female roles evolve to fill in gaps in social and familial responsibility. The activity and ability of Amy Dorrit reflects a system of gender roles and domain which can change fluidly in response to social
circumstances. Even the most 'feminist' of the characters in *Little Dorrit*,
Miss Wade, is viewed with some sympathy; in allowing her to tell her story
of mistreatment and suspicion in the 'History of a Self-Tormentor,'
Dickens reveals many of the motivations behind anti-patriarchal activity.
Despite these 'admissions,' however, the novel harshly condemns female
separatism as anti-family and wholly misguided by anger and hatred;
women may have understandable grievances against men, but, the novel indicates, they should forego attempts to right those wrongs because evil, in
fact, sows the seeds of its own destruction.

Ironically enough, this is true, but not in the exact way that Dickens
indicates, as many of *his* extreme warnings and characterizations worked
against the very ideological stands out of which they grew. Moreover, the
hasty denials of women's rights and ability to redress wrongs that one
finds in Whyte-Melville and Dickens could not outweigh the substantial
ideological effect of the admissions that accompany them. Irrevocably and
even though he often seems to resist acknowledging it, there was a new
space in Dickens's own discursive matrix that allowed for changes in gender constructs in response to individual needs and as one tactic, among
many, that could be used against institutionalized oppression. One need
only think of the extraordinary contrast between the fixity of characters
such as Rose and Nancy from *Oliver Twist* (1838) and the dramatically
burgeoning fluidity of characters such as Betsey Trotwood in *David Copperfield* (1850) and Madame Defarge in *A Tale of Two Cities* (1859) to perceive my point.

But in isolating such mutations and implicit accommodations, I am not
suggesting that there was a perfectly linear and quickly accelerating breakdown in Victorian patriarchy or the mindset fundamental to it, for through
hard work and concerted efforts to enhance their visibility, aggressive and
organized women became both more and less threatening, differently
threatening, as they became more effectively demanding and more familiar.
Their motivations could be understood by some men even as their demands
were often resisted and their activities feared. And it is this interplay of resistance and accommodation that accounts for many of the peculiarities of
Great Expectations. In it one finds rich, complex characterizations of transgressive women; the novel pays close attention to changing social circumstances allowing gender roles to metamorphose. At the same time, one

finds a thematic overreaction to collaborative efforts by women and certain extreme representations that are clearly anti-feminist, even brutal. In a first person narrative filtered through a male consciousness, it is telling that the sources of the most pronounced and continuing forms of threat, both in the hero's childhood and young adulthood, are women; even more importantly, they are strong and vital women with whom the reader is at times invited to sympathize, but in many other instances, urged to fear.

Even though Magwitch is the first figure in the novel whom we actually see threatening young Pip, more immediate and persistent threats to his health and happiness come from his sister, Mrs Joe. She is 'given to government,'[33] a gynecocrat, as it were, whose tyranny extends over both her husband and young brother.

> My sister, Mrs Joe Gargery, . . . had established a great reputation with herself and the neighbours because she had brought me up 'by hand.' Having at that time to find out for myself what the expression meant, and knowing her to have a hard and heavy hand, and to be much in the habit of laying it upon her husband as well as upon me, I suppose that Joe Gargery and I were both brought up by hand. (14)

As in Aytoun's representations above, her threats are both physical and psychological, for during her 'ram-pages' of anger and destructiveness, she alternately abuses Pip by thrashing him with the ironically named 'Tickler' and vocally wishing him dead. As Pip indicates above, she does so as well to her husband, even managing to combine her abuse of the two when she throws Pip at Joe: 'I often served as a connubial missle' (15).

Elihu Pearlman has argued convincingly that the threat to social and familial equilibrium which Mrs Joe embodies originates in her appropriation of traditionally masculine behaviors. 'The props which define her are distinctly phallic,' Pearlman notes, remarking pertinently that many of the words used to describe her, such as 'Ram' and 'Buster,' 'suggest that Mrs. Joe has arrogated masculine sexuality to herself'.[34] But Pearlman's claim that because 'Mrs. Joe's masculinity and her prediliction toward violence are her defining characteristics' then 'In some part of Dickens's imagination, she is a man, even though one who is costumed as a woman'[35] is not quite on target. Rather, her biological sex and the gender transgression which her appropriation of masculine characteristics indicate accentuate her villainy. Mrs Joe is not 'an example of a bad father'[36] as Pearlman argues, rather she is an example of a particularly threatening type of woman for Victorian men, one who has effectively garnered power and who uses it as tyrannically as men have used their power in the past: the gynecocrat who, like Lydia Gwilt and Hester Dethridge in Collins's novels, punishes representative members of an oppressive patriarchal social order.

But while Mrs Joe's cruelty is certainly as monstrous as that of Dickens's earlier villainnesses, she is not portrayed simplistically or without subtlety. Unlike Sairey Gamp, who is simply greedy and destructive, Mrs Joe's transgressions are contextualized, arguably even accommodated. The threat to male equanimity which she poses as the novel unfolds comes not from her attempts to acquire power—which is a *fait accompli*—but from her continuing misuse of it; after all, she fills a power void that is not of her own making. Joe is 'a mild, good-natured, sweet-tempered, easy-going, foolish, dear fellow—a sort of Hercules in strength, and also in weakness' (14). While such qualities may be laudable from the perspective of an abused boy, they are not very useful ones in the running of a household. We get an intimation of the actual necessity of Mrs Joe being the way she is in her husband's characterization of her as a 'master-minded,' for he just as decidedly declares, 'I ain't a master-mind' (58). Indeed, the appropriateness of her assumption of power is indicated when Pip describes her appearance on a trip to town; she carries 'a basket like the Great Seal of England' and several other articles which she displays 'much as Cleopatra or any other sovereign lady on the rampage might exhibit her wealth in a pageant or procession' (112–13). In describing Mrs Joe as a 'sovereign' in the tradition of Cleopatra and indeed, Victoria, the novel works to recognize the legitimacy of and thereby validate her power even as it criticizes her misuse of it.

Of course Mrs Joe is hardly a sympathetic character, and while the novel allows that she fills a certain void, she is also a figure who is punished for her cruelty and abuse of power. Kurt Hartog argues that 'At the center of Dickens's portrayal of women in *Great Expectations* lies a stark and melodramatic image: women, lacking the capacity to love, become destructive to themselves and to men. Like predators, they must be held firmly, even violently in check. Orlick "tames" Mrs. Joe by smashing her skull with convict chains'.[37] Certainly her inability to love and nurture, as women in particular 'should,' contributes to Mrs Joe's culpability, making her one of Dickens's many portrayals of parent figures who fail miserably in their duties toward dependents: Old Martin in *Martin Chuzzlewit*, Lady Dedlock in *Bleak House*, Mr. Dorrit and Mrs. Clennam in *Little Dorrit*, and Mr. Murdstone (and David's own mother) in *David Copperfield*. But Hartog is perceptive in recognizing a specific gender component to the transformation of Mrs Joe. Like Merry Chuzzlewit, who is effectively turned into an angel by Jonas's abuse, Mrs Joe becomes cheerful and repentant after being beaten brutally by Orlick. She brings him before her daily to see if he forgives the abuse that she once leveled at him: 'She watched his countenance as if she were particularly wishful to be assured that he took kindly to his reception, she showed every possible desire to conciliate him, and there was an air of humble propitiation in all she did, such as I have seen pervade the bearing of a child towards a hard master' (139). Her self-debasement and apologetic actions continue; on her deathbed, she puts her arms around Joe's neck and says, '"Pardon," and once "Pip"' (306). Is the novel degrading and punishing her solely for being a formerly assertive woman? I recognize the point is moot, but would argue that here the 'gynecocrat' may be begging forgiveness only for her abuses of power, not her assumption of power; after all, she acts in the scenes above with an extreme deference that fully disgusts Pip and that in the representational economy of the novel, seems the mirror image of the extreme indifference to the needs of others that she had demonstrated earlier. Both are portrayed as shocking and inappropriate. In dramatizing Mrs Joe's behavior as excessive in both her abuse of power and renunciation of all power, the novel sets the stage, so to speak, for the 'moderate' ideal it will offer the reader.

Unlike many of Dickens's earlier novels, *Great Expectations* works to avoid a simple 'if . . . then . . .' response to empowered women, for it arrives at a synthesis in which a woman's activity, vocal ability, and agency are retained even as her good will and noncombativeness are emphasized. Biddy serves as the text's 'ideal,' one who would be unimaginable in a Dickens novel from earlier decades. Clearly she is as intelligent as Pip, for she teaches him at his first school and then keeps up with him in his later studies; we are told that she catches knowledge 'like a cough' (141). Pip reflects, 'In short, whatever I knew, Biddy knew. Theoretically, she was already as good a blacksmith as I, or better' (141). Later hers is a voice of common sense and 'reason' that attempts to check Pip's flights of fancy; in doing so, she fully reverses Victorian gender stereotypes which attribute fancifulness to women and rationality to men. To be sure, she is something of a domestic angel; her housekeeping duties and nurturing ability are inevitable Victorian components of the 'balance' that she represents. But even though she never attempts to be 'everybody's master' as Mrs Joe did and does not interfere in matters at the forge, as was characteristic of her predecessor, she nevertheless fills the same power void—she gives 'herself a deal o' trouble' (503) with Joe to explain to him how to think and act, and later, with characteristic gentleness and directness, tells Pip what to do also, that he 'must marry' (517). In short, Biddy can be seen as a substantial evolution in the Dickens heroine; she has the domestic ability of a Ruth Pinch or Mary Graham, the activity of an Amy Dorrit, the intellectual ability of a Dickens hero such as David Copperfield, and far less reticence in expressing opinions than any of her female forerunners. While clearly no 'feminist' ideal from a late twentieth-century perspective, Biddy is an individual whose abilities and assertiveness demonstrate how far Dickens (and by implication, Victorian society) had come in the twenty years since he created the physically and psychologically threatening 'strong-minded woman' who plots to take over the Chuzzlewit family by 'man-slaughtering' her husband and locking her brother-in-law in a madhouse.

But in exploring the compromises and accommodations rendered in the characters of Biddy and Mrs Joe, I have yet to explore the loci of greatest fear and attraction in the novel. While strong women acting on their own or with male approval may be accommodated with relative ease, women together—those communities recognized as discursively disruptive by Auerbach, applauded for producing social change by Greenwell, and branded as dangerous and virulent by numerous male writers—still generate intense anxiety in Dickens, evoke fears of conspiracy and desire out of control. The 'communities' represented in the collaboration of the American feminists and of the British nurses in *Martin Chuzzlewit* and of Miss Wade and Tattycoram in *Little Dorrit* reappear in a new guise in the community of Miss Havisham and Estella in *Great Expectations*. In looking at diachronic permutations in these pairings, it is clear that Dickens's perceptions of the potential intensity of *women*-generated threats to men persisted over the course of decades, even as the parameters of those representations changed dramatically with the evolution of a discursive context. *Great Expectations* helps reveal the reciprocal relationship between literary (and other cultural) representations and the society to which they are inextricably connected. In the mid- to late-1860s the dialogue surrounding and concerning the Contagious Diseases Acts helped bring into focus certain gender-inflected notions of culpability and punishability, but several years before the passage of the Acts, *Great Expectations* anticipated much of the complexity of this debate as well as effectively contributed to a discursive matrix enabling it. As Edward Said explores in *Culture and Imperialism*, 'cultural forms like the novel or opera' do not 'cause' people to go out and oppress.[38] But we are right to recognize the complex ideological ties between representations and the racist, sexist, homophobic, and imperialist practices that they may help enable. Dickens's novel both reflected and reinforced a set of discursive norms that not only failed to hinder the punishment of prostitutes, but in fact supported it ideologically.[39] At the same time, the scope of his novel is wide and within its many voices *Great Expectations* captures the very site that would prove the most effective point for challenging the CDAs.

There are several components of *Great Expectations* that we might say 'enabled' the passage of the Acts. After all, Estella is portrayed as a form of vicious prostitute who toys with men and their affections, manipulates them to meet her economic, psychological, and perverse erotic needs. Draining sexual attraction of its emotional content, she uses her beauty and body as one might a tool or, more accurately, a weapon; early in the novel she taunts Pip with 'Am I pretty?' even though she considers him a 'little coarse monster' (94). She later watches him fight Herbert Pocket, which brings a 'bright flush' to her face, and rewards Pip with a kiss. He immediately recognizes the tawdriness of this encounter, thinking 'the kiss was given to the coarse common boy as a piece of money might have been . . . it was worth nothing' (104). Of course here it is Pip who feels 'cheap,' who is disgusted by his contact with the young woman who gives kisses away without love, but even if she is the one actually 'paying' in the scene above, Estella is portrayed as the morally corrupt participant, whose 'bright flush' indicates a morbidity, a (deviant, of course) sexual subjectivity, and specifically, a propensity for public display that is wholly consonant with the images of diseased women in the passages quoted earlier.[40]

Indeed, Estella uses her body 'to deceive and entrap' numerous men (337). Insensitive and corrupt(ed), she finally breaks Pip's heart by marrying Bentley Drummle. Pip argues with her that Drummle has 'nothing to recommend him but money,' that she 'throws away her graces and attractions on a mere boor, the lowest of the crowd.' 'Well?' is her impassive reply (336), even as she later admits that his money in fact encourages her to take this 'fatal step,' to, in Pip's words, 'fling herself away upon a brute' (390). The rhetoric of these conversations leaves little to the imagination; Estella is selling her body to a wealthy man and in doing so commits a criminal offense which leaves her open to judgement and punishment.

But if Estella is prostitute-like, what does that make Miss Havisham? Not a 'madam' exactly, for she strongly opposes Estella' marriage to Drummle. Even so, Miss Havisham's characterization if quite telling, for certainly she is cast as the unhealthy proprietor of a house of corruption. Kristeva's analysis of the 'diseased' and 'abject' comes to mind as Pip describes the grounds of Satis House, which contain a 'rank garden . . . overgrown with tangled weeds' (73), entered through a door 'encumbered with a growth of fungus' (430). Compared to the 'Queens' Gardens' of Ruskin's *Sesame and Lilies* (1865), where the thoroughly deferential and devoted wife is both the token cultivator of and most ornamental flower in a well-tended domestic flowerbed, Miss Havisham's domestic garden, both within and without the house, clearly lacks a proper gardener. Her rotten wedding-cake covered with fungus and spiders symbolically indicates a corruption of domestic arrangements. Satis House may not be a brothel, but it is clearly a house of diseased desires.

Indeed, the anxiety which Auerbach argues attended most Victorian male representations of female cohabitation and cooperation is evident at Satis House as well; in fact, the 'satisfaction' gleaned there seems quite erotic for Miss Havisham:

> She was even more dreadfully fond of Estella than she had been when I last saw them together; I repeat the word advisedly, for there was something positively dreadful in the energy of her looks and embraces. She hung upon Estella's beauty, hung upon her words, hung upon her gestures, and sat mumbling her own dreadful fingers while she looked at her, as though she were devouring the beautiful creature she had reared. (327)

Not only is there a 'dreadful' eroticism portrayed, but also an implication of contagion; Miss Havisham and her house are described similarly: 'in shutting out the light of day, she had shut out infinitely more; that, in seclusion, she had secluded herself from a thousand natural and healing influences; that her mind, brooding solitary, had grown diseased' (428). Reflecting the mid- to late-nineteenth century medicalization of conceptions of same sex desire, Dickens's representation works to pathologize an emotional attachment that fails to serve the interests of the nuclear family and the reproductive mandate of an industrializing and colonizing nation. But perceptions and representations of desire between women had their own special inflections; as Lillian Faderman has explored, many of the aspects of 'disease' commonly attributed to erotic attachments between women can be traced directly to their renunciation of and challenge to patriarchal power and influence.[41] Lesbians presented (and present) a clear and unequivocal threat to the fundamental principle underlying patriarchy: male social, political, and sexual centrality—indeed, men's necessary, defining, and 'natural'-izing presence. Estella charges her mentor with teaching her 'that there was such a thing as daylight, but that it was made to be her enemy and destroyer, and she must always turn against it' (331); keeping in mind the equation in *Little Dorrit* of 'light' with wise and healthy patriarchal management of women,[42] this metaphor reiterates the linkage between Miss Havisham's active transmission of contagion and her virulent hatred of men.

The representation in *Great Expectations* of autonomous and antipatriarchal women as sick and dangerous vividly captures the larger social linkages that Walkowitz, Banks, and Kent suggest above, for in a broad sense, Miss Havisham's disease is that of the nineteenth-century feminist, an active discontent; like a venereal infection, it is represented as poisoning the system, both the individual body and the social body. And in *Great Expectations,* as in the case of the prostitutes mentioned above, anti-patriarchal women are constructed as 'punishable' because of their conscious agency in the passing of contagion, for the novel portrays Miss Havisham's and Estella's lives as ones devoted to making Pip's and other man's existences miserable. Like the venereal infections of prostitutes, the 'blight' (331) that is upon the women of the novel is transmitted to men through the channel of romantic machination. Pip's life is infected by his contact with the inhabitants of Satis House; his mistaken expectations and the havoc that these wreak on his potentially happy existence with Joe and Biddy originate in the evil maneuverings of the women: 'Does she grow prettier and prettier, Pip?' Miss Havisham asks; when he answers affirmatively, she murmurs, 'Break their hearts, my pride and hope, break their hearts and have no mercy!' (108). In Pip's words, Miss Havisham 'practise[s] on the susceptibility of a poor boy' (389), a metaphor indicating both the entrapment of an innocent male in an evil woman's snare and susceptibility to a form of infection. Of course, Pip *is* susceptible, but for the most part because of an abuse-filled childhood that contributes to his intense desire for Estella's approval. His easy contraction of disease can thus be traced back even further to an unhealthy childhood with Mrs Joe. Certainly the novel never exonerates Pip for his own cruel, vain, and foolish actions, but it consistently demonstrates that his infectious discontent results from contact with dangerous, virulent women whose perversity and malice destroy men's lives and happiness.

Why attraction and abhorrence often go hand in hand is a subject beyond the scope of the present study; here I can only point out that the dynamics of the novel consistently mirror that of the CDAs, as *Great Expectations* portrays Estella as both highly desirable and detestable. And in this combination of antagonism and attraction we find one key to understanding the violence which is manifested toward Miss Havisham and Estella, as well as the women who were brutalized under the CDAs. Exciting and dangerous, admired and abhorred, they are punished in a manner that one might say 'befits' their crimes. Josephine Butler often and effectively decried the forced medical examination of prostitutes as a form of legally sanctioned sexual assault.[43] Similarly, Hartog describes the fire which finally consumes Miss Havisham as a symbolic act of rape perpetrated by Pip.[44] The imagery of fire taken in connection with the way Pip clings to the older woman as she burns makes the scene one of violent sexuality, or more precisely, heterosexuality, as the formerly dominant agent in a women-centered, erotically charged, anti-patriarchal community is punished by an imposition of male/female sexual contact: 'the closer I covered her, the more wildly she shrieked and tried to free herself . . . I knew nothing until I knew that we were on the floor by the great table' (431). Estella's fate is not dissimilar, for the mistreatment that Pip received at her hands is 'appropriately' repaid in the beatings that she endures from Bentley Drummle; the 'sadist' is repaid sadistically. Just as Mrs Joe does slavish penance to the man whom she once scolded, so too are the women of Satis House cleansed of their disease through what the novel portrays as a dose of their own medicine.

Indeed, collaborative actions among women was so fundamentally threatening to a still substantially self-righteous and highly defensive male power structure that *Great Expectations* does not even present or represent an ideal community of women who might be spared punishment. Even so, it is a work that, as I demonstrated above, accommodates certain solitarily transgressive female figures and that never loses its attention to and sympathy with personal histories which help account for present actions. In doing so, the novel effectively captures points of opposition within the same cultural/discursive matrix. In the words of one commentator on prostitution from 1861, 'Woman, waylaid, tempted, deceived, becomes in turn the terrible avenger of her sex. Armed with a power which is all but irresistible . . . the law of retaliation is hers.'[45]

As the sister in the anecdote which opened this chapter seemed to ask, who exactly is victimizing whom here? One of Josephine Butler's most effective arguments against the CDAs was that *men* were substantially responsible for the transmission of venereal diseases to 'innocent families,' not the prostitutes who were treated so harshly; in 1870, she protested 'it is unjust to punish the sex who are the victims of vice, and leave unpunished the sex who are the main cause, both of the vice and its dreadful consequences'.[46] In a *Westminster Review* article from the same year, essayist John Chapman argues angrily that 'Men steeped in sin themselves have dared to stone' the prostitute; they have 'hypocritically cloaked their own sensuality in the outward garb of punishing the being whom they alone have brought to shame'.[47] Particularly effective sites of resistance were created as questions of double standards and male responsibility for abuse crystallized around the CDAs debate. But even in the early years of the decade, Dickens's representations of Miss Havisham and Estella dramatized much of the complexity of these issues. Amanda Anderson had suggested that Dickens was particularly acute in 'insisting that circumstances or context were to blame' in his portrayals of fallen women,[48] ones who serve as 'both victim and embodiment of threatening forces in the social environment'.[49] Even Pip partially exonerates Miss Havisham by recognizing that 'in the endurance of her own trial, she forgot mine' (389). Her anti-male activity is understandable, even if not clearly forgivable, because there is a history behind it, a chain of responsibility leading directly back to men. In telling us that Miss Havisham became isolated, eccentric, and eventually revenge-minded through the agency of Compeyson and her half brother, the novel shifts some of the blame for the misery it dramatizes onto the shoulders of abusive men. Theirs too was a disease of discontent, cruelty, and unhappiness that they pass along to Miss Havisham by exploiting her romantically; if Miss Havisham is contagious, she was infected by men, who by implication, are also responsible for the eventual transmission of the same disease to Estella and Pip. Of course, we are told that Miss Havisham's abuse at the hands of Compeyson results partially from her own stubbornness and disregard of the advice of Matthew Picket; the novel implies that she, like Merry Chuzzlewit, should have allowed herself to be better managed by wise men. Clearly Dickens does not (dares not? cannot?) dramatize a case of a victimized woman who rightfully and appropriately redresses her grievances against men. Nevertheless, a site of resistance is there, a shifting of blame, that no matter how undercut and resisted it may be in the novel and throughout the press coverage of the CDAs debate, would eventually lead to the repeal of the Acts. Indeed, to respond with violence against individuals who are no more 'guilty' than many men is to open up one clear path for challenging an entire patriarchal social order; the CDAs provided a secure vantage point for the continued undermining of a theory and set of practices centering on claims of seamless wisdom and unassailable moral authority. While, following Foucault, one must acknowledge that there is no real 'outside' to discourse, no objective exterior to cultural contests, yet there certainly is an 'outside' to explicit theoretical constructs and legally codified power structures. Such enabled the oppositional tactics and articulations of Victorian feminists.

But, of course, Dickens himself was neither 'outside' of patriarchal privilege nor of a reliance on patriarchal theory. Thus Anderson makes the cogent point that while 'Dickens exhibits some self-consciousness about the scape-goating mechanisms directed toward the fallen, . . . he does not significantly transform the dominant paradigms'.[50] Indeed, Estella is thoroughly tamed and conventionalized by the end of the novel, and Satis House itself is wholly destroyed. When Pip returns to the garden grounds in the printed ending to the novel, he notes 'There was no house now, no brewery, no building whatever left, but the wall of the old garden. The cleared space had been enclosed with a rough fence, and looking over it, I saw that some of the old ivy had struck root anew, and was growing green on the low quiet mounds of ruin' (518). This image of destruction and rebirth serves to highlight dramatically the cleansing and transformation of Estella through the violence of her marriage with Drummle.

Yet the image does imply some small sense of synthesis: it is the 'old' garden ivy, after all, that is growing 'anew'. Time does not stand still; nothing is wholly static, securely fixed. And this small sense of continuing dynamism, this incrementality, should neither be overlooked nor dismissed. *Great Expectations'* mishmashed accommodation of and harsh reaction against female empowerment makes it a particularly useful indicator not only of disconcerting activity and ideological instability, but also of the very slow processes of social change. . . . For as under-emphasized as it may be, the shifting of blame that is represented in the novel not only led to the dismantling of the CDAs, but was part of a larger paradigm shift that also allowed for new property rights acts in 1870 and 1882.

So, *was the glass, is the glass, half empty or half full?* To my mind, the gross exaggerations and half-hearted admissions of Aytoun and Whyte-Melville quoted at the beginning of this chapter tell us much more about the effectiveness of the mid-Victorian feminists than about any incapacities that the writers wished to emphasize. At issue were new forms of female and feminist subjectivity at a time when feminine object-hood was idealized by—overloaded with meaning by—nervous, defensive, but also self-subverting men. Potent threat, begrudged admissions, and violent reactions characterized the era; the changes produced by the interplay of these forces were clearly less than radical, but did represent small steps in the progressive breakdown of one particularly oppressive, legally codified social structure: Victorian patriarchy. Dickens's novels taken together offer us compelling evidence of the extent to which an individual consciousness can be shaped by an inherently conservative but still polyvalent discursive matrix, as well as the ways fiction itself not only reflects but also helps simultaneously construct and disrupt what is broadly termed 'social reality.'

NOTES

1. George Whyte-Melville, "Strong-Minded Women," *Fraser's* 68 (November 1863): 667.
2. Whyte-Melville, 668.
3. Whyte-Melville, 668.
4. Whyte-Melville, 667.
5. Susan Kingsley Kent, *Sex and Suffrage in Britain, 1860–1914* (Princeton, NJ: Princeton University Press, 1987), 184.
6. Mary Poovey, *Uneven Developments: The Ideological Work of Gender in Mid-Victorian England* (Chicago, IL: University of Chicago Press, 1985), 150.
7. Dora Greenwell, "Our Single Women," *North British Review* 36 (February 1862): 68.
8. Greenwell, 71.
9. Greenwell, 75
10. Greenwell, 81–82.

11. Greenwell, 87.

12. W. E. Aytoun, "The Rights of Woman," *Blackwood's* 92 (August 1862): 186.

13. Aytoun, 186.

14. Aytoun, 183.

15. Nina Auerbach, *Communities of Women: An Idea in Fiction* (Cambridge, MA: Harvard University Press, 1978), 5.

16. Auerbach, 14.

17. Barbara Ehrenreich and Deirdre English, *For Her Own Good: 150 Years of the Experts' Advice to Women* (New York: Anchor Books, 1978), 110.

18. Ehrenreich and English, 134.

19. Whyte-Melville, 675.

20. Julia Kristeva, *Powers of Horror: An Essay on Abjection*, trans Leon S. Roudiez (New York: Columbia University Press, 1982), 20.

21. Kristeva, 70.

22. E. M. Sigsworth and T. J. Wyke, "A Study of Victorian Prostitution and Venereal Disease," in Martha Vicinus (ed.), *Suffer and Be Still* (Bloomington, IN: Indiana University Press, 1972): 80.

23. Sigsworth and Wyke, 92.

24. Kent, 66.

25. From the *Lancet*, November 7, 1857, quoted in Keith Nield's introduction to *Prostitution in the Victorian Age* (Westmead, UK: Grcgg International, 1973), np.

26. This was written in 1859 by James Miller, Professor of Surgery at the University of Edinburgh, and is quoted in Lynda Nead, *Myths of Sexuality: Representations of Women in Victorian Britain* (New York: Basil Blackwell, 1988), 117.

27. William O'Neill, *The Woman Movement: Feminism in the United States and England* (Chicago, IL: Quadrangle, 1969), 37.

28. Judith Walkowitz, *Prostitution and Victorian Society: Women, Class, and the State* (Cambridge, UK: Cambridge University Press, 1980), 194.

29. Olive Banks, *Faces of Feminism: A Study of Feminism as a Social Movement* (New York: Basil Blackwell, 1981), 66.

30. Kent, 73.

31. Michel Foucault, *The History of Sexuality*, Volume 1, trans. Robert Hurley (New York: Vintage Books, 1978), 100–101.

32. Poovey, 173.

33. Charles Dickens, *Great Expectations* 1861 (New York: Signet, 1980), 58. Future references to this text will be inserted parenthetically.

34. Elihu Pearlman, "Inversion in *Great Expectations,*" in Robert Partlow (ed.), *Dickens Studies Annual* 7 (Carbondale, IL: Southern Illinois University Press, 1978): 193–194.

35. Pearlman, 194.

36. Pearlman, 194.

37. Kurt Hartog, "The Rape of Miss Havisham," *Studies in the Novel* 14, No. 3 (1982): 248.

38.   Edward Said, *Culture and Imperialism* (New York: Vintage, 1993), 81–82.

39.   For a differently focused (yet in the following pages, quite useful) discussion of the ways Dickens's "depictions of prostitutes and fallen women . . . dramatize predicaments of agency and uncertainties about the nature of selfhood, character, and society" (1), see the whole of Amanda Anderson's superb *Tainted Souls and Painted Faces: The Rhetoric of Fallenness in Victorian Culture* (Ithaca, NY: Cornell University Press, 1993), but especially pages 66–107.

40.   For a more thorough discussion of *Great Expectations'* "deeply saturated perversity" (220) as it is reflected in the men of the novel, see William A. Cohen's "Manual Conduct in *Great Expectations*," *ELH* 60, No. 1 (1993): 217–259.

41.   Lillian Faderman, *Surpassing the Love of Men* (New York: Morrow, 1981), see especially pages 231–294.

42.   My discussion there and here draws, of course, on Luce Irigaray; see especially *Speculum of the Other Woman*, trans. Gillian C. Gill (Ithaca, NY: Cornell University Press, 1985), pages 243–364.

43.   For more detail on Butler's work and perspective, see my discussion below, but also Walkowitz, especially Part 2, and Banks, Chapters 5 and 6.

44.   Hartog, 260–261.

45.   This was published in *The Magdalen's Friend and Female Homes' Intelligencer* in 1861, and is quoted in Nead, 110.

46.   This is quoted in Patricia Hollis, Ed., *Women in Public 1850–1900: Documents of the Victorian Women's Movement* (London: Allen & Unwin, 1979), 208, and comes from Butler's *Personal Reminiscences of a Great Crusade;* see also the writers mentioned in note 43 above.

47.   John Chapman, "Prostitution: Government Experiments in Controlling It," *Westminster Review* 37 (1870): 143.

48.   Anderson, 68.

49.   Anderson, 78.

50.   Anderson, 199–200.

Analysis of Application

"Great Expectations and Harsh Realities" explores the reciprocal relationship between novelistic representation and political activity during the second half of the nineteenth century. "History" is presented as a three-dimensional construct here, rather than posited as a two-dimensional, linear timeline. Within the text of Dickens's *Great Expectations* and in a variety of other media, this essay reveals a clash of discourses concerning and changing reactions to feminist demands and associations, arguing that historical change occurs as individuals and groups react polyvalently to previous articulations and activities.

The essay explores the historical context surrounding *Great Expectations* by probing journalistic portrayals of and references to "strong-minded women" and by investigating political skirmishes over the Contagious Diseases Acts, passed in 1864 and suspended in 1883. Dickens's novel is revealed to be thoroughly enmeshed in a confused and volatile set of social discourses concerning individual and collective demands by women for greater access to social power structures. While the essay does not posit a cause-and-effect relationship between the novel and the passage of the acts, it suggests, via the theories of Michel Foucault and Edward Said, that literary representations participate in and can lend their support to a climate of concrete political activity and reactions. Texts are made by, but also help make, the real world.

This essay is also enmeshed in its own dialogue with feminist interpretations of Dickens's novel and with feminist methodologies, which gives it a sense of focus and overarching purpose. A single essay or reading cannot simultaneously address all the various possibilities for analyzing a work: gender, class, race, sexuality, and so forth. Yet "Great Expectations and Harsh Realities" demonstrates that in a focused discussion, the critic can still move beyond an exclusively gender-based argument to include readings of sexuality, sociopolitical history, and post-structuralist (here Foucauldian) theory. And beyond the way this essay demonstrates possibilities for a synthetic methodology, it also shows that politically charged analysis of a text can still draw productively on precise details from within the text itself: Direct quotations, references to scenes and symbols, and other supporting evidence are used in the development of the argument. Furthermore, such details are used to set up not only a sociopolitical context for the discussion but also a literary-critical one, with references to previous works that both support and diverge from the analysis set forth. Thus Dickens, his novel, and the essay itelf are all revealed to be involved in broad dialogues on gender, representation, and social change.

Critical analysis today has many possible emphases and points of departure; this breadth of possibility can be daunting, or energizing, or both. The essay's final reference is to its readers' perspectives on the glass being half empty or half full when considering feminist "advances" during the nineteenth century; the same diversity of view is possible vis-à-vis our own context of change in critical methodologies. Perhaps it is best to remember simply that this is an exciting time in the history of literary and cultural criticism, one of great vitality and some volatility. Your work as a critic is to make that vitality your own as you, too, participate in energetic discussions and engage reciprocally with a context of expectations and realities—yours, your instructor's, and, always, your readers'.

Credits

Index